FIGHT FOREVER
THE BALLAD OF KEVIN AND SAMI

J.J. MCGEE

ILLUSTRATED BY
JAIME SHELHAMER

Copyright © 2025 by J.J. McGee

First Edition

Cover Art by Eunice Lai

Interior Art and Back Cover image by Jaime Shelhamer

Edited by Kristina Snowden

Designed by Jonathan Snowden

All rights reserved.

This unauthorized book is not affiliated with WWE, Sami Zayn or Kevin Owens. No endorsement is suggested or implied.

No part of this book may be reproduced in any form or by any electronic or mechanical means, including information storage and retrieval systems, without written permission from the author, except for the use of brief quotations in a book review.

Library of Congress Cataloging-in-Publication Data has been applied for

ISBN: 978-1-7349459-7-3

This book is dedicated to the memory of
Michael "Llakor" Ryan,
who should have had first shot at writing it

and

My Mother,
who was looking forward to reading it.

CONTENTS

Introduction	7
ORIGIN STORIES *(1984-2002)*	13
THREE WAY DANCE *(2002-2003)*	27
PLEASE DON'T GO *(2003)*	39
GRAB THE BRASS RING *(2004)*	47
ACTION FIGURES *(2004-2005)*	56
JUST WRESTLE *(2005)*	67
ACROSS THE SEAS *(2006)*	81
MAN UP *(2007)*	92
HANDS IN THE AIR *(2008)*	105
YEAR OF THE WOLF *(2009)*	118
MOMENT OF CLARITY *(2009)*	129
BITTER FRIENDS, STIFFER ENEMIES *(2010)*	145
FIGHT WITHOUT HONOR *(2010)*	157
FUCK RING OF HONOR *(2011)*	172
VIEW FROM THE TOP *(2012)*	185
NOTHING WITHOUT YOU *(2012-2013)*	197
SEPARATION *(2013)*	212
OUR EVOLUTION *(2014)*	225

RIVAL *(2015)*	245
UNSTOPPABLE *(2015)*	255
TIME HEALS ALL WOUNDS *(2015-2016)*	267
PAYBACK *(2016)*	276
BATTLEGROUND *(2016)*	286
THIS IS OURS *(2016-2017)*	297
HELL IN A CELL *(2017)*	311
KEVIN'S HEAVEN *(2017-2018)*	325
THUNDERDOME *(2019-2020)*	339
KARMA *(2021)*	353
INTERLUDE *(2021-2022)*	366
MIND GAMES AND WARGAMES *(2022)*	371
ROYAL RUMBLE *(2023)*	384
THE FINAL CHAPTER *(2023)*	397
AFTERWORD	408
CODA: THE STORYTELLERS *(2024)*	410
NOTES	421
ACKNOWLEDGMENTS	433
ALSO FROM HYBRID SHOOT	435

INTRODUCTION

Long story short

It's March 10, 2016, and Mike "The Miz" Mizanin sits in his director's chair in the ring, smirking at his guest. Sami Zayn, newly on the roster and building toward his first WrestleMania match, sits across from him, looking slightly baffled, rather annoyed, and just a tiny bit condescending.

Miz asks him to answer the question everyone's been asking since he showed up to thwart Kevin Owens' latest rampage: "Who is Sami Zayn?"

Sami takes a breath and begins, "I've been doing this a long time. Fourteen years—"

Miz cuts him off, waving his hands impatiently to indicate he should skip to the good stuff. "Can we move it along? Fast forward to your relationship with Kevin Owens."

Sami blinks. He thinks for a second. Then he says, deadpan: "All right, to make a long story short, the history with Kevin and I goes back thirteen years."

For the world of wrestling, it's almost understated, the dry delivery of the fact that "fast forwarding" to the point where his career and Kevin's became intertwined shaves only the barest fraction of time off

INTRODUCTION

his history. There is no making this long story short; from nearly the beginning, it has been one narrative, one career.

This book is an attempt to let that long story be long and unpack two decades' worth of storytelling.

Powers of Two

In his book *Powers of Two: How Relationships Drive Creativity*, Joshua Wolf Shenk argued that "creative dyads"—pairs of people—have been responsible for some of the greatest achievements in human history. He looked at pairs like John Lennon and Paul McCartney, Pierre and Marie Curie, Steve Jobs and Steve Wozniak, Ann Landers and Dear Abby, and the way the synergy between two people can drive creativity.

It's a shame Shenk didn't dip into professional wrestling for examples, because here's one of the amazing things about that genre of sport/art/entertainment: *professional wrestling is quite possibly the only inherently collaborative artform in the world.*

That is to say, all other creative enterprises that can be done in tandem can also be done solo. A song can be sung by one voice; a dance can be performed by a single dancer; a play can be delivered by a lone actor. There's even solo synchronized swimming, as technically it's the music that's being synchronized to, not the other swimmers. Professional wrestling, however, literally requires collaboration to create the illusion of combat.

Even the nearest thing to solo professional wrestling—those rare matches with dolls or "invisible opponents"—requires the creation of an implied partner for the audience's vision. A professional wrestler needs an opponent to create a match, and any match that isn't a novelty one-off is created from the chemistry between two or more wrestlers. Solo professional wrestling is nothing more than acrobatics in a ring. It's the collaboration and interchange between people that powers a wrestling match.

In Kevin Owens and Sami Zayn, wrestling has one of the most coherent and long-term collaborations that has ever existed in

INTRODUCTION

wrestling.* Over the course of their twenty-year career, the longest they've ever gone without being in the ring together was the two years from the beginning of Sami Zayn's WWE tenure to when Kevin Owens joined him and instantly launched into a feud with him.

The vast wrestling database of Cagematch.net logs the number of matches they've been in together at over 300—and Kevin estimates it's at least double that, thanks to the sheer number of matches with tiny promotions that have never been recorded.[1] This puts them in a small and distinctive group of wrestler pairs who have had careers that evolved together across the tag and singles division, going back and forth between tag partners, allies, and rivals. Putting aside pairs of wrestlers who grew up in the same family, complex rivalry/friendships that span decades are rare.

Even rarer are wrestlers who have taken that kind of partnership all the way to the top promotions in the world, climbing up through regional indies to reach the highest national and international levels together, their characters' relationship evolving in the process.

Arguably only Kenny Omega and Kota Ibushi's shared career has achieved the same continuity and complexity as Kevin and Sami's—and it is far from a coincidence that both Omega and Ibushi have mentioned Sami as a friend who shares their vision of wrestling. This kind of story is not merely generational, it is historical. And a historical narrative deserves to have a history written about it.

Each chapter of this book will focus in-depth on one match Kevin and Sami created together, the fictional story leading up to and away from it, and some of the real events connected to it. As we move from one match to the next, you'll hear about the triumphs and losses, the disasters and miracles, the heroes and villains—both in the fiction and in reality—and follow along as two men create a story that spans decades—and beyond.

---

* When talking about himself and Kevin, Sami consistently refers in interviews to "our career," not "our careers." It's a revealing description.

INTRODUCTION

A Note on Terminology

A professional wrestler is a weird chimera, the fusion of a real person and a fictional character into a quasi-mythical being. Sometimes the real person and the fiction overlap so close to completely that there's little difference—for example, Bobby Lashley seems to share Franklin Roberto Lashley's background and basic personality, differing only in that Franklin Lashley knows when he walks to the ring who will win a match, while Bobby Lashley doesn't. Other times the real person and the character overlap so little that it becomes a source of comedic disjunction to consider that the mayor of Knoxville and the Undertaker's demon brother share the same physical body. There's a huge range of possibilities, and it's one of the enduring ironies of this book that its two subjects fall on totally opposite ends of the spectrum.

The name on "Kevin Owens'" birth certificate is Kevin Steen, and until he came to WWE he wrestled under that legal name, the fictional and real people tightly interlinked. When he made the leap to WWE in 2014, he kept his first name (almost unheard-of at the time) and so Kevin has always been Kevin, in reality and fiction, in the indies and in WWE. He's one of the most solidly *real* wrestlers in the world, and it's always clear that this Kevin is the same Kevin who wrestled in IWS in 2003. There's no disjunction or major shifts in character between Kevin Steen the real man, Kevin Steen the indie character and Kevin Owens the WWE character. Kevin is Kevin is Kevin, always.

Then there's the other side of the equation. When Kevin was using his legal name as his wrestling name, his tag partner was wrestling under a mask as a character so cartoonish that no one could ever think he was authentic, a "Mexican luchador" who spoke almost no Spanish. Where Kevin has always linked himself with his parents, his wife, and his children, to the point of using them in storylines, promos, and sometimes even matches, for a long time his friend and rival's legal name wasn't even widely known, and his non-wrestling privacy has always been fiercely protected. Fans have respected and embraced this, to the point where it's a common fannish game to completely de-link the indie character and the WWE character and insist on their utter separation. It's a game I love to play myself, but here for a moment I

INTRODUCTION

must pause and state it clearly: Rami Sebei was El Generico is Sami Zayn.

This book dances on the line between fiction and reality at times, because these two love to smudge that line, then re-draw it, then obliterate it once again. So depending on the situation, "Kevin Steen" or "Kevin Owens" might refer to the real person or the character; "El Generico" might refer to the magical-realism Mexican luchador or the person who played him. I'll try to keep it clear with context, but—

You know what? You're a wrestling fan. You're used to these blurred lines and narrative games. You can handle it.

Let's go.

ORIGIN STORIES
(1984-2002)

TWO OF THE greatest Quebec wrestlers of all time were born two months apart in 1984.

One of them was born in Marieville, a small town of around six thousand people about a twenty-minute drive east of Montreal. The other grew up in Laval, the largest suburb of Montreal, a bustling city of three hundred thousand. One was French-Canadian, the other the son of Syrian immigrants. One was raised Catholic, the other Muslim. One grew up in a French-speaking family, the other spoke Arabic at home. You could hardly imagine two different children of Quebec, with no heritage, religion, upbringing, or even native language in common. All they shared when they met was a love of wrestling and an ambition to be the best, and that would be enough to launch them on a decades-long quest to reach the top, a journey defined both within the ring and backstage by the same questions: *Can we be stronger together? Can we succeed together? Can we reach heights together that we never could separately?* And those questions would be answered—

Well, we're getting way, way ahead of ourselves. Let's back up to 1995, when a man in Marieville made a momentous decision that would change the world of professional wrestling forever. Security systems technician Terry Steen stopped by Depanneur Video du Coin, the local corner store, and rented a VCR tape of *WrestleMania XI* to watch with his 12-year-old son.

The opening match featured Lex Luger and the British Bulldog, Davey Boy Smith, tagging together against the Blu Brothers. The incredibly muscular Luger and Smith, at that moment about halfway through their brief eight-month stint as a tag team, came to the ring in sparkling jackets decorated with Old Glory and the Union Jack, carrying the American and British flags. The Blu Brothers, identical twin mountain men in matching gear, were escorted by their "Uncle Zebekiah" Colter. The Allied Powers delivered twin slams to the hapless hillbillies on their way to victory, and Terry Steen's son Kevin was instantly intrigued.

That intrigue turned to obsession when the heavyweight title match between Diesel and his former tag team partner Shawn Michaels rolled around. Michaels—cocky, sexy, and sneering—ripped off his mirrored red chaps to transform into a dynamo in the ring, lightning-fast and agile, leaping off turnbuckles and over ropes in a doomed attempt to defeat his former bodyguard and friend, performing feats that young Kevin had no idea a human could do.[1]

The next day he went to the town's municipal pool and raced around breathlessly regaling every single child, from friends to total strangers, about this amazing new thing called *professional wrestling*. He was met with varying levels of boredom and bafflement, but it didn't deter him at all: Kevin was in love. And the two matches that had kindled that love? A tag match pitting a unified, indistinguishable pair against two distinct individuals, and a grudge match between tag partners turned rivals. Kevin had seen what he loved about wrestling, and would spend much of his career, especially the parts he shared with the future Sami Zayn, echoing aspects of those two matches.

From then on, Kevin was driven. Before wrestling, he had been a fairly aimless kid, picking interests up and putting them down again, unfocused and restless. After seeing Shawn Michaels on the screen, all he wanted was to become like his hero. He dressed in full Heartbreak Kid regalia for Halloween, blissfully, prepubescently unaware of the more lurid implications of Michaels' gear: "I looked like a twelve-year-old stripper," he remembers ruefully in an interview with Johnny

Gargano, who laughs and admits he did the same.[2] Growing up in a Francophone family in Quebec, his English had been rudimentary until discovering wrestling. One day in English class, during a tedious lesson in names for body parts, he suddenly made the connection that the *elbow* the teacher was talking about was the same thing as the *elbow drop* he'd heard commentator Jim Ross talk about. "Jim Ross is teaching me English!" he thought in amazement.[3] Once he realized English would help him understand wrestling, it wasn't long until he had amassed an impressive English vocabulary, albeit one that included words like *slobberknocker*, which he had no idea wasn't standard English until he tried using it in casual conversation.

And of course, he wanted to learn wrestling. He nagged his parents to let him take wrestling lessons until they finally gave in and let him sign up for a school at age 14. It wasn't exactly a hard sell. Impressed by his determination and focus, his mother and father were eager to encourage him in his newfound passion.

His mother, Suzanne, took the initiative. After coming across an advertisement for a wrestling school, she got him enrolled when he was 14. Serge Jodoin's school operated out of a barn and was nothing fancy, but it covered the basics, and on the first day Kevin suffered his first setback in wrestling—he couldn't figure out how to take a back bump, no matter how hard he tried. Frustrated that his enthusiasm hadn't translated into instant success, he went home after the first day and told his mother he was thinking about quitting. His parents, however, encouraged him to keep at it and keep fighting, and he set up a mattress in the back yard and practiced bumping over and over until he got the hang of it. This was the first, but far from the last, time that Kevin would get discouraged with his wrestling career. But it was also the first, and far from the last, time he would set his teeth and dig in, refusing to change course.

Once he got past that first physical hurdle, the rest started to fall into place. A month later, he was on his way to mastering the basics of wrestling when the roof of the barn collapsed onto the practice ring (luckily empty at the time) and the school was forced to close. With no other formal wrestling schools in the area, Kevin's training came to an abrupt end for about a year.

As he looked for another place to train, Kevin picked up other favorite wrestlers—at one point his bedroom was literally wallpapered from floor to ceiling with Steve Austin posters, and he was particularly fond of Chris Jericho, although Shawn Michaels would forever be the wrestler of his heart. He started attending live WWE shows, though only WWE shows, as he considered rival WCW "the enemy" and, with the fierce and dogged loyalty that would mark key points through his career, refused to watch a minute of them.[4]

A young Kevin in HBK gear.

The biggest show he went to was *Survivor Series 1997*, where he witnessed the infamous Montreal Screwjob in person. That fateful *WrestleMania XI* tape from years before had featured an "I quit" match between Bret Hart and Bob Backlund that Kevin had found boring, and as a result he had taken a firm dislike to the Hitman, unmoved by the fact that Hart was a fellow Canadian.[5] At Survivor Series, when Kevin's beloved Shawn Michaels got Hart into his own sharpshooter submission and the referee quickly (too quickly) announced that Hart had tapped out, Kevin—nearly alone in the entire roiling audience—was ecstatic. As Hart spat in Vince McMahon's face and enraged fans booed the CEO, Kevin was cheering loudly, and he swears that Bret Hart saw him in the audience and flipped him off. In a special on the WWE Network, Kevin smiles fondly while retelling the story, delighted at the memory of that most wrestling of joys, savoring the lamentations of your enemy.[6]

A concerned Sami attended the same show.

Elsewhere in that same arena, witnessing that same Screwjob but with a very different reaction, was another fifteen-year-old: a gangling, awkward redhead. Rami Sebei was a diehard Bret Hart fan attending his very first live wrestling event, sitting in the cheapest of the cheap seats with an obscured view, which must have made the bewildering events unfolding even more baffling. Watching his idol apparently tap out to his own submission gutted him. The arena was filled with confusion and sadness, and Rami—always sensitive to the mood of a crowd—felt all that pain and anger.[7]

It's a magical moment, these two future stars both witness to one of the most defining moments in wrestling history, each of them supporting opposite sides. One can't help but hope that young Rami glimpsed that one obnoxious Shawn Michaels fan jeering at Montreal's anguish and hated him with all of his heart.

Rami had come much earlier to wrestling than Kevin. He had grown up watching professional wrestling in part because his father had been an amateur wrestler in his home country of Syria.[8] That didn't mean the family had money to spare for their son to train formally, however. When Rami decided to get trained, there was no wrestling school—not even one in a barn. Instead, he paid someone a few dollars a week to teach him how to take bumps on the frozen Montreal grass. It was all just for fun at the start, a wild silly thing to do, like skateboarding. When his mother met his trainer and hesitantly asked if her son could possibly make a living in wrestling, Rami's jaw dropped at the trainer's assertion that yes, he was probably good enough to make money at it. It doesn't seem to have crossed his mind before then that his lark could earn him income. It was only when he went to shows at a local promotion, International Wrestling Syndicate (IWS), and watched other people wrestle that he started to think, *Maybe I can do this.*[9]

The next step was to have an actual match and create an in-ring character.

His first matches were in FLQ, the Federation de Lutte Quebecoise, under the ring name "Stevie McFly," a persona created in part from his favorite movie, *Back to the Future*. Stevie McFly had no wrestling gear and performed in jeans, bowling shoes, and a t-shirt—the name manages to frame it as part of the gimmick, but it seems likely he also legitimately had no formal gear. The few Stevie McFly matches captured on video are such low quality that his face is nothing but a pale smudge under a blur of coppery hair, but there's no mistaking the

ORIGIN STORIES

kinetic floppy energy of his body, the wild precision of his dropkicks and moonsaults, the way he lurches out of pins with one hand thrust in the air like an eager schoolchild with all the answers. His physical skills are already there, but Kushida from NJPW is the only wrestler who has ever made "guy who likes *Back to the Future*" work as a character, and there isn't room for two in the world of professional wrestling.

It's in another promotion, the International Wrestling Syndicate (IWS), that he created the character that he spent the next ten years perfecting.

Well, "created" might be too strong a word. At first it was just handed to him, when the IWS booker needed a torture victim.

"You do realize, now you're stuck with the mask"

Of all the matches and moments described in this book, El Generico's first match in 2002 is the only one I've never seen with my own eyes. It was never released on DVD and may well be lost forever. However, thanks to the work of Michael "Llakor" Ryan, the IWS publicist at the time, the match lives on. An amazing writer with a gift for dancing on that fine line between fiction and reality, winking to either side but never quite choosing one, Llakor's match summaries sparkle and illuminate. In 2005 Llakor wrote up his memory of El Generico's first match under the title "I Am El Generico's Father," with a vividness that makes the reader feel like they have ringside seats for the birth of one of the greatest characters in wrestling.[10]

Apparently, IWS promoter PCP Crazy F'N Manny (that's not a judgment, that's his name) had a problem. One of his badass heels, TNT, needed to demonstrate how cruel and sadistic he was by twisting someone into an agony-wracked pretzel, and they couldn't find just the right person for the job. Manny had a volunteer for the duty—an eager red-headed kid who'd been hanging around backstage clamoring for a chance at his first IWS match—but hesitated. Surely if the audience's first impression of this kid was as a hapless victim, they'd never take him seriously again? Inspiration struck and Manny handed the erstwhile Stevie McFly a spare mask. By hiding his face under the mask, he could debut again later with his *real* character and no one would connect him with the loser who got destroyed by TNT. Someone grabbed a magic marker and scrawled a bunch of gibberish-Spanish fake tattoos on his body, and soon ring announcer Brian the Guppie was introducing the IWS audience to "El Generico, the Generic Luchador."

It was a clever plan, and its only flaw was underestimating how much wrestling fans love losers.

When El Generico—skinny, cheerful, hands waving wildly and beaming from ear to ear—gets into the ring and yells "Olé!" a scattering of fans call it back to him. Delighted at the response and oblivious to the growing annoyance of TNT, the luchador yells "olé!" again and gets a slightly louder response. When he does it again, TNT loses what little patience he had and drops him with a vicious lariat from behind, then plants a foot on his neck and yells "Olé *now*, you son of a bitch!"

And somehow in this moment, a magical connection is made between the Generic Luchador and the audience.

He does get in some impressive offense, some wild flips and tumbles over the top rope, each move punctuated by a breathless "olé!" But he's been sent out there to suffer, and oh, how he suffers. He claws at the air, he gasps for breath, he drums the mat with his heels. TNT gets him in a surfboard submission and he flails his arms in a vain attempt at breaking the hold. He suffers so dramatically and so piteously that the audience's hearts go out to him, this random and generic unknown, and they start chanting "Olé!" at TNT with all their might. Llakor has called this a "Tinkerbell Moment," after the moment in *Peter Pan* where the audience is suddenly addressed directly and told that Tinkerbell will die if they don't clap for her.[11] Wrestling is at its most magic when the spectacle immerses the audience so fully that they truly believe their support can help a wrestler win, and in Le Skratch that night El Generico discovered that he was one of the most convincing Tinkerbells in professional wrestling.

TNT continues to murder El Generico, El Generico continues to writhe and choke, and the audience gets louder and louder. And oh, did I just say that wrestling is at its most magic when the audience believes their support can help a wrestler win? There's an even deeper magic: those moments when an audience's support actually *does* help a wrestler win. TNT, seeing the fans leaping up and hearing them calling out, makes a decision on the fly. He gives up in disgust and walks away, letting the referee count him out. The mysterious masked wrestler lies crumpled, motionless in the ring, brutalized and beaten.

But victorious.

The crowd kept chanting "olé!" as he staggered to the back, this most generic of luchadors who had on his very first night achieved something most wrestlers never do: change a loss into a win through the sheer power of the love they inspire in the audience.

Manny looked down at him—we have to imagine him smiling under the mask there on the stretcher, aglow with the joy of connecting with the audience, of realizing he could call forth such a response—and said, "You do realize, now you're stuck with the mask?"

"Stuck" was the right word—he wanted nothing to do with the gimmick at first and kept wrestling outside IWS as Stevie McFly.[12] He even added an ill-advised third character, "Big Larry," an attempt at playing a "thug" wannabe, "street" slang and all. But people wanted to see El Generico, and eventually the mask became the default.

It is one of the enduring mysteries of professional wrestling that a character who should have been deeply offensive—a Mexican wrestler played by a Canadian with no Mexican heritage as an idiot who speaks no English or Spanish—largely managed to avoid offense. There's no denying there were times that Generico's actions crossed the line into racist stereotyping, and there were plenty of times commentators riffed on the character in racist ways. But those became fewer and fewer as years went by, because the man behind the mask chose to frame El Generico as a sort of holy fool, a good-hearted soul who didn't understand English but also didn't understand evil. His unworldliness and lack of comprehension kept him apart from it all: the cruelties and crassness of the wrestling world seemed to be things that he simply didn't quite know were wrong, as if he took all the low blows and spitting and snot-spraying to be the quaint and confusing customs of his foreign friends.

Sami has never spoken of his thoughts and feelings on wearing a mask for a decade—he almost literally *can't*, since he and Generico are still separate beings, even though that insistence has worn down to the flimsiest and most threadbare of tissue at this point. But one important thing to remember about El Generico is that he was created in July 2002, just ten months after the 9/11 terrorist attacks and that the man behind the mask is Muslim.

Although Sami has never spoken about the early days of El Generico, we can look at another Muslim wrestler, Mustafa Ali, and see some interesting parallels and differences. Ali, probably the second most famous Muslim wrestler after Sami, started wrestling in 2004, and at first also wrestled under a mask as a high-flying babyface, specifically because he wanted to avoid being cast in the inevitable "foreign terrorist heel" role that Muslim wrestlers always had been. But bookings for the masked daredevil "Alto" were few and far between (Cagematch.net lists only seven between 2004 and 2007) and eventually he unmasked and began playing the villainous "Prince Ali."* Promotions started booking him more often, but the feeling that he was making money by stoking hatred toward his religion haunted him. He remembers coming to the ring and confronting a small boy, who put his fists up as if to fight him, his face contorted with fear and rage. Ali was stricken, wondering, "Did I just teach this kid to hate people like me?" It was a struggle every Muslim wrestler has faced, and one every Muslim wrestler has to find a way to confront.

Ali was wrestling in the United States rather than Canada, and more importantly, with his black hair and olive skin tone he matched the stereotype better than Sami did. It would probably have been easier for Sami to escape being typecast as a "terrorist," but that brings its own difficult issues of authenticity. Should he lean into his Muslim heritage or elide it? Which path is more of a betrayal of one's background? Safer to dodge the question entirely and play a character completely disassociated from yourself.

The creation of El Generico was a fluke, a lucky stroke of destiny. The *continuation* of El Generico, on the other hand, hints at a person

---

* It's ironic that Ali couldn't get bookings when he wrestled masked, while Sami found his bookings increased as El Generico.

who was searching for a way to avoid being forced to weaponize his religion into a gimmick. His first attempt, Stevie McFly, used his red hair and pale skin as its own kind of mask to perform as the most generic of white dudes. And Big Larry did something similar, posing as a poser appropriating another ethnicity. But in El Generico he found a way to keep his civilian self almost entirely private from fans and hone his gift for channeling the love of an audience through a perfect cartoon cypher.

To the extent that El Generico managed to rise above being an offensive stereotype, we can see the efforts of a man who knew how harmful stereotypes could be and tried his best to transcend them.

The Golden Boy in the Gilded Cage

I started this book with a promise that each chapter would focus on one time that Kevin and Sami were in the ring together. Since this chapter covers the years before their meeting, it makes sense that there'd have to be two matches, one for El Generico and one for Kevin Steen. But there is no match for Kevin in this chapter, even though he had been wrestling for years by the time Stevie McFly and El Generico were having their first matches.

Here's why.

After Kevin's first wrestling school closed because the barn it was held in collapsed, he went for about a year without any training. Then one day in 1999, when he was using a school computer to look up wrestling-related things instead of doing classwork, he came across exciting news: Jacques Rougeau, also known as "The Mountie" and one half of the WWE[13] tag team champions the Quebecers, was opening up a wrestling school in Montreal. He walked out of class on the spot and called his mother to beg her to enroll him in the school. She did—after scolding him for skipping class—and his parents took him there for auditions in September.[14]

According to Kevin, Rougeau was completely blown away by Kevin's physical skills. When he found out Kevin could do a 450 splash, he decided that Kevin was never going to lose a match—and indeed, he appears to have lost only once at a Rougeau-promoted show, and that was in a tag match where it's doubtful he took the pin. Kevin was Rougeau's golden boy from the beginning, and at first Rougeau's lavish praise was naturally flattering. After all, he used to work for the top promotion in the world! He held a title there! Kevin was sixteen when he started training with Rougeau in 1999, star-struck and full of hope that with The Mountie's help he was on a fast track to the big time.

There was only one problem with Rougeau's school, just one small flaw:

It was incredibly boring.

Rougeau apparently believed the best way to learn to do a match was to memorize a set of moves and then do them the exact same way every single time, with no improvisations. That way there could be no mistakes and wrestlers would never be caught calling moves in the ring. Rougeau held three shows a year, and his wrestlers would practice the same match over and over until it was engraved in their muscle memory, until they could do it with their eyes closed while thinking of something else. Then he'd hold the show, the wrestlers would do the matches they'd been drilling for four months, and that would be it.[15]

Rougeau's shows for his promotion, Lutte International/International Wrestling 2000 (IW2000), always had a large crowd at them, often numbering in the thousands—a press release at the time refers to 3500 as a "disappointing crowd."[16] The Rougeau family were wrestling royalty in Quebec, generations of the family wrestling and promoting. Rougeau often booked wrestling friends like King Kong Bundy and Jimmy Hart on his shows, another major draw. And as his former students liked to point out, he also gave away a lot of tickets at local businesses.[17] At the height of the Attitude Era, Rougeau offered a deliberate throwback style. As a news release of the time put it, he produced "a 'family value filled old fashion wrestling show', without the extracurricular shenanigans from the major leagues."[18] That meant cartoonish characters (at one show, for example, the construction-worker-themed Bull Dozer wrestled the stockbroker-themed Dow Jones), appearances by clowns, local radio station mascots and Mr. Potato Head, and of course, "what is a Lutte International 2000 card without the obligatory midget match?"[19] It was a circus and the actual matches were not the focus. Kevin managed to dodge getting a themed gimmick by the simple strategy of being merely spectacular: he was dubbed "The Kid" (Or "Le Kid" depending on the language) and he was there to dazzle, do 450 splashes, and win. He delivered consistently, but he must have felt like something was missing.

At seventeen The Kid was wrestling in front of thousands of fans, and he was winning all the time, but the matches were sterile, soulless, hollow. "I felt like a robot," he says, "going through the motions."[20] His audience was often uninterested in the wrestling, and there was no sense of creativity or art to what he was doing. There was no real collaboration, not between the wrestlers and not with the audience.

Maybe most importantly, there was no *story*.

Ironically, it was here in Rougeau's school, moving through the motions of the same match over and over for months, that Kevin probably started to develop his own wrestling superpower. He must have come to value psychology and narrative like a man craving water in a desert. If there were only an overarching *reason* that connected these matches! If only he had some idea why his character was *doing* this 450 splash! Was it because he was arrogant? Because he was insecure? Kevin was devouring WWE at a time when wrestlers like the Rock, Steve Austin, Kurt Angle and Mick Foley were delivering captivating character work, and it's easy to imagine him trying out character flourishes in his matches, groping for something to keep his interest. When you get in trouble if you throw a kick instead of a punch, you learn to slip character work into the margins of the matches, to focus on the nuances instead of the moves.

Entirely by accident, Jacques Rougeau was helping to forge one of the greatest storytellers in wrestling.

Kevin was learning some incredibly valuable lessons between 2000 and 2003. He learned to start creating his own stories to explain his characters' actions rather than waiting for the promoter to tell him what they were. He learned that winning all the time didn't mean very much if there was no narrative behind those wins. As time went on, Rougeau started leaving his most reliable student in charge of organizing things like music, lighting, and staging, and Kevin learned how important those details were to creating an impact. He had no memorable matches in those three years to summarize in this chapter, but in this airless, hermetically-sealed atmosphere, he learned exactly what he wanted to do if he ever got a chance to wrestle at the top levels. It's a vision he has carried with him through his whole career.

Pieces in Place

By late 2002, Kevin Steen and El Generico were fully trained, their characters complete and their physical skills perfected. During these earliest years, the men behind the characters had each learned invaluable and mutually complementary lessons. Sami had learned the joy of connecting with a small, raucous crowd from bell to bell, of suffering and struggling in a way that wrings the heart and forges an emotional bond between wrestler and audience. Kevin had learned to look beyond the match for creative fulfillment, to create character and narrative continuity between matches when the audience wasn't engaged and the matches were leading nowhere. Put them both together and you'd have an unstoppable storytelling engine. If they could just cross paths.

In December, they did.

THREE WAY DANCE
(2002-2003)

AS WE START THIS CHAPTER, it's time for me to face a certain issue head-on: the name "Sami Zayn" didn't exist until 2013. It's an odd retcon to refer to the man behind El Generico's mask as Sami. But this book isn't a biography of Rami Sebei and Kevin Steen, the real people behind their characters. Their private lives and personalities don't enter this book except where they happen to intersect with the front-stage story.

On the other hand, neither is it exactly a history of *just* the characters. Inevitably, some backstage events that breach the illusion of fiction are important to the story. I'm not going to spend this book stoutly insisting that El Generico was actually from Tijuana, but I'm also not going digging for the "real" backstage dirt about the Ring of Honor locker room.

What this history covers is the on-camera events, slipping backstage just enough to include the information that has become an open part of the Kevin-and-Sami story via interviews and behind-the-curtain official footage. So to maintain a sense of continuity, the person who was El Generico and who became Sami Zayn will be called "Sami" from now on.

Wrestling: it's weird.

A Meet-Cute in 2002

In the latter half of 2002, Sami was tearing up bars and church basements as El Generico and Stevie McFly, while Kevin was dying of boredom in Jacques Rougeau's school, waiting for his big break to come. Other students got fed up and walked away to start wrestling in other promotions and vent to wrestling magazines about how Rougeau never even showed up to his school, leaving the wrestlers to learn by training each other,[1] most notably two wrestlers called Kid Kamikaze and Beef Wellington[2], who became the bridge between Rougeau's school and IWS.

Beef Wellington and Sami shared a sense of humor and a voracious love of wrestling. They loved the grimy, free-wheeling, bloody and comedic wrestling that IWS was doing. Together they devoured tapes of wrestling from around the world, eventually becoming tag team partners and real-life roommates as well. While they watched tape from Japan or California, they talked about wrestling, and this is where Sami first heard about the prodigy still trapped back in Rougeau's school.

Kevin's talent was undeniable at that point. He was Rougeau's star, showing off by performing all the moves of his favorites, from RVD's split-legged moonsault to Brock Lesnar's F5. He appears to have struck some amount of awe into everyone in the Montreal wrestling scene, and it was taken for granted that if anyone in the area were ever to make it to WWE, it would be Kevin Steen.

One assumes Sami took this as a challenge.

In December 2002, a group of former Rougeau students went to an IW2000 show, and Sami went along. Kevin's very first impression of Sami was not promising. "He was in the crowd with some of my friends that I had trained with. Honestly, I remember thinking that he was kind of annoying. He was jumping around, being loud and obnoxious."[3]

"Annoying, loud and obnoxious" is not exactly a great first impression, but it's unclear what exactly "loud and obnoxious" means here. Here's my guess based on what we know of Sami and of the situation: Sami was marking out.

THREE WAY DANCE

Remember, the typical audience at one of Rougeau's shows was thousands of people, mostly families with small children, who weren't really wrestling fans and had come because they were given free promotional tickets. If you've been to a wrestling show with a large but disengaged crowd, you know that low humming rustle of sound, which rises and falls but never really peaks in excitement. A person who's enjoying a match loudly and enthusiastically stands out. A person jumping around and yelling about a match is, let's be honest, going to come off as practically sarcastic. For Kevin, Sami's over-the-top energy could well have felt obnoxious, even taunting. *Who the hell is that guy losing his mind over there?*

Kevin recalls that once he actually got to know Sami he realized, in his words, "he wasn't doing it on purpose, putting on a show or trying to get attention,"[4] which tells us at first that's exactly how he took it, as mocking the Rougeau wrestlers by over-performing the role of *excited fan*. No, it was just Sami. That was just who he was.

On Sami's side, the connection was immediate, no re-evaluation needed. Other refugees from Rougeau's school had told him that Kevin was incredibly talented but arrogant, a jerk. Sami found him anything but. "We instantly clicked. We got along famously right away. I remember thinking, 'Why is everyone saying this guy's a jerk?'"[5] They had only barely crossed paths, and neither had ever seen the other wrestle, but the obnoxious loudmouth and the arrogant show-off may have recognized in each other someone as opinionated and self-confident—and talented—as themselves.

As they entered 2003, Kurt Angle was the WWE champion. Triple H was Heavyweight Champion. Booker T and Goldust were tag team champions. Ring of Honor had just come into existence. And Kevin was still biding his time doing his memorized matches, waiting for that promised audition. But the escapees from Rougeau's school were banging on his door and calling him to come out and play, and soon Kevin had to find out what he was missing.

The Forbidden Wrestling

The reason Kevin hadn't yet realized what he was missing was simple. Jacques Rougeau barred his students not only from wrestling outside the school, but from even attending shows held by other promotions. He claimed it was because he didn't want to give credibility to the smaller promotions, but it seems plausible he might also have not wanted his more talented students to get a glimpse of other styles of wrestling and realize there was more out there than doing the exact same match for four months. Kevin's appetite for wrestling was as voracious as Sami's, but his palate was much more limited at that age: as a child and young teen he consumed only WWE. He seems to have felt vaguely that because Rougeau had been a WWE star, the style he was teaching *must* be the proper style. When he started watching ECW's rougher, more hardcore matches in the early 2000s, he surely started to suspect there were other ways of approaching the art. His friends wrestling in IWS surely were telling him so. By 2003, after almost four years in Rougeau's school, his hunger to really wrestle was growing undeniable.

There was an extra complication. In August 2002, Kevin tore his ACL mid-match. He felt his knee give way and considered halting the match, then decided to gut his way through it. The fact that Bret Hart happened to be in the audience may have had something to do with that decision. Hart consoled him after, told him he was impressed and reassured The Kid that he would heal up just fine, but the end result was one of the worst injuries Kevin would ever face in his career. The eighteen-year-old required surgery, and the knee would never heal perfectly, leaving him with a nagging injury that even becomes a major plot point down the line.* The Canadian healthcare system didn't prioritize a teenaged athlete, so he didn't get that surgery until May 2003.[6]

So he resolved to get a taste of the forbidden wrestling, and that taste would change his life.

In early 2003, a friend finally got him to watch a tape of an IWS show. Kevin was instantly enchanted by how much fun everyone seemed to be having and the way the wrestlers were interacting with

---

* Therefore, in a weird coincidence, both Kevin and Sami sustained one of the most severe injuries in their career wrestling in front of Bret Hart, over a decade apart.

the crowd, creating art together on the fly.[7] There were drunk and rowdy fans, broken light bulbs and barbed wire, botches and improvisations, and not a single Mr. Potato Head in evidence. But he was banned by Rougeau from attending other shows. There was only one solution:

Sneak in incognito.

On March 15, 2003, Kevin donned a bright red Big Evil shirt in his attempt to be inconspicuous and slipped into the bar Le Skratch to watch IWS's *Know Your Enemies* show from the audience.

Le Skratch is dark and chaotic, already a dramatic contrast from the large, well-lit arenas Rougeau typically booked. Action spills out of the ring and into the crowd regularly; the floor must have been tacky with beer almost instantly, the air thick with alcohol fumes and the stench of sweat. The main event is a nearly thirty-minute two-out-of-three falls hardcore match featuring tables and a lot of blood. A segment in the middle features guest appearances by a couple of porn stars—IWS was owned by an adult film company—one of whom had previously "been suspended" for flashing her breasts to the audience. The audience happily chants "Tits! Tits! Tits!" as she dodges the faux-horrified promoter to take off her shirt once more and run around the ring before exiting through the crowd.

Definitely not a "family value filled old fashion wrestling show." It's dirty in every sense of the world, seething and messy and vibrant.

El Generico happens to have two matches this night. He's in the very first match against Kamikaze Kid, one of Kevin's friends from Rougeau's school. Later he'll meet the challenge of Steve Royds for a second match, at the end of which a chastened Royds will gift him with the gold-spangled scarlet-lined cape that Generico wore for the rest of his career.[8] Kamikaze Kid is wearing an orange shirt with the sleeves cut off and "Westmount Playboy" on the front. Generico is in black trunks with "Olé" magic-markered on his chest (the "O" has a smiley face inked into it) and "I am Hot" on his back (another smiley face in the middle). They start by taking turns posing on the turnbuckles, playing to the crowd, seeing who can get the crowd going more.

According to commentary, apparently Kamikaze recently went to Tijuana to learn some *lucha libre* moves, and now he shows off a variety of arm drags, headscissors, and suplexes. He blocks most of Generico's offense, making the match basically his technique and viciousness versus Generico's heart and will. Eventually things break down into a brawl, Generico's limbs fanning the air wildly as he swings and staggers. Generico stumbles out of the ring, dazed, and Kamikaze Kid pulls off a springboard corkscrew plancha that leaves them both sprawled on the concrete floor right in front of Kevin.

As the camera moves to take in the crowd, you can see Kevin in his Big Evil shirt. He's jumped to his feet to applaud and point triumphantly at Kamikaze.

El Generico impressed Steen with his athleticism.

Then it's Generico's turn to impress. As they struggle out on the floor, Generico throws his opponent into a piece of scaffolding, then climbs to the apron and springboards from one rope across the corner to the other, somersaulting onto Kamikaze Kid.

Kevin leaps to his feet again, applauding, chanting "holy shit!" in sheer delight. Generico—Sami—stops and poses in front of the audience, throwing up his hands to acknowledge the cheers, cupping a hand to his ear: *let me hear you*. The crowd starts to sing, and although we can't see Kevin anymore, it's hard to imagine he could have resisted joining in.

Is El Generico aware that he's posing directly in front of Kevin Steen, there in the audience trying to be stealthy? Surely he is. It must have been Quebec's worst-kept secret that Rougeau's prodigy had infiltrated Le Skratch and was there in the third row, and it seems likely that both Kamikaze Kid and Generico were pulling out all the stops to impress him with his first IWS match.

When Generico finally gets the pin to end the match, the camera pans to follow his exhausted celebration. Behind him you can see the audience applauding. A few people have jumped to their feet as they clap. One of them is Kevin.

There's something charming about the fact that Kevin's first appearance in IWS is as an audience member, cheering for the daring exploits of El Generico. The symmetry is satisfying, since his first glimpse of Sami was in the crowd—"jumping around, being obnoxious"—at his own show.

Since the very beginning, they have been each other's biggest fans.

A Taste of Freedom

Kevin walked away from *Know Your Enemies* smitten. "I thought everything they did was awesome and I literally thought, 'These are the best wrestlers in Quebec, I *need* to wrestle *those guys.*'"[9] He was determined to wrestle outside of IW2000. He knew he needed more ring time than a match every four months, and he wanted to share the ring with the grungy free spirits of the Quebec indie scene. But he had a problem, and that problem was that Kevin is immensely loyal.

OK, I can hear those of you who know Kevin Steen and Kevin

Owens' vast history of abrupt betrayals snickering in the distance. In this area, however, the character is not the real person turned up to eleven, as most wrestlers put it. Kevin's heel character, authentic as it feels, is a deliberate inversion of Kevin's real-life personality, which is stubbornly faithful once he's committed to someone or something. Faithful even to a fault, as in this case where it was becoming increasingly clear that his skills were stagnating. Kevin was determined to see things through with Rougeau, even if the gilt of his early hero-worship had worn away. By 2003, he was responsible for training other wrestlers, for setting up at venues and handling the technical aspects of the shows, and he was reluctant to walk away from those responsibilities. He also still truly believed that Rougeau's school was the only way to get to WWE, a belief that he half-knew was false, but he had no idea how else one would ever get there. And Rougeau had said there would be no wrestling allowed outside of IW2000.

By August 2003, his knee was healed and he was ready to wrestle again. How to get the experience he needed so badly while not turning his back on his chance at the big time? Sure, he could slip into a show without it getting back to Rougeau, but there was no way he could get away with actually wrestling incognito. He was stuck. And then, a strange lucky break: Jacques Rougeau got sick.

It's unclear what the illness was, but it was severe enough that he suspended shows indefinitely, and attention-consuming enough that when Kevin asked if he could use this time to wrestle in other promotions, Rougeau didn't bother to say no. Within days Kevin appeared at the IWS show *Born to Bleed* to make a dramatic open challenge to the IWS roster that was accepted by one half of the current tag team champions, eXesS69.* It was the first time he had ever cut a promo on a microphone, because Rougeau didn't teach promo skills.[10] He was put on the very next IWS card in September.

The match starts off slow, and Kevin remembers with some bitterness the fans chanting "boring" at first.[11] They also chant "Jacques Rougeau!" which one can assume is not meant as a respectful tribute to

---

* He simplified his name to "Exess" in 2005 and I'll refer to him as that from now on, because it's much less unwieldy.

the former tag team champion. Exess is one of the best high fliers in Quebec, and this is Kevin's chance to show that the knee surgery hasn't slowed him down and he still belongs in that group, so the pace of the match starts at "brisk" and quickly ratchets upward.[12] Kevin breaks out his picture-perfect moonsault, his somersault guillotine leg drop, his package piledriver. Exess counters with northern lights suplexes, springboard DDTs, a phoenix splash. It's all fast and flashy and the crowd ends up shrieking along with it despite themselves, until Kevin gets a little too cocky and Exess rolls him up for a win. The victorious Exess helps Kevin to his feet to acknowledge him, and the commentary crowd is noting with satisfaction this respectful conclusion when Kevin attacks Exess from behind with a low blow. He throws Exess into the ropes so his neck gets tangled in the ropes in truly alarming fashion, then whallops him in the head with a chair and spits on his crumpled body on the floor.

So not a babyface debut, then.

The former Kid distinguished himself from the IWS regulars by loftily refusing to do hardcore matches, positioning himself as a "pure" and elitist wrestler, and promptly picked up the nickname "Mr. Wrestling." Like the "Jacques Rougeau" chants, it was anything but a compliment from the grungy hardcare fans. It made perfect sense, therefore, that his next opponent would be the very least elitist of IWS wrestlers, the embodiment of the fans' energy, El Generico. They were booked in a singles match for the very next event, *Blood Sweat & Beers*, a month after Kevin's debut.

The same day as his IWS debut, Kevin had a match with Stevie McFly in another promotion, MWF. So he'd shared a ring with Sami already, but the MWF match was a six-way match for the title, and if they had touched in the ring at all, it must have been a fleeting contact. The two had quickly gotten the measure of each other and started to realize they'd met someone who was their match in the ring, not just physically but in storytelling skill. They were eager to have a singles match together and see what they could do, and probably aware that Kevin's time of freedom might be limited before Rougeau reeled him back in. They must have been looking forward to that first singles match.

At the last second, the promoter added a third person to make it a three-way dance.

Admittedly, the third person was Pierre-Carl Ouellet, better-known as PCO, Jacques Rougeau's former tag team partner, who had become a mentor to Kevin when Rougeau was missing in action at his own school. PCO had also recently debuted in IWS, and Manny probably wanted to put him in a high-profile but non-title match. Kevin and Sami could hardly complain about having a former WWE champion and friend put into the match, but they did ask what the reason was.[13] Told it would all make sense in the future, they shrugged and went with it (spoiler: it does not seem to have made much more sense in the future). Next show they could have their singles match, they were told and had to be content with that. But in that request to be given a reason one can read a certain level of disappointment that they didn't get to share the ring one-on-one.

The match itself expresses that disappointment in concrete form, because the whole fight is structured around the question, "Can Kevin and Generico manage to have a singles match despite PCO's presence?"

Three Way Dance

The match starts with PCO beckoning the two younger wrestlers into the ring. The ring announcer claims El Generico is 157 pounds, and that is a generous estimate. Looking at him, you might think for a moment that he had abs before you realized no, those are actually his ribs outlined through his skin. He's got "Olé" written on his chest and "Please buy my shirts!" on his back. Kevin is wearing a red t-shirt and black trunks, hair cut short, looking brash and young. Neither he nor Generico have even the slightest scruff on their chins. They are wrestling babies. PCO is a dramatic contrast. At 35 he's almost twice their age and quite possibly twice their weight, a solid rectangle of muscle waiting behind them, arms akimbo, while they argue.

Because that's how Kevin and Generico have decided to spend some of their first moments in the ring together: arguing. Kevin suggests they work together to take out the former tag team champion.

THREE WAY DANCE

El Generico, hands flying wildly, explains by gesture that no, he will be the one to take out the monster all by himself. Kevin shrugs and leans back against the ropes to watch as PCO takes Generico and hurls him bodily out of the ring. Then he holds the ropes open for the chastened luchador, who re-enters the ring and seems to agree that maybe teamwork is best after all.

They start charging at PCO, but at first they do it one at a time, and he clubs them down one after the other. Eventually, almost as if by accident, their attacks start to sync up, and they manage to knock PCO to his knees. Teamwork! When PCO recovers, they flee the ring, only to get bowled over by a somersault plancha from the behemoth. PCO picks them both up and tosses them back in the ring, preparing to climb in and continue his path of destruction. But this is where PCO has made his first mistake. He's given Kevin Steen and El Generico the ring together alone, possibly for the first time ever, and they're in no hurry to give it back to him.

When PCO tries to get back into the ring, Kevin leaps forward and kicks him off the apron. He tries again, and Generico jumps forward and knocks him off with a hip attack. Frustrated, PCO tries a third time, and this time Kevin and Generico work together to shut him out, draping him across the lower rope and taking turns holding him in place so that Kevin can hit an arcing senton and then Generico a soaring moonsault. Together they put their shoulders to the slab of muscle and heave mightily until PCO tumbles to the floor again. Delighted at their successful teamwork, El Generico poses for the crowd, pointing to acknowledge Kevin and doing a small victory lap around the ring, a victory lap that comes to an abrupt end when he walks directly into a superkick by Kevin and crumples to the mat.

Kevin and Generico have gone from arguing to teamwork to triumph to betrayal in three minutes, a speed run through some of the major themes of their entire career.

As PCO sits outside the ring, betrayer and betrayed throw a flurry of moves at each other, each unable to get the upper hand. They're evenly matched, they're trying everything they've got, they're getting the measure of each other—and then they see that PCO has decided, once again, to get onto the apron and try to re-join the match.

Without any hesitation or communication, as if by reflex, Kevin and Generico jump forward together and kick him off the apron again.

PCO comes to rest on the floor and rolls over to sit on the concrete, looking up at the ring. He's got a wry grin on his face. Years later, talking about working with the two of them, he'll say that from the beginning they "always knew where they were going."[14] You can see it there, in the way he sits, smiling, and lets Kevin and Generico go to town, sailing around the ring in wild arcs, the three way dance turned into a tango, a waltz, a foxtrot for a moment.

When the two younger wrestlers spill out of the ring and brawl into the crowd, he joins in, creating mad chaos in which Kevin leaps off a balcony and flattens them both. Kevin suplexes PCO outside the ring and then it's back into the ring for Kevin and Generico, grabbing for a little more time to show off and to test each other, just a little longer. Finally, though, PCO loses his patience and plows back into the ring to hurl Generico into near-orbit and then into a turnbuckle. Kevin, who has stood by watching his rival get destroyed, lunges forward and also meets with little success. Unable to work together for any length of time now, neither of them can make any headway against the massive former WWE champion, and in the end PCO destroys Kevin with a senton and gets the win as Generico fails to scramble in and break up the pin in time. The luchador collapses next to Kevin on the mat and they both lie there as PCO celebrates his victory. Yet there's a sideways triumph to the moment. They managed to get enough time together in the ring to test out their chemistry, and the audience ate it up, not just the sequences with PCO but also those with just the two of them. "The crowd was on fire and it was just *magic*," Kevin will recall years later.[15]

Maybe more importantly, there are glimmers of a theme in this match, a theme that works not just at the fictional level. Former champion PCO is practically the physical embodiment of the WWE, he's the pinnacle. He's been to the top of the mountain. He's got everything they don't: brawn, height, finesse, experience. He took each of them apart separately and left them defeated and broken.

But if they could work *together*...

PLEASE DON'T GO
(2003)

BY NOVEMBER 2003, Kevin had been free of Rougeau's wrestling school for three heady months full of free-wheeling wrestling, filthy bars and drunk fans. He'd probably learned more about wrestling as an art form in those three months than he had in three years at Jacques Rougeau's school. He was learning how to improvise and adapt to an audience on the fly, how to react to the mood of the moment. In a week, he and El Generico were going to wrestle one-on-one for the first time, at Payback's a Bitch, where they could see how they worked in the ring together, just the two of them.

And then disaster struck, disguised as opportunity. Jacques Rougeau called Kevin with some big news.

Opportunity Strikes

First, he was starting IW2000 shows again. His health was better and he was ready to start booking arenas, giving away tickets, and hiring radio station mascots. He needed The Kid back.

Second, WWE would be coming to Montreal in the spring, and Rougeau had been promised a tryout dark match for two of his most promising students. Kevin would be one of them, there was no question of that. But of course, this meant that playtime was over. If Kevin wanted that WWE tryout, he had to stop doing all of this indie bar-wrestling nonsense and *commit* to his career.

Just before his singles match with Sami, Rougeau told Kevin to get back in his gilded cage, latch the door, and sing.

You might be raising a dubious eyebrow at the suggestion that there was any chance a nineteen-year-old kid was going to land a job in WWE so easily. Once Kevin had more experience, he realized the idea had been ludicrous. But Quebec wrestling in the early 2000s was an island, cut off from American wrestling and the rest of Canadian wrestling by geography. In 2003, Kevin had no idea what exactly one did to become a WWE wrestler and being sponsored by a former WWE wrestler seemed as reasonable a way as any other. He knew he had the talent, and believed—with a confidence that was warranted but ill-informed—that if he could just get official WWE eyes on him he could surely land a spot on the roster.

Now he was distraught. He'd been working for that tryout year after tedious year. To abandon Rougeau now, when he was so close, was unthinkable. But he had been learning so much and having so much fun! It didn't seem fair that he had to stop evolving to get a chance at the big leagues. It didn't seem right.

He talked to his parents and he called up PCO and asked for advice, but neither could give him a definite answer. PCO told him that he had the drive to make it with or without Rougeau and he should follow his gut instincts.[1] Kevin's parents were more cautious, reluctant to see Kevin sever ties with a powerful figure like Rougeau, but told him he should follow his heart. Which left him pretty much exactly in the same place.

Trying to buy himself a little time, he asked Rougeau if he could at least appear on the shows he was already booked for. In a 2014 interview, remembering it, Kevin unconsciously seems to become his nineteen-year-old self for a moment, and his usual confident body posture goes closed-off and nervous. He leans forward to look up imploringly at the Rougeau of his memory, stammering "Can you at least let me finish off the shows I... I... Like, I have a show this weekend, can I at least do that one?"[2] Magnanimous in victory, Rougeau granted him that one IWS show. Kevin could fulfill that one obligation, but after that all his energy would go toward the tryout. No more goofing around. Back to memorizing the same match for four months in preparation.

Kevin agonized as he got ready for what he knew would be his last IWS match. The night before *Blood Sweat and Beers*, he finished his midnight shift at the local gas station, then went straight to Rougeau's school to train his students. He had responsibilities at the school, after all, people depending on him. Was anyone depending on him in IWS? His duties and his dreams both lay with IW2000, so why did it feel so terrible to consider giving up wrestling in bars and bingo halls for a few dollars a match? He met Rougeau and argued with him for hours, but Rougeau wouldn't back down from his position: the wrestling for "shit companies" had to stop.[3] He knew he should go home and get some sleep before the show, but he was too jangled and upset, so instead he went to Le Skratch and hung out with the IWS wrestlers, helping set up.[4]

He must have been a mess: red-eyed and bleary with no sleep, torn in two, feeling guilty when he considered abandoning Rougeau but also feeling selfish that he was ditching IWS for the fame and fortune that surely awaited him. When re-telling the story, he's mentioned that various IWS wrestlers urged him to walk away from Rougeau's school and stay with them.[5] What he didn't know, as he helped to set up the ring and get into his gear, was that the news of his situation had filtered out into the audience, and the word was spreading. Soon enough everyone knew that this was Mr. Wrestling's last match.

Please Don't Go

Remember how El Generico's first match changed the pre-determined results of the match, turning his defeat into a victory? Kevin and Sami's first singles match, in the bar Le Skratch in November 2003, also changes the course of history. Kevin enters the ring knowing this will be his last IWS match, and he leaves the ring—

Well, let's get through the match first.

Kevin Steen waits in the ring as El Generico dances his way in. *OLÉ SHIT* is written on the luchador's chest, and when he takes off his sparkling cape you can see *I AM HOT* written on the back, with the "hot" underlined twice. The match is about twenty minutes long, and it's nonstop action, the two of them throwing every move they might ever have wanted to perform out there, because this will be their only chance. They trade submissions—El Generico's hands claw the air like a desperate kitten in Kevin's chinlock, Kevin complains bitterly in a strangled voice from an STF. They dodge each other's moves, anticipate each other's responses; this is the kind of match about which commentary would usually note "you can see these two wrestlers know each other so well" and talk about their long history.

It's their first singles match.

El Generico dances, he shows off, he exhorts the crowd to stamp their feet and sing. They move from submissions and technical sequences to high-flying moves: Generico does a soaring spaceman moonsault that leaves him tumbled and tangled up in chairs and fans. Kevin does a frog splash from the turnbuckle and eats concrete as Generico utterly fails to be there and break his fall. Generico climbs the scaffolding near the ring to leap onto the ropes, grab Kevin standing aghast on the turnbuckle, and plant him in the ring. They start to trade kickouts. Generico, exhausted after a nearfall, slams his heels on the mat, and the crowd responds by banging their hands on the ring and singing.

Generico manages to get a foot to the ropes after Kevin hits his finisher, the package piledriver. Kevin just barely kicks out of Generico's brainbuster finisher. Usually finishing moves are "protected," meaning someone doesn't casually kick out of them in a non-title match, but there's not much reason to protect your finisher from someone you'll never wrestle again, right? Generico misses with a 450 splash, Kevin misses with a moonsault, and then they just lie on the mat for a long time, breathing heavily. They're too evenly matched; it feels like they might never actually find a way to end the fight. It feels like they might not want to. They laboriously pull themselves to their knees and start trading exhausted punches, their anger slowly raising them back to their feet as they pummel each other. Kevin hits Generico with a second package piledriver, but Generico manages to kick out again, then gets a

PLEASE DON'T GO

desperate rollup and the pin. The match—Kevin's last IWS match—is over.

The wrestlers crawl to opposite sides of the ring, using the ropes to haul themselves to their feet. There's a long, awkward moment while Kevin sulks and Generico acknowledges the crowd's applause. Both of them are studiously not looking at each other. Then Generico wobbles, wavers to the center of the ring and holds out his hand for Kevin to shake at the end of their first, last, and only match.

And maybe it still was their *last and only* match when Kevin, inevitably, brushes aside his hand and staggers to leave the ring. But the fans in Le Skratch call an audible at this point and change history. Tipped off about Kevin's terrible dilemma, they raise their voices and start chanting "please don't go!" for Mr. Wrestling.

Kevin hears the chant.

You can see the moment Kevin realizes what they're chanting. He stops dead for a second, halfway through the ropes, and listens as the IWS fans beg him to stay. Then he shoves himself through the ropes and leaves the ring, walking slowly toward the back, his head down.

Behind him in the ring, El Generico is watching him leave.

I mentioned earlier that Kevin has said that various IWS wrestlers argued with him, telling him not to go back to Rougeau. When he lists their names, they include friends like Beef Wellington, Green Phantom. He never says that anyone named Rami or Sami or El Generico asked him to stay. But by the end of this fight it's clear that the match itself is El Generico's argument, constructed in his most eloquent language, which has never been English or French or Spanish or even Arabic, but wrestling: *Look at what we can do together. Stay here and let's fight forever. Please don't go.*

Dreams and Goals

By the end of the match, Kevin was exhausted and sleep-deprived, all his nerves frayed and snarled with unbearable tension. On his way to the back, his father, who had been hesitant for him to break ties with Rougeau, grabbed his arm and said "I've never seen better. This was a great match. You do what you think is right."[6] Kevin stumbled through the backstage curtain and the second he was out of sight of the crowd he burst into tears, falling to his knees.[7] It was all too much—the crowd's chants, his father's words, the match itself—"I had chemistry with this guy that I never even knew could exist between two wrestlers," he says later, looking back.[8] He couldn't bring himself to say goodbye to that, not even for a WWE tryout.

He called Jacques Rougeau and explained himself. In a last desperate attempt to have the best of both worlds, he said he'd be happy to keep working for Rougeau, but he *had* to keep wrestling in other promotions too. Rougeau hung up on him, closing the door on any attempts to flit in and out of that gilded cage at a whim.[9]

So that was that. As far as nineteen-year-old Kevin knew, he'd given up his best chance at ever being in WWE. It was time to start figuring out how to move forward from there. He made a video promo addressing IWS, explaining that Rougeau had gotten him a WWE dark match and tryout, but only if he quit wrestling for IWS. In the video, he's up against a stucco wall, looking straight into the camera. "I really, really want that dark match... but not this way. I want that dark match on my own terms, not on somebody else's," he says in the grainy footage. In the background you can hear the distant sounds of a match or maybe a training session happening. "I'm gonna make my own path to greatness, and I'm gonna start in the IWS, and I'm gonna make it on my own."[10]

He was almost completely correct.

Stung by Rougeau's abrupt dismissal, Kevin concluded "I'm gonna wrestle everywhere I can. Every single place that'll take me, I'll wrestle. And I'll get *so* good that whatever [Rougeau] could have given me I'll take on my own."[11] In the following three months, he wrestled more matches than he had in the last three years.[12] He was wrestling almost every weekend, sometimes twice, for a veritable alphabet soup of small Quebec promotions: IWS, EWR, NCW, MWF. And either Stevie McFly or El Generico was on every one of those cards too.

Sami didn't have a car and Kevin did, so it was just convenient for Kevin to drive both of them to the shows they were attending every weekend.[13] Every Saturday morning, he must have driven west along the long, flat, hour-long route across fields and woods to get from Saint-Jean-Baptiste, where he was living with his grandparents, to Montreal, cutting through the city to reach the suburbs of Laval on the other side and pick up a drowsy red-headed wrestler with a tendency to oversleep or forget his gear. All winter they ranged up and down the St. Lawrence River, from Montreal to Quebec City, three hours away, wrestling in Knights of Columbus halls and bars and basements. They wrestled in Kevin's hometown of Marieville in front of twenty-three people.[14] Years later, after El Generico's retirement, Kevin will record himself driving to a show alone and mention that he doesn't like listening to music while driving. He'll add wryly that some people think this proves he has no soul, an opinion that one can easily imagine a teen-aged Sami Zayn expressing vehemently from the passenger seat, hands flying.

They were far from the only wrestlers scouring the Quebec area for experience, so there must often have been other wrestlers along for the ride, but now and then it must have been just the two of them. It was on these trips that they grew from acquaintances into friends.[15] And inevitably, in between—one assumes—arguing about the Montreal Screwjob and ska, there must have been discussions about the future, and if it were possible to break out of the Quebec scene into the larger world of wrestling, and maybe even claw one's way to the very top.

Each of them discovered in the other a kindred spirit of ambition welded to creativity, a person who refused to just wish for success but swore to make it happen.

In interviews, both Kevin and Sami have often referenced the difference between dreams and goals, explaining how a dream is just something you hope might happen, but a goal is something that you're actively working toward, something you believe you can *make* happen. "I remember telling [Sami] that for me WWE wasn't really a *dream* anymore. Because when I was a kid, it was a dream. But then when I started wrestling, it became a *goal*. I think there's a difference between having *goals* and having *dreams*," Kevin says in one interview, weighting those key words with significance.[16] When asked in 2015 to give advice to young Arab wrestlers hoping to get to WWE, Sami says they should keep in mind that "dreams are just dreams, unless you put the work in. It can't just be a dream. It has to be a *goal*. Know the difference between a dream and a goal."[17] Recalling a time when Kevin was discouraged in Ring of Honor, Sami says Kevin had to remember that "this is a goal, not a dream. If you want to achieve this, you have to go after your *goals*."[18] And again, giving an aspiring wrestler advice in 2015 at San Diego ComicCon, Sami says "If this is your *dream*, if it's something you fantasize about, then that's all it'll ever be. There's a very big difference between a goal and a dream."[19] That precise phrase can be officially traced all the way back to 2005, in an interview with Slam Wrestling, where Kevin stresses that "what makes me different than other Quebec wrestlers is if I know I will make it to the top, it isn't a dream, it is a goal."[20]

Based on the nearly-identical phrasing Sami and Kevin use, and the weight they give those words, I think it's safe to say this idea of having goals and not dreams dates back even earlier than 2005. It goes back to long car rides through the icy Montreal night in the winter of 2003, and conversations between two battered and exhausted wrestlers on their way home after another show in a bingo hall or bar, talking about the future. Kevin came to realize that Jacques Rougeau had offered him nothing but dreams. Now, with Sami, he had found someone who shared his goals.

But first, they had to break out of Quebec.

GRAB THE BRASS RING
(2004)

IT TOOK a severed artery and some blood drinking to get Kevin and Sami to the United States.

They spent the first half of 2004 wrestling in just about every promotion in the Quebec area, piling up the miles on the road and minutes in the ring. In June, El Generico took on current IWS champion PCO and actually managed to wrest the IWS Championship from him, helped by a distraction. It's El Generico's first title win—okay, Stevie McFly had won the MWF Provincial Title, but it's *El Generico's* first, and Sami's first top title—and the IWS crowd is delirious with joy, screaming and pounding on the ring for their beloved underdog champion and his glorious reign of…three minutes. Because as El Generico starts to make his way out of the ring through the sea of jubilant humanity, a figure attacks him, rolls him back into the ring, and package piledrives him.

It's Kevin, come at this very moment to call in the promoter's promise that he'll get a title shot, before the sweat is even dry on the new champion's skinny chest. The crowd chants "Fuck you, Steen," but it's no use. The bell rings, and despite a flurry of desperate offense by El Generico, fifty-six seconds later Kevin holds aloft the IWS's top prize. He parades around the ring, taunting the furious crowd, taking a solid deliberate step on Generico's stomach on the way.

Ah, Kevin attacking his compatriot just after he wins a major championship and ripping it from him almost immediately; I'm sure we'll never see that happen again.

By mid-2004 Kevin and Sami had wrestled just about everywhere there is to wrestle in the St. Lawrence Valley. They were ready to make the jump to the rest of the world, but that was easier said than done. The Quebec area is isolated geographically, both from the United States and the rest of Canada: a five or six hours' long and expensive drive to Toronto, Buffalo, New York City, or Boston. It's also isolated culturally and linguistically, and before 2004, the only wrestlers from the larger wrestling world that the Montreal area had seen were the former WCW and WWE wrestlers who came to wrestle for their friend Jacques Rougeau's promotion. None of them were showing up in IWS.

In mid-2004 a shift was taking place, a shift on two levels. First, the

United States started to come to Montreal wrestling, and second, Montreal wrestling started to go to the United States.

Building Bloody Bridges

Total Nonstop Action (TNA) and Ring of Honor (ROH) were both founded in 2002 in the vacuum created by the demise and co-option of WWE's biggest competitors, WCW and ECW. As both promotions gained momentum through 2003 and 2004, they created a new class of wrestlers, elite globe-trotting technicians who weren't as cut off from the rest of the wrestling world as WWE wrestlers were. In 2004, Quebec promoters managed to start booking some of those high-level names to make the trek north, and as two of the most promising wrestlers on the Quebec scene, Kevin and Sami ended up crossing paths with most of them. It wasn't IWS but another promotion, Elite Wrestling Revolution (EWR), that started breaking down those barriers. Christopher Daniels wrestled Kevin in April 2004, AJ Styles showed up to fight El Generico that September, and Kevin met Steve Corino in the ring in November. Elsewhere in Montreal, promoter Marc the Grizzly brought in Samoa Joe for a July show to wrestle Kevin.

Through all these encounters, they won respect from some of the best in the world and made connections that helped them out later. Kevin gamely told the famously stiff worker Samoa Joe that he was free to beat him up legitimately if he liked ("I don't know why the fuck I said that," he recalled much later, laughing at his past self. "I thought it sounded smart at the time."[1]) Joe shrugged, said "All right," and proceeded to kick him in the face so many times that by the end of the match Kevin's face was swollen and unrecognizable, but when later asked to vouch for Kevin by the promoters of Jersey All Pro Wrestling (JAPW), Samoa Joe said "Book him. The arrogant little prick is almost as good as he thinks he is,"[2] and Kevin was in. Steve Corino was so impressed by Kevin's poise and skill that he would remember him in a year and bring him out to Japan to wrestle for Zero-One. People went back to the States knowing there were some wrestlers in Quebec who could really work, inclined to hire them when their names came up again.

And then there was the blood-drinking.

The tireless efforts of IWS's publicist Michael Ryan had landed a few of their wrestlers bookings at JAPW and Combat Zone Wrestling (CZW). In July, Arsenal, Evil Ninja #2, Green Phantom, and Sexxxy Eddy made the long drive down to Delaware to participate in the CZW show *Ultraviolent Tournament Of Death III: Banned ... My Ass!* If the name of the show doesn't get the mood across, the names of some of the matches will: Thumbtack Strips Death Match, Barbed Wire Boards Death Match, Panes Of Glass Death Match. In the semifinal, a light tubes match, a piece of glass sliced an artery in Sexxxy Eddy's arm, causing blood to geyser out. On the spur of the moment, utilizing true wrestler's instincts for the spectacular, Eddy flexed his arm to jet his blood into his own mouth, as if he were decanting wine from a wineskin. This would have been show-stopping all on its own, but Eddy wrestled in nothing but a gold lame thong and red bowtie, and the contrast between his look and his actions must have taken it all to a transcendental level.

From that moment, Sexxxy Eddy was a made man in CZW. Fans wanted to see more of him, and the CZW promoter made it worth his while to come by also giving more spots to his Canadian compatriots. On September 11, 2004, Sexxxy Eddy, Excess, Kevin Steen and Sami Zayn drove the seven hours to Philadelphia for a four-way match at the night show of CZW's double-header *High Stakes II*.

The border crossing into America to wrestle was always a fraught one for Canadian wrestlers, because of course none of them had visas to work in the United States. Kevin has talked about how one always had to be casual, but not *too* casual, politely respectful but not suspiciously tense. They learned over time to keep their gear in the trunk and to claim they were going to do cosplay at a convention if some zealous border guard took a look. Quebec wrestling historian Pat Laprade remembers that Sami was their go-to for interacting with the guards because he could cheerfully announce he was training to be a wrestler, and the guards would say *"You're going to be a wrestler?"* Sami would answer "Well, I hope so!" and the guards would look at the skinny youth, laugh at the joke, and let them pass.[3] We don't know for sure how that very first crossing into the United States went for Kevin and Sami, but it must have gone smoothly enough, because here they were, in Philadelphia, wrestling for an American crowd for the first time in their lives.

CZW had two shows on that day, an afternoon and evening show. The IWS contingent was wrestling in the evening, so they attended the afternoon show. It featured four wrestlers from California's new young promotion Pro Wrestling Guerilla (PWG), including two of its founders, Super Dragon and Excalibur, and it was a high-energy, excellent match that impressed the watching Canadians to the point where Sami turned to Kevin and announced "Oh, we're fucked. We can't keep up with this, this is great."

Kevin notoriously didn't pay much attention to non-WWE wrestling, but even he had heard of PWG by now, because fellow IWS wrestler Beef Wellington had quickly become one of their major fans. A year after its founding, PWG was starting to establish itself as a promotion to watch, bringing in stars and building compelling cards in front of white-hot audiences. The IWS wrestlers knew they also had a four-way dance coming up that would undoubtedly be compared to the PWG match, and they knew they wanted to break into that South California market. If they topped the PWG match, it might hurt their chances of ever working in that promotion. The four Canadians looked at each other. "What are we going to do?" someone asked.

Kevin answered, "Everything we can."[4]

Sexxxy Eddy enters first, as befits a CZW legend, to a huge pop from the crowd. El Generico—glittering cape flying as he dances—gets a much more muted reception, as do Kevin and Exess, as none of them have ever spouted blood in the ring like a breaching whale.

The match starts with Generico gesturing at the others to wait, then taking a quick calibration of the audience with a cry of "olé!" A smattering of "olés" ring back at him, and Generico does his little helicopter dance around the ring to reward them, at which point Kevin charges past him to attack Sexxxy Eddy in the opposite corner, immediately setting himself up as Heel of the Match.

The pace of the match starts off at "fast" and accelerates steadily from there as headscissors, dropkicks, superkicks, tornado DDTs, split-legged moonsaults, and yakuza kicks are thrown about with wild abandon. Kevin does a soaring tope con giro and flattens Eddy; Generico immediately does a twisting plancha onto Eddy and Kevin; Eddy instantly scrambles back into the ring and does an Asai moonsault out so far that he almost cuts himself in half on the barricade. Package piledrivers and double pumphandle orange crush bombs and other moves even more complex than their names fly, and by sixteen minutes in, the audience is on its feet and chanting *C-Z-Dub!*, stamping so loudly that it sounds like thunder. At this point, this is probably the largest audience Sami has ever wrestled in front of, and while Kevin's had larger at Rougeau's school, never one this large *and* this raucous. And they've got them wrapped around their four Canadian little fingers.

Kevin busts out his Steenalizer—a terrifying move where he basically picks up a wrestler, rolls them into a ball, and then hurls them backwards over his head into the unknown. As the crowd is still reeling from that murder scene, Generico drops Exess on his head onto the turnbuckle. The crowd gasps and starts chanting "holy shit!" People are jumping up and down in the stands. Sexxxy Eddy charges at Generico, who proceeds to dump him on his head on the turnbuckle as well. The crowd howls, and Generico, high on murder-adrenaline, drops to one knee in the center of the ring, throwing his arms out to exhort everyone to cheer more. They oblige!

When Eddy finally manages to hit his finisher and win the match, the crowd bursts into chants of his name. He lifts up the fallen Generico, they bring Exess into the ring and salute him, everyone hugs except for Kevin, sulking in a corner. Generico and Eddy notice he's not joining in and beg him to hear the crowd cheering. Generico points to them, and as he does, the chants suddenly, astonishingly coalesce into a yell of "IWS! IWS!" Seven hundred people chanting together for a promotion surely almost none of them have been to? Eddy, Excess, Generico and Kevin have not so much grabbed the proverbial brass ring as they've dismantled the entire merry-go-round and left wreckage strewn about the Pennsylvania countryside. Kevin eventually moves as if to shake Eddy's hand, then spits messily in his face and stalks out. As the remaining three take a bow, the crowd chants "Please come back!" Commentary says quellingly, "These fans say that to everybody, don't they?"

From the announcer's box the promoter, John Zandig, grabs a mic. "Sounds like you people like the Canadians, huh?" he notes to applause. "Let me tell you, anytime you guys wanna come back to CZW, it's open arms from us." He throws his arms wide. His face looks a lot less welcoming than his words sound.

So that's Kevin and Sami's first match in the United States, an absolutely wild affair that proved these IWS wrestlers could grab the attention of the crowd and get them chanting for an entirely different promotion. Maybe it's not surprising that from that match on, they and CZW had something of a love-hate relationship. After all, they'd been brought down from Montreal to put CZW over, not IWS. From that date, CZW booked Montreal wrestlers regularly, but the promoter badmouthed them in promos and booked them sloppily at best, with no care to giving any sense or consistency to the matches. The relationship would never be a good one, and a great deal of this simmering animosity seems to have stemmed from that first match in 2004, when the IWS wrestlers grabbed the crowd and conjured up a chant for the wrong promotion from the ether between them.

If that's an example of a promoter responding badly to being shown up, here's a counter-example.

Super Dragon and Excalibur, two of the founders of PWG, were in the four-way dance in the afternoon that the IWS wrestlers had gone out of their way to top. Super Dragon watched Kevin, Generico, Eddy and Exess blow away the audience and instantly hated them for trying to top his match.[5] But the weekend after that CZW show, Super Dragon found himself at a Jersey All-Pro Wrestling show with various IWS wrestlers. He was booked to wrestle Beef Wellington, Sami's roommate, which must have been a thrill to Beef since he was the one who had introduced PWG to his friends. Kevin was defending the IWS title against Exess, and Generico was in a light heavyweights tournament.

As the wrestlers milled around backstage, Sami Zayn decided he was going to give Super Dragon and Beef Wellington some advice on their upcoming match.

Super Dragon is apparently intimidating in or out of character, but Sami is not an easily intimidated person, especially when there are opinions to be given about calling a match. He draped himself over their shoulders, offering useful suggestions, and it is a tribute to Super Dragon that he was able to appreciate that this pushy kid who had shown up his team last week seemed to have some good takes on match construction.

After the show, Sami and Super Dragon stayed in touch on Instant Messenger, and within a couple of weeks Sami suggested a deal: if PWG would pay to fly a couple of IWS wrestlers out to Los Angeles, they would wrestle for free.

It's an audacious suggestion, coming from a barely-twenty-year-old wrestler that Super Dragon knew only as the wrestler who deliberately set out to outshine him in CZW and who had a lot of opinions about structuring a match in JAPW. It has an added benefit that if they didn't get paid, they wouldn't require one of those pesky work visas. It's a gutsy move. When I think about it, and about Sami's approach to self-promotion, I always remember a story that Kevin tells about young Sami and his Nintendo.

Apparently when Sami was six or seven, he desperately yearned for a Nintendo. When his father finally bought one for the family, he could hardly believe it. "Oh my God, I'm gonna play the Nintendo! Oh my God, I'm gonna play the Nintendo!" Kevin describes him chanting to himself over and over in anticipation. The machine was unboxed and set up and young Sami was in an agony of longing to finally play it, but his older brother got first shot at it. Sami sat there quietly, watching his brother play, waiting for his turn to finally, *finally* come. He waited and waited late into the night, sitting patiently for five hours, and eventually his brother finished playing… and pressed pause and turned off the TV to go to bed, leaving the game unsaved. Sami couldn't take his turn without losing his brother's game, and it dawned on him at last that he was not going to get his turn for a long, long time.[6] The story as Kevin tells it ends with the image of a tiny forlorn Sami staring at the forbidden Nintendo, but I've always suspected the story actually ended with a moral, a lesson learned.

Something along the lines of Sami saying "and *that's* when I learned never to patiently wait for someone to hand over the thing I want," as he hits "send" on the message to Super Dragon suggesting he buy Sami a plane ticket so he can fly to California and wrestle for free.

Whether he was amused or impressed or both, Super Dragon took him up on it. He wrote back, telling Sami that he'd pay for two plane tickets to come to PWG, one for Sami and one for another IWS wrestler, to come out and have a match.

Sami looked at the IWS roster, at all of his friends and compatriots. At his roommate and future tag partner Beef Wellington, who had introduced him to PWG and yearned for a match there.

And Sami invited Kevin to come to California with him.

ACTION FIGURES
(2004-2005)

BACK IN 2018, Kevin Owens and Sami Zayn shot a commercial for Mattel action figures of the two of them. In the video showing the making of the commercial, they goof around, playing with their figures, which are programmed to respond to each other as a tag team. "Kevin Owens, I've got your back," announces the Sami figure, and Kevin exclaims "Oh! You've got my back!" as they break into laughter. Later, Sami explains that "We were both playing with action figures well into our late teens."

As he doubles over with giggles, Kevin looks straight into the camera and says deadpan, "We were nineteen years old."[1]

He's not exaggerating, either. An ancient IWS promo reveals El Generico and Beef Wellington, in their early twenties, happily playing with action figures of Maven and Kevin Nash, putting together a match in which Maven triumphs because Nash tears a quad.[2] Kevin tells a similar story about how he was in his family basement at age seventeen, attempting to re-create the iconic shattering-glass sound of Steve Austin's entrance by throwing a mug at the wall. However, he didn't consider the relative sturdiness of ceramic and ended up hurling the mug *into* the wall, leaving it embedded there.[3] One assumes this was a moment that tested his parents' faithful support of their son's dreams.

ACTION FIGURES

One fascinating thing about wrestlers is that so many of them started off as fans, thrilling to wrestling stories, immersed in that narrative. For example, in August 2004, Kevin and Sami finished wrestling a show and drove the nearly six hours to Toronto to go to SummerSlam. Looking at the card, you might expect the two of them would be excited about the triple threat between Edge, Chris Jericho, and Batista for the Intercontinental Championship, or about the Undertaker challenging John Bradshaw Layfield for the WWE Championship. And maybe Kevin was, but Sami apparently never cared who held titles. He was interested in one match on the card: Matt Hardy fighting the demon Kane, with the victor to gain Lita's hand in marriage. The morning of SummerSlam, though, Kevin couldn't wake up his exhausted friend. Finally, yelling "We gotta *go,*" he flipped the thin hotel mattress so that Sami tumbled into the gap between the bed and the wall. There was a pause, a series of confused disembodied thumps as Sami woke up, and then a plaintive sleepy voice came from the gap: "I just... want Matt Hardy and Lita to be together."[4]

It's a funny story, but it's also a revealing look at Sami's storytelling priorities, which put relationships over titles, melodrama over belts. Almost every wrestler has imagined from an early age what it might be like to win the Royal Rumble, to be King or Queen of the Ring, to climb the ladder and grab the Money in the Bank briefcase. To rescue a damsel in distress from a demon's clutches. In a way, a modern wrestler making it to the main roster of WWE is a fan who's succeeded at getting their original character made canonical. Playing with action figures or practicing a dramatic entrance at age nineteen is comedic, but it's also a way for wrestlers to think about match construction and storytelling, as Sami explains in the Mattel commercial. "I came up with, as a kid, a lot of different ideas and delved into this whole world of becoming a match-maker" while playing with action figures. It's play with a serious goal.

By late 2004, twenty-year-olds Kevin and Sami were starting to go about the serious playful business of figuring out how their characters might work together, like making action figures fight or team up for tragedy and glory. They were starting to write a story.

Olé!

"We're getting on a *plane*? To *wrestle*? Oh my God."

On the car ride to the airport in November 2004, Kevin and Sami were unable to believe this was real. The flight was only Kevin's second time on a plane ever. The first had been earlier the same year to a weekend training camp for WWE's developmental property Ohio Valley Wrestling (OVW), run by the legendary Jim Cornette, where Kevin had realized once and for all that Jacques Rougeau's school had never been a possible path to WWE. Now he was on the way to board a plane that *someone else had paid for* to fly to Southern California to wrestle—okay, to wrestle for free, but still! They were flying to what they saw as the other end of the world[5], the land of Hollywood and Disney, magic and illusion. The two twenty-year-olds bubbled with excitement. "Even if the plane crashes on the way back, we'll be happy! We made it!"[6]

They were booked on the card as a tag team against two local SoCal wrestlers. Despite sharing the ring now and then for over a year by late 2004, Kevin and Sami had rarely if ever been an actual tag team together.* They were two of IWS's top singles wrestlers and had dramatically opposite moral alignments, so it had never made sense to be a tag team in their base promotion. This would require a different kind of match construction. They must have talked about it on the ride to the airport and on the flight itself, possibly as they squabbled over the armrest: how would brutal opportunist Kevin Steen and kinetic clown El Generico manage to work as a tag team? Why would they be working together? How would they co-exist?

As it turned out, they hadn't needed to plan.

When they arrived at the Silverlake Jewish Community Center, they learned that the team they were supposed to be wrestling against, Scorpio Sky and Quicksilver, were apparently stuck in traffic and unable to make it to the show in time, though Kevin and Sami suspected this was an excuse and that the SoCal wrestlers simply

---

* Cagematch.net claims never, but again, Kevin notes there are a lot of matches from this time that didn't make it into Cagematch.

didn't want to share the ring with two unknowns from Montreal.[7] Whatever the reason, their opponents weren't there, so a tag team match was off the table. Could the Canadians wrestle each other in a singles match instead?

Oh yes, the Canadians could do that.

As they waited for the show to start, they peeked out at the Southern California crowd, and Sami felt uneasy. His nerves weren't solely from the prospect of facing a new crowd in a new promotion, but for a very specific reason: he was worried how the Angelenos would respond to El Generico.

Describing the match years later, IWS publicist Llakor (keeping carefully if winkingly to the fictional), claims that El Generico was nervous because he had been banned from Mexico after almost killing someone with a brainbuster as a young wrestler. "Los Angeles might not be in Mexico, but in all other respects it was a Mexican city," he wrote. "The traditions of lucha libre were honored and respected there. El Generico wondered how he would be received. How would a crowd of Los Angelinos react to a man who had been banned from Mexico, who had violated the cardinal rules of lucha libre?"[8]

Llakor never *quite* broke kayfabe in his writing, but he did often try to express some fundamental truth about the situation in a fictional way, so it seems likely that what Llakor was referring to there was the unease of Sami Zayn, the Muslim-Canadian wrestler who was about to go out in front of a crowd of South Californians while wearing a luchador mask and playing the fool. Would he be booed out of PWG? Was this going to be a disaster?

Going up against Kevin instead of two local wrestlers was probably a relief. This way every aspect of the match was either in Sami's hands or the hands of someone he trusted. Still, he was probably uneasy as he went through the curtain to the ring to stand in front of PWG fans for the first time.

El Generico, however, doesn't look uneasy. Instead he looks confused as it's explained that their opponents couldn't make it. Kevin paces around him like a caged animal as the ring announcer notes that he's heard these two Canadians "fuck shit up in the ring" and that they're not exactly the best of friends.

"No, we're not," agrees Kevin, moving to lean against the ropes directly behind Generico's puzzled back.

"So you guys are gonna wrestle *each other* and show these SoCal motherfuckers what you guys can do!" the announcer says, and Generico seems just on the verge of understanding what's going on when Kevin clobbers him from behind before the bell can even ring.

The audience groans and laughs, though without much sympathy, as the hapless Generico gets stomped. "Now you applaud!" Kevin announces over his body, and there is polite applause.

The story of the match is simple: Kevin thinks he has a chance to pick up an easy win against El Generico, and comes to realize that not only are they evenly matched, the luchador might actually be better than he is. When El Generico does his around-the-world arm drag, where he spins disorientingly behind Kevin before hurling him by his arm to the mat, Kevin's jaw drops and he blurts out a perfectly-timed "What the fu—!" before getting tossed by his surprisingly-skilled opponent. He charges at Generico, bellowing like a wounded bull, only to get caught in a hurricanrana and tossed again.

A lone voice in the audience calls out "olé!"

Generico dodges a haymaker from Kevin, grabs him and does a tornado DDT off the turnbuckle. He's a spinning dynamo, dodging and tossing. Kevin rolls out of the ring in a panic to go sit on some laughing and startled fans. There's applause, louder and less merely polite this time. The audience seems to be getting the idea that despite the mask and funny name, El Generico is not merely a comedy act.

For his part, Kevin is at his most efficiently brutal, countering moves left and right to slam Generico into the mat whenever he tries anything too fancy. When Generico goes for a second turnbuckle tornado DDT (helpfully telegraphed by calling out "dos!") Kevin catches him out of the air and drops him across his knee in a backbreaker that drags gasps from the audience.

It's here as well, in this first singles match in America, in front of a fresh crowd, that Kevin seems to be honing one of his finest skills: making his babyface friend shine. He demands attention from the crowd where Generico can't ("Watch this!" or "Check this out!" he keeps yelling, refusing to let anyone lose interest), and his every move seems designed to make sure the audience comes to see Generico as not merely ludicrous but also heroic. Kevin does a somersault leg drop to the back of Generico's head and goes for a pin, but Generico manages to kick out. As Kevin sits in annoyance, Generico clutches his head and drums the mat with agonized boots, and the audience picks up the rhythm, clapping. Kevin jumps up and kicks the luchador, then puts his hand to his ear tauntingly. "What?" he mocks, "he needs you!"

The audience responds with a garbled growl of rising annoyance. "You suck, man!" yells a lone voice, and Kevin quips back an emphatic "No I don't!" as Generico suffers at his feet. Other people yell taunts, but Kevin is always ready with a retort. Clearly there's no way to shut him up with insults. At precisely the halfway mark, Kevin puts Generico into a chinlock and, as the luchador flails and struggles, he yells at the audience "What do you think of Generico now?"

And the audience finally figures out the only response that will shut Kevin up.

One person starts singing Generico's theme song, lifting the olé chant up to the ceiling of the community center, and most of the audience immediately joins in. What a feeling that must have been for two Canadian kids who had walked in unsure if they would be booed out of the ring. Despite the punishing chinlock, Generico's hands make eager grabby motions at the crowd, pulling more song from them like a magician summoning handkerchiefs out of the air. Kevin, of course, shows no delight at all. He shakes his head as if he's being attacked by a swarm of gnats, unable to summon any cutting response to the music as Generico fights his way out of the submission and renews the attack.

They keep going back and forth, Kevin's unmovable brutality and Generico's irresistible resilience too evenly matched. Something is going to have to break the stalemate. Kevin gets knocked to the floor and as he staggers and sways, Generico's boots drum a quick tattoo on the mat and he runs to slingshot off the ropes and head back. The people around Kevin suddenly realize that he's about to come over the ropes and there's a general cry of "oh shit" as everyone scatters to get out of the way of the hurtling luchador.

As he and Kevin pick themselves off the mat, everyone spontaneously starts to sing again.

Kevin stops Generico's momentum by dodging a brainbuster, then shuts the audience down by hitting a package piledriver, and the audience yelps in shock and goes silent as Kevin drives the luchador's head into the mat. Generico goes limp, lying unmoving as Kevin goes for the three-count—but at the last second Kevin pulls him up to break the pin. He's apparently having too much fun to stop just yet, and informs the audience that he's going to piledrive him again.

Unfortunately for Kevin, Generico is now mostly-dead and has gone so floppy that Kevin can't get him to stand up enough to actually take his finishing move. "Get up," he says in annoyance, then is hit with inspiration. "Maybe that olé chant will help him!" he says, and waves his finger cheerfully as the fans immediately start singing. "C'mon! Olé! C'mon!" he exhorts the crowd as Generico slowly staggers to his feet, dragged up out of near-death by the song. But as Kevin grabs Generico to piledrive him again, Generico flips over his head in a sudden burst of energy. "Fuck!" he yells as Generico grabs him and suplexes him into the turnbuckle. Another suplex, a brainbuster, and Kevin is defeated by his underestimated rival, his own hubris, and the energy of the crowd.

Oh, and a song. I'm sure it had already cropped up elsewhere in the past, but I believe this match is the first example of Kevin working to make the audience sing the Olé song, the song that will eventually follow him everywhere. In the future, he and Generico will generally enter to it as a tag team. Once they're enemies, he will spend a huge amount of time belligerently telling crowds he never wants to hear it, which will only make them sing it louder. In the end, it will become almost as much his song as Generico's. In 2016, when Sami Zayn and Kevin Owens are in the ring together for one of the first times on the WWE main roster, the crowd immediately starts singing the olé chant. Kevin claps his hands and beams at Sami. "You think they're singing that for *you?*" he exclaims. "That's so nice!" His sarcastic faux-delight barely hides a deeper joy, because he knows the song isn't just for Sami, but for the two of them together.

But that's in the distant future. Back in 2004, the PWG match was a success. Southern California sang for El Generico and cheered for Kevin's defeat. Kevin remembers climbing the stairs to the locker room after the match and thinking with each step, "that was the most fun I have ever had in my entire life."[9] As enemies, they'd made California sing. The next challenge was to see how they worked as a tag team. Time to play with a new configuration, a new dynamic. Do these action figures work as well as a team as they do as rivals?

Pull and Push

The American bookings were starting to come fairly quickly now. They and the other IWS wrestlers were regulars in CZW and JAPW, and after their first PWG match, Super Dragon was happy to book them again. But they were generally booked as a package deal—their singles match in PWG was an aberration. It was increasingly clear that they were going to be on American cards as a tag team a lot of the time. From late 2004 to early 2005 Kevin and Sami had a series of tag matches in three different promotions where they got to really work out their dynamic as allies rather than enemies.

They could have basically "rebooted" their characters to be friends. Wrestlers do that all the time, simply shift character to meet the requirements of the program they're in. But they made the more complicated choice to try and hold their characters steady across the various promotions they were working in, and to continue that character development in IWS as well. So how do this innocent weirdo and vicious egomaniac work together? The answer was simultaneously "very poorly" and "brilliantly."

Kevin and Sami had been in the ring together as two-thirds of a trio once in EWR, in Quebec, but CZW's *Cage of Death 6* on Dec. 11, 2004, is the first time they ever wrestle together as a two-man tag. They face off against Super Dragon and Excalibur from PWG, but before the match starts Kevin addresses Generico to make their relationship clear. "It's no secret that you and I aren't friends," he says to the confused luchador. "But this isn't about you and me. Tonight, this is about representing our home fed, IWS, at CZW's biggest fucking show of the year!" Generico's hands waver back and forth between him and Kevin and he squints, trying to follow his English. Kevin pats him neutrally on the back and Generico apparently decides that they're actually friends now. He pulls Kevin in for a big hug, leaving Kevin baffled and annoyed as the match begins. After Generico eats the pin, Kevin helps him to his feet, hugging him in turn before kicking him in the crotch and package piledriving him. Because they're not friends.

A week later, they're back in California in PWG, teaming up against Scorpio Sky and Quicksilver, who don't seem to have had any problems with traffic this time around. El Generico has apparently forgotten that Kevin is not to be trusted, and Kevin yells bullying "encouragement" at him from the ring apron, loudly noting his mistakes. This time it's Kevin that takes the pin, but unlike Kevin, Generico doesn't hold that against him. When Santa Claus comes to the ring and hands the luchador a flannel shirt as a present, Generico goes to his knees in awe at the soft cotton splendor of the gift, then begs Santa to give Kevin a shirt as well. Santa is dubious (Kevin is, to put it mildly, on the naughty list), but eventually gives way before Generico's pleas. Kevin puts on his shirt, then notices Generico is having some problems figuring out how to wear a shirt, lurching around with his head stuck in it and his arms waving aimlessly. Kevin helps his tag team partner out, arranging the shirt properly so that Generico can get a good look at him as he kicks him in the crotch and package piledrives him. Because they're definitely not friends.

The basic dynamic of these two matches is the same: El Generico thinks Kevin is his friend, but he's not, and the match ends with Kevin teasing friendship and then annihilating him. This is all well and good for the occasional team-up by two singles wrestlers, but it's not sustainable for a regular tag team. If they wanted to establish a team dynamic, they had to figure out how these two work as actual friends and allies, how to make their wildly different characters a true team. They chose to ramp up Generico's affection and tone down Kevin's violence just enough that they could get along while retaining their face and heel alignment, and that remained the default for their tag team dynamic over the next four years. They would swerve heel for a time, and gradually evolve into a long-term babyface tag team, but the fundamental structure of "El Generico is a better and kinder person

ACTION FIGURES

than Kevin Steen" would remain the unstable dynamic that kept their alliance crackling with an irresistible energy for years.

They also needed a finishing move and some wins, which they found in the next promotion they went to.

That promotion, called Chikara, was founded in 2002. By February 2005, it was starting to hit its stride in terms of goofy creativity when it brought Beef Wellington, Kevin Steen, and El Generico down for their Tag Team World Grand Prix, held in the basement of a fire station in Emmaus, Pennsylvania.

It's there in that Pennsylvania fire station basement that Kevin and Sami get their first win as a tag team, and it's there that they debut what becomes their tag team finisher move. Called the Assembly Line, it's their individual finishing moves stitched together: Kevin hits an opponent with his package piledriver, then rolls the semi-conscious wrestler diagonally to Generico, who hits a brainbuster and leaves them ready for the pin.

"The Assembly Line"

Package Piledriver — Hand Off — Brainbuster

It's also there that they debut what becomes a key feature of their tag team dynamic. Having won, they celebrate in a distinctive fashion, where Generico is effusively affectionate and Kevin is alarmed and annoyed by that affection. Kevin helps Generico up from the mat and they embrace, but the exhausted Generico's head dips a little too close to Kevin's crotch and Kevin recoils; Generico hurls himself into Kevin's arms and Kevin backs away with his arms waving, sputtering in horror. The whole spectacle is given a surreal tinge by the fact that it's fairly easy to see that it's *Kevin* who's directing this display, suggesting with a nudge that Generico drop his head a little too low and surreptitiously tugging the luchador close so that he can rebuff him. They're clearly working on their dynamic, figuring out what's funniest and works best for their characters. In a strange way, though, the fact that we can see Kevin being the initiator of the affection actually works for their characters as well. Over the next few years, the two of them engage in a complicated dance of dependency and rejection where Kevin especially is always pulling and then pushing, embracing and then spurning his partner. There's a homophobic edge to their shenanigans, but over time the relationship will become more complex, the affection more unabashedly sincere, and Kevin's inability to accept it will move from comedic to tragic.

But in 2005 it's all playful and silly. They go on to win their second match of the tournament, with more goofy celebration, and when they eventually lose Kevin doesn't even get around to kicking and piledriving Generico. Because… maybe they're friends?

They're twenty years old and playing with their characters as you might play with action figures, putting them into matches and seeing what happens. *If I do **this** then you could do **this**… If **this** happens then maybe we could…* Fantasy-booking where they might go, these carefully-crafted personas. It's easy to imagine them making up ludicrous scenarios, trying to top each other.

Here's me beating Jeff Hardy for the Intercontinental title in a ladder match.

Here's me giving a stunner to Stone Cold Steve Austin.

Here's us winning the tag titles in the main event at WrestleMania.

JUST WRESTLE
(2005)

Do or Die

KEVIN STEEN and El Generico get their first win as a tag team on Feb. 19, 2005, in a fire station basement in Pennsylvania. They do the first Assembly Line and their first victory celebration. Later that night they get their second win in the same tag team tournament.

These two wins are actually their second and third matches of the day, because earlier that day they had their very first matches in Ring of Honor, kicking off their first stint in the promotion that would eventually become their home. So let's rewind to those for a second.

Ring of Honor's *Do or Die IV* was an afternoon taping in New Jersey. El Generico was in a four-way match with Arik Cannon, Eddie Vegas, and Josh Daniels. Kevin had a singles match against B-Boy. The crowd had clearly heard of both of them through their appearances in other east coast promotions. There's a robust outburst of "olé" at one point and a decent "Mr. Wrestling" chant as well. Kevin comes to the ring in a shirt over a singlet, but wrestles in the singlet only, a gear choice that will become relevant soon. Neither of them wins, though Generico does manage to avoid taking the pin.

So in one day they had singles losses in one promotion, drove an hour and a half, and got two victories as a tag team in another. This day turns out to be emblematic of Kevin and Sami's 2005, in which they each have disastrous singles runs in Ring of Honor and close off the year as a tag team in other promotions. Because they only shared the ring once in their first ROH run, much of this chapter details out-of-ring frustrations and setbacks they faced during this year—but those frustrations and setbacks played a huge role in shaping how they approached wrestling storytelling.

From 2007 to 2013, Kevin Steen and El Generico were such beloved fixtures in Ring of Honor that it's difficult to believe their first time there went poorly. However, it's hard to overstate just how inauspicious this first run was. Between the two of them, they had sixteen matches in Ring of Honor in 2005, and just one win—and that one victory was El Generico beating Kevin in a dark match that was never aired. Their win-loss record wasn't the real problem with that year, though.

Before we get to that, however, we have to rewind just a bit more to November 2004. While that *Do or Die* match in February was Kevin's first Ring of Honor match, and El Generico's first Ring of Honor match, it wasn't *Sami's*.

On November 8, Kevin, Sami, and Beef Wellington drove from Montreal to Revere, Massachusetts, to attend the first night of Ring of Honor's *Weekend of Thunder* show. This was Kevin's first Ring of Honor show, and the main event was Jushin Thunder Liger facing Bryan Danielson—two wrestlers Kevin and Sami would share the ring with in the future. Their big PWG match in California was in a week, and they must have felt like they were on the cusp on breaking through because they brought a VCR tape of some of their matches to give to the Ring of Honor booker.

The only problem was, they weren't sure who that was.

Uncertain how to proceed, they approached one of the Ring of Honor wrestlers that they knew, CM Punk, whom they'd crossed paths with fleetingly a week earlier in All Jersey Pro Wrestling. Punk pointed them to Gabe Sapolsky, the ROH booker, and they handed over their tape. Sapolsky told them he'd heard of them but hadn't seen their work yet, and he'd give it a look.[1] It must have felt like a shot in the dark, but it paid off. Sapolsky gave Kevin a call a few weeks later, asking if he was free to work at the upcoming Final Battle show on December 26.

It wasn't a big role: they needed someone to wrestle a short match against Jay Lethal as a masked thug of a faction called the Embassy. Kevin had just re-torn the meniscus of the knee he'd injured back in 2002, so Sami took his place, debuting (rather ironically, on more than one level) as an anonymous masked wrestler called Weapon of Mask Destruction #2. Deliberately steering clear of most of El Generico's traditional moveset, he instead cribs a bit from Kevin, doing a powerbomb and a moonsault from the turnbuckle, which are much more his compatriot's moves than his own. Still, there are moments where you can see the luchador shining through in the way he tilts his head or holds up fingers to appeal to the ref after a nearfall. "This guy definitely looks very generic," commentary notes archly. It's only a six minute match, but by about four minutes in, there are scattered but noticeable "Let's go Weapon" chants in the audience.

Kevin was at the show, watching from the sidelines, glad for Sami and miserable for himself, worrying this Ring of Honor chance would pass him by. Austin Aries beat Samoa Joe for the Ring of Honor title, CM Punk and Steve Corino beat Alex Shelley and Roderick Strong to retain the tag team titles, and Kevin wondered if he'd ever get his chance to prove himself at this level.

He'd get more than one, it turned out, because Sapolsky started booking them about once a month through 2005, starting in February. When ROH was within reasonable driving distance of Montreal, on the east coast, Kevin and El Generico tended to be on the card—always as singles wrestlers, always in separate matches, with only one exception during the year.

Things started to go wrong from the very beginning for a host of reasons.

"What Am I Fucking Doing Wrong?"

Kevin and Sami were an odd fit for Ring of Honor, especially in the mid 2000s, when ROH had a very distinct aesthetic for its wrestlers: they tended to be athletic, well-proportioned (neither extremely muscular nor wiry), clean-cut and short-haired. There were other wrestlers who didn't fit that mold, but Kevin and Sami demolished it entirely. El Generico—weird, floppy, skinny, masked and mute—was unlike almost anyone in Ring of Honor at the time. Kevin hewed closer to the short-haired and beardless ideal, but he had never been a gym devotee, and he never had a particularly chiseled physique. Around 2005 was when he started actively struggling with his weight. "I don't drink, and I don't do drugs, but I *eat*," he remembered ruefully in his official Ring of Honor shoot interview in 2013. "That's my thing. I fucking get upset, and I eat."[2]

It's a fair bet he was upset often in 2005, because his and Sami's run in Ring of Honor wasn't going well. There were many reasons for this, and only one of them was that they didn't have the right look. They also seem to have struggled in a locker room with a stricter sense of protocol than they were used to, one where their buoyant confidence could rub people the wrong way. Sami was "overly familiar," and made himself "too comfortable too quickly,"[3] immediately treating everyone as equals and ignoring locker-room hierarchy. In 2008 Kevin was told by a ROH wrestler that Sami was "too happy to be a wrestler," too likely to come to the back overflowing with enthusiasm for how well his match had gone[4], and this attitude was probably there in 2005 as well. For his part, Kevin seems to have seethed on his friend's behalf: even years later he got agitated and angry remembering people's dismissal of Sami, calling them "full of shit" and "repulsive."[5]

Sami was also hobbled by the mask. The top of the card in Ring of Honor in 2005 was held by gimmick-free technically brilliant athletes. The character of El Generico was getting reactions from the crowd but watching his matches gives the distinct feeling that he's seen as a comedy act and is unlikely to be booked as anything else. The ceiling was low and he was bumping his head on it already.

Kevin's major struggle was a different kind of character-driven one. Specifically, he didn't mesh well with ROH's narrative style, which was focused primarily on combat-for-combat's sake and not the psychologically-driven storylines he was used to. When he asked how he should wrestle a match, he was told "You know, just go out there and wrestle."[6]

This didn't work well for either Sami or Kevin, but especially not for Kevin, who has always needed narrative like oxygen. He wanted to know whether he was a heel or a face, what his character's reason was for wrestling, and what his relationships with the other wrestlers were. "Just wrestling" gave him little to work with, and as a result, he struggled to connect to the match and the audience. Match by match, the "Mr. Wrestling" chants grew fainter as Kevin… just wrestled.

CM Punk, known for his stints on commentary where he viciously mocked most of the rest of the roster, dubbed Kevin's package piledriver finisher the "Mr. Peeper Driver." It was a reference to an SNL character, a scrawny half-monkey subhuman who wore a singlet-looking red shorts and suspenders and enjoyed dry-humping people. Considering the package piledriver always began with the opponent's head jammed between Kevin's legs, the nickname was a brilliantly savage belittling of Kevin's intelligence, appearance, masculinity, and humanity, all in one fell swoop. Other members of the commentary team started using it. Fans started using it. And in this case, catching on wasn't a good thing. It was going to be a challenge to get anyone to take a move called the Mister Peeper Driver seriously, and Kevin wasn't achieving the connection with the audience that might have provided an antidote.

The whole difficult year is epitomized by one awful moment for Kevin in April 2005, revolving around, of all things, a t-shirt. Since even his earliest matches in Rougeau's school, Kevin had always wrestled wearing a shirt, which fit the casual cockiness of his character. The Ring of Honor crowd, however, viewed wearing a shirt as a sign that a wrestler was hiding that he was out of shape. This problem was exacerbated, of course, by the fact that Kevin increasingly *did* look out of shape and was growing more and more unhappy and defensive about it. Generally, ROH wrestlers wore trunks, tights, or shorts with a bare chest, the better to show off their muscular physiques. The other option, which let a wrestler cover up a little more, was the skintight wrestling singlet. When Kevin started in Ring of Honor, he abandoned the shirt for a traditional singlet, but felt uncomfortable and bland—

"when I don't have the shirt, I just feel like I'm this Wrestler Dude"[7]—and it seems to have thrown him off.

That, combined with his frustration at not having a clear narrative reason for his actions, put him at a distinct disadvantage in the ring. On the ROH message boards Kevin was getting roasted by a vociferous and outspoken set of commenters who had taken a strong dislike to everything about him—his skillset, his character, and especially his look. "I read the message boards religiously," Kevin remembers, "and I was just getting *destroyed.*"[8] He distinctly remembers people piling on to critique a specific spot in a specific match he had with Jimmy Jacobs —a match that never even happened. Kevin fumed helplessly. "I have no fucking chance with this company! They're making shit up to hate me!"[9] His frustrations also turned inward as he wondered, "what am I fucking doing wrong here?"[10] It must have been upsetting, and Kevin's already told us what he does when he's upset. It was a vicious cycle, a loop of frustration, negativity and calories.

In April he tried to break out of it. His third match in Ring of Honor was coming up, and he was unhappy with how the first two had gone. Outside of Ring of Honor, things were moving much more smoothly. Just the month before, Steve Corino had brought him to Japan to wrestle for Zero-One and he'd had a shot at the PWG Championship against Super Dragon on the west coast. But somehow things weren't clicking in Ring of Honor. Trying to find some way to get his head back into it, he asked booker Gabe Sapolsky if he could wear a shirt for his next match. Sapolsky said it was fine, but when Kevin was walking around the arena before the show, CM Punk—soon to become the ROH champion—got onto the PA system and announced to the entire building in a booming voice, "Kevin Steen, this is God. You're a pro wrestler. Don't wear a t-shirt."[11]

Kevin was stung—not just from the insult, but even more from the implication that Sapolsky had been talking behind his back about him. Not surprisingly, his match that night—in which he wore a singlet— went badly.

Watching the match, the viewer can hear people in the audience heckling him, though their insults are indistinct. Kevin stops and heckles back, but the exchanges don't have the enjoyable snap of a heel working a crowd—how can they, when Kevin isn't sure whether he's a heel or a babyface? Kevin's on the verge of having *go-home heat*, the dreaded crowd alchemy when people aren't booing you because they want you to lose, they're booing you because they don't want you there at all.

Kevin came to the back winded from the match, sweaty and exhausted and miserable, and he made a terrible decision. He met Punk's eyes and said "Are you happy now?"

Kevin claims he meant it as a joke, but if he was still out of breath and defensive, it's pretty likely it came out as more of a snarl than a quip. Whatever the tone, mouthing off to a wrestler so much higher up in the hierarchy was a breach of locker room etiquette, and Kevin knew immediately that he would have to be put in his place. Punk loudly and at length dressed him down for being disrespectful, Kevin apologized, and the year moved on.

The anecdote is important not because it reveals any long-standing beef between Kevin and Punk—both of them have said publicly the exchange was no big deal—but because it epitomizes how awkward and ill-omened all of Ring of Honor in 2005 was for Kevin and Sami. The most telling detail from the whole story occurred right after Kevin said "Are you happy now?" to Punk. Instantly stricken and knowing what was coming, he added quietly, "Oh, please don't." Punk looked at him and said calmly, "No, I have to," then took a breath and launched into his tirade.

It's a moment that reveals the hierarchies at play. Punk wasn't even truly angry but was required by locker room code to re-assert his status over this newcomer who had addressed him as an equal. "It was like he was telling me it was a show," Kevin remembers.[12] It was a performance, a kind of kayfabe as surely as the in-ring performance was, part of a complex code of dominance and deference that neither Kevin nor Sami seemed to speak fluently.

"Have a Brain"

In July, Kevin and Sami found themselves booked to have a singles match together, the opening match at Homecoming. It was an opportunity, but more than that, it felt like a test. It was a chance for them to have the ring together and prove that they... Prove that they *what?*

They weren't exactly sure. The first match of any show is an important but difficult position: the wrestlers should get the crowd warmed up and enthusiastic, but if there's too much flashy showboating or drama in the match, the crowd might peak too soon and be flat for the rest of the show. "Are we gonna go balls-out in the opener or are we gonna be smart?" they wondered.[13] Were they supposed to show that they could dazzle or that they would be reliable hands?

By that point, they were isolated from the rest of the locker room—Kevin has stated bluntly that nobody was talking to them.[14] Only one person went out of his way to come to them and offer advice, and that was CM Punk. He'd become Ring of Honor champion in June *after* getting an offer from WWE, kicking off the original "Summer of Punk." Showing up after his win in a suit for an immediate heel turn, he signed his shiny new contract on top of the Ring of Honor title, then reigned in contempt until August, when he lost the title and moved on to WWE. Kevin and Sami's singles match fell right in the middle of that white-hot summer, and here was the champion, seeking them out when no one else would speak to them, to magnanimously impart some words of wisdom.

"I want you guys to do good," Punk told them, "but... have a brain."[15] The implication was clear—it was best to be conservative and not show off. After six months in the Ring of Honor locker room they knew that when the champion gives you some friendly advice, you follow that advice. So they played it safe and cautious and the final result was a perfectly fine match. The crowd gives them some perfectly fine applause, except for one male voice that keeps cutting in with a flat, joyless "Fuck you, Steen." It's a perfectly fine match.

But it was too late for a perfectly fine match to keep them on the card in Ring of Honor. It was probably too late at that point for anything to have kept them on the roster.

They were called in for one last show in August, and Kevin, feeling fatalistic, decided that he'd heel it up.[16] He had nothing to lose now, after all. The difference is palpable, electrifying. He immediately pulls the eye in a way he'd struggled to do for the last six months. His actions between moves are no longer neutral, they're riveting; his selling is no longer "realistic," it's magnetic. Halfway through the match a thundering "Mr. Wrestling" chant starts up. Kevin, who had gotten almost no response from the crowd for months, stops dead for a moment on hearing it. He looks gratified and dismayed at once: *Where have you been? It's too late now.*

And it was. Sapolsky told both Kevin and Sami he'd be in touch if there was anything more for them. It was clear this was a polite dismissal. When the *Homecoming* DVD came out in September and their singles match had been left off the DVD, it must have given a distinct air of finality to their time in Ring of Honor.

The year had been full of huge milestones for both Kevin and Sami. Kevin had wrestled in Japan for ZERO-ONE, and Sami had made it to Europe, wrestling in England and Germany for Internationa Pro-Wrestling (IPW) and Westside Xtreme Wrestling (wXw). Kevin had feuded with Super Dragon through the first half of 2005 in a series of brutal hardcore matches that cemented him as a PWG favorite. In August, just a few weeks after their one match together in Ring of Honor, Kevin had beaten AJ Styles for the PWG Championship on the same night that El Generico and his tag partner Human Tornado had won the tag titles. The two Canadians went up to the roof of the building after the show and sat looking out at the night sky of Los Angeles beyond the palm trees, holding their titles, full of gratitude that PWG had entrusted them with championships.[17] They'd piled up new experiences and proud achievements through the year.

But their run in Ring of Honor had been a disaster.

It was the first major setback on the road they had planned for their career. Until Ring of Honor in 2005, events had progressed in a series of natural upward steps, from Quebec to the East Coast to California. Ring of Honor had been the next logical step… and they had failed. They were going to have to regroup and think about a new approach.

The first part of their re-evaluation was to keep expanding their reach laterally. If they couldn't take that step up to Ring of Honor, they'd wrestle everywhere else. They'd made some connections in Japan and in Europe; in 2006 they'd spend even more time overseas.

"Maybe we don't *need* Ring of Honor," they decided with a mix of pragmatism and bravado.[18]

The second part of their path forward was a major leap in both their characters and their storytelling.

The Kevin Steen and El Generico Show

In 2004, Kevin and El Generico had wrestled in nine IWS shows. The next year was a very different story: wrestling regularly in JAPW, CZW, PWG, and ROH meant they were on the road many weekends, and by September 2005, they'd only wrestled three shows in their "home" promotion in Montreal. They were on the card for IWS's September show *Blood, Sweat & Beers*—Kevin wrestling an old nemesis, Damian, in a last man standing match, and Generico teaming up with Beef Wellington to take on Shane Matthews and Jagged, the current IWS tag team champions. Generico and Beef were still roommates and had already tagged a few times in 2005, in both CZW and IWS. This match marked their second attempt at the IWS tag titles.

As El Generico comes to the ring, he's mobbed by fans high-fiving and hugging him. Commentator Peter LaSalle notes that it's been a long time since they've seen El Generico in IWS, calling him a "world traveler and international superstar" who has "graced us with his presence" this evening. It's affectionate, but the respect and sense of distance are a huge shift from the way Generico was once treated as the scrappy little underdog the fans created.

As the two teams start to wrestle, Kevin Steen suddenly shows up on commentary.

"Oh look!" he says, "it's Beef Wellington, the guy whose ass I kicked last month!" Not only did he beat Beef, he apparently had talked a lot of trash at him, saying he was a disgrace to IWS. He's got little to say about Generico but does note when Generico is wrestling that "the match is so much better when Beef isn't in it!" He brags that the IWS champs have to share their two titles, but he has two titles all his own. Commentary grudgingly admits that Kevin is the PWG Heavyweight Champion and the CZW Iron Man Champion, adding that Generico also holds a PWG title. Kevin tells everyone the web page to buy PWG tapes and pretends he doesn't know where IWS tapes are sold. Then, having established himself as a preening egomaniac who thinks he's become too good for IWS, he takes his leave.

The match rolls on. Matthews' nasal foghorn voice, one day to become familiar to a world of fans as Matt Menard, the voice of the Jericho Appreciation Society and AEW commentary, booms from the apron. Generico does an Asai moonsault, wiping out both of the tag team champs on the floor below. He and Wellington do a double ass punch (Wellington's signature move) from the turnbuckle. Everything seems to be going well, but in the end Generico is knocked out of the action and Wellington takes the pin. They stagger out together, propping each other up. It's the last time Generico and Wellington will ever be allies in IWS.

In the main event, Damian comes out first, waiting in the ring as Kevin enters. Kevin is, it must be noted, wearing a shirt over his singlet. Damian launches himself at Kevin with a suicide dive before Kevin can get to the ring, and the match is on.

It's a wild match that brawls out into the crowd numerous times. Kevin sends Damian into a wall with a fallaway slam and fans scatter. Peter LaSalle and Brian the Guppie on commentary explain that Kevin is a "current Ring of Honor competitor," which they may not know is false; Kevin wrestled for Ring of Honor last month but will not be on the roster again for a year and a half. "He wrestles all over the United States now," they add, which is true and emphasizes how both he and Generico have apparently left IWS behind. Kevin rolls under the ring and comes up bleeding. He gets his hands covered in his own blood and deliberately smears scarlet on chairs, a vending machine, an ATM. "Oh, we're gonna have to pay for that," sighs LaSalle. At one point, Damian asks for chairs and fans start throwing them into the ring, a smattering at first that becomes a steady hail of folding chairs, at least fifty of them in the center of the ring in a terrifying shifting pile which Damian and Kevin pick their way across as they fight. Kevin does a 450 splash, misses, and crashes directly onto the pile of chairs.

Brian the Guppie leaves commentary to go to the ring and make everyone clear out the chairs, which vanish as fast as they appeared. And just in time for Beef Wellington, Generico's tag team partner, to appear and interfere in the match. He distracts Kevin, allowing Damian to knock his rival out, dragging him out of the ring and onto a table. Two leaping stomps off of scaffolding later and Damian is the last man standing.

The winner clears out, leaving Beef to drag the semi-conscious Kevin into the center of the ring so he can stand over and berate him. "How fucking dare you question how much the IWS means to me? For three and a half years I've made this company the most important thing in my fucking life," he yells, but his rant is cut short when Kevin kicks him in the balls. Kevin props Beef up in a corner of the ring and grabs a chair, raising it over his head to strike Beef down.

The relationship between Steen and Generico was always complicated.

The crowd yells in surprise and delight as El Generico jumps into the ring, grabbing the chair from Kevin and saving his partner. Generico shoves Kevin backwards into the opposite corner from Beef. As he does, Kevin starts screaming at him: "This isn't about you and me!"

Generico goes back to check on Beef, then has to turn as Kevin advances, shoving him back into the corner as he spits insults and tells Generico to get out of the way.

"It's not between you and I!" Kevin yells.

Generico stops dead, staring at him. His fingers splay wildly, clench, spring open again. He sways as if caught in a sudden high wind.

"It's not between you and I!" Kevin yells again.

And El Generico pivots without hesitation and Helluva Kicks Beef Wellington on the other side of the ring. Kevin steps forward and puts a heavy hand on Generico's shoulder as the luchador pants for breath, exhausted with emotion. Generico turns to him and they hug.

There are both groans and applause from the audience, but the overall mood turns sour as Kevin grabs the mic. It squeals with feedback and he starts ranting about how IWS mics are trash, the ring ropes are shoddy, and the fans need to shut up. Grabbing Generico's head, he says "I wish you could speak so you could tell them everything. We've been traveling up and down the fucking road together and I *know* what you think!" He claims they're both tired of being held back by IWS management and being seen as egotistical just because "we succeeded where all of you failed."

It is, of course, ironic that Kevin and Sami are framing themselves as too good for IWS when the fact of the matter is Ring of Honor has stopped calling them. This isn't a success, this is a failure, and they are completely aware of it. They're playing bullies who have come back to torment their hometown, but only because they couldn't cut it in the big city in real life.

Kevin bends over Beef Wellington and tauntingly informs him that Beef is just jealous that they've worked in PWG and he hasn't, and he never will, because he's nothing but a joke. Beef lashes out feebly and Kevin laughs, then sics Generico on him to pummel him. Please spare a kind retroactive thought for Beef Wellington, who introduced these two to each other, who introduced both of them to PWG and is now being beaten up and mocked by the pair.

At one point in the promo, Kevin notices that some fans are moving for the door. He stops and says to them, "Don't leave yet. Because the

Kevin Steen and El Generico Show..." He pauses dramatically, pleased with himself, pleased with the phrase. "...has just begun."

He's not talking about this one event. He means more than even all of IWS. He means the entire world has become the Kevin Steen and El Generico Show. When Kevin threw that "It's not about you and I" in Generico's face, Generico refuted him in the simplest, most direct fashion possible. Without words, he made it clear: *it is in fact about you and me. Everything from here on is about you and me.* Once in NXT and able to speak, Sami will make it explicit. Addressing an absent Kevin Owens in 2015, staring straight into the camera, he will say "Everything you've done for the last twelve years, it's been about *you* and *me!* And that's how it's gonna stay for the next twelve years!"

Faced with the painful fact of their separate failures in Ring of Honor, Kevin and Sami respond by binding themselves together going forward. It's an alliance that has been forming for years, but it takes its final form on this night, when Generico turns heel for the first and only time to become Kevin's partner. They're a unit now. In shoot interviews, Kevin casually uses "us" in striking places: for example, talking in 2014 about Sami's ROH match as Weapon of Mask Destruction, he says "It was very gracious of Green Phantom to loan us his mask."[19] He speaks sometimes as if they were a single wrestler.

This is not just a practical alliance, it's a narrative strategy, a response to the struggles of 2005 in Ring of Honor. "I didn't know what I *was* in Ring of Honor," Kevin says to Gabe Sapolsky years later.[20] Without a narrative or motivation, both of them floundered. From this point on, each of them defines himself by the other. Whatever happens to one influences the other. They are each other's character arc. If El Generico is in Japan, it affects Kevin's character. If Kevin wins the Universal Championship, it affects Sami's character. They become a sort of binary star system, each of them pulled by the other's gravity into a stable orbit, circling each other forever. Their path is determined—often invisibly—by the other's motion.

In the simplest and most elegant way possible, they have ensured that they will never have to "just wrestle" again.

ACROSS THE SEAS
(2006)

AS 2005 ENDED, Kevin and Sami regrouped in Montreal, still reeling from the setback they experienced in Ring of Honor. El

Generico had turned heel to team with Kevin in IWS, and they had turned the world into the Kevin Steen and El Generico Show.

So it's slightly ironic that in 2006 they barely teamed up together at all.

They had only two matches together as a two-person team that year, one in IWS (to complete their feud with Damian and Beef Wellington) and one in CZW. Their return to IWS as big-egoed bullies turned out to be fleeting—they were only there for four shows in 2006. And out of the nearly one hundred matches each of them put on that year, they shared the ring in any way less than ten times. All of that is because their other strategy for recovering from their Ring of Honor debacle was in full force, as they dedicated themselves to traveling as widely and as far as possible, gathering experience and making connections. Despite the lack of time their characters spent in the ring together, their alliance was stronger than ever, focused as always on their goal of reaching the heights. Somehow.

"An Evil Stand-Up Comedian"

Sami had already done two tours of Europe the previous year, in March and November. In 2006, Sami and Kevin would go there twice together and Kevin would make it back once without him.

The first trip was in February, when PWG put on shows in Germany and England. These were PWG's first shows outside of the United States, so a fair amount of pressure to perform must have fallen on the wrestlers. In Germany, El Generico and his new tag partner Quicksilver had an unsuccessful shot at the tag team titles. Kevin had lost his PWG World Championship two months earlier and was in a match to become the number one contender again versus Chris Bosh. Kevin had heard that the German fans hated him and was a little uneasy, and indeed the match started with people turning their backs on him, flipping him off, or calling him "Mrs. Wrestling." But by the end there were fairly equal dueling "Let's go Bosh"/"Let's go Steen" chants. He was winning people over, turning go-home heat to enjoyment.

In England, Kevin and Generico were in a singles match together.

ACROSS THE SEAS

Kevin likes to tell a story about a time when he and Sami were traveling together in 2005, on the way to Los Angeles.[1] In the middle of a grueling money-saving itinerary that involved driving from Montreal to Albany, New York, then flying to Philadelphia, then Dallas, then Los Angeles, he spotted his childhood idol, Stone Cold Steve Austin, sitting and waiting for a flight. Flustered, eager to meet his beloved Texas Rattlesnake, he ran back to the gate where Sami was waiting to gather him up. Not wanting to alert other people to the presence of Austin, he muttered quickly under his breath to Sami that Austin was here, urging him to come with him. Sami stood up and ambled along after him, but he hadn't heard Kevin clearly, which became obvious when he stopped Kevin and asked, game but a little concerned, "Who are we fighting?" Once the situation was cleared up and Sami was unlikely to start a brawl with Steve Austin, they went up to him and introduced themselves, explaining they were fans and also wrestlers, and asking Austin if he had any advice for them. The legend's advice for Kevin, delivered in his best laconic fashion: "Never stop running your mouth."

By this match in early 2006 it's clear to see that Kevin has taken Austin's advice to heart, because he never once stops running his mouth.

The match is in a hall in Kent, with a ring mat that's threadbare in spots, like a worn Persian rug, and emits puffs of dust whenever someone takes a bump. PWG's video of the match literally starts mid-sentence, with Kevin on the turnbuckle telling the audience "Just convert! Convert to Kevin Steen." He puts on El Generico's cape to pose when introduced to the crowd, causing the luchador to point accusingly at him. They've barely started the match when he stops to inform a woman in the crowd, "You're kind of cute," then indicates the man next to her and adds, "much too cute for that guy." He chest-chops Generico so hard that it sounds like a whip-crack, then blows on his own hand in exaggerated pain to cool it off. When the crowd does the Ric Flair "whoo!" in response to the chop, he does a bit of a Flair strut in the middle of the ring. Later, a slap to Generico's face gets a chant of "one more time" going, to which Kevin says in mock-annoyance "Are you never satisfied?" The chant shifts spontaneously to "ten more times!" and you can see Kevin lighting up, gratified at the interplay.

Sami, let it be known, is not having half as much fun. Later he would describe it as one of his least favorite matches and like "being attacked by an evil stand-up comedian."[2] You may be wondering, "Didn't he turn heel at the end of the last chapter? Why does he sound like the babyface in this match?" and the truth is that the IWS heel turn… it didn't really stick outside of IWS. In all other promotions he remained the unshakable natural babyface he had always been, because even in 2006, years away from his greatest moments, the El Generico character had already become such a finely-honed instrument for gathering and channeling the love of the audience. In this match, however, he finds his ability to gain the sympathy of the audience thwarted at every turn by Kevin's quips and comebacks. It's like Kevin's countering all of his moves in the same way he loves to counter Generico's turnbuckle DDT into a backbreaker, taking all of the luchador's momentum and using it for himself. It's not that the crowd has turned on Generico, not at all—they're singing "Olé," they're cheering his moves. It's just that whatever he does, Kevin undercuts him by making the audience laugh and love him despite their boos.

He gets Generico down on the mat and grinds his elbow into the pitifully flailing luchador's face, but then when the referee chides him, "Watch the point of the elbow in the face!" Kevin looks at his elbow intently and says, "I'm watching it and it's fine." The audience dissolves into delighted laughter, and Generico's babyface momentum is gone again.

Jumping to his feet, Kevin says to the audience as if suddenly inspired, "Chant my name a little bit!" They immediately do so. He's having the time of his life after a 2005 spent wrestling to go-home heat in Ring of Honor and strong heel heat in IWS, playing with the crowd like a cat with a catnip toy, giddy with delight. The only heckle that actually seems to get under his skin is when someone in the crowd calls out for a "Mister Peeper Driver." Kevin turns and says in a voice laced with plaintive exasperation, "That doesn't *exist*." The fan says "CM Punk says it does," and Kevin responds "CM Punk is full of shit," and kicks El Generico in the head. "How about *that?*" he says, and then it's back to the fun.

It's not all putdowns and wordplay: from about the halfway point on, the pace picks up and the humor diminishes. Kevin does a cannonball to Generico as he dangles helplessly upside-down from the turnbuckle. Generico does a moonsault onto Kevin as he's tangled in the ropes. The last third of the match is a full-on sprint. Kevin gets out of the ring and Generico tumbles over the ropes onto him, scattering fans everywhere. Everyone jumps up, and when Generico gets to his feet they start chanting "one more time!" Generico stops dead—at last, a "one more time" of his very own!—and jumps back into the ring to somersault off the turnbuckle onto Kevin again. There are suplexes and Helluva Kicks and Kevin even breaks out the 450 splash that used to be his staple, to the ecstatic shrieks of the audience. It's not enough to keep Generico down, but the package piledriver that follows is.

The audience ends up on their feet, chanting Kevin's name. Sami may have hated the match, but it's hard not to feel like Kevin needed and deserved a few matches where he was the one gathering up the crowd's energy, a feast after a pretty lean time.

That said, going forward Kevin generally moderated his wisecracks when he was heeling it up and let his opponent get some nourishment as well.

New Connections

Kevin went back to Germany in May for a couple of wXw matches, but as a duo, most of the summer was spent wrestling for PWG, CZW, and IWA Mid-South. In PWG, Kevin spent those months trying to get back the World Championship and failing. El Generico and Quicksilver were chasing tag gold, which they would finally achieve in December. There were a lot of losses for both of them that year, but they were putting on good matches, getting in the ring for the first time with an impressive list of wrestlers whose names were destined to become inextricably linked to theirs in many different ways. El Generico and Quicksilver had a match with the Briscoe Brothers, who will become extremely important to the narrative very soon. During his May trip to Germany, Kevin first wrestled Pac, who would become extremely important to Sami Zayn's story in about a decade. In one three-way tag match, El Generico (teaming with Quicksilver) and Kevin (his violent feud with founder Super Dragon turned to an alliance) shared the ring with the Kings of Wrestling, Chris Hero and Claudio Castagnoli, for the first time. At PWG's *Battle of Los Angeles* Kevin had his first match with CIMA of the Japanese promotion Dragongate. Kevin and Generico had shared a card with Tyler Black already in IWA Mid-South, but in 2006 Kevin wrestled him for the very first time, long before he became Seth Rollins and a thorn in his side.

Another name became prominent in 2006: Colt Cabana, one of the few allies they had managed to make during their first Ring of Honor run. Cabana advised them to not take no for an answer from ROH booker Gabe Sapolsky, to keep reminding him that they were out there and interested. Sami took his advice to heart, calling him regularly and eventually saying bluntly, "What do we need to do to get back?"[3] Meanwhile, Kevin was still CZW's Iron Man Champion, though his patience with the promotion had frayed. When ROH and CZW did an invasion angle in March and all the other CZW wrestlers defended the honor of their home promotion, Kevin decided instead to cut a promo running down CZW and begging ROH to take him back.[4] Cabana reported that Sapolsky was impressed by their initiative, but there wasn't any spot for them yet. So they bided their time.

Kevin and Sami's association with CZW came to a bumpy end in August at the show Trapped, when Kevin told promoter John Zandig that he was about to go on a tour of Europe followed by a tour of Japan, and he wouldn't be around to defend the Iron Man title so it would be best if he lost it. Kevin and El Generico were in a three-team barbed-wire cage match that night, teaming with fellow Canadians Franky the Mobster and Lufisto. Zandig, distracted by other matches and not paying much attention, suggested that Generico pin Kevin to win the title. Sami quickly demurred. "Oh, no no, I don't want it. I have... other things."[5] Besides, he was on the same team as Kevin, and that's not how any of this works. As Sami tenaciously argued the details, Zandig got fed up and yelled "Fuck the match!" This caused Sami—for whom there is perhaps no greater sin than to not care about the details of a match—to break into raucous, jeering laughter, mimicking him: "Yeah, *fuck* the match! Who gives a *shit* about the match?" Finally, Kevin, exhausted and eager to be finished with CZW, suggested that Lufisto—also on his own team—pin him to win the championship. Delighted at the idea of a female wrestler pinning Kevin Steen, Zandig agreed, and one barbed-wire cage match later, Kevin and Sami were done with CZW.* They were free to head off to tour Europe together.

This trip was for two weeks through Italy, Germany, and England in September. The Italian leg of the trip was a whirlwind of mishaps and memories, starting when Kevin and Sami arrived in Milan and realized they'd been sent to a different airport than the one they were supposed to be picked up at. They had no contact information for the promotion that had hired them beyond the name "Luca." Exhausted, jet lagged, and uncertain what to do, they called the other airport and asked them to make an announcement, then made a sign with their names on it and fell asleep underneath it on an airport bench. Eventually a search party of wrestlers found them, among them an Irish wrestler named Rebecca Knox, still many years away from being "The Man" Becky Lynch. The group bonded quickly, which was good, because it soon became clear that the promotion they were there to wrestle for, International Wrestling Zone (IWZ), had some problems. To put it mildly.

Sami, Kevin, Becky and the other wrestlers had been brought in to kick off the new promotion with its first three shows. However, the IWZ promoter was a man with a lot of money and not much knowledge of wrestling, and all of the staff including "Luca" were literal teenaged wrestling fans, doing their best but woefully unprepared to run a promotion. They didn't know how to promote and advertise shows beyond putting up some posters, so the shows were held in large arenas with a few dozen in attendance. They hadn't hired enough wrestlers to make a full card, so there were only four matches a night. Concerned that the fans weren't getting their money's worth, the

---

* Between 2008 and 2012 they'd wrestle there five more times between the two of them, but only sporadically.

wrestlers decided to add a battle royale to the end of each show, so everyone was wrestling two matches a night.

Despite the extra work, the wrestlers were all having a blast, especially since the promoter had made reservations for them in much more luxurious hotels than any of them were accustomed to. He'd also paid them all up-front, so everyone was flush with cash, young, and in Italy. During the three-show run, Becky and Kevin even had a match together—and if you're keeping track, that means yes, Kevin wrestled both the future Becky Lynch and the future Seth Rollins for the first time in 2006, over a decade before the two of them met and became WWE's power couple.

The night of the third and final show, Sami decided he'd better speak to the promoter. He didn't think it was fair that the wrestlers were putting on two matches a night and he wanted to suggest the promoter pay them for the extra work. The promoter, however, blew up at the idea: he'd brought these foreign wrestlers in, booked them nice hotels, and now they wanted even more money when they had failed to draw a huge crowd? "You're not Rey Mysterio!" he ranted, furious that the masked El Generico hadn't proven as big a draw as the WWE legend. "People ask if you're Rey Mysterio and when you're not, they leave!"[6] Unable to be any more Rey Mysterio than he already was, Sami couldn't placate him, and left him still-fuming to prepare for their last show.

Just before the show started, Sami went to the locker room and discovered that his wallet—with all the money he had, about 2,500 dollars—had gone missing. By the end of the show, it was clear the promoter had also gone missing. Baffled, the troupe of wrestlers headed to their hotel, to discover that the promoter had canceled their reservations and disappeared, presumably along with Sami's wallet.

Broke once more but undaunted, Sami and Kevin decided to explore Italy on their own. They went to Venice with one of the Italian wrestlers from the tour they'd made friends with, the Italian Warrior. The Italian Warrior's day job turned out to be as a gondolier, and he treated his Canadian friends to a romantic gondola ride around the city.[7] Then they went to Rome, which quickly became one of Kevin's favorite cities... and on the train ride back to Milan to catch the flight to Germany, they spotted the rogue promoter on a platform. He went pale with shock at the sight of the two Canadians that he thought had left the country a week ago, then turned and bolted off through the crowd, leaving Sami to shrug and tell Kevin not to bother chasing him.

Moving on to Germany, they wrestled a show with wXw, and Sami got in the ring for a singles match with a British kid called Pac (a childhood nickname from the fact that he had a six-pack as a pre-teen)[8] in a discotheque in Essen. They tear the ring apart with Frankensteiners, hurricanranas, wild cascades of flips. The sound levels are wonky, and the camera, perched on a second-floor balcony, picks up the constant babbling hum of people at the bar, their glasses and silverware clinking. After the bell rings and an incongruous disco light starts up, bathing their bodies in patterns of red, blue, and green, you can see Generico reach out and clasp Pac's upper arm, a check-in and a salute. The background buzzing chatter goes on unabated, a bar full of people oblivious to the fact that two of the greatest wrestlers of their generation just had their first match together.

After Italy and Germany, they went to England for a couple of IPW: UK shows, including one featuring a three-way match between Pac, El Generico, and Kevin, which one can only assume was amazing.* And it was in England that an extremely important event happened—Kevin fell in love.

Not with a British woman, however. No, Kevin had fallen in love over MySpace, the pre-Facebook social media site.

He had spotted a picture on a friend's page of a woman so beautiful he felt compelled to message her out of the blue, something he insists he had never done before. The woman, Karina, responded, and they clicked immediately. "She *instantly* went on my Top 8," the list of contacts on MySpace a user considered most important.[9] By the time he and Sami were heading home, he was desperate to meet her in person, but there was a complication: he had already sent a tape of his work to the Japanese promotion Dragongate, and they had booked him for a two-month tour that started almost immediately after the European tour ended. He landed in Canada, went to Illinois for two

---

* This match is one that appears to have gone unrecorded or missing, alas.

shows for IWA Mid-South (wrestling Claudio Castagnoli in their first singles match together), and then was off to Japan with no time to meet Karina in person.

He was going to feel like he was missing out in more ways than one during the next two months.

Lonely in Japan

Kevin's Dragongate run was fun... when he was wrestling. He even got to share the ring with cruiserweight legend Jushin Thunder Liger: "That made my whole trip worth it."[10] Unfortunately, there were long stretches where he *wasn't* wrestling, and the language and culture barriers meant he didn't know how to get around to experience much of Japan. He ended up terminally bored, kicking around the dojo and pining for Karina. They were trading messages on Instant Messenger and MySpace constantly, but it wasn't the same as finally meeting her face to face.

Even worse, while he was in the middle of his time in Japan, Sami got a phone call from Gabe Sapolsky, the Ring of Honor booker. Impressed by Sami's tenacity, he offered him spots on the card at two shows in November and December, including *Final Battle*, ROH's big end-of-the-year show. Kevin would still be in Japan for the November show, so he couldn't have made that one... but he would be back in the States before *Final Battle*, which suggests Sapolsky booked only Sami.

Kevin was distressed—El Generico was back on the Ring of Honor card and he wasn't. "Fuck, this kinda sucks!" he remembers moping. "If Generico's gonna be there, I wanna be there too!"[11] Was this going to turn into a full-time roster spot for Sami? Was Kevin going to miss his chance? Sami and Beef Wellington had been green with envy at his Japan stints[12], but this one now seemed less like an opportunity and more like a trap. He wavered between bravado and anxiety, going from messaging Karina "Fuck Ring of Honor, I don't care, let Generico do it!" to walking down to the ocean and staring out across the waves to the east, heartsick, missing the woman he'd never met and the friend who might be leaving him behind.

But he did get back to Montreal eventually, where he met Karina at

ACROSS THE SEAS

last and took her out for their first date (at McDonald's). El Generico was in the opening match of ROH's *Final Battle* against Jimmy Rave, Christopher Daniels, and Davey Richards. And at some point in late 2006 or early 2007, when Kevin was out on another dinner date with Karina, his phone rang.

Sami was on the other end, so excited that Kevin couldn't make any sense of his gabbling for a minute, but eventually he figured out that his friend was telling him Gabe Sapolsky had booked the two of them in a match against the Briscoe Brothers in February. They were getting a second chance with the top indie promotion.[13]

Kevin must have been visibly overjoyed when he hung up the phone, because Karina, remembering his messages from Japan, said "I thought you didn't care." Kevin instantly responded "Oh, I was fucking lying, I totally do!"[14] and Karina must have found Kevin's distinctive mix of bluster and vulnerability endearing, because they'd be married within months.

But for now, it's February 2007. Donald Trump has just challenged Vince McMahon to a hair versus hair match at *WrestleMania*. Jeff Hardy defended his Intercontinental Championship on *Raw*. Dusty Rhodes is about to be inducted into the Hall of Fame. John Cena is a double champion, holding the WWE Championship and (with Shawn Michaels) the World Tag Team Championship.

And Kevin and Sami are about to head back to Ring of Honor, this time as a tag team.

MAN UP
(2007)

Dem Boys

FEUDING with brothers always brings out the best in Sami and Kevin. There's something about the tension between the one tag-team extreme, those bound by literal blood since birth, and the other extreme of oddballs thrown together by circumstance. Facing down brothers throws Sami and Kevin's weaknesses and strengths into sharp relief, because unlike siblings they always have the option to sever their ties, deny their bond. Throughout their history, brothers have forged them into a team, broken them apart, and brought them together again. Three pairs of brothers in particular have played major roles in shaping their story.

In February 2007, they meet the first of those pairs.

Ring of Honor booker Gabe Sapolsky had brought Sami and Kevin on as a tag team to fight Jay and Mark Briscoe, at the time on their way to becoming three-time Ring of Honor tag team champions. "You've got fifteen minutes," he told them. "Go nuts."[1] This was already a big shift from "have a brain." Considering Kevin and Sami's previous struggles with backstage etiquette and their desire to become Ring of Honor regulars, they approached the Briscoes with caution.

Here's how negotiating a match goes when there is a power difference between the wrestlers: the lower-status wrestler asks the higher-status wrestler what they'd like to do in the match and then does what they suggest. If the higher-status wrestler is feeling magnanimous, they'll ask if there are any spots or moments the other wrestler would like to get in and find a way to include them in the match, but such generosity is certainly not required.

Sami Zayn, rather notoriously, has never been good at following this guideline. He tends to open these discussions by telling everyone how the match should go, then listening to feedback and ignoring most of it, hands fanning the air as he deflects suggestions.[2] In a PWG match with celebrated former WWE tag champions Paul London and Brian Kendrick, he was so sure of the right way to call the match that Kendrick eventually literally threw his hands up and announced he was done arguing and would do whatever Sami decided, but he was no longer emotionally invested in the match.[3] The people involved in Sami's first few big WWE matches remember him walking into planning sessions and announcing to the room full of wrestlers, every single one of whom had seniority over him, how the match was going to go.[4] It's an off-putting approach, no matter how much Kevin defensively notes that "98.5 percent of the time, he's right."[5] In the world of wrestling, being right about match construction is rarely as important as being respectful to people who outrank you.

Jay Briscoe was the same age as Kevin and Sami, and Mark was a year younger, so they didn't outrank the Canadians in that sense. But the brothers had both been in Ring of Honor since the very first show five years earlier, and thus had a huge amount of seniority compared to two guys brought in to wrestle one match after a disastrous first run. So when Kevin remembers that he went up to Jay before the show—the first time he'd ever spoken to him—and followed proper protocol by asking him what he wanted to do in the ring, you can be sure that either Sami wasn't by his side or that Sami was restraining himself with all his might in order to keep from blowing their second chance.

And all this talk of protocol and etiquette, seniority and status, makes clear what a gift it was when Jay just grinned at Kevin and said "Well shit, man... Let's go out there and fucking kill it!"[6]

And fucking kill it they did.

The two teams were well-matched and complementary, with Jay and Kevin providing the brawling and Mark and Generico adding a more wild and high-flying style. Interestingly, the Briscoes had started off in Ring of Honor wearing singlets and, well, "just wrestling," as skilled technical wrestlers. They had taken a hiatus from Ring of Honor, and largely from wrestling in general, in 2005, because Mark was injured and Jay was unwilling to wrestle without him. As a result, they entirely missed Kevin and Sami's first snake-bit run in ROH. The brothers came back in 2006, while Kevin and Sami were regrouping and touring the world, without the singlets and with a lot more personality. Embracing what can only be described as a "redneck gimmick" based on their real lives as gun-loving chicken farmers, the two brothers had begun to evolve toward the wild-eyed, dreadlocked, bandanna-wearing iteration that would become their most well-known. In 2007, when Kevin and Sami came back to Ring of Honor, that transformation had only just begun, though Mark was already using what he came to call his "Redneck Kung-fu" strikes and blows. It's easy to imagine that in the Canadian duo they could see another pair eager to get past "just wrestling" into something more character-driven, more urgent.

The difference between Kevin and El Generico's 2005 matches and their 2007 matches is visceral and immediate from the opening bell of their first match with the Briscoes. Everything crackles with energy, and the crowd is instantly dragged along for the ride as the upstarts try in vain to halt the momentum of the veteran brothers. As the brothers team up to beat down El Generico, Kevin fumes dramatically on the apron, holding on to the tag rope—which he accidentally pulls free from the turnbuckle. He stares at it for a moment, then uses it to try and lash at Jay's back, only to have Jay grab it and use it to garrote Generico, to Kevin's horror. Generico flails wildly for Kevin's reaching hand, finally scrambling between Jay's legs to make the tag, and the crowd leaps up with him. Kevin dropkicks Jay from the turnbuckle, bodyslams Mark, backdrops Jay, then does a murderous-looking cannonball to Mark in the corner. You can see in his face the elation of knowing that this time, things are going right, this time things are *good*. The brothers tumble to the outside and Kevin climbs the turnbuckle and does a swanton onto them both, knocking them to the floor. Scrambling back onto the apron, he leans backward and locks his arms around the ropes, staring out at the crowd and bellowing as though his excitement is too expansive to contain within his body. The frustrations of 2005 are just a distant memory now.

Some of the difference comes from Sapolsky giving them free reign, some of it comes from Kevin and Sami returning with a year's worth of wide-ranging experience under their belts. A lot of it is the talent of the Briscoe Brothers. But some of it is also the special alchemy of tag team wrestling. Years later, Kevin will be interviewing the Super Smash Brothers, and Player Uno will mention that once upon a time he didn't want to be in a tag team, but now he would fight tooth and nail to keep from being split up. Kevin will nod and smile, then say with emphasis, "Tag team wrestling is the *fucking best.*"[7]

It's in 2007, against the Briscoe Brothers, that he really learned that. For all their experience and globe-trotting, before 2007 Kevin and Sami had never spent any length of time in a tag division of any sort, with any partner. In IWS they'd been the top stars, not tag wrestlers. El Generico had been tag champion twice in PWG, but PWG's all-star format and monthly shows make long-term rivalries and stories difficult to build: when teaming with Human Tornado and Quicksilver, Generico never faced the same opponents more than three times. Kevin and Sami wrestled the Briscoe Brothers *six times* in tag matches in 2007. Add the matches where they faced one of the brothers, either as singles or in a tag match, and they faced at least one of the Briscoes ten times that year. Four of those matches were title matches. One was the first ladder match ever in Ring of Honor. Their names were inextricably linked throughout that year, turning in some of the most exciting tag team wrestling ROH fans had ever seen. And Kevin and Sami learned how to tell riveting tag team stories here, in Ring of Honor's tag division, starting with this match against the Briscoes in February.

They lost that match, of course. The Briscoes were slated to win the tag titles in their next match, a week later. But that wasn't the real victory. After the match Sapolsky greeted them backstage by announcing they were in. They were on every card from now on, and Kevin immediately called Karina and burst into tears of relief and joy.[8]

Things were going to be different this time around, because two brothers from Delaware were willing to give them a fresh start.

Writing in the Margins

When the Briscoes successfully defend their titles in May at ROH's first-ever pay-per-view, Steen and Generico show up after their win to challenge them to a title match. Kevin charges through the crowd to the ring and Generico is basically dragged along in his wake. The luchador jumps into the ring looking like he's trying to stop Kevin from doing anything rash, but Mark Briscoe intercepts him with a punch and all four start to brawl with increasing frenzied hatred as the crowd freaks out. They have to get pulled apart by the emptied locker room, and the fans boo angrily. Kevin seems to be caught up in bloodlust, but his heart is singing. "Oh shit, this is working!" Generico leaps off a turnbuckle onto a crowd of wrestlers and the crowd erupts into screams. Kevin wades back in to hurl himself at Mark, thinking "This is it, we fucking did it! *We did it!*"[9]

The feud with the Briscoes is magic for Kevin and El Generico. They get a chance to cut backstage promos and they lean into the impromptu comedy of them. In one Kevin explains he was worried about this upcoming "Race to the Top" tournament because he isn't a good runner, until someone explained to him it was actually a series of matches! Behind him, Generico tips his head to the side and gives us a knowing look behind the mask: *It was me. I told him that.* They use whatever is lying around at the armories and community centers as prop comedy. Here's Kevin in a random wheelchair demanding that Generico lace up his boots as he talks about destroying the Briscoes. Generico smiles loopily up at him as Kevin boasts that his tag partner is actually a vicious killing machine, flexing his noodly arms to show off his muscles.

Their backstage promos are hilarious, but any risk that they might get pegged as a "comedy tag team" is shattered by their in-ring action, where they are fearless, reckless, ruthless. They and the Briscoes beat and bloody each other over and over in a dizzying carnival of violence that lasts for months, through street fights, cage matches, last man standing matches, two out of three falls matches. All four of them do monstrous things to each other, hurling each other through tables, chairs, ladders, the crowd itself. They crack chairs over each other's heads with a gleeful abandon that might make a modern viewer shudder. One of the things that made Steen and Generico versus the Briscoes so magical was that they created the unshakable impression that they really, truly hated each other and wished each other dead—not for any ginned-up reason, but just by instinct, like a pair of mongooses meeting two cobras. It was on-sight and to-the-death every single time they crossed paths.

The other storytelling tool Kevin and Sami brought to the table at this time was a byproduct of that IWS betrayal of Beef Wellington from 2005 and Kevin's cry of "It's not between you and me!" Whatever is going on in the ring, whoever they're facing, they manage to communicate that the relationship between them is a dynamic thing, full of tension, always worth watching. There is *always* something between their characters, something that burns or hums or purrs but is never silent and never complacent.

Across six months in 2007, Kevin and Sami tell two stories. The first is the official story of how Kevin Steen and El Generico feud with the Briscoe Brothers, struggling and scratching and eventually falling short. It's the story that was booked, the story made up of the matches on the cards.

The second story is the story of Kevin and El Generico's partnership and why we should care about it. After that first match with the Briscoes, Sapolsky had intended to split Kevin and Sami up, making them singles wrestlers in different factions. Kevin, however, argued for keeping them together in the tag division. "I think we should keep teaming. I think we have something here. Our dynamic is different."[10] As the story with the Briscoes is unfolding, Kevin and Sami write their own story into the margins of the first, as they unpack and explore that "different dynamic."

Again and again in the years and promotions to come, we'll see examples of Kevin and Sami writing in the margins of the narratives they've been given, like two restless students jotting notes and doodling pictures in their textbook. They develop a gift for adding these little notes here and there through a match, or during their entrance, or after the action is over: small moments that add to the Story of Kevin and Generico/Sami, sometimes even in the total absence of the other person.

This narrative begins as soon as they know they're going to be booked full-time in Ring of Honor. In April, they have a match with Jay Briscoe and Erick Stevens—Stevens taking Mark's place because Mark has legitimately suffered a concussion. When Stevens "gets injured" and taken out of the match, Jay fights alone until Mark suddenly, unwisely shows up to make the tag. Kevin and Generico proceed to target Mark's head with absolutely brutal, pragmatic precision. Kevin mocks the mother of the Briscoes, sitting in the first row. Generico helps Kevin try to re-concuss Mark, and eventually they pin Mark for the win (note their Assembly Line finisher, a brainbuster/package piledriver combo, basically means dropping someone on their head *twice*). They're merciless heels in the match from bell to bell.

But when the match is over, El Generico goes to check on Mark Briscoe in apparent concern.

Kevin drags him roughly away, but it's an important moment, establishing that even though this team is fighting as heels, they disagree on tactics, and the luchador is a kinder person than Kevin. As the feud progresses, Generico is dragged again and again into brawls and sneak attacks on the Briscoes, and he joins in with gusto... but once the matches are over, there's a hint of respect, of remorse, of a humanity that Kevin lacks. After they lose their first title shot, at ROH's second PPV, Kevin seizes a ladder and smacks Jay with it. Grabbing Generico, he barks, "That's what I do! That's what you need to do!" As Generico staggers, a fan's voice offscreen suddenly yells, "Generico, you're so much better than this!" They ignore him, but you have to imagine they were thrilled to hear proof their character work was taking root.

When they win, Kevin is buoyant, his disagreements with Generico forgotten. After a bruising street fight where they come out on top, he challenges the Briscoes to a steel cage match for the titles, announcing "Ladies and gentlemen. This building has just transformed itself into one giant crystal ball. Because what you have in front of you right now is a clear indication of the future." And he's right in just about every sense *besides* the sense he means, of them being fated to beat the Briscoes for the tag team titles. They lose that cage match, and then the very next night they lose a two-out-of-three-falls match against the brothers in two falls, like six other teams before them have.

It's when they're suffering setbacks that things get strained between them, as it continues to become clear that El Generico's moral compass is calibrated quite differently from his tag partner's. At the end of that two-out-of-three-falls match, a dejected El Generico stands in the ring in front of the Briscoes, while Kevin sags against the ropes behind him. Mark offers Generico a handshake, and the crowd bursts into chants of "Shake his hand! Shake his hand!" By this point in August, Steen and Generico have been feuding with the Briscoes for six months, and the crowd has come to love the scrappy luchador and despise Kevin. This match had three babyfaces—at one point the crowd switched almost without transition from "Fuck 'em up, Briscoes, fuck 'em up!" to a boisterous olé chant—and a single heel who got yells of "Go back to Canada, you motherfucker!" They want the luchador to show and receive respect.

Generico hesitates, looking at Mark's outstretched hand, then back at Kevin. He steps forward and shakes both brothers' hands, and the crowd explodes in delight, while Kevin explodes in rage. "What are you *doing?*" he screams. Generico wordlessly begs the crowd to support his friend, and they immediately start a loud "Mr. Wrestling" chant until Kevin, his face almost childishly twisted in tears, steps forward and shakes his rivals' hands... and then kicks them both in the balls. Generico turns around to see the Briscoes crumpled and is comically confused as Kevin jumps out of the ring and starts to rummage beneath it. A fan's voice, thick with both a New York accent and disdain, sneers "He's gettin' a fuckin' ladder," and indeed, he is. Dragging it into the ring, he shoves one end at Generico. Generico hesitates, and Kevin bellows at the top of his lungs, "Grab it! Grab it! *Grab it or I'll fucking kill you!*"

Generico does grab the ladder, and Kevin uses it to plow down the Briscoes. Then he seizes their titles and hands one to Generico, climbing the turnbuckle to pose with the other. Generico, who is a good guy but still a wrestler, stares longingly at the title in his hand, then slowly walks out with it, trailing along in Kevin's wake.

Kevin had been using ladders as weapons over and over since their first title shot in June, so it only makes sense (wrestling sense) that the feud would reach its final climax in Ring of Honor's first-ever ladder match. The match was scheduled for ROH's third PPV as the main event: Kevin and Sami went from less than nothing to main-eventing in eight months, a truly meteoric rise. The show was titled *Man Up*, after the Briscoes' rallying cry of "man up, boys!"

It was time for the Canadian boys to man up as well.

Ladder War

The match kicks off with a wild brawl through the crowd. Kevin is in a red and black singlet—he won't start wearing shirts in the ring until 2012. El Generico is also in red and black; in 2006 the earliest version of his mask gave way to a black mask with red outlining on the face, one that he will have with slight variations for the rest of his career.

The brawl spreads like wildfire through the crowd. Wrestlers are hurled into chairs like bowling balls into pins. I count at least seven chairshots to various heads. El Generico might have more morals than Kevin, but he certainly doesn't hesitate to join in the general head-cracking violence. By the time the four of them battle back to the ring the crowd is revved up and ready to go, which is good because twenty-two minutes of relentless action await them. There is almost no stop for breath, yet the match is paced well enough that it escalates smoothly all the way through, driven on by the hatred and ambition of these four men.

The match is insane. Nobody seems to have informed any of the wrestlers that any given spot was complete and utter madness, so they just do them all.* Mark leaps from the ropes and dropkicks Kevin off

---

* Eleven years later, Kevin and Sami will walk into the planning session for one of their first WWE ladder matches and suggest so many reckless spots that Chris Jericho will

the ladder, and that's just the first warm-up spot. The brothers toss Generico back first into a ladder propped up against a turnbuckle and both ladder and luchador crumple dramatically. It's quickly apparent to everyone but the rage-blinded wrestlers that the ladders they're using are far too short and flimsy to reach the belts suspended far above the ring. A wrestler would have to stand precariously at the very top to reach them, but they keep trying anyway. As Mark scrambles up a ladder, Kevin tips him backwards onto the previously-crumpled ladder to create a writhing pile of metal and flesh.

While being pulled out from under the ring, the ladders have become tangled in the streamers thrown by fans. Now gaily-colored crepe keeps getting twined around the steel as the wrestlers use them to batter each other. The resulting image is incongruously festive.

Kevin manages to make it just a few steps from the top of the ladder. El Generico, at the base of the ladder, is trying to guard him from the Briscoes. As Kevin stretches a desperate hand upward, Jay leaps forward and tackles Generico, driving him backward and into the ladder. The ladder jolts over and Kevin drops down as straight as a stone: no drama or theatrics, just the finality of gravity.

Eventually Jay realizes none of these ladders will do. He spots a bright orange maintenance ladder, conveniently left standing in a corner of the arena, and calls to the crowd to bring it to him. They grab it and joyously crowd-surf it to the ring to be set up. It's tall enough to reach the titles; we're clearly entering the final act of the match.

The violence ratchets up accordingly. The brothers start to climb the ladder, but Kevin grabs one of the smaller ladders and knocks them off. He wedges his ladder between the maintenance ladder and the turnbuckle, creating a bridge, and manages to deliver a package piledriver to Mark onto the bridging ladder, destroying it. Generico sees his chance and makes a run up the ladder, his fingers brushing the belts for the first time. Below him, Jay wedges a second bridging ladder between the turnbuckle and the main ladder as Generico's

---

finally flat-out veto them: "Sami and Kevin were convinced that they needed to build an apparatus and take some kind of ridiculously stupid bump or else nobody would care," he will remember years later on Talk is Jericho while talking to Jon Moxley's

fingers reach upward. Jay drags Generico down and does his signature Jay Driller to him onto the bridging ladder. In technical terms it's an underhook reverse piledriver, but in essence it means Jay drives Generico headfirst into the ladder.

As Generico lands on the ladder, his legs are wrenched by his momentum into an involuntary split. The luchador is flexible, but not *that* flexible, and El Generico—Sami—comes to rest on the mat clutching at his thigh. The action surges on without him.

Generico down on the mat.

Kevin takes his turn running up the ladder, but Jay meets him at the top. The two trade blows as the crowd shrieks and commentary yells "It's time to man up!" Kevin finally cannot hold on to the ladder and plummets back down through the twisted metal at the bottom. Jay struggles to unhook the titles, which are attached by an unusually (one might say suspiciously) sturdy apparatus. After an agonizing sixty seconds that seems longer, he gets them free. The Briscoes are still the champions. Kevin and Generico have failed in their fourth attempt at the titles.

The crowd starts chanting "Thank you Briscoes" and "Match of the year." On the mat below Jay, Kevin and Generico have their heads together, one assumes discussing the fact that Sami can't walk at the moment. Eventually they stagger to their feet, and Kevin, staying in-character, shoves Generico away in fury and walks out, leaving Generico to limp out gingerly on his own. If he is upset at having to leave his injured tag partner unsupported and alone, it doesn't show on his face.

At this point, all hell breaks loose.

There's a commotion in the crowd and four figures jump into the ring: Tyler Black, Jimmy Jacobs, deathmatch legend Necro Butcher, and Jimmy's love interest Lacey. Although many in the audience don't know Black—this is his Ring of Honor debut—you probably know him as the future Seth Rollins. Kevin wrestled him for the first time in 2006. Right now he's a skinny little punk in black pants. His partner, Jimmy, is wearing white trunks and a white trench coat, his shiny chest bare beneath it. Necro Butcher's fist is wrapped in barbed wire and he attacks Jay, punching his forehead and leaving bloody gashes behind.

This is the debut of the faction called The Age of the Fall, one of the most visually spectacular wrestling debuts ever, though you might not know it from the released DVD of *Man Up*, where the video stops abruptly as the new faction stands over Jay Briscoe. But that isn't where the show actually ends, because at this point they tie Jay's feet to the cable that had held the tag titles and hoist him, dangling head-first, above the ring.

Head wounds already tend to bleed copiously even if all the blood *isn't* rushing to the victim's head. As Jay hangs upside down, his blood starts to splatter the ring: first a trickle, then a flood. Jimmy Jacobs steps directly into the stream of blood, letting it pour over him as he delivers his introductory rant. "Love doesn't save!" Crimson flattens his well-coiffed hair, oozes thick scarlet stripes down his snowy coat. "Nothing saves!" He takes Lacey's arm as he harangues the audience, tacitly encouraging her to join him in the torrent; she smiles at him, a tight-lipped "you're fucking kidding me" grimace, and declines to come closer. Jimmy tips his head back, mouth open, letting blood paint his lips and streak his bare chest. The crowd roils.

Backstage, everything is in chaos. Sapolsky is freaking out in mixed horror and delight at the grisly spectacle, panicking that Jay might pass out completely. It must have been mayhem, everyone staring at the monitors in aghast admiration or running around trying to get control of the situation.

When Kevin is asked what he remembers from that promo, he replies: nothing. He wasn't paying any attention to it, because he was worried about Sami, hobbling from his strained thigh. "I wasn't really concerned with what was happening," he says, dismissing the pandemonium that was unfolding around him. "I was more concerned about my partner being hurt."[11]

There they are, the two of them backstage, surrounded by bedlam, checking in on each other. They've pulled it off. Two years ago they left Ring of Honor in disgrace, and now they've cemented themselves as one of the most exciting acts in the tag division. In six months they've had some of the year's most memorable matches. And they've put together a small stealth story arc across those six months that established El Generico as a sympathetic babyface while keeping Kevin Steen a hateable heel. As Kevin stormed from the ring, the commentary crew had noted "I guess we will see in the weeks to come just what the future of Steen and Generico in Ring of Honor is"—but now the audience wants to find out.

They're invested, and Kevin and Sami are on their way to the top.

HANDS IN THE AIR
(2008)

Goals in Conflict

KEVIN AND SAMI spent most of 2007 feuding with the Briscoe Brothers and establishing themselves as a force to be reckoned with in Ring of Honor. That wasn't the only place they were wrestling, however. At the same time they were telling the story of their failed attempt at winning the tag titles, they were busy in other promotions, most notably PWG.

Over the years, many bookers and promoters dismissed El Generico as a goofy comedy act, but PWG was one of the first to treat him as a top star. He started 2007 as a tag team champion with wrestler Quicksilver, but they had to vacate the titles when Quicksilver suffered a career-ending combination of concussion and staph infection. Shortly after that, in February, El Generico won the PWG Championship for the first time—a year and a half after Kevin had, as his partner almost certainly reminded him.

Between getting a permanent roster position in Ring of Honor and winning PWG's top title, February 2007 must have been a heady month for Sami. He lost the PWG title to Bryan Danielson five months later on July 29, but earlier that night he and Kevin had won the PWG tag titles for the first time. That meant Generico was the first wrestler to ever hold both PWG titles simultaneously, albeit for only a few hours.

He would eventually go on to hold both simultaneously one more time, one of only two wrestlers to ever achieve that to date.

Kevin is the other.

They held the PWG tag titles for three months, basically through the end of their feud with the Briscoes, and lost them during PWG's second tour of England in October 2007. After the match is over, Kevin addresses the crowd and tells them that since El Generico is fighting Bryan Danielson for the World Championship the next day, he's going to ask Pac to team with him and try to win back the titles he and Generico had just lost. He notes that if he doesn't win them back, "I'm not sure when you guys will see Kevin Steen in PWG again."

The next night in Germany, he and Pac failed to unseat the champions. Kevin disappeared from PWG for five months after that. Even more strikingly, that night marked the last time Kevin wrestled outside of North America for six years. From late 2007 on, his range was limited to America and Canada. The reason, however, was not pique but something very different: his wife, Karina, gave birth to a baby boy in December 2007. They named him Owen, after Owen Hart, who was one of Kevin's favorite wrestlers in part because he seemed so likable.

Kevin was 23 years old, Karina even younger. None of Kevin's cohort had children, so this was all new territory for him. As they were holding Owen for the first time in the hospital room, the baby started to cry. They called a nurse and asked what was wrong, and the nurse looked at them, said "He's probably hungry," and walked out of the room without any further explanation or assistance.[1]

Attempting to dress Owen, Kevin was struck with terror at how fragile his son's newborn limbs were, sure that he would somehow break bones with the hands that caught flying wrestlers on the regular. He spent nights dozing fitfully on a windowsill in Owen's room to give Karina a break, ready to spring into action when needed. And of course, money became even tighter.

His parents helped—for a time the young parents moved in with Kevin's mother and father when they could no longer pay the heating bills—but Kevin felt a new pressure beyond the sheer ambition of his early wrestling days, a pressure that would goad him for years. He had to provide for his family now, and wrestling was not a reliable way to do it. He was working in a warehouse to try and pay the bills, but he was unwilling to travel every single weekend to the States and leave Karina to get by alone.

He had to prioritize Ring of Honor, which meant he was forced to cut back dramatically on other bookings. He appeared more often in IWS, becoming their top champion again for most of 2008, but shows outside of Montreal had to be ruthlessly trimmed. Kevin has said of PWG in this era that "If PWG was a person, it would be your best friend."[2] Now he was forced to spend less time with that "best friend" and treat wrestling more as a job.

And what of his actual best friend?

While Kevin was digging in with ROH and IWS, trying to make ends meet and raise his child, Sami was expanding his range, trying to get wider experience. In 2008 he did three different runs in Japan with Dragongate and wrestled in Germany, England, and Switzerland. In Wolverhampton, UK, he wrestled a curly-haired Canadian wrestler named Kenny Omega for the first time, just a month after Omega wrestled Kota Ibushi for the first time to kick off their career-spanning story.

More than ever before, Kevin and Sami were following different paths, their goals diverging for the first time. There's no evidence this led to any hard feelings between them, but it must have been difficult for both of them at times to feel like the person you had tethered your character arc to was spinning off on a different orbit. There's a moment on the *Fight Owens Fight* DVD released by WWE where some of Kevin's oldest friends list the many reasons why people thought Kevin might not make it to WWE. Pac laughingly mentions his personality, noting "He can be a bit of a prick." Seth Rollins admits he always worried Kevin's weight would keep WWE from taking him seriously.

Sami mentions Kevin's decision to put his family first. "The pressures of being a family man start to mount and mount... I was—I don't want to say skeptical, but I was concerned" that he might never make it to WWE.

This is the time when those pressures first started to mount, but they'd shape 2008 in unexpected ways.

"You Don't Need Him, Steen"

Despite their divergences, Sami and Kevin still were able to touch base almost every month in Ring of Honor, where they were generally booked as a tag team. They finished the feud with the Briscoes on an emotional cliffhanger: Kevin churlish in defeat, shoving an injured Generico away to stalk to the back seething, as commentary wonders what will become of them. Sami's injury was relatively minor—he didn't wrestle for a month, which is an unusually long time for him at this point in his career, but it means he's back at the very next Ring of Honor show to be in a four-way match against Nigel McGuinness, Hallowicked, and Tyler Black, the annoying emo boy from Age of the Fall, who will one day, as Seth Rollins, confess he never thought Kevin would make it. On the same card, Kevin has a shot at the top title against current champion Takeshi Morishima. Generico is there at ringside, cheering him on with every ounce of strength in his body. But when Kevin falls short, he pushes aside Generico's reassurances and storms off.

The next night, Adam Pearce, the leader of the faction the Hangmen Three, calls out Kevin. The faction had a penchant for both ornate robes and dastardly deeds, and they had a deal for Kevin, who they suspected shared a love of the latter, if not the former. Pearce reminds everyone they are feuding with the masked wrestler Delirious, having recently stapled his mask to his face, and that Kevin also has an annoying masked wrestler he might want to transcend. Generico's "complete and utter existence is that of a *loser*," Pearce says, and Kevin nods thoughtfully. Pearce has noticed Kevin's growing annoyance with the luchador and suggests he might prefer to team up with "people who are as vicious as you," turning the Hangmen Three into the Hangmen Four. And as a welcoming gift...

The curtain parts and Pearce's faction members enter, dragging the limp and wobbly body of El Generico between them into the ring. The crowd boos as they prop Generico up and Pearce bellows "let the dark side within you come out! Strike him down, Kevin Steen! Now is your opportunity!"

It's ridiculously corny, wrestling melodrama in its most pure and uncut form. What saves the segment is El Generico's face as Kevin puts his hand on the top of the masked head and balls up his fist, preparing to club him down. Behind the mask, his eyes are wide and terrified, but he doesn't protest or plead. He looks up into Kevin's face and then closes his eyes tightly and bows his head, accepting the inevitable. Kevin looks away, biting his lip, irresolute. Pearce growls "Do it! What are you waiting for?" then adds, "You don't need him, Steen!"

Which is, of course, the line that causes Kevin to turn and punch Pearce instead.

The whole faction starts pummeling Kevin. Generico is down and unable to help but Kevin fights on alone. The crowd is jumping with delight. Delirious, the other wrestler the Hangmen have been targeting, runs out to help, and they clear the ring of the bad guys. There's a dramatic pause and Kevin grabs the mic to point to Generico and yell "Hangmen Three, let me tell you something. There's only one person in Ring of Honor who's gonna have fun smacking around this guy, and that's me!" He drags Generico halfway to his feet and Generico, overjoyed, wraps his arms around Kevin's waist and hangs there like a particularly ornate championship belt. The tension between the two is resolved for now. Where before the team was aligned heel despite Generico being basically babyface, now the team would be aligned babyface with Kevin more or less still heel.

They feuded off and on with the Hangmen Three through the end of 2007, never fully getting the best of them. As that feud was ending, Goth triumphed over redneck as the Briscoes lost the tag team championship to the Age of the Fall. But the tag division would have to wait for a little while for Kevin Steen and El Generico.

"Actually, I Did It"

By the beginning of 2008, Kevin and Generico's tag team status was somewhat precarious. They cut promos together, they often were ringside to support each other, they tended to feud with the same factions

—for example, both of them had fights with members of the Hangmen Three early in the year as that feud wound down. But for the first three months, across seven Ring of Honor shows, they didn't tag together once.

Kevin was flirting a bit with the top of the card at the time. In February, he won a tournament to become the number one contender for the ROH World Championship. Unfortunately, that made him the contender against current champion Nigel McGuinness, who was gathering intense heat by refusing to wrestle, claiming injury after injury. Ironically, many of the injuries were legitimate ones, but McGuiness worked them into heel heat by making it look like they were excuses. As Kevin waited and waited for his match with Nigel, he got a variety of high-profile singles matches that elevated his status in the promotion. Sami was touring the world and getting a wider range of experiences, but Kevin's focus on Ring of Honor was paying dividends.

Keeping tag team members equal is a daunting task. There tends to be a Marty Jannetty to the Shawn Michaels in any tag team, and fans are quick to decide who's the Heartbreak Kid and who's the one about to get kicked through a barbershop window. When a tag team features two wrestlers with very different styles and personalities, as Kevin and Generico had, keeping them equal is an even bigger challenge. This is one of the constant tensions of Kevin and Sami's creative partnership —they're always competing, striving to outdo the other, but if one were actually to leave the other behind, he would risk being left adrift without his lodestar, his foil. Over and over in their history, either Kevin or Sami will ascend so far and fast on their own that they risk losing touch with the other entirely. Over and over again, they will find a way to come back together, whether as enemies or allies.

This is the first time that tension becomes overt in their relationship.

You can see it in the moment Kevin wins that number one contendership. Generico hurls himself into the ring, knocking his winded tag partner flat with the force of his exuberance. He leaps up and dances around the ring, gesturing wildly at Kevin for the audience as if to say *Look at him, look at how great he is*. He cradles Kevin's head in his arms, pressing a kiss to his temple, and fetches a microphone for the victor. Kevin touches his forehead to Generico's as he rises to his knees. His mouth twisted with emotion, he says, "Generico... we did it!" and throws his arms open wide for a huge hug.

Then in the middle of the hug, he suddenly seems to think twice. "Well, actually... I did it," he says, pushing Generico so that he tumbles backwards like a surprised red panda. There it is, that tension between *we* and *me*, between solitude and connection. If Kevin is heading to the top of the card as a singles wrestler, where will that leave his quirky masked partner?

Kevin spends the beginning of 2008 caught between the tag and singles divisions. The very night after he wins the number one contender's spot, he and El Generico show up to challenge for the tag team titles as well. From the Briscoes to the Age of the Fall, the tag titles have fallen into the hands of the No Remorse Corps faction, specifically Davey Richards and Rocky Romero. After their first title defense, Kevin and Generico interrupt the celebration to remind them that the Briscoes had "manned up" and given them a title shot, and they challenge the NRC to do the same. Richards grabs the mic and manages, in a twenty-second promo, to mock Kevin's weight three times, starting at calling him "tons-of-fun" and quickly progressing to the more direct "fat boy."* Kevin shrugs and he and Generico charge the ring, but Richards and Romero run away, laughing. Kevin and Generico never got that title shot from the No Remorse Corps, but their challenge kept them in the tag team division, even as Kevin chased the top singles title.

Meanwhile, in PWG, Kevin started to re-appear after a few months off to take care of Karina and Owen. He and El Generico won the tag titles for the second time there in March, a month after their challenge to the No Remorse Corps in Ring of Honor.

A month after that, on the night of Kevin's first failed attempt at the top title, the Briscoes won back the tag championships from the No

---

* Richards will cross paths with Kevin more than once in the future, but the fact that in their very first Ring of Honor interaction Richards immediately dismisses him as overweight will set the stage for an eventual feud in 2012.

Remorse Corps. Kevin and Generico's reference to how the Briscoes accepted their challenge hints at where the story might be going from here. It seemed likely that Steen and Generico were slated to come after the Briscoes' titles once Kevin was done feuding with McGuinness, and this time they might actually win them. As a callback to the red-hot rivalry of 2007, it made perfect sense. After months of the tag titles being tossed around without much of a storyline, Ring of Honor could enter the summer of 2008 with a sure-fire angle in the tag division and end it with a big feel-good win. In PWG, Kevin and Generico lost the tag titles shortly after this, which would also make sense if they were getting ready to focus on Ring of Honor as champions. All the pieces were in place for the summer of Steen and Generico.

Unfortunately, Mark Briscoe discovered he needed surgery on a damaged wrist immediately after he and Jay won the titles. They defended the titles once with a stand-in for Mark, but after that match Jay said he was unwilling to hold the titles with anyone but his brother, so they were vacated. The summer plans for an exciting program where Steen and Generico finally win the big one off their old nemeses lay in ruins. Because Steen and Generico had been in the tag division only sporadically through the beginning of the year, they had no real heat with any other tag team. The one team they *had* confronted, the No Remorse Corps, had just entered an angle where Davey Richards was about to betray his faction and break up the team, so that was a no-go. Gabe Sapolsky had to come up with a new feel-good story for the summer.

So Ring of Honor announced a one-day tournament for the tag team titles.

Kevin and Generico are the scrappy underdogs all the way through the tournament, wrestling three matches in one evening. They come into the first match already banged up, and commentary notes that Generico's shoulder and Kevin's knee are both in bad shape. You may remember Kevin's bad knee from 2000, when he injured it at the age of 16 and it never healed well. It's his go-to for storytelling psychology, the limb that every enemy targets if they want to bring him down. The same is true of Generico's shoulder, which has always been his weakness and will lead in the future to Sami's longest absences from wrestling. Unfortunately, their first opponents are Go Shiozaki and... Ring of Honor champion Nigel McGuinness, who Kevin's been feuding with most of 2008 and who is a master of targeting vulnerable body parts. Shiozaki brutalizes Generico's shoulder for eight full minutes as the luchador tries to get back to the corner to make the tag. The audience is already entirely on Kevin and Generico's side, and this inflames them. When Kevin gets the hot tag, he actually gets McGuinness in a submission hold and makes the champion tap out, winning them the match but so infuriating McGuinness that he grabs a chair and pummels Kevin's knee with it, leaving the unlikely victors barely able to make their way back from the ring.

The second match is with Chris Hero and Adam Pearce, old enemies who are more than happy to stomp Generico's shoulder and crack Kevin's knee some more. Only a distraction and a lucky rollup get Kevin and Generico the win. They're walking wounded, almost unable to stand, and they still have to face the Age of the Fall in the finals.

The crowd hates Black and Jacobs' mopey shenanigans. They've been rooting for Steen and Generico for months, and the weight of narrative is on the Canadians' side. They think they see where this tournament is going. Surely Steen and Generico will be able to pull it off. When Generico's shoulder is so badly hurt that he can't continue and is sent to the back, they're pretty sure they're getting one of the most reliable of wrestling tropes: the scrappy partner running back to the ring to save the day. Kevin is fighting alone and the crowd is simply begging him to endure until his partner can make it back. It's a gutsy performance. Kevin's anguish and endurance are heartwrenching. When Generico comes flying back in like an avenging angel, everyone goes nuts.

And then Age of the Fall cheats, gets a quick rollup pin, and wins the tournament.

The audience goes *insane* with rage. As Jacobs and Black attempt to cut a triumphant promo, the fans thunder "Shut the fuck up!" over and over, so loudly they drown them out. Someone throws a half-filled cup at the champions. Then it's a popcorn box. Soon a steady torrent of food, drink and debris is raining down on the winners as the audience screams hatred at them. Eventually the beer-soaked, popcorn-pelted new champions swagger out, and El Generico emerges from beneath the table he used for shelter to rejoin Kevin. They limp out together, leaning on each other as people gather around to thank them, to reach out and touch them as they walk by. "This isn't over!" Kevin swears, his voice breaking into tears.

Ring of Honor had its tag team feud for the summer again.

Through the summer of 2008, Kevin and Generico feuded with the Age of the Fall faction members, overcoming every obstacle thrown in their way until they finally got their title shot on September 19, in Boston, Massachusetts. Once again they main event the card for the tag team titles.

As the match starts, commentary reminds everyone that Kevin promised he'd have a Ring of Honor title by the end of the year. He's tried over and over to oust Nigel McGuinness, but the tag division is where he's focusing his energies now. Everyone in the match is in black and red, but there's no mistaking any of them: El Generico in red and black mask and tights, white mask ties fluttering; Kevin in his red-and-black singlet with the moonsaulting figure on the front; Tyler Black in no-frills black trunks with a cascade of long dark hair; Jimmy Jacobs with black hair gelled and styled so a single red forelock falls onto his forehead, wearing red trunks with artfully ripped black mesh over them. If an '80s New Wave band member decided to wrestle, he'd be Jimmy Jacobs.

The match starts with a flurry of tags in and out, warming the Boston crowd up. Not that they need much warming—they're frenzied with the desire to see the Age of the Fall punished and Steen and Generico elevated. When Kevin gets a chance to chop Black's chest and yank on his hair, the crowd yells "fuck him up, Kevin, fuck him up!" and pounds on the metal barricades to fill the arena with thunder.

The match settles into a protracted stretch of babyface suffering as Age of the Fall cuts Generico off on the far side of the ring and tortures him. Kevin can't seem to help arguing with the referee, which of course causes the ref to turn his back on the ring and the galling sight of Black and Jacobs doing dastardly things to the suffering luchador. It's like wrestling a pair of very emo eels that slip away after every tormenting move. Generico reaches wildly for Kevin's corner, his long fingers fanned out, arms windmilling as he gets pulled back. The crowd sings the Olé chant at the top of their lungs, urging him on, taunting Jacobs and Black with it as Kevin stretches his hand out in desperate urgency.

When Generico finally knocks his tormentors to the floor and makes that tag, the crowd erupts. Kevin immediately does a somersault tumble over the ropes to bowl over both opponents, then powerbombs Jacobs onto the apron. The action ticks up a level from "frenetic" to "insane," including a spot where Black charges at Generico, who tosses him over his head and right into the arms of Kevin on the turnbuckle. Kevin hoists him up, then jumps from the turnbuckle to drop Black across his knee stomach-first. Black flops wildly in the middle of the ring, retching for breath, only to be hit in quick succession with a swanton from Kevin off one turnbuckle and a splash from Generico off the opposite turnbuckle. The crowd is sure they're going to win with this, and howls in agony when Black kicks out. Black manages to recover enough to hit his finisher, God's Last Gift—a complex move that basically involves hooking Kevin's leg, dumping him on his neck, then having him in the pin as the move ends—and that would probably have ended the match except that Generico flies in from out of the ring to break up the pin at the last possible second.

As the pace accelerates, Kevin gets Black into a sharpshooter submission and it looks like Black is going to tap, but Jacobs hurls himself onto Kevin, biting his nose and breaking the hold.

Finally, the critical moment arrives. Black leaps off the ropes with a forearm but Generico dodges and he catches Jacobs with it instead. Kevin superkicks Black to fall against Jacobs in the corner, and Generico does his running big boot—called a Yakuza Kick in 2008, not yet the Helluva Kick—to both of them. Black falls out of the ring, and Generico hurls the stunned Jacobs backwards into Kevin's grip.

Kevin gets Jacobs into position for the package piledriver, then stops and looks wildly around the arena. This is clearly it, the moment when they succeed or fail. The crowd noise is deafening.

When the Assembly Line goes off without a hitch, Kevin's piledriver giving way to Generico's brainbuster and the pin, the crowd takes a huge collective breath and counts along with the referee. At "three" a roar goes up and nearly every single person in the arena leaps to their feet, their hands shooting up, a thicket of ecstatic arms. Kevin, who has been struggling to keep Black from breaking up the pin, jumps to his own feet and staggers around the ring for a second as if he doesn't know what to do with himself before falling to his knees.

Two boys from Montreal.

Both Kevin and Sami remember this win as one of the greatest in their career. Sami specifically mentions the hands leaping into the air, the involuntary spasm of joy pulling everyone upward as one in that instant. "It was such a real emotion."[3] When Kevin talks about it, he becomes uncharacteristically incoherent, stumbling over his words. "Everybody in that crowd forgot for a second that... you know... it wasn't—" He breaks off before he can say the word *real*, tries again: "forgot that this was *supposed* to happen. Like, what they saw..." He pauses, searching for words. "That emotion was so *real*," he finally says, exactly the same way Sami does.[4]

"Even for us," he adds, and you can see that too, the way that true and genuine emotion transports everyone in the arena, both the fans and the wrestlers, out of the fakery of wrestling and into the deepest reality of it.

Kevin crawls over to where Generico is lying and they embrace, listening to the ovation as the referee drapes the titles across their bodies. They both slowly rise to their feet, each of them staring down at the title in their hands, then look up and lock eyes, staring at each other in amazement. The crowd lifts up their voices to sing Olé, and, as if the song prompted it, Kevin and Sami come together in a huge hug, Generico lifting the title above his head in triumph as Kevin wraps his arms around him. It's a beautiful scene, one of the most powerful in a career full of powerful moments, created by two boys from Montreal.

And, of course, also by their sworn Hot Topic-themed enemies. Because behind the scenes, Sami and Kevin had become fast friends with Jimmy Jacobs and Tyler Black. The four of them would regularly share a hotel room, dubbed "The Scrub Room" by Colt Cabana, where they would sit and talk all through the night after a show about the world of wrestling and how they were going to change the future. How they were going to *be* the future.[5]

But for now, the new champions had to defend their tag titles against all comers, from the Briscoes to the Age of the Fall to a new and ruthless tag team on the scene.

YEAR OF THE WOLF
(2009)

The Hunt Begins

KEVIN AND EL GENERICO'S first Ring of Honor feud, the one that put them on the map, was with Jay and Mark Briscoe. In a more narratively perfect world where Mark wasn't injured, they would have won the titles from the brothers. But the fiction of wrestling intersects with the real world of physical bodies, of injuries and tragedies, and Kevin and Sami would only share the ring two-on-two with the Briscoes five more times in their careers. Two of those times were in late 2009, as new champions. It's possible they were gearing up for a full-blown feud—the Briscoes were starting to have a mean-spirited edge to their wrestling, hinting at a heel turn that would have made a feud with the babyface champs crackle—but Mark got injured again and that became impossible. Meanwhile, the former champs, Jimmy Jacobs and Tyler Black, were starting to have conflicts that would soon cause the end of their alliance. Ring of Honor needed a new tag team to challenge the unlikely odd couple of Steen and Generico, and they needed it fast.

Enter the American Wolves.

The American Wolves were Davey Richards and Eddie Edwards, two wrestlers recruited by Larry Sweeney to become the tag team for

Sweeney's faction Sweet 'n' Sour. We first see them backstage attempting to kick a sandbag in two as Sweeney yells about this groundbreaking debut. Richards and Edwards were visually the antithesis of Steen and Generico: muscular, clean-shaven, scowlingly intense, deliberately lacking any personality beyond hunger and ambition. They were ruthless opponents who honed in on the weakness of their prey with a single-minded focus, and Steen and Generico would become their prey immediately after their creation. That same night they jumped Kevin and Generico in the middle of their non-title match with Age of the Fall, taking a lead pipe to Kevin's knee and leaving him in so much pain that he was forced to tap out to Jacobs' guillotine choke.

The next night, at Ring of Honor's traditional year-end finale show *Final Battle*, Kevin and Generico defended their titles from Jimmy Jacobs and his ally Delirious, representing Age of the Fall while Tyler Black tried to become the number one contender for the heavyweight championship. After the loss, a frustrated Jacobs cost Black his match then turned on him. The two of them would spin off into a feud with Black as a newly-minted babyface, starting his climb up to the top of the card with a bang. For now, they exit Kevin and Sami's story, but they'll both be back.

Elsewhere on the card, the Briscoes had a match against Kensuke Sasaki and Katsuhiko Nakajima. After the match, Richards and Edwards rush the ring, attacking Jay and Mark. They handcuff Jay to the ropes and demolish Mark's knee with a chair, writing the already-injured brother off the show for a while. El Generico and Kevin, chair in hand, come running in to confront the Wolves, who clear out of the ring and regroup on the ramp. The tag champions pause, eyeing the Briscoes: Mark writhing in the corner clutching his knee, Jay still handcuffed to the ropes. There's a long, fraught pause while the Wolves laugh mockingly on the ramp, waiting for Kevin to use the opportunity to hit one of his old enemies with the chair. Instead, Kevin throws the chair down and goes to Jay to help unhandcuff him, limping on his old bad knee with its ancient ACL tear, re-aggravated by the Wolves the night before.

Richards and Edwards, on the ramp, stop laughing. Their eyes light up as they realize the tag champion has thrown away his weapon, that he's wounded and vulnerable, and they charge back into the ring—this time to attack Kevin's knee. The Wolves are chased away with some help, Kevin is left hobbling and furious, and the feud that will define the Ring of Honor tag division for 2009 is in play.

Steen and Generico would face the Wolves five times two-on-two in 2009, a rivalry that would establish the new tag team and push the champions to their breaking point—and beyond.

The Wolves were nipping at the champions' heels from the very first ROH show of 2009, inexorable and unrelenting, though the oily and duplicitous Larry Sweeney is in their corner as a manager, which keeps their vibe from being as purely vicious as it would become later in their career. There's some weasel in their wolf: Richards kisses a confused El Generico's boots, groveling to trick him into letting his guard down so Edwards can blindside him. They're a mix of cunning and cruel, yanking on Generico's mask ties, hooking their fingers into its eye holes and dragging him around. Their sneers could cut glass. Anyone who felt like they didn't deserve a tag title shot in their fifth-ever match probably was silenced after this bout, because the skill of the Wolves and their chemistry with Steen and Generico was undeniable from the opening bell. There's a crackling enmity between Richards and Kevin especially, while Edwards dishes out violence with a cool ferocity that matches up perfectly with Generico's limber suffering. The vibe between the two teams is different from the visceral hatred with the Briscoes, the repugnance with Age of the Fall. As champions, Steen and Generico were classic heroes, embattled and besieged by their wily foes, and there's a growing desperation to their matches as they struggle to hold them off.

The first match in January, Steen and Generico won largely due to a lucky distraction and a quick roll-up. The Wolves were not going to give up that easily.

For the next two months, Steen/Generico and the American Wolves faced each other over and over in various combinations. As one part of a larger faction, The Wolves had a ready supply of compatriots to step in and help out. For their part, Steen and Generico had a rotating set of loose allies or at least enemy-of-my-enemies who could team with one or the other—for a couple of shows, for instance, Jay Briscoe helped Kevin out when the globe-trotting Generico was wrestling in Poland. This means Edwards and Richards were constantly working together with Kevin and Sami backstage—which is valuable because it gives us a glimpse of their creative process.

In 2012, Kevin had Eddie Edwards as a guest on The Kevin Steen Show. Kevin's rapport with Eddie is easy and relaxed—a sharp contrast to Davey Richards' time on the show, which was cordial but strained—and Eddie reminisces about calling matches with Steen and Generico. Eddie remembers their planning sessions as rancorous affairs, filled with bitter arguments and vehement disagreements.

Oh, not with the American Wolves. Between Kevin and Sami, the tag team partners themselves.

Eddie paints a vivid picture of the Wolves sitting in growing impatience as Sami and Kevin bickered endlessly over the minutiae of a match, wrangling every single detail at length, even as the match before theirs was going on. He remembers Davey turning to him at one point and muttering "I'm just gonna choke Generico out, I'm just gonna grab him and choke him out."[1] He seems to have meant as the end to the match, but one can't help but get the impression that Davey was contemplating not waiting until the match. Eddie's affection for the duo is clear but so is his exasperation. Kevin responds by defensively claiming that he and Sami were doing it on purpose, that bickering was their "schtick" and they knew people expected it of them: "It was a thing we were doing because we knew people liked it." Eddie responds with a fond but firm "uggggh" before adding more politely "I don't know if we liked it," remembering thinking "Can we just figure out what we're doing, please!"

Whether other wrestlers found it amusing or annoying, this obsessive tweaking of details has remained a hallmark of working with Sami and Kevin through their careers, to the point JBL claims he quit being one of WWE's backstage agents—the people whose job it is to mediate between wrestlers and the bookers and writers—specifically because he could no longer bear to listen to Sami Zayn's in-depth discussions about his character and his storylines. "Everything was questioned. Everything," he complained in an interview with his friend and fellow agent Road Dogg.[2] Road Dogg commiserated, noting that "Kevin is the same way. Every single thing needs to be talked out and talked about a lot, and I'm talking about from the reversal of an Irish Whip to, well now do you put your feet here?"

This endless haggling and wrangling over the details was especially ill-suited for the time and place they were in. Jon Moxley writes in his memoirs about the indie attitude that it's "a sign of weakness" to go over the details of a match too carefully beforehand. "There's a weird, old-school ego thing that goes on between 'call it in the ring'-minded guys, and it's admittedly stupid," he explains. "Neither guy is gonna want to be the first to get too excited or have an idea."[3]

Kevin and Sami—bubbling with excitement and overflowing with ideas—must baffle wrestlers who prefer to play it cool and disinterested. Even separately they probably come across as over-eager, and when they're working together that trait is accentuated to the point of potential derangement for anyone working with them. But it pays off over and over again, including in 2009, as the American Wolves closed in on their prey. Richards and Edwards honed in on Kevin like they were cutting a vulnerable caribou out of a herd, targeting his knee over and over in every match leading up to their next title shot.

Predator and Prey

By March, Kevin comes through the curtain limping already, but also at a dead run to the ring to pummel their tormentors. This second title match is a no disqualification match, which does not favor the champions, to put it mildly. Kevin struggles and suffers dramatically all the way through, constantly hobbled by the fact that he needs his knees for every move. His signature submission move, the sharpshooter, requires him to squat while twisting his opponent's legs under him. By March 2009, he screams with pain while executing it, his demands for his enemy to tap sounding more like pleas to end his own agony. He finally does manage to get Richards to tap out, however, leading to a win but also a coldly efficient post-match beatdown by the Wolves. By the end of it, Generico has been put through a table and Kevin is tied to the ropes, arms spread as the Wolves ruthlessly beat his knees with chairs. There's blood trickling down his face as he howls with pain and anger, spitting bloody mist at the Wolves whenever they draw close. The Wolves finally clock his head with both chairs at once (they're angled so the chairs themselves catch almost all of the impact) and he sags unconscious against his bonds. El Generico crawls from the wreckage and to Kevin's side as the sneering Wolves leave. He cradles his partner's lolling head as the referees untie him, then hovers anxiously as his partner is carried out. It's high melodrama, with a feeling of impending doom: how much more can the champions endure?

Next month, in April, the American Wolves close in for the kill.

This match is a tornado tag match, which means all four wrestlers can be in the ring at the same time, there are no legal men and no tags, and anyone can be pinned or submitted. Once again, this format isn't ideal for the champions because the Wolves are masters at cutting off and separating their prey. It's also a "tables are legal" match, which is an invitation to mayhem. Richards and Edwards get thrown through tables first; wood splinters and metal snaps over and over. At one point the Wolves throw Kevin from the turnbuckle into a table, which Kevin takes absolutely knee-first, his bandaged knee taking all the impact. Kevin and El Generico set up two tables on top of each other behind a turnbuckle but then get pulled away, leaving the tables standing there, ominously. And indeed, after Generico puts Edwards through yet another table with a wild splash to the outside, Richards shoves Kevin as he unwisely climbs the exact wrong turnbuckle, sending him hurtling through the two stacked tables. Edwards recovers enough to low blow Generico and get him up on his shoulders so Richards can drive the luchador through a table. The exhausted, battered Generico can do nothing but lie there, tangled in the twisted metal braces of the destroyed table, as Edwards gets the pin and takes their titles away.

"They are broken men," commentary intones as referees check on the crumpled former champions. The story for the summer of 2009 is in place: Can Steen and Generico win back their titles? And what toll will this chase take on their bodies and souls?

The toll on the bodies was immediately apparent, as shortly after this El Generico was gone for a couple of months to rehab an injured knee. While he was gone, Kevin tried to win the titles from the Wolves with temporary partners Jay Briscoe and Bryan Danielson, but neither attempt succeeded (and in fact his alliance with Jay ended in angry recriminations after an accidental low blow by Kevin to Jay). So by the time Generico returned, Kevin was even more banged up, even more desperate and exhausted.

Continuing the run of terrible match stipulations, Steen and Generico's first rematch with the Wolves was a submission match. Between Generico's short-term knee injury and Kevin's career-long knee injury, their disadvantage was glaringly obvious as the Wolves honed in on their joints and did their best to dislocate them. It was Generico who eventually tapped out, but both of them were shambling, limping messes. Yet they wouldn't give up, hunting the Wolves as the Wolves had once hunted them, constantly kicking and scratching at Edwards and Richards for another chance.

In late June, they got a non-title match against the Wolves. If they won the match, they would get to choose the stipulation for their last chance at the titles. If they lost the match, they would not get another chance at the titles at all. When they won and finally got the freedom to choose whatever stipulation they liked, they went with the one type of match they had experience with where the Wolves did not, the one that had made their name in Ring of Honor two years ago against the Briscoes.

Steen and Generico were to take on the American Wolves for one final chance at the tag team titles at the second-ever Ring of Honor Ladder War.

Please Don't Die

It's important to be clear here that every match Steen and Generico had with the Wolves was one of the best on its card, very often *the* best on its card. They were all well-paced, full of action, athleticism, and emotion. Every one of them is worth watching.

The Ladder War match is on another level altogether.

Some of it is the emotion: the agonizing desperation of Kevin and

El Generico to retake their titles, the ruthless determination of the Wolves to keep them. Some of it is the physical danger, the sheer and simple daredevil recklessness of what they do with those ladders. But there was an extra real-world factor that bumped up the stakes of the match. The night before the big show, Eddie Edwards legitimately broke his elbow, a severe break that left his arm in a straight cast. You might think that would mean a forfeit, or at least a more cautious style—but you would only think that if you didn't know the four men involved in creating this match.

When Edwards comes to the ring, it's immediately obvious that this is no fictional injury. To begin with, the cast is awkwardly swaddled in bandages, both to keep it from being damaged and to prevent it from accidentally hurting any of the other wrestlers. It looks radically uncool and uncomfortable, which of course makes Edwards instantly ten times cooler for wrestling through it.

As the match begins and the two teams brawl around the ring, it is also clear that Kevin and Generico are not targeting the elbow, as they would if it were a fictional injury.* It's not because they've developed any sense of mercy, mind you, as the brawl begins with Kevin biting Edwards' nose, and when Edwards complains loudly, Kevin screams "I'm gonna rip off your fucking face!" They don't cut Edwards any slack at all—he takes bumps landing flat on his back, one arm spread wide and the wrapped one held close to his body, his teeth gritted. He does moves that would be risky and painful if he *didn't* have a broken elbow, his real determination shining through the superficial fiction.

The Wolves manage to handcuff Kevin, who is forced to watch helplessly from the corner of the ring as Generico fights on, outnumbered. He struggles to his feet, fighting back in true Kevin style, spitting and kicking crotches with his hands behind his back, eventually hurling his whole body at a ladder as Edwards tries to climb one in a run for the titles, sending them both tumbling. Generico finally gets the

---

* In his interview with Edwards on *The Kevin Steen Show*, Kevin mentions fans will sometimes ask him why he and Generico didn't target the elbow in this match, "Why do you *think?*" he responds with an incredulous look at the camera, saying without words, *Because we're friends and working together, you idiot.*

key for the handcuffs from a struggling Sweet 'n' Sour faction-mate, Shane Hagadorn, and frees Kevin.

The two of them start building a... contraption. That's what Kevin always calls them, the complex Rube Goldberg mayhem machines built of ladders and chairs that are eventually set off like firecrackers in the final stretch of a match.

Picture the ring in your mind, a ladder in the middle. Kevin and Generico set up tables on either side of the ladder, creating a line that cuts diagonally across the ring, table-ladder-table. For good measure, they prop up a ladder-bridge outside the ring, resting from the ring apron to the barricade and add a table on top of it. A spectator looking at this setup might well be filled with trepidation about what the payoff to this elaborate construction might be.

That spectator would be right to worry.

The contraption.

One by one, the ladders and tables are used to violent ends. Generico and Richards grapple on top of the ladder in the middle of the ring until Generico climbs to the top of the ladder, grabs Richards, and does a somersaulting sunset flip to hurl him into the table. Edwards retaliates by climbing the ladder and tossing Generico back first into the other table.

The ladder wobbles and falls over, sending Edwards crashing to the mat as well, wincing in pain as he tries to keep his arm steady. He starts to set up the ladder again, but realizes it can't reach the titles anyway. He dodges an attack by a chair-wielding Kevin, then spots the bright orange maintenance ladder and calls for Hagadorn to bring it to him.*

At this point the fans, moved by the sight of Edwards wrestling injured, decide to ignore that he's a heel and start raucously chanting "Ed-die Ed-wards!" and pounding on the barricades. Once the ladder is set up and Kevin lurches back, chair in hand, to stop him from climbing it, the crowd reverts to cheering for Steen and Generico, but it's one of those moments where the audience puts aside the facade just long enough to show their real appreciation, and it's wonderful.

Kevin promptly whacks Edwards square across the head with the chair, because favoring someone's elbow doesn't mean sparing their brain. As Edwards reels, Kevin starts climbing the huge orange ladder that will take him to the titles.

Up and up he goes, to the very top. Just as he gets there, fingers reaching upward toward the prize, Edwards tips over the ladder.

Kevin falls for what seems like an hour, a long frozen moment, and crashes—inevitably—into the table and ladder bridge that he and Generico set up a while ago outside the ring. He lies tangled in the wreckage, washed in the howls of the crowd, unmoving as Edwards and Generico right the ladder and each scramble up a side, meeting at the top. They start to brawl, each of them swaying precariously with every punch. The audience starts to chant "Please don't die!" over and over. Eventually Edwards manages to grab Generico's leg and pull it through the ladder. Generico's knee brace, a remnant of his recent surgery, gets caught there, and he can't extricate his leg. He dangles helplessly and Edwards clings to his leg, pinning him in place. They're stuck there, the man wrestling with a bad knee and the man wrestling with a broken elbow, as Richards clambers up the ladder and over his

---

* Did the Briscoes have this exact same realization at the first Ladder War, two years ago? Yes. But don't ask wrestlers to remember such things when a dramatic realization works so well.

teammate to finally reach up and retrieve the titles. The American Wolves have defeated Steen and Generico for the final time.

There's wreckage and rubble everywhere, wood and steel fragments littering the ring. Davey Richards storms around waving his belt, blustering, threatening Generico as the luchador disentangles his leg and slithers painfully down the ladder to the mat. Eddie Edwards lies on his back, taking careful breaths. His title is brought to him and he clasps it to his chest, his face gray and clammy. He lifts it to his lips for an instant before he's helped out.[4]

Kevin pulls himself out of the pieces of ladder and chair on the floor and crawls into the ring to El Generico's side. Other wrestlers come out to guard against a post-match Wolves attack and help the losers leave the ring. Two of them are Matt and Nick Jackson, the Young Bucks, mostly invisible right now but already great backstage friends with Kevin and Sami, about to become a major part of their story.

El Generico and Kevin are truly broken men now. Their attempt to reclaim the titles has failed and there will be no further attempts. The management of Ring of Honor is in flux in late 2009, and it's becoming clear that Kevin and Sami are not going to get another title run in the future. This is a recipe for disaster—and worse, a recipe for stagnation and aimless drifting. In wrestling, a disaster is infinitely superior.

Kevin has some ideas about that.

MOMENT OF CLARITY
(2009)

The Ring General and Captain Continuity

KEVIN HAS NEVER TALKED at length about the creative process with Sami, but there are moments here and there that provide clues. For example, there's that conversation with Eddie Edwards where Edwards remembers how Kevin and Sami bickered and wrangled over every single detail of their matches.[1] Then there's his interview with Jay Lethal, where Kevin admits that Sami can be hard to work with because he has such a strong idea of how a match should go, but adds that "ninety-eight point five percent of the time, he's right."[2] Or his talk with Jimmy Jacobs of Age of the Fall where he notes "I literally didn't get any input into any of my matches for a very long time," because Sami decided all the details of the matches they were both in (and, I suspect, some of Kevin's matches that he *wasn't* in but happened to be around for).[3]

At first glance, these statements don't add up. How could they argue endlessly if Sami was almost always right and ended up being the person who decided how the match would go? What were they arguing about, then? The answer to this conundrum lies in the different strengths that each of them brought to their alliance.

Sami has always been the bell-to-bell guy, the "ring general" who gauges the audience and the situation and decides how the match will go in detail. He has an uncanny intuition as to how the audience will react, how to get the desired response from them. When it comes to the storytelling between the ropes, Sami is one of the best in the world.

Kevin, on the other hand, is the big-picture guy. He's the continuity stickler, the one who remembers the history of the feud, the character arcs over time, the rise and fall of the long-term story. He's even worked this into his WWE character, who clings to past feuds and slights while other wrestlers let the past flicker by like light across a goldfish's bowl. When it comes to understanding long-term narrative rhythm, Kevin is nearly unparalleled. He and Sami's bitter arguments are almost certainly about how to implement Kevin's long-term story ideas into a specific match, how to make character beats happen within the ring itself.

Sami has called himself and Kevin the "Lennon/McCartney of pro wrestling"[4]—not in the sense that one is like John Lennon and the other like Paul McCartney, but in the sense that their creative partnership is to the world of wrestling what Lennon and McCartney were to the world of music, an unparalleled complementary pair. To run with the musical metaphor, it is as if Kevin were the musician with ideas for the most epic, sweeping concept album, complete with motifs and hooks, while Sami is the genius at putting those motifs and hooks into the specific individual songs in ways that catch and wring the audience's hearts. Either of them are brilliant separately. Put together, they're transcendent.

It was in late 2009 that Kevin's gift for long-term storytelling truly blossomed, and—combined with Sami's genius for crafting perfectly-calibrated matches—the result was one of the greatest stories of modern wrestling.

Setting the Stage

In September 2009, Steen and Generico had their final shot at the tag team titles, and they failed. Their nine-month feud with the American Wolves had come to an end. They could both read the room, and they could tell there was little chance they'd have another shot at the tag titles. Faced with the possibility of sinking down the card, Kevin came up with a plan. If he and Sami weren't going to have another tag team run, why not break up the team? Sami was reluctant, but Kevin eventually talked him around to it.[5] It was a chance for the two of them to sink their teeth into a long, intense story, one that would transform El Generico and Kevin Steen from a comedy duo into a tragically betrayed hero and a violently psychotic villain. Done right, it could catapult them to the top of the card. And they knew they could do it right.

Kevin sat down and wrote an entire story, a full program from beginning to end. He decided all of the major character beats, the build and the payoff, from the agonizing treachery to the final triumph, a blood-soaked melodrama of despair and vindication. It was also cleverly designed to be the epitome of writing in the margins. Many of the major story beats took place as run-ins or moments that happen after matches. This gave Ring of Honor's creative team a great deal of freedom—for example, if some other wrestler needed to win a match in February, he could fight Generico, because Kevin had written the luchador as sinking into a deep depression and correspondingly long losing streak. A few matches during the year were inked in—and Sami surely already had some strong opinions of what should happen in them—but long stretches of the feud were very much plug-and-play, a modular narrative that could take place around and between other storylines. It was flexible and adaptable, designed to be appealingly easy to book the rest of a promotion around.

Kevin took the idea to the Ring of Honor booker.

The booker at this point was Adam Pearce, last seen wearing a glittery robe and attempting to seduce Kevin to the dark side as the leader of the Hangmen Three. When former booker Gabe Sapolsky parted ways with ROH and Pearce took his place, in late 2008, Kevin's first reaction had been dismay. "I thought Generico and I would be done with Ring of Honor very soon. Because I was not friends with Adam Pearce and I did not think he liked us, and I think I was right at first."[6] But Pearce had proven willing to listen to wrestler input and had warmed up to the perfectionist pair. He had his doubts about this sprawling epic but was willing to take a chance on it.

They needed two more wrestlers to help out with the feud and provide backup, stand-ins for matches, someone to play off in promos. Sami and Kevin had already asked their friend Colt Cabana to be El Generico's confidant through his harrowing year. Cabana, largely known as a comedy wrestler, was happy to try a more dramatic role. That left the opposite role of the evil mastermind companion for villain Kevin Steen. They considered going with Roderick Strong, but then Adam Peace got in touch with them with a proposition. Ring of Honor was about to hire Steve Corino—were Kevin and Sami interested in having him as Kevin's evil mentor?

Kevin was more than interested, he was ecstatic. He'd been a fan of Corino's since seeing him in ECW, where (like Kevin in IWS) he'd played a character who styled himself a pure wrestler and refused to do anything hardcore in a hardcore promotion. He and Corino had wrestled each other back in 2004, in Quebec, and Corino had been impressed enough with young Mr. Wrestling to invite him to come to Japan on a tour with him in 2005. They'd drifted out of contact since then, but Kevin had always wanted to work with him again,[7] and now he was being offered the chance to have a year-long story with him.

In the months leading up to the September ladder match, Kevin started laying some character groundwork. His knee, constantly targeted by his enemies, weakened until it was barely able to hold his weight. His promos started to take on a self-recriminating edge as he wondered why they hadn't been able to win their titles back, wondered if he was the weak link in this team. His hair was becoming shaggy, his beard unkempt, his eyes haunted.

All the pieces were in place on the night that Kevin and Generico lost the tag team title bout to the American Wolves on September 26, 2009.

That same night, the owner of Ring of Honor introduced their new Executive Producer, Jim Cornette.

"He could have seen something in me!"

Kevin and Sami's first reaction to Cornette's arrival in Ring of Honor was excitement. One of the greatest talkers in the history of wrestling, the legendary manager of the Midnight Express tag team? "Awesome. He's got a great mind to help us, and it's gonna be great to have him here," they thought.[8] Kevin had even met Cornette before, back in 2004, when he'd spent a weekend training at OVW, Cornette's promotion at the time. When he and Sami introduced themselves backstage that first night, Kevin was gratified to discover that Cornette remembered him from that weekend. Now was the time to make a good first impression on the legend and get him on board with the angle Pearce had approved. Kevin wrote out the details of the story in an email—it must have been pages and pages long, brimming with meticulous detail—sent it off to Cornette, and waited for a reply.[9]

And waited.

And waited.

Eventually it became clear that there was going to be no response from Cornette. Sami had left immediately after they failed to recapture the titles to go on another tour of Japan and then of Europe, leaving Kevin to do two shows on his own. The first was a match with Roderick Strong, and after the match Cornette approached them, complimenting Strong effusively for the great match. Kevin waited patiently for his turn—only to have Cornette finish complimenting Strong, turn around and walk away without speaking to Kevin. "He doesn't even look at me. I don't even exist."[10] Something had gone horribly wrong between Kevin and Cornette almost immediately, a dislocation that would have long-reaching implications for both of them and for the future of Ring of Honor.

It's possible it was a lost cause from the very beginning, that nothing could have salvaged the relationship. Cornette has mentioned that former booker Gabe Sapolsky had warned Adam Pearce that "you will spend the majority of your time dealing with Kevin Steen and El Generico, and their various issues and ideas and problems and complaints."[11] Pearce had passed that assessment on to Cornette, perhaps before he even met the duo. Getting an extremely detailed email about the booking for an epic storyline would only have confirmed that Sapolsky and Pearce had been correct.

From the first backstage handshake, things had misfired. Cornette was baffled by the El Generico character, mystified by the amount of energy and devotion Sami was pouring into the persona. As far as he was concerned, El Generico as a top star was an absolute non-starter because he didn't speak. Cornette had no patience with a wrestler that didn't have the ability to cut a promo, to explain motivations, to connect to an audience through words.[12] With Kevin it was his looks. Cornette has mentioned specifically the scraggly beard, the disheveled hair, noting that he couldn't imagine him as a champion unless he first were to "lose some weight, fucking buy some new clothes and fucking trim [his] beard up and look a little neater."[13]

Oh, what's that you say? You remember from eight paragraphs ago that Kevin was deliberately growing his hair and beard out to communicate his despair and self-doubt? Yes, well, by the time Cornette got the mail explaining the plan, it was too late, his mind was irrevocably made up on Kevin Steen.

And maybe even that wouldn't have mattered. The hair and beard and general air of neglect may have been deliberate choices, but Kevin's continuing struggles with his weight were not. Jim Cornette remembered meeting Kevin as a 19-year-old, and any promise Le Kid might have had in 2003 was outweighed, quite literally, by the changes in his body. When Cornette looked at Kevin, he saw a "fat guy wearing bike shorts and a t-shirt."[14] A slob. A failure.

Cornette was neither the first nor the last person to be unable to see any brilliance in Kevin because of how he looked, but he has always been one of the most painful to Kevin. In his 2013 shoot interview for Ring of Honor, *Hell Rising*, he points out that Cornette had worked with Mick Foley and understood what a genius *he* was. He backtracks awkwardly, stammering slightly as he clarifies that he's not saying he's on the level of Foley. What he's implying they have in common is clear: Mick Foley was unkempt and overweight, but Cornette could still see what a good mind he had. Kevin looks at the camera, exasperated and bitter, but there's an old hurt still lurking under his words when he says "This is a dude who appreciated Mick Foley. He could have seen something in me!"[15]

By the time Sami came back from Japan, it was clear Cornette held Kevin in contempt. Sami appears to have responded to this contempt by simply shunning Cornette, refusing to communicate with him unless absolutely necessary. One of Cornette's additional complaints quickly became that Kevin did all of Sami's communicating for him. "Steen takes up all of the wind in the room," he recalled, "and they were kind of joined at the hip also. Steen was pretty much Generico's agent."[16] Looking back, Kevin remembers being baffled by Cornette insisting on talking to Sami, hounding Kevin to get him to return his calls: "It's because he doesn't want to talk to you!" he snaps at his memory of Cornette. "I was talking *for* him, why would you need to talk to him?"[17]

It's a fascinating difference between the two wrestlers. Kevin, whose father was deeply involved in his son's life and attended every match he could, seems to have spent much of his career hoping to find a mentor that would support him with the same level of enthusiasm. Sami, whose relationship with his father seems to have been supportive in general but absolutely separate from wrestling—his parents didn't see him in the ring until 2013—appears to be sublimely uninterested in being mentored. When authority figures don't have faith in Sami, he appears to shrug and continue doing exactly what he was planning on doing. If Cornette didn't see his and Kevin's worth, then he had no further use for Cornette. About the only time he's mentioned Cornette in any way was in 2022 during the Bloodline story, when Cornette said that Sami had become his "favorite person to watch on television," to which Sami responded on Twitter with a bewildered "My... dawg?"[18]

Kevin, however, holds a grudge. His bitter, wounded resentment toward Cornette shaped his time in Ring of Honor in striking ways, and it all stems from these few months in late 2009, when Cornette couldn't see past his appearance to value his mind.

Bridge Out Ahead

If Jim Cornette had been able to look beyond the hair, the beard, and the body, he might have realized that Kevin was doing some quietly brilliant storytelling in the leadup to Ring of Honor's final show of the year, *Final Battle*. He was playing not just with wrestling tropes, but with a certain kind of fan's "insider knowledge," weaponizing the modern fan's self-awareness against them to lead them inexorably to the depressing conclusion that Kevin Steen's knee was shot and he was facing at least a long hiatus—or possible retirement. He wasn't just "selling the knee" in the ring, he was selling it at the meta-level.

Using the fact that Sami was touring Japan and Europe through much of the fall of 2009, Kevin went to work. His backstage promos were increasingly bleak. "I don't know what to expect," he says somberly in October before a match with Roderick Strong, noting that Generico is in Japan and he's alone, and "I've been relying on Generico for *so* long." He loses that match when he can't make the pin quickly enough, losing precious seconds as he grabs his knee, wincing in pain.

The next month, he met his friend, Colt Cabana, in a first-round tournament match to determine a contender for the top title. At this point, of course, plans were very much in place for Cabana to play a huge role in the upcoming story. As they shake hands, Cabana notes that Kevin looks lonely and asks him where Generico is. Kevin, smiling through gritted teeth, tells him he isn't lonely at all. The match is weird and truncated—only six minutes long—because just a few minutes in Kevin tries to do a dropkick and falls awkwardly on his bad knee. He struggles through the match, and it's clear the referee is moving back and forth between Cabana and Kevin, communicating with each of them. It's how wrestlers deal with legitimate injuries in the ring, using the ref as a go-between to adjust the match to the injury. The watching Ring of Honor fans, all of whom, of course, know the secrets and tricks of wrestling, understand that this means Kevin is truly struggling to get through the match. Cabana gets a quick pin (also a common happening when a wrestler is legitimately injured) and whispers something to the ref as his hand is raised. The ref goes to check on Kevin, clearly because Cabana has surreptitiously asked him to check on his friend, and Kevin has a long talk with a trainer as he sits on the apron, his face drawn with agony, as Cabana tries to celebrate, sneaking worried looks at Kevin. To a savvy audience member, one "smartened up" to how wrestling works, it's clear that Kevin—the real person, not the character—is struggling with that knee.

He's not. Well, no more than usual, since that is the knee that never healed well. But he and Cabana are using the audience's own knowledge of the sleight-of-hand of wrestling against them, letting them think they've peeked behind the curtain, unaware that all they're seeing is another curtain. Soon the message boards were ablaze with speculation that Kevin's career could be over.

The last piece needed for *Final Battle* was an opponent to be the foil for battered, existential-dread-filled Steen and Generico. And who better than the two bounciest, flippiest, entropy-defying and youngest of tag teams, the Young Bucks?

The Young Bucks. Matt and Nick Jackson, hailing from Rancho Cucamonga, California—the second pair of brothers to change the course of Kevin and Sami's story. Inspired by the flashy theatrics of the Rockers and the daredevil abandon of the Hardy Boys, they had started as backyard wrestlers. Matt founded his own promotion when he was nineteen and Nick was fourteen. By the time they showed up in Ring of Honor in 2009, Matt was twenty-four and Nick a shocking nineteen, and their rubber-ball wrestling style and tongue-in-cheek antics (a typical move was to do a sequence of dazzling flips across the ring, only to end in a comically anticlimactic backrake) made them seem even younger at times.

They were also a combination of visionary and mercenary that meshed well with the little group that had come to be known as the "Scrub Room" of Kevin, Sami, Tyler Black [Seth Rollins] and Jimmy Jacobs. Bursting with ambitious energy, they joined the other four in late-night hotel-room discussions about professional wrestling, and their goals of conquering and changing it.

Kevin and Sami had met the Bucks in the ring now and then in the past—a six-man tag in PWG, a greased-lightning four-way match between Generico, Kota Ibushi, Jigsaw and Nick Jackson in Chikara—but it was in Ring of Honor, in June 2009, that they had their first match as two tag teams.

It was only the Bucks' third match in Ring of Honor, and the audience wasn't sure they liked these Hardy Boys wannabes. But their chemistry with the former tag champions crackled, everything clicked into place, and by the end the crowd was chanting "please come back" for the brothers. Kevin and Generico won the match, but Kevin shook their hands with grudging respect. Generico lifted their hands in the air, and they cleared out to let the Bucks enjoy the applause. There had been a distinct feeling that these reckless scamps could be the future of Ring of Honor.

On his way out, Kevin let Generico go through the curtain, then paused, looking back at the ring for a long moment. His face was opaque and surely in June he didn't know how instrumental the Bucks would be in his story, but it's not hard to imagine him thinking if the Bucks are the future of the promotion… what does that make him?

In November, Generico was back from his tour, and he and Kevin had their second match of 2009 against the Young Bucks. They win, but this time the tone is gloomy. As their names are called, the audience starts to chant "Mr. Wrestling." Generico gestures to the audience and then Kevin, calling his attention to the chant, and Kevin laughs wryly. "That's for me?" he says, and it's clear he finds the nickname painfully ironic. He's hobbling more than wrestling. There are miscommunications throughout the match: Matt throws Kevin into Generico's raised boot, Nick dodges Generico's kick and Kevin gets kicked instead. "Kevin Steen can't quite keep up, especially with those knee problems," commentary notes.

They have another match with the Bucks the following week, but this one is in PWG for the tag team championship. Kevin hasn't been wrestling often in PWG since the birth of his son—this is only his second match there in 2009—but it marks one of the first examples of a storytelling trick Kevin and Sami will use more and more in the next few years.

Basically, PWG's all-star roster approach, its looser style of storytelling, and its high level of creative control for wrestlers make it an excellent way to augment stories that are going on elsewhere or to embroider their characters' personalities and backstories. For example, it was in PWG that El Generico picked up nearly all of his backstory, most of it added around 2009 in a feud with noted child-hater Chuck Taylor. To heighten the conflict between them, Generico suddenly had an entire orphanage of Mexican children that he was wrestling to support and Taylor was trying to deprive. Los Angelinos de El Generico became the final piece of the luchador's personality, cementing his babyface credentials. Wrestlers tend to come to PWG from other promotions, often bringing those feuds and rivalries with them. In 2009, Kevin and Sami used PWG to extend and embellish their ROH story, confident that the PWG audience would be aware of what was going on in Ring of Honor.

The PWG match with the Bucks deepens the anguish. There's a feeling of desperation to it as Kevin and Generico try to win back the tag team titles, constantly hamstrung by Kevin's injury and his despair. This time, for the first time ever, they lose to the Young Bucks. As the champions celebrate, Generico crawls laboriously to his tag partner's side. Kevin's face is bloody from being superkicked, his eyes glazed. Generico buries his face in Kevin's chest. There's a distinct feeling that time is running out for the tag team.

By this point, Kevin and Generico's fans were filled with dread and sadness. They could read the signs, and the signs indicated that Kevin had been just limping forward on his bad knees until he could have a final match with Generico at *Final Battle*, reach some kind of closure with his tag team partner, then disappear for surgery—maybe forever.

The possibility that Kevin might have been deliberately mis-writing those signs, like a cartoon villain changing "Bridge Out Ahead" to "Bridge Fine Ahead" and cackling to himself, was too implausible for most fans to consider.

In early December, Kevin fought Claudio Castagnoli in Chicago, trying desperately to take top place in Ring of Honor's ranking system. The backstage promo before his match is dismal. "It's so bad since the Ladder War that I've pulled this baby back out," he says, showing the camera his knee brace. "I'll be real honest, that number one spot could mean that I still have a reason to be here." He notes that he's had a lot of shots at the top title but never won it. "I'd really like to hold that title before..." He trails off, his eyes sad. "Before it's all done."

Colt Cabana pops into the frame to check on him, his face worried. "That's my buddy Colt," Kevin says fondly after he leaves, before promising to go down fighting.

Which he does.

After his defeat, he grabs the mic and thanks the Chicago fans, telling them that he always appreciated their reception of their first

Ladder War with the Briscoes, and that even though he probably shouldn't be wrestling right now, he felt like he needed to come to Chicago to say thank you to them. The audience applauds, full of grief.

He's lying, he's lying, he is a lying liar who lies. And everything is in place for the final payoff to the months' worth of deception and misdirection.

Bridge out ahead.

Final Battle 2009

The night before Final Battle, Kevin and El Generico wrestle two big guys from the Embassy, Erick Stevens and Bison Smith. Smith, as hulkingly strong as both the animal and the video game character whose name he bears, proceeds to crush El Generico into paste. Kevin, on the apron, holds out an urgent hand for the tag, but Generico looks at his injured partner, then squares his shoulders and keeps battling Bison. "Please tag! Please tag!" Kevin screams as Bison destroys the luchador. "Oh my God! Please tag!" You can hear it in his anguished voice—he's helpless, useless, a burden on his tag partner, who doesn't trust him to make the save. He finally makes a blind tag, tapping Generico without his knowledge or consent, and charges in to try to help, but it's no use, and they lose the match.

Commentary says, "Get that surgery, Steen! Heal up!" as the pair try to exit the ring. Kevin holds the ropes open for Generico, but Generico doesn't see it and gets tangled up in the ropes in an exhaustion that would be comedic if it weren't so sad. Kevin shrugs, with a look on his face that's both affectionate and bitter, like "I can't even do this right." They stagger out with Kevin leaning heavily on Generico.

It's the last time they will ever leave the ring together in Ring of Honor.

When Kevin and El Generico arrive at *Final Battle*, Dec. 19, 2009, Kevin is a mess. He's limping, shaggy, his beard unkempt and his eyes mournful. In a promo later that evening he's going to inform Colt Cabana that he looks like this because he couldn't bear to look at his own face in the mirror anymore. If his hero, Shawn Michaels, once famously lost his smile, Kevin has lost his sneer, that cocky bravado that had gotten him through so much. His mind seems to be elsewhere. The New York audience senses an ending and is determined to give him a loving sendoff.*

He doesn't even attempt to start the match, just cedes the ring to Generico, who stands there, baffled and worried for a moment before turning to face the Young Bucks—so young! So flippy! So annoying!—who had just defeated them last month. Even when Kevin holds out his hand for the tag, there's a look of weary resignation on his face, as if he feels obligated to get in and give the audience a show, but knows he has no business being in the ring in this condition. He's clearly struggling to get through the match, his body betraying him with every move. He wrestles with a desperate melancholy—and if you don't believe melancholic wrestling is possible, I urge you to watch this match. When the Bucks kick out of his pins, he looks disappointed not because he hasn't won but because he so desperately needs this match to end so he can finally rest.

For their part, Nick and Matt Jackson bounce around the ring, seemingly untouched by pain or injury or exhaustion as Kevin struggles to keep up, limping along on sheer willpower. Worst of all, they seem to be having fun wrestling, something Kevin and Generico most definitely are not.

Eventually they wipe out Generico and then hit Kevin with their finisher of the time, More Bang for Your Buck, in which Matt does a rolling fireman's carry, then scrambles up the turnbuckle as Nick does a 450 splash and caps it all off with a moonsault. It's a dizzying, show-off cascade of moves, a finisher no one in Ring of Honor had ever kicked out of at that point; they both pile on top of him for the pin and Kevin kicks out anyway, as if he doesn't know how to quit even though maybe he should.

Astonished and infuriated, the Bucks just start superkicking him. He wobbles and goes to his knees, staring at them blankly, unable to either fight or fall, until they both kick him simultaneously and he goes down in a heap, blood at the corner of his mouth.

---

* I've spoken to various people who were fans of Ring of Honor at the time and they insist that Kevin had totally bamboozled them and they were sure he was about to retire.

This time he stays down for the count, Generico can't get there in time to save him, and the match is over. The Bucks celebrate briefly and then evaporate (for such flashy little punks, they have an odd gift for conveniently evaporating after key matches), leaving Kevin and Generico in the ring.

Kevin eventually manages to get to his feet. He humbly accepts the applause of the crowd, gets a microphone, and starts what is obviously a retirement speech, note-perfect in every respect. He looks back over his and Generico's careers in Ring of Honor. He admits that lately he's been struggling. "You can blame it on the injuries, the weight gain, the pressure of having a family that depends on me, but I know for a fact that I'm not the man I was," he says as the audience calls out support.

Generico is sitting on his knees in the middle of the ring and Kevin limps around him as he speaks, effusively thanking everyone who ever helped him in Ring of Honor, with just enough snark (he thanks all the shitty wrestlers he worked with who inspired him to be better, for example, before thanking all the great ones who taught him so much) that it feels authentic. He thanks the Briscoes and Nigel McGuinness, and you can feel the crowd's collective heart breaking, because he would never thank his enemies if he weren't actually leaving, right? He thanks the fans—both the ones who supported him, and the ones who didn't, saying "I appreciate every emotion you've invested in me." His expression is open and vulnerable; it's as if he's allowing the fans to see past his abrasive character to glimpse his genuine self, here at the end. The crowd is in anguish, calling out that they love him. "Don't go!" rings out a lone, desperate voice.

Kevin smiles wistfully. And turns, finally, to Generico.

His voice trembling, he manages to quaver "And last but not least, to you, I just want to say—" before Generico jumps up and throws his arms around him, interrupting him. They stand in the middle of the ring, both of them sobbing so hard that you can see their bodies shaking with emotion.

It is in this precise moment that Kevin Steen has a complete and total break with reality, his mind shattering under the weight of his despair and self-loathing and guilt. He has what he will call a "moment of clarity," and it's a moment that will change everything.

MOMENT OF CLARITY

He enters the hug in one reality, and exits it in a very different one, rearing back and finishing his sentence with "—*I hate your fucking guts,*" and kicking Generico square between the legs. The crowd makes an utterly indescribable noise, a mix of horror, shock, and sorrow that congeals into seething anger as Kevin leaves the ring and picks up a chair.

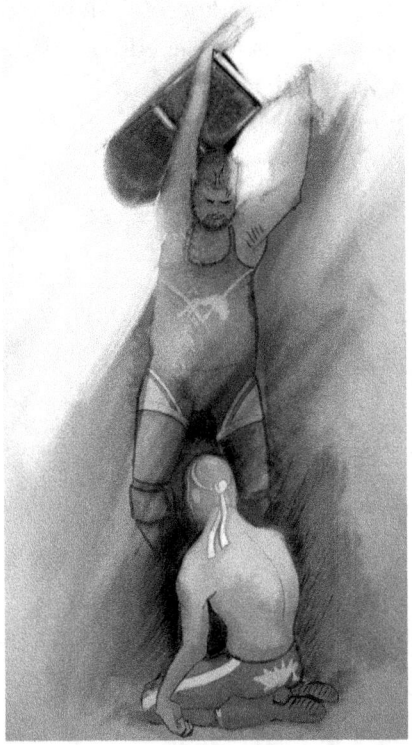

A break with reality.

He comes back and looms over Generico for a long, awful moment, chair raised. On his knees, Generico stares up at him in silence, as though he absolutely can't believe this is happening. As if the world is over. He doesn't raise his hands or even his shoulder, he doesn't even flinch as Kevin brings the chair down uncompromisingly across his head.

He drops without a sound.

Kevin drops the chair and sags in relief, his face rapturous as he lets go of any guilt at being a burden, any shame about his physical condition, any responsibility to his friend. El Generico lies unmoving on the mat. It's a moment that etches itself into the mind, an image that will haunt both of them for the rest of their lives.

Colt Cabana, Kevin's "buddy," runs into the ring to confront him in shock. Kevin grabs him and kisses him on the mouth, then rolls out of the ring and strolls past a long line of furious faces, angrily raised middle fingers. As Colt kneels by Generico's side, Kevin stops at the curtain, looking back at the chaos he's caused.

He blows the audience a laughing kiss, then steps back from the light into the darkness and is gone.

BITTER FRIENDS, STIFFER ENEMIES
(2010)

"Should I be ashamed of this?"

KEVIN'S YEAR-LONG program with El Generico is jammed full of moments, piled up one after another in a wild frenzy of storytelling: fraught staredowns and brawls, chairshots and blood and anguish. The first major moment after the betrayal is his backstage promo with Colt Cabana, a masterpiece of unnerving psychology.

When Cabana bursts in on him, Kevin is devouring an apple with huge, sloppy bites, sighing in near-orgasmic bliss. His face is that of a man who has been denying himself for a long time and will no longer restrain himself from anything. He jumps to his feet, smiling broadly as Cabana confronts him. His joy brings

An apple, devoured.

Cabana up short as Kevin explains, with the lucid cheer of complete insanity, that this is the greatest night of his life. That he had come to the ring planning to retire, sunk in depression and despair, but when El Generico put his arms around him he had experienced a "moment of clarity," comparing it to the moment an alcoholic realizes that their dependency is making life unbearable—but in this case, that dependency was not on alcohol, but on El Generico himself. "But I didn't need twelve steps," he says. "I needed one. And that was a chairshot to his head." Cabana stares, appalled. "You should be happy for me," Kevin insists, his smile wild between messy bites of apple. "No, man. Not all," Cabana mutters in bewildered horror.

This promo, and his explanation for his actions, resonate through Kevin's many future betrayals across the coming decades. One thing it makes clear is that Kevin's sudden attacks on people he cares about, from El Generico to Sami Zayn to Chris Jericho to Kofi Kingston to Big E to Cody Rhodes, are almost always impulsive, unpremeditated. Every time, no matter how much he might try to claim it was planned after, it's the sudden shattering of a brittle ego under the weight of friendship. It's as if when he makes friends or allies, some karmic rubber band gets stretched tighter and tighter until it snaps, rebounding into a total rejection of any responsibility or humanity. It happens over and over in Kevin's career but never as violently as this time with El Generico.

Kevin's character post-betrayal is incredibly unsettling. His is not the cool, controlled "insanity" of so many wrestling badasses. No, Kevin skitters, he lurches, he looms. He's erratic and uncontrollable, an insatiable monster of gluttonous glee. He kisses wrestlers, he slobbers on camera lens, he bites and licks and consumes everything in his way. When Steve Corino returns from Japan and takes credit for inspiring Kevin's embrace of evil, the two go on a rampage together through the roster. When a young trainee wrestler confronts them backstage, telling Kevin he should be ashamed of himself for his betrayal, Kevin strikes him to the floor, then kneels over him, punching him. "Should I be ashamed of *this?*" he demands with each punch. "Should I be ashamed of *this?*" Looking up at his mentor, he says "Steve, should I be ashamed of this?" and for a moment the question isn't rhetorical, it's sincere, almost plaintive. *Should I be ashamed?* Corino assures him that he has no need to feel shame, and Kevin smiles, reassured, before starting to kick the hapless trainee's ribs in.

El Generico, meanwhile, has lost all joy in life. Betrayed, abandoned, he sinks into a deep depression. We see him in the background as Cabana cuts a promo in the locker room, picking listlessly at his bootlaces, unable to find the will to tie his boots. The emotional shock of Kevin's betrayal even follows him into the ring. In his first few matches in 2010, Generico can barely bring himself to wrestle, losing match after match when he becomes visibly distracted by his sorrow. Backstage, he's gone from a comic to a tragic figure. When an interviewer asks him if there's anything he'd like to say to Steen, he struggles to speak, then gives up with a heavy sigh, looking into the camera with a silent sadness more eloquent than any words: *Kevin always used to do the talking for me.*

Teaming up with Cabana helps a little. When they come to the ring, Generico does all the things he used to do—he touches the fans' hands, he points upwards as he enters the ring—but it's clearly going through the motions without any real joy. He tends to tag out immediately after taking any offense, all the fight visibly crushed out of him. Cabana's fun-loving shenanigans, hugs, and dances barely seem to touch Generico's despair. What does reach him is seeing the other wrestlers in the match hurt Cabana, which awakens some spirit within him and gets him to actually fight for a moment. But it's a spark that gutters out the moment he's confronted with his former friend.

Which of course, he inevitably is. Kevin talks a lot about how he just wants to be free of El Generico (or *Him*, since he refuses to use his former friend's name), but it's clear that his attempt to make a clean break has only left them more entangled than ever. He finds himself at war with anyone who dares to defend the luchador and call him a friend. This quickly comes to include nearly the entire Ring of Honor fan base, as they discover that singing Olé or wearing a Generico mask will reduce Kevin to a frothing yet oddly impotent fury. Before a match with Kenny Omega, Kevin solemnly informs the audience that on the advice of his doctor, no Olé chants are to be sung during his match, then buries his head in his hands when they immediately start to ring out.

Nothing Without Him

The pacing of Kevin and Generico's feud was stellar, a masterpiece of the slow build. Of the four wrestlers involved in the storyline—Kevin, Generico, Cabana and Corino—none of them had a match against each other for the first two months of 2010. Kevin and Generico don't share the screen at all, and Generico's lack of language combined with Kevin's refusal to speak his name means neither of them even says the other's name in all that time. Yet the feud's temperature always remains at a steady boil because Cabana and Corino provide a constant bridge between the two. At one show, Cabana interferes to stop Kevin from brutalizing the Human Tornado, Generico's former PWG tag partner. At another, Corino appears on the ramp post-match to ominously inform Cabana to be careful who he chooses to defend. This leads inevitably to a match between Cabana and Kevin in February at ROH's 8th Anniversary show, nine weeks after Kevin attacked Generico.

Nine weeks! The build to the first match in this feud took longer than many entire feuds in wrestling.

El Generico has a match earlier in the card against Davey Richards, his old nemesis from the American Wolves. Cabana comes to the ring with him and does his best (in vain) to psych up the visibly reluctant and dispirited luchador. As a good example of the modular nature of the storyline, Generico could have been facing anyone at all in this match because the essential point was his relationship with Cabana. However, since it's Richards, commentary gets a chance to remind everyone that losing the titles to the Wolves was what sent Kevin into his spiral of despair, and Generico's inability to stay fired-up enough to get the win, tapping out to Richards's submission hold, has extra resonance when it's against his old rival.

When Cabana comes out later the same evening to meet Kevin, he comes alone. Kevin has written KILL and HIM on his wrist tape, and it's pretty clear that "HIM" is not referring to Cabana. A few minutes into the match, Kevin falls heavily out of the ring and onto his wounded knee, and Cabana grabs the mic and yells at him that he's faking it. Kevin's face twists in pain and he hesitates, at which point Corino runs in to demand Kevin get back in the ring. He throws him back in the ring and grabs his throat, yelling "For me, Kevin! You know what you have to do! Do it for me, Kevin!" Kevin's face is filled with an almost childlike uncertainty, and when Cabana attacks Corino and drives him from the ring, he just stares at Cabana. Cabana tells Kevin to "start being a man, the man you are in there," smacking his chest, and Kevin turns away and buries his face in the turnbuckle.

At which point Generico comes flying into the ring, and at the precise moment Kevin turns back around to confront Cabana he comes face to face with his old friend for the first time since *Final Battle*.

Everything goes still for a long, long moment. Generico stares at Kevin, and Kevin looks anywhere but at Generico's face, his eyes veering wildly around, slipping away from that accusing look. For all his bullying and blustering, in that moment his face is more pathetic than evil. The moment is shattered by Corino attacking Cabana with a chair. When he drops it Generico grabs it and advances on him, but suddenly Kevin jumps in between them, shielding his mentor with his own body. He stands, wavering, unable to put his weight on one leg, and they stare at each other. Again, it's amazing how *unrushed* all of this is, how much time is given for fraught moments to unfold and breathe.

Slowly, slowly, slowly, Generico lowers the chair, unable to hit Kevin.

So, of course, Kevin grabs the chair from him and starts to pummel him.

As he leaves with Corino at his side, he still looks somehow at sea, but there's a wicked smile pulling up one side of his forlorn face as he looks at Generico crumpled in the ring. The scene ends with Generico on his knees in the middle of the ring, mask ties drooping in despair, as Cabana holds the chair and mimes his explanation that Generico needs to find the inner strength to put his demons to rest by hitting Kevin with it. But Generico can't. Not yet.

Each show, the storyline progressed, bit by bit, built up largely through encounters after bouts, add-ons slipped into the spaces between matches. The wrestlers interfered with each other's matches, did run-ins, cut ominous promos at each other almost every show, as El Generico inched closer and closer to being willing to stand up to Kevin. It was a story told in the spaces between other stories, and that ended up being its saving grace because Jim Cornette had not been won over by Kevin and Sami. If anything, his opinion of them had curdled further, and Cornette's power backstage was on the rise through the first half of 2010. Kevin has said the only reason they were able to tell the story was that behind the cameras, Cornette was focused on the top of the card and didn't have any time or energy to care about a wild melodrama written in the margins of the midcard.[1]

For now, at least.

In front of the cameras, Kevin grows bolder. He keeps complaining in promos that he just wants Generico to leave him alone, while the dispirited luchador clearly yearns to never see Kevin's face again but keeps getting dragged back in as they torment him and his friend. Kevin shows up after Generico passes out in Chris Hero's brutal submission hold to taunt the wobbly luchador, daring him to hit him. "They want it!" he says, waving at the audience. "You want to see him hit me?" he asks Detroit as Cabana yells "Hit him!" and the audience roars its approval. "But you're not going to hit me," he informs Generico's miserable eyes. "You're just like those women who get beaten by their boyfriends but don't leave because—" His voice turns mockingly shrill, "'*They love him.*'" Cabana rolls back into the ring with a chair and hands it to Generico, begging him to shut Kevin up, and Kevin gets down on his knees and bows his head in mocking submission as Generico wavers, until Corino shows up to break the stalemate. He's constantly yelling cruel taunts at Generico from the ramp. "You're nothing without me!" he screams in a fury one time as Generico fumes in the ring. "You're *nothing* without me!"

When Corino and Generico have a scheduled match, Corino vows backstage "Tonight, I'm gonna destroy you." When he comes to the ring in a suit and tie, Generico is baffled until it becomes clear that the destruction Corino plans is of the spirit and not the body. He starts off with "If you died tomorrow, no one would care," and it escalates from there, to the point where some of what he's calling Generico gets bleeped out—and let's pause for a moment to contemplate what it might take to get censored in Ring of Honor in 2010. None of this cruel invective raises a response from the dejected luchador, who merely stands and looks at him in sorrow, until Corino's final line. "One last thing," he sneers. "Kevin Steen was right." With vicious emphasis, he spits the next line.

"You will *never* be *anything* without him."

And that's it, the raw nerve under the skin of narrative, the jolt of reality that gives energy to the fiction. Can the real people behind their respective masks succeed without each other? Is any success achieved together somehow lesser? Is one of them doomed to be left behind as the other soars to the heights? Generico visibly flinches at Corino's words, and it's this accusation that finally goads him to punch his tormentor rather than all the slurs and abuse that have gone before.

Cabana eventually gets Corino and Kevin to agree to a tag match against him and Generico. A week before that match, Cabana and Generico beat the American Wolves, and Generico, who seems to have snapped out of his funk, is celebrating when Kevin runs into the ring with a chair and starts assaulting Cabana. He tries to slap Generico but Generico—finally taking some initiative—blocks the blow and spits in his face. He seems ready to fight Kevin—but Corino attacks him from behind and the audience is denied that catharsis.

A week later on April 3—almost five months after the initial turn—Kevin and Generico share the ring for a match for the first time, but Generico is still not emotionally ready to fight Kevin. Even when Cabana pins Kevin's arms behind his back and begs Generico to hit him, Generico stands with his fist pulled back, wavering, unable to do it. The match eventually ends in a disqualification when Kevin attacks Cabana with a chair, then gouges at his sliced-open forehead as a wounded El Generico crawls into the ring. Kevin starts licking the blood from Cabana's face as the audience shrieks and chants "You sick fuck!" at him.

Slowly, Generico pulls himself to his feet, staring aghast at the monster his friend has become. Kevin drags Cabana over to him and carefully wipes his hand across Cabana's blood-soaked face. After holding it up so everyone can get a good look at it, he slaps Generico across the face with a hand dyed with his friend's blood.

Generico goes to his knees, more at the emotional force of the blow than the physical. Kevin turns back to Cabana, laughing, and so doesn't see Generico in the center of the ring, slowly rising to his feet, shaking with righteous rage as the crowd cheers. Kevin turns just in time to get kicked straight in the face by Generico, finally driven beyond all reason. He pummels Kevin—we see delightful glimpses of Kevin's startled face between punches as it dawns on him he might have made a terrible mistake—and is going to deliver the turnbuckle brainbuster to him but Corino pulls him to safety. The Ring of Honor trainees jump into the ring to try and stop him, only to have Generico scythe through them in a berserker rage, handing out brainbusters to everyone. Kevin stands on the ramp, shaken and appalled, as Cabana triumphantly demands one more match, one beyond any DQ or any rules. And so a street fight is booked for the next big show in Chicago —*Bitter Friends, Stiffer Enemies 2*—as Kevin and Generico move ever closer to the inevitable singles match that will bring closure to the feud.

The street fight is an operatic tour de force, a chaotic scarlet wallow of hatred. All four come dressed for the occasion in their own ways. Hometown boy Cabana is in a Dick Butkus shirt, El Generico decked out in navy track pants and an incongruous white A-shirt in flimsy cotton. Kevin wears a Guns 'n' Roses t-shirt and shorts instead of his singlet, making him look more like WWE Kevin Owens for the space of this match.

Steve Corino comes ready for a street fight dressed in a crisp immaculate white shirt and slacks, both of which end up artistically soaked in blood as the fight progresses. Suffice to say the brawl through the crowd *begins* with Kevin giving Generico a low blow and then prying open the agonized luchador's legs to gnaw on his crotch. By the end, Kevin, Corino and Cabana are all dripping scarlet—Generico's mask, of course, makes it nearly-impossible to bloody his face, but his arms and chest are painted with his enemies' blood in bold crimson swaths. The finish features Cabana getting Corino in a submission while Generico grates his lacerated face across a barbed-wire bat. On the outside of the ring, Kevin is frozen in horror at the sight of what his former friend has become—what his actions have made Generico into.[*] As Kevin stares, paralyzed with shock, Generico puts the bat on the mat beneath Corino's face, takes a chair and smacks the

---

[*] The cameras didn't capture this character beat, but Shane Hagadorn describes it on

back of his head, driving it into the barbed wire. The referee is forced to stop the match and give the win to Generico and Cabana.

The victors celebrate in front of the audience (some of whom are visibly shell-shocked at the gorefest) and leave Kevin to crawl into the ring and cradle his fallen mentor, his pale blood-spattered face a Jackson Pollock canvas of madness as he vows horrific revenge.

The build continues through May, a rising bloody shriek of violence as Kevin grows increasingly unhinged. Kevin and Cabana have a Last Man Standing match in which he does a moonsault onto Kevin while he lies on a carpet of thumbtacks, buried in chairs. Cabana loses that match when Corino's thirteen-year-old son Colby runs in, dressed as a luchador, to beamingly hand over a barbed-wire bat. Kevin jams the bat between Cabana's legs and then scrubs it across his face until he passes out from the pain, giving the victory to Kevin. Yet the very next night in PWG, El Generico wins the tag titles with his *new* tag team partner, WWE former tag team champion Paul London, a booking coincidence (or possibly not) that surely rendered Kevin's win over Cabana hollow.

This Ends Now

Finally, it's June 19, 2010. The scene is *Death Before Dishonor VIII* in Toronto, where Kevin Steen and El Generico have their first singles match since Kevin turned on Generico exactly six months ago to the day. The fans have been waiting all year to see Kevin get his comeuppance and the luchador to get his revenge, and the six-month anniversary seems the perfect time for it.

Ring of Honor shows at the time were generally structured to have a slow build up through the card—opening matches were the bottom of the card, the lowest-status wrestlers. But as the first match's combatants (Cheech and Cloudy AKA the tag team "Up in Smoke") start to make their way down the ramp, they are suddenly bowled over by a furious El Generico, who shoves them aside to leap in the ring. The

---

his podcast with Jeff Schwartz, "An Honorable Mention," in episode 111, which covers this show.

luchador, incandescent with rage, bellows "Steen! Now!" It's a huge shift in a character that has gone from a mute comedy act to a heroic avenging angel. It's also a clever way to obscure that Jim Cornette was never going to book this showdown in a prominent position on the card—this way it feels like it could have been a main event except for Generico's furious impatience. "Steen! Now!" he demands again at the top of his lungs, and the Ring of Honor audience that had been dawdling for the opening act hurriedly scrambles to their seats.

Steve Corino appears at the curtain to inform Generico that Kevin Steen doesn't waste his time on opening acts. He's gunning for the world title now and has no time to waste on anything but the main event. As he's explaining all this, however, Kevin himself pushes Corino aside and rushes the ring. "Kevin, no! No!" Corino screams, as his protege and the luchador go forehead-to-forehead in the ring, vibrating with hatred.

"Steve, it's fine!" Kevin yells without taking his eyes from Generico. "This ends *now!*"

The audience shrieks in delight as the two of them start in with the wild hockey punches that will be a hallmark of Kevin and Sami's fights in the future. They know their wrestling tropes, they know that Kevin's rage-blind impatience is going to cost him this match. Yes, it will end now, as Kevin says, but surely not in the way Kevin wants.

The beginning of the match is all El Generico, of course, fueled with righteous rage and out to destroy his former friend. He sails over the ropes to crush Kevin as Kevin tries to flee this newly-energized nemesis and hurls him into the ring, where Kevin clings to the bottom rope like a rabid koala, panicking as Generico tries to drag him to the center. When Generico attempts his tornado DDT from the turnbuckle, however, Kevin counters it and slams the luchador back-first across his knees, snuffing out the audience's "olé" chant. When he shoves Generico's head into the bottom rope at the corner and then stands on his head, bouncing up and down, the audience starts chanting "Fuck you, Steen," which he responds to with a vicious-looking cannonball and a long laugh at the audience's frustration.

Commentary says solemnly, "The ones you love always hurt you the most," which seems a decent summary of the feud.

Generico tries his tornado DDT again and this time Kevin shoves him when he's on the top turnbuckle, causing him to crotch himself. When Generico finally manages to pull off one of his most spectacular moves, a dive through the corner ropes into a DDT, the crowd goes crazy, pounding on the metal barricades and chanting "ROH!" at the top of their lungs. The pace picks up until there's a sudden back-and-forth flurry of moves—a Helluva Kick, a suplex, a lariat—and for a moment both wrestlers lie on the mat, gathering their energy. The audience can feel things are moving into the third act of the match, and they are ready.

As the action winds up, there's an amazing sequence where Generico goes for his brainbuster and Kevin somehow counters it, hoisting Generico up into the package piledriver and driving him down onto his head. It's his finishing move.

Generico kicks out, running on sheer fury.

He finally gets his astonished tormenter up on the turnbuckle, in position for his ultimate finishing move, the brainbuster onto the turnbuckle. The crowd is on its collective feet waiting to see Generico deliver this long-awaited vengeance. Kevin desperately starts gnawing on Generico's fingers, struggling against his fate, and when the referee steps closer to warn him against biting, the referee gets bumped. For a moment, his back is turned.

Kevin grabs the turnbuckle wrench which has been hidden in the turnbuckle and smacks Generico in the head with it.

All the air goes out of the crowd as Kevin grabs Generico and does a neckbreaker off the top turnbuckle with him. The luchador lies motionless as the referee turns around, sees the pin, and counts to three.

The match is over and Kevin did not get the comeuppance he so richly deserved.

The audience is deflated as the dazed Generico is helped from the ring, as Kevin leers and sneers at them all. It's up to the rest of the card to get the audience back into the show as events move on, leaving Kevin and Generico's feud behind.

At intermission, the crowd is milling around the arena, leaving the ring surrounded by mostly-empty seats as the crew cleans the mat and tightens the ropes. Suddenly Kevin comes flying out of the curtain, in full retreat from an enraged El Generico, who pursues him around the ring, hurling him into barricades as startled fans rush back to ringside for the second time this evening. Generico has Kevin on his knees in the middle of the ring and is hoisting a chair to hit him when Corino appears and stops him. Then Cabana joins the fray. By the time Generico has grabbed the ring announcer's necktie* and is throttling a struggling Kevin with it, the message to the thrilled and singing audience is clear.

You thought this was over after six months?
Oh, we're just getting started.

---

* The necktie was a reference to the former ROH champion Bryan Danielson, who had been hired by WWE under the name Daniel Bryan in 2009… and fired just a week prior to Death Before Dishonor for strangling the ring announcer with his own necktie during a brawl. The firing would be temporary, and this would be far from the last time Sami drew parallels to his career and that of the man known as the American Dragon.

FIGHT WITHOUT HONOR
(2010)

J.J. MCGEE

Writing in Blood

THE FIRST HALF of 2010 told the story of how the betrayed El Generico rose from his depression with the help of his friend Colt Cabana, and how Kevin Steen sank further into madness at the encouragement of his mentor Steve Corino. In the second half of the year, the story shifted and darkened further as they built toward the climax at *Final Battle 2010*. Cabana had spent six months trying to convince Generico to confront Kevin, but after losing to him in June, Generico started to become obsessed with ending his faithless friend. And Kevin had started the feud claiming he wanted to be free of his former tag partner, but by the middle of the year his motivations seemed more tangled and torn.

At their next singles match, a month later at the show aptly named Hate, Kevin seems determined to not just beat but humiliate Generico. The looming and leering have intensified. He uses his bulk to pin Generico against the turnbuckle, nuzzling at the luchador as he squirms frantically, trying to escape. He gouges at Generico's eyes, then licks the tears of pain and fury from his fingers with relish. He's annihilating the boundaries between them, invading not just his space but his body. The fans are simultaneously thrilled and unnerved by his erratic actions, especially when he starts to threaten anyone who dares to wear a Generico mask to a show. Seeing a black-and-red mask in the audience inevitably sends him into a meltdown of impotent rage, one that often ends with a desecrating kiss that tends to horrify the audience more than his bloody matches. There's an undeniably erotic edge to all of it—not sexual but erotic, at that dark borderline where death and love, hate and bliss, are nearly identical.

The day after Hate, Kevin has a match for the Ring of Honor world title against current champion Tyler Black. After leaving the Age of the Fall, Black had made his way to the very top of the card and won the top title, and in mid-2010, his path crossed Kevin's once more. Unfortunately for Black, by this point Jim Cornette was making a lot of the creative decisions, especially for the top of the card. Cornette's idea of a babyface champion was earnest and noble, and Tyler Black...well, let's just say "earnest and noble" has never been the strength of the man who would one day become Seth Rollins. The fans were not sold on him, as Kevin pointed out in the build to their match. "When you were beaten and bruised and broken, then they *loved* you," he explained with a mad earnestness that felt more genuine than Black's humble babyface persona. "They were behind you when you were chasing that title, and I just want to take it and help you get them back." It's one of the strongest early examples of the genre-savvy aspects of Kevin's persona, this awareness of the cliche that "heels retain, faces chase," because faces are always more beloved when they're struggling to win a title. He promises that when he finally gets that title and can "strap it around my *fat fucking waist*"—spitting the words with vitriol—"I'm going to rain a hell on this place that's going to make everyone regret ever offering me a contract!"

That doesn't happen—not quite yet—but his match with Black is a bloody psychological thriller in which Kevin teaches the champion the twisted joy of mayhem and suffering. The match ends with Kevin on his knees, defeated, soaked in his own blood and laughing as Black stares at him in horror—and something darker. In a promo after the match, Kevin calls Corino on the phone, still dripping blood, to tell him that he'd achieved what he'd wanted to. "Oh, he loved it. When he saw the blood... We did it," he says, as calmly triumphant as if there weren't still rivulets of fresh blood running down his face. The pieces for a heel turn for Black were in place, though it never came to fruition because Black signed with WWE shortly after, cutting short any character arc the match may have launched. The case could be made, however, that Seth Rollins carried the lessons Kevin had taught him with him into WWE, where their paths would cross yet again in the future.

But for now Kevin went back to his feud with Generico, one that was growing more intense and claustrophobic by the week. It was getting more and more attention from fans and critics, too, attention that would eventually win it Feud of the Year for 2010 in the Wrestling Observer Newsletter awards. Unfortunately, all of that buzz and excitement meant it started receiving attention from another source as well, a far less welcome one.

To this point, Kevin and Generico's feud had been given space to breathe and unfold because the executive producer of ROH, Jim Cornette, was focused on the top of the card and paid little attention to it. Booker Adam Pearce did most of the work with Kevin, Sami, Cabana and Corino to set up the storyline and organize the matches necessary to tell it. However, in the middle of 2010, Pearce was replaced as head booker by Hunter Johnston (AKA the wrestler Delirious). Delirious seems to have deferred to Cornette and left major decisions to him, meaning that just as Kevin and Generico's storyline approached its fever pitch, Cornette was consolidating more and more power within Ring of Honor. This was bad news for Kevin and Sami.

Cornette already didn't like them in the least, seeing them as two loudmouth, high-maintenance control freaks who looked all wrong to be wrestlers. The extra difficulty lay in the reason Cornette had been hired in the first place: not just to produce or to book but to attempt to broker a sale of the promotion to some corporate entity who could maintain it. By mid-2010, the Sinclair Broadcast Company was showing interest. Sinclair was about to embark on a decade-long quest to acquire different media properties,[1] and it was interested in picking up the large amount of live television a wrestling promotion could provide. All Ring of Honor needed to do was prove it could provide a steady flow of broadcast-ready content and the sale might proceed.

There was nothing at all "broadcast-ready" about Kevin and Generico's blood-soaked, deeply profane feud. Cornette asked them to tone it down, but the boundary-pushing violence was the defining heart of the feud, and there was no way they were going to dial it back, no matter how much the executive producer raged backstage. In September, the four major characters met again in a chain match, meaning that members of each team were required to be chained together as the match began.

El Generico insists on being chained to Kevin instead of Corino, and Kevin laughs maniacally as he and his former partner are manacled together. Strap matches and chain matches often function as metaphors for characters who can't seem to get free of each other, wrestlers locked in a vicious cycle of violence, and in this match the chains are entirely on-the-nose as Kevin and Generico get literally linked together with steel bonds. All three of the non-masked wrestlers end up gushing blood from head wounds once more, of course (one can almost hear the howls of fury from Cornette offscreen). Generico's need to destroy his former friend has begun to consume him, and the formerly happy-go-lucky luchador ends up gnawing on Kevin's bloodied head, then running his dripping hands over his masked face. The camera closes up on his gory fingers before he goes back to his frenzied death-dance with Kevin, locked together in hatred and violence. By the end of that match, Corino's son Colby has managed to cut the straps keeping Kevin and Corino chained, which they use to tie Cabana up and brutalize him as Generico struggles to shield his friend. Eventually Corino is forced to tap out, but the real victory belongs to Kevin when Generico attacks him after the match and he manages to rip off the luchador's mask.

The crowd gasps in horror and excitement. El Generico's unmasked face was literally never seen, not even outside shows. Almost no fans knew what he looked like.* Generico hides his face in the ring apron so quickly that not a glimpse of anyone looking like Sami Zayn can be seen, and Cabana fetches a towel to hide his face as they beat a hasty retreat. Kevin, howling with evil glee, props the empty mask on a chair —literally the same chair Kevin hit Generico with at Final Battle 2009, painstakingly tracked and curated by Shane Hagadorn.[2] Corino, still covered in blood, kneels by the chair and Kevin wipes the blood off his face with his fingers like an artist with a grotesque palette, writing "Die Generico" on the back of the chair in scarlet letters.

The last stretch of the Feud of the Year has begun, and the stakes are at their highest.

Higher even than the wrestlers had intended.

"Get Rid of Kevin"

Shortly after Adam Peace left ROH, Kevin got a phone call from Jim Cornette. Cornette wanted to discuss how exactly the feud was

---

* I've spoken to a fan of Ring of Honor at the time who chatted regularly with the red-headed guy who helped set up the ring before shows and assumed he was part of the ring crew. When Sami Zayn debuted in WWE, she had a Moment of Revelation.

going to end, and he had some ideas. Specifically, he had the idea to make their climactic match at Final Battle 2010 a "mask versus career" match. If Generico lost, he had to unmask.

If Kevin lost, he had to leave Ring of Honor.

The final end of the feud had never been in doubt. Cornette explained that after Kevin lost, he would "go away for a while," at which point Kevin broke from his frozen paralysis to stammer "Uh... um... I'm— I *go away for a while?*"

"Yeah, yeah! Six months..."

Rendered almost incoherent with horror, Kevin groped for words. "Wh... but... my, my, the—my life? Money? The— the— the world? My— the— people? The— my child and wife?"[3] Six months without his usual paycheck was alarming enough, but that faltering "the— the world?" revealed Kevin's other, deeper concern. That's six months out of the prime of his career, six months on the shelf after a feud meant to launch both him and Sami toward the top of the card. It would be a tragically wasted opportunity—and that's even if the hiatus was limited to six months. Kevin suspected that Cornette hoped to make that absence even longer. Maybe even permanent.

It was payback time for Kevin's demands on Cornette's attention, his insistence on controlling his story. "That was to throw him under the bus," Jimmy Jacobs remembers when asked about it in an interview along with Steve Corino, and Steve agrees, "Yeah, they really were making an example out of us."

"It wasn't a storyline when it happened," Jimmy adds. "They were like 'Get rid of Kevin.'"[4]

On the phone, floundering, Kevin asked Cornette, what if I don't agree to this? Only to be told, of course, that not agreeing wasn't an option. He wasn't the booker, after all. His approval was not required for this ending.

And Kevin was forced to admit that the frenzied intensity of the storyline the four of them had created did require an outsized punishment for the monster he'd crafted of his literal sweat and blood. Kevin Steen had to be punished, had to be banished. "I figured, in a way... how else could Generico and I's feud end, but by something like that?"[5]

Still... *six months* is a huge stretch of time. Long enough for the fans to forget about him. Long enough for El Generico to move on and move up to the top of the card, free of his nemesis. Months of scraping by and pinching pennies and watching his friends progress without him. Too much.

But there was nothing he could do.

Final Battle

The last three months of 2010 were a long shriek of bloody violence, building inexorably to the final show of the year, Final Battle. Robbed of his mask, El Generico became a spirit of vengeance, showing up like a specter in all-black gear to confront Kevin, single-mindedly bent on destruction. Kevin carried the mask with him everywhere, taunting fans with it, spitting on it, blowing his nose on it, or using it to create Generico-proxies. For example, in a match with the bearded Grizzly Redwood ("The Littlest Lumberjack"), Kevin jammed the Generico mask onto his head and quickly destroyed him, then draped himself across the still body to gaze dreamily into the mask's eyeholes as if imagining it were Generico he'd just murdered. They were on a path to darkness and ruin, both of them sprinting toward the final battle.

Both Steve Corino and Colt Cabana grew weary of their friends' bloody-minded pact of destruction. Where Cabana had once begged his friend to stand up to Kevin, by October he was sickened by the violence, desperate to extricate himself from it all. Corino was alarmed by Kevin's willfully putting his entire career at risk, unable to convince him to back off. He began begging *Generico* to voluntarily unmask, framing it as a smarmy attempt to save Generico, but underneath that he was clearly worried about his protege's future. Eventually Corino and Cabana wrestled an "I Quit" match, where if Cabana could make Corino quit he would agree not to interfere in Generico and Kevin's feud anymore. Kevin accompanied Corino to the ring wearing a straitjacket to restrain him from interfering, limiting him (for a while) to maniacally laughing commentary like informing Corino "You're getting a little creative! I like it! It's turning me on a little!" Eventually Corino liberated Kevin from the jacket, only to end up trapped in it himself as Cabana hit him in the head with a chair, then powerbombed him through a table. Covered in blood, with Cabana sawing at his head with jagged fragments of table, Corino finally admitted defeat and quit.

Standing over him, Colt announced "This is done," and Corino echoed him: "It's over." All of it dramatic enough on its own, but takes on an extra layer of tragedy with the knowledge that all of the wrestlers involved knew how this was actually going to end for Kevin. Corino desperately wished he actually could save Kevin's career, while Cabana and Generico found themselves in the horrible position of costing a friend his job. In a way, the storyline was too compelling, too bloody and intense to end without punishment. By crafting the narrative and playing its villain to perfection, Kevin had written himself out of his own story.

All of which brings us, at last, to December 18, 2010, and *Final Battle* in New York City. Kevin and Sami have planned the match in meticulous detail, each seemingly-chaotic spot actually part of a complex narrative machinery. They take time to talk to the camera crew, explaining where they need to be and what moments they need to capture from which angles. Jake Manning, operating a camera that night, remembers them as "very particular of how the spots would come off."[6] That painstaking attention to each detail is one of the things that people cite as annoying about Kevin and Sami, and it's clearly not limited to this one climactic match. Years later, after the infamous Festival of Friendship in 2017, the magician hired to be part of the spectacle will remember Kevin as "quiet and intense" and "precise," and mention specifically that he "wanted everything to be perfect."[7] One can easily imagine him applying that same quiet intensity to this match, the culmination of over a year of planning. It had to be perfect.

It's the last match of the night, but it's not the main event. Adam Pearce had told Kevin and Sami that it would be the main event, but once Pearce was gone Cornette, once again, changed the plans.[8] Traditionally, the top title match is the main event, and so Davey Richards versus Roderick Strong, who had defeated Tyler Black a few months ago to become champion, was the main event match on the posters.

FIGHT WITHOUT HONOR

Kevin and Generico's match was dubbed an "unsanctioned match without honor," technically not on the card at all—after the title match the show was announced as officially over, so they were the last match of the night but not the main event. This semantic shell game stung both Kevin and Sami's pride unbearably—to have worked so hard for over a year, to have been a major draw on the card for so many shows, only to be denied the main event through petty word games? It was another slight that was added to Jim Cornette's pile of transgressions.

On that night, though, the audience does not care at all whether this is the official main event or not. It's clearly the highlight and climax of the show—of the year—and when Kevin comes to the ring tauntingly wearing his former tag team shirt, they're ready with a full-throated response. El Generico arrives all in monochrome, in black tights, a black-and-white mask, and a black trench coat he got during a stint in Dragongate. The coat is lined with golden cloth, and when Generico leaps into the ring it flares around him so the luchador looks like a sunbeam trapped in a storm cloud. The crowd throws a dizzying rainbow arc of streamers, and the image is complete, the theme of the match set by the sheer visuals: can Generico shake off the darkness of the last year and find the brightness that had once been his?

He goes on the offense at first, of course, soaring out of the ring in a wild tope to flatten his nemesis. He quickly finds a chain and wraps it around Kevin's head before kicking him in the face. Kevin is immediately fountaining blood. He's one of those people who lose all color when they bleed, so his face is a ghastly chalk-white under the scarlet, making everything even more eerie as he rubs his own blood on himself, licking it off his arms as the crowd shrieks in gleeful horror.

Somehow bloodying Kevin turns the tide of the match against Generico, which makes sense in a dark way. By embracing mayhem and violence Generico has entered Kevin's twisted world. Soon the luchador is thrown into a ladder, and Kevin pins him face-down to the mat with one knee, wiping the blood from his own forehead to scrawl words on Generico's squirming flesh. He whacks Generico with a chair across the back, then straddles him and begins ripping at the mask above one eye, exposing his forehead.

As Kevin rips at the mask and El Generico struggles against him, the torn mask is pulled askew and for the first time in the luchador's career it's possible to glimpse the face of the real person beneath it. It's a gruesome violation, a tearing of the boundaries between fantasy and reality. El Generico is so carefully constructed, so zealously maintained as a character, that it feels as if Kevin is ripping the very skin from his face. Over and over again in this feud we've seen Kevin, Corino, and Cabana—often all three at once—covered in their own blood. But El Generico has been spared that grisly fate, because it's nearly-impossible to cut your forehead while wearing a mask. Because of the mask, it's likely Sami had never bladed before. But Kevin sentons a chair against Generico's head, and soon the exposed side of Generico's face is a crimson welter of blood.

He staggers and hangs on the ropes, and the audience, getting a good look at him, goes weirdly quiet. The bloody ruin of the mask and face combined is uncanny, unnerving.

Kevin, on the other hand, hasn't seemed to realize that Generico is bleeding yet. He pulls Generico's old red-and-black mask out from where he stuffed it into his shorts at the beginning of the match and turns it into a hand puppet, taunting Generico in a squeaky little voice. "Oh no!" he shrills, "Kevin Steen is going to kill you!" He punches Generico with the mask, then stuffs it back into his shorts and mimes humping Generico's face, leering at the groans of the audience. Only then does he realize what the audience has already seen, that Generico is bleeding, and his mouth drops open in delight.

Seeing Generico's blood unleashes an orgy of gleeful wallowing: Kevin licks the blood from his hands, rubs it into his hair, bathes his arms in it. Some people in the audience cheer, but most have gone unnervingly still. It's not the flat emptiness of boredom or disapproval, it's a truly unsettled silence, full of a complex mix of fear and anticipation. When Kevin goes so far as to stick his bloody hand up his shorts, they make an awful keening sound. You can see hands shooting up reflexively to cover heads, clasp over mouths. Kevin drags Generico to the ropes to display to the audience like a gory, limp trophy, caressing his bloody face with an almost tender pride in his handiwork. The crowd stares at them, completely enthralled and horror-stricken. In the back, Jim Cornette is "flipping shit," fuming about how this is "killing pro wrestling, look at this, this is garbage wrestling."⁹ Steve Corino watches him and is so furious that he wants to quit Ring of Honor. Cabana tries to calm him down as they wait together for the cue to play their final roles in the feud.

Dragging Generico around like a wounded kitten, Kevin sets up the ladder on its side so it's basically just a rigid foot-high bar of steel with no give at all. Hauling the luchador to his feet, he kisses his former friend on the mouth in a cruel taunting farewell and prepares to suplex him onto the ladder.

And here's what I mean about the precise clockwork that ticks beneath the bloody melodrama in this match: it's thirty-two minutes long from bell to bell, and this moment is set exactly sixteen minutes into it, a pinpoint pivot. Because it's this mocking executioner's kiss that galvanizes El Generico and turns the tide back in his favor. He reverses the move and it's Kevin who ends up thrown back-first onto the ladder, crushed against the unyielding steel, and Generico rises up trembling with rage, and the enraptured crowd starts to sing with all their hearts. *Olé. Olé, olé, olé.*

The momentum has shifted again, and Generico in fairly short order unleashes a barrage of moves against Kevin, to the audience's joy. He suplexes Kevin onto a chair, he hurls him off the turnbuckle and through a table. He even does Kevin's own finishing move to him, package piledriving him before giving him a brainbuster on the apron, and it looks like he might finally be able to pin Kevin, but then Steve Corino shows up and pulls the ref out of the ring, breaking up the count and saving his protege's career for the moment.

Corino rummages under the ring and comes up with The Chair, the battered chair that Kevin had smashed over Generico's head a full year ago, had written on in Corino's own blood three months ago. He holds it high over his head so everyone can see the red-lettered "Die Generico" scrawled on it, preparing to strike Generico with it. Before he can, Colt Cabana runs in and saves Generico, grabbing the chair away from Corino and giving Kevin a good whack with it before tossing it down and chasing Corino backstage. The supporting players have had their moment, and now Generico and Kevin are left alone in the ring. The fateful chair lies nearby, its role not quite over.

Bloody and truly weary—the match has gone on for almost a half hour now—Generico and Kevin continue to battle around the ring, running through a few referees before finally, *finally*, Generico gets him in position to deliver his finishing move, the brainbuster off the turnbuckle. But here things go badly, as both wrestlers are so exhausted that Generico can't make sure Kevin falls forward into the ring, and instead Kevin tumbles wildly sideways off the turnbuckle and crashes out of the ring to the floor. Kevin's weight nearly crushes Generico against the ropes before he goes flying, and the camera catches a glimpse of blank shock on Kevin's face as things go wrong. The move bashes up his sternum so badly that he'll be in pain for months to come. Luckily the match is almost done, as Generico rolls him back in the ring and pins him.

At this point Kevin has taken Generico's finishing moves, he's taken his own finisher, he's been thrown into ladders and drenched in his own blood. But the villain is still running on spite and hatred that can't be quenched, just as much as the person playing him is running on adrenaline and the imperative to bring resolution to the story he's sacrificed so much for. He kicks out.

Stunned, Generico is at a loss, until he spots the chair lying in the ring, the chair daubed in blood, with its history of pain. The requirement to end the cycle is clear—the story began with a chairshot to the head and only that can put Kevin down.

As Generico picks up the chair and steels himself to deliver the finishing blow, Kevin—on his knees, helpless as Generico had been a year ago—suddenly produces that familiar red-and-black mask and offers it up to him.

Generico takes the mask from him, staring at it for a long moment as Kevin begs for mercy, his hands clasped piteously. The audience isn't going for it: for starters, they know their wrestling and they don't trust Kevin for one second. They know if Generico wavers it'll be all over, there'll be a low blow or a chair shot and Kevin will be triumphant, Generico will be forced to unmask, justice will never get served. And especially after the last half hour, after the last *year*, they know that wrestling is rarely about mercy. They want justice.

Generico drops the mask and lifts the chair high, and we can see in

Kevin's face the final, crushing knowledge that there's no escaping his fate, that he's orchestrated the very event that will now destroy him.

When his former friend brings the chair down across his head, he drops without a sound. It might have been nearly a relief, to at last lie still after thirty minutes of grueling exertion. After the last year.

Too exhausted to stand, Generico has his hand raised by the referee as his music starts to play. He's radiant with victory as he struggles to stand, as he goes to find his old familiar mask on the mat and clasp it to him.

Sami's commitment to the El Generico character was always complete and total. But now and then there's a fleeting glimpse of the real person behind the mask, behind the character. One of them is here, at the end of *Final Battle*, at the end of their defining feud, as Generico celebrates his freedom and Sami faces the knowledge that Kevin will be gone for at least six months—possibly even longer. Possibly forever, because everyone suspects Cornette will try to find reasons to not bring him back. It's possible this is the last time they will ever be in the ring together in Ring of Honor.

Now and then, after a risky spot or a difficult match, you can catch wrestlers doing a check-in—surreptitiously clasping hands to send the message *I'm all right*. If you look closely you can see that as Generico struggles to stand, as he rises and collapses again, he is trying, over and over, to get a check-in from Kevin. His hand brushes Kevin's wrist as if by accident. As he fumbles with his mask his fingers use it as a screen to tap at Kevin's hand, hidden by the cloth. There's a terrible urgency to it, and it's clear Kevin is not giving him the signal that he's okay. Kevin is lying there bloody and battered, and he is not responding to Sami's tactile pleas for a response. Finally, as the referee lifts his hand, Generico stumbles and goes down to his knees, and—as if by accident—one of his legs ends up across Kevin's calf, pressing down in a final attempt at some kind of communication, an acknowledgement, a possible reassurance.

Colt Cabana appears with a towel, which he uses to shield Generico from the eyes of the audience as he changes from his ripped and bloodied black mask back to his cheerful, bright old mask. As he comforts and supports his friend and the audience cheers, the vanquished villain rolls, agonizingly slowly, to the side of the ring.

Steve Corino arrives as well and crouches next to Kevin as if to guard him, but Generico and Cabana pay no attention to Kevin, because he must be utterly ignored in this moment for the story that they've all expended a year of blood and pain and effort to create to be complete, for Generico to be free.

Generico emerges in his red-and-black mask, the blood wiped away, his identity restored, and the audience lifts up its voice in song: *Olé. Olé, olé, olé.*

The crowd cheers and sings, Cabana and Generico celebrate, paying no heed to their fallen enemy, and Kevin lies on his stomach with his face buried in his arms. He's lost. He's injured and in pain, and he's being sent away in defeat. You can see his whole body shaking with sobs. Still crouched next to him, Corino rests his hand on the back of his head, very gently, so he's not totally alone.

Generico meets Kevin's eyes one time and waves goodbye, then staggers from the ring in triumph, leaving Kevin staring after him. His face is caked in dried blood. Tears have cut pale tracks down through the gore. He spent a year insisting he wanted to be free of El Generico, and now the luchador is free of *him*, and it is nothing he ever wanted.

The audience tauntingly sings "Na na na na, hey hey hey, goodbye" at Kevin as Generico leaves, but the moment Generico passes through the curtain it's like they suddenly realize that this means Kevin is leaving, he's really leaving and they don't actually want that at all. "Please don't go," they start to chant, and then "Thank you Steen." Kevin staggers to his feet as they plead with him, takes a moment to soak in the cheers, and then responds by flipping them all off and bellowing "Fuck you all!"

The crowd bursts into jubilant, raucous applause as Kevin rages from the ring, honoring his refusal to accept any form of pity. He storms out, grabbing and mauling the abandoned black-and-white Generico mask as his last act. He pauses one last time to stare back at the audience, baffled and wretched, and then he's gone.

Aftermath

That night, after the fight of his life, Kevin drives the six hours back to Montreal. His wife and son sleep in the backseat as he drives through the clear, freezing-cold night.[10] Most likely he drives straight north from New York City, through the woods of upstate New York. After Albany it's mostly long empty stretches of road, with the High Peaks Wilderness to his left and home still a long way to go. As he drives, he goes back over the match in his mind and sees all the places that it could have been better. It was the culmination of a year of his career, it was the best he had to give, and it wasn't *perfect*. The coming year stretches out ahead of him, devoid of Ring of Honor, of his salary, of his art. All of his work and dedication have ended with him unemployed, heading into the unknown. He tries to console himself with the thought that surely Sami will be booked at the top of the card from now on, that at least his friend will benefit.[11] It's a bittersweet consolation.

As he drives away from *Final Battle*, he looks out at the darkened woods, his chest bruised and his heart aching, and he thinks, "Maybe I'll just quit."

FUCK RING OF HONOR
(2011)

American Legion Post #308, Reseda, California

LUCKILY FOR KEVIN AND SAMI—LUCKILY for wrestling—Pro Wrestling Guerrilla was there for them during Kevin's time away from Ring of Honor in 2011. Banned from ROH, a punishment for both the character and the real person, he needed a way to get through that hiatus. When re-negotiating his contract before Final Battle, Kevin had made explicit in the document that the absence would be only for six months, that they were required to bring him back by June.[1] So he had to find a way to get through those six months. Just half a year.

For the last few years his appearances in the California promotion had been sporadic, as he focused on his family and his Ring of Honor work. But he'd had a match with Japanese wrestler Akira Tozawa in December 2010, just before Final Battle, that had reminded him how much fun PWG matches could be. Faced with the possibility of simply quitting wrestling altogether, he rallied himself, thinking "fuck this, I'm going back to PWG, and this is what's going to keep me alive."[2]

PWG had truly come into its own in the last few years, becoming famous for some of the best bell to bell wrestling in the world and some of the best wrestling audiences in the world too, especially in the cramped and grungy venue of the American Legion Hall of Reseda, California. Its stark white walls, its Art Deco ceiling lamps hanging from the polished wooden beams, its incongruous mirrorball hanging above the ring, would be emblematic of great wrestling for over a decade until its demolition in 2019.[3] As he faced early 2011 with no Ring of Honor bookings, Kevin consoled himself that at least he would have PWG as a lifeline, both financially and emotionally. It was also the only place where he and Sami could continue to have high-profile matches, continue their story.

Since their return to Ring of Honor in 2007, Kevin and Sami had been nearly inseparable in the promotion, first as a tag team and then as rivals. After *Final Battle 2010* and the *Fight Without Honor* to conclude their year-long feud, Kevin and Sami found themselves disconnected for the first time in years, as El Generico's Ring of Honor trajectory was forced to continue without his partner and nemesis.

Kevin and Sami only shared the ring five times in this whole year, two of them for Montreal promotion NSPW of which no video appears to be available, and three for PWG. Yet in this year of disjunction and hiatus, those three PWG matches are some of the greatest matches of their career. Each of them is distinctly different, sharp and polished as diamonds, showcasing some of the best that wrestling has to offer. And each of them helps get Kevin and Sami through this year.

When PWG suggests Kevin make a tag team with Tozawa, the

Nightmare Violence connection is born. And so, on All Star Weekend in May, Kevin finds himself in the ring with El Generico, currently tagging with Ricochet.

"This is the first time Kevin and Generico have met up since *Final Battle*?" Chuck Taylor asks on commentary as the wrestlers come to the ring.

"Yep," says Excalibur, who is also the PWG booker.

"Did you... watch *Final Battle*?" Taylor says.

"Yep," says Excalibur.

There's a thoughtful pause, and then Taylor asks, "Are you sure booking this match was a wise choice?"

Wise or not, any questions about how things stand between El Generico and Kevin are put to rest when Generico does his traditional olé salute, then pivots without any transition at all into punching Kevin, resulting in the two of them throwing frantic hands until their shaken tag team partners pull them apart.

Tozawa and Ricochet spend the whole match emoting "Look, we came here to beat people up and have some fun, okay? This is way too intense." And that is part of the story of the match, that Ricochet and Tozawa just want to *fight*, free of the agonizing baggage Generico and Kevin are lugging with them.

It turns out to be a good, vicious match, with one of the highlights being Kevin catching his tag partner out of the air and using him to batter his enemies, swinging the startled Tozawa around in a fireman's carry, his arms and legs lashing at Generico and Ricochet. Dropping his partner, Kevin climbs up onto the turnbuckle in triumph and the crowd goes wild, pouring love toward him. There are no barricades at Reseda, the fans are pressed right up against the ring, their excitement and adoration radiating from them.

Kevin soaks it up like sunlight, glowing. Even when he and Generico square off and things turn dark, as when Generico takes particular pleasure in kicking him until he releases a submission hold on Ricochet as Kevin literally spits defiance at him—even then, the match is fun. The stakes are low compared to the grinding, emotionally exhausting story of the year before, and the chemistry between all four is energizing. Kevin's enjoying himself, teaming with and pitted against three of the best wrestlers in the world, in front of one of the best crowds in the world, and the match is full of a violent energy that is exactly what Kevin needs right now.

When it comes to an end, the four of them stand in the middle of the ring, and Tozawa offers Ricochet his hand. They shake, and Tozawa turns to Generico next as Kevin shakes Ricochet's hand in turn. That leaves only Kevin and Generico, and they stare at each other for a long, painful moment. A chant of "hug it out" starts up in the hopeful crowd, but neither wrestler reaches out, and Generico retreats cautiously, refusing to turn his back on Kevin.

Left in the ring with Tozawa, Kevin horrifies him by dropping into a *dogeza*, the deepest, most respectful form of bow. The *dogeza*, which I assume Kevin learned during one of his Dragongate stints, is an extravagant gesture, lavishly over-the-top, totally unanswerable. Wrestlers will do this for a Japanese audience as they're about to leave Japan, to thank every single one of them for *years* of support. It's extreme, it's hardcore, it's the barbed-wire-bat of gratitude, and Tozawa claps his hands to his head in horror for a moment in response before Kevin takes pity on him and stands back up to hug him. This moment, and the deep emotion it hints at, tell us a great deal about Kevin's state of mind at the beginning of 2011, and the darkness he had to work to shake off.

It was May, he was almost to June, *at last*, and his return to Ring of Honor. He'd been training hard and watching what he ate, leaving him 40 pounds lighter, eager to come back. But would the fans remember him and welcome him after six months away?

Like Jesus

Storylines in Ring of Honor had moved on without Kevin, of course. Roderick Strong started off the year as champion, and Generico got a title match with him in January. They put on a great match, but Generico lost and did not get another shot. Kevin, following the ROH news from home, was frustrated that his friend hadn't been pushed higher up the card and was instead "relegated to opening contests and just... bullshit."[4] It felt increasingly like their year of bloody work had gained them nothing.

As the first half of the year went on, Generico ended up in the title scene for the ROH TV title, their mid-card title. It had been held by Eddie Edwards, who then lost to Christopher Daniels. Generico started feuding with Daniels over the title as Edwards moved up and won the top championship from Strong. Clearly, winning the TV title could be a step toward the main-event title, so as Generico moved toward his title shot, that must have been cause for optimism—and perhaps more frustration for Kevin, who was running wrestling seminars in Montreal and growing increasingly restless at his exile.

But as always, Ring of Honor was only one of the many places El Generico was appearing. He did tours in Japan, England, Germany. He popped up for shows in Peru and Chile. Notably for his future, he had a couple of dark matches for TNA, at the time one of the few other televised wrestling shows in the US. Nothing came of it then, but it was a sign people were noticing him outside of Ring of Honor and the indies, a hint that maybe he could be catching the attention of people at the final goal of WWE. Was he getting ready to make that leap to the next level? It must have seemed a possibility, to both him and to Kevin.

Elsewhere in ROH, in Kevin's absence evil mastermind Steve Corino had experienced a change of heart and spent the first half of 2011 trying to atone for his wicked deeds. He called himself a "recovering evil person," an addict to violence, and spent most of his matches visibly struggling not to cheat. Eventually he was joined by Jimmy Jacobs, Kevin and Generico's old nemesis from Age of the Fall, and together the two reformed villains tried to overcome their addiction to mayhem.

At June's *Best in the World* show, Corino and Jacobs inform the crowd there's another person who hopes to ask for a second chance. As they wind up for the reveal, Kevin's sitting in the balcony in a hoodie, waiting. Walking in, he had felt like a total stranger.[5] The company is under entirely new ownership. It's been six months since the Ring of Honor fans have seen him—an eternity in wrestling. Would they react with apathy?

When Corino says Kevin's name, Hammerstein Ballroom erupts

FUCK RING OF HONOR

into a roar of delight. Kevin stands up and rips off his hoodie, throwing his arms wide as if to gather up every bit of their adulation, joy etched on his face and in every line of his body. He runs down to try and get in the ring, but Jim Cornette intervenes and blocks him. Kevin pleads with Cornette to listen to the fans and let him in, he clasps his hands and begs, but no, he's turned away, to the crowd's annoyance.

But wait! When Corino gets defeated by Michael Elgin soon after, Kevin comes running in to save him and Jacobs, then grabs the mic and announces that there's something he's been waiting for months to tell all of Ring of Honor—the fans, the wrestlers, everyone. He starts his statement in the confessional tone Corino and Jacobs have been using to try and recover from being evil. "My name is Kevin Steen," he says, his eyes cast down, penitent and almost bashful. Then he lifts his chin, throws out his chest, and bellows "And *fuck Ring of Honor!*"

It seems almost unbelievable, but according to Kevin, Cornette thought that this would make Kevin a heel.[6] At a superficial level that makes sense. Surely denouncing the thing the fans love would make them hate him? But what Cornette failed to realize is that much as the fans love Ring of Honor, they don't *identify* with the people running it. Cornette expected that given the choice between a person fed up and frustrated in his workplace and his boss, people would identify with the boss.

It's a major miscalculation.

Kevin yells "fuck Ring of Honor" with all the weight of six months of legitimate anger and gloom behind it, and the crowd reacts as they always do to authentic cries from the heart by wrestlers, by falling instantly, irrevocably in love with him. They cheer deliriously as he attacks Corino and Jacobs, threatens Cornette and owner Cary Silken and is eventually carried out bodily by security, lifted aloft with his arms outstretched—"like Jesus," Kevin says happily later, if Jesus were prone to flipping people off with both hands as he passed.[7] A furious Jim Cornette swears on his mother's grave that Kevin Steen will never enter a Ring of Honor ring again. The audience, meanwhile, is still buzzing with love for their rabble-rousing berserker hero. It's the beginning of a schism between the fans and the official narrative that will never quite be reconciled.

The very next match is El Generico winning his first and only solo title in Ring of Honor, the TV title off Christopher Daniels, in a match where he somehow manages to do a coast to coast senton all the way across the ring onto Daniels, who is hanging in the tree of woe position. When he wins, he's showered with streamers from the delighted fans as he kisses his title.

It's a glorious night for both of them, and if this were a movie, it would make a great triumphant ending. But there are very few endings in wrestling, and mid-2011 Ring of Honor is a particularly ill-omened time to try and have closure. The company's sale to Sinclair has finally gone through, and Cornette is determined that there's no place for non-English-speaking luchadors, profane and bloody-minded brawlers, or people who don't look like… well, like Davey Richards, who beats his former tag partner Eddie Edwards that very night to become Ring of Honor champion. Worried about the pending sale, well-aware of Cornette's disdain for him, Kevin had made sure to put in his contract that he had to be brought back by June.

He had not, however, put in the contract that they were required to keep bringing him back after that.

Battle of Los Angeles

After his triumphant return at *Best in the World*, Kevin was informed that he won't be wrestling in Ring of Honor until December. Another six months of exile.

"That really punched me in the face," Kevin says when he remembers it. "I was really upset. It's six more months--again? Fuck! I thought I made it through this!"[8]

He thought he was done, but he was only halfway there, and the first half was already hard enough. Despairing and depressed, he proceeded to gain back every one of the forty pounds he had lost looking forward to his return, plus a few more. Realizing that a year of his career in Ring of Honor had been frittered away, his mood soured even more, to the point where he admits he was unbearable to be around.

Meanwhile, El Generico didn't defend his title for two months, then lost it in his first defense—hardly an ideal run. But if Ring of Honor was frustrating or infuriating to them, at least they still had PWG. Kevin won the PWG World Title in July, beating Claudio Castagnoli. And in August, shortly after Generico lost his lone Ring of Honor singles title, they found themselves facing each other in the ring once more. It's not a title match, but rather the final match of the *Battle of Los Angeles* tournament. But it's their first time one-on-one since *Final Battle*, eight months before.

If *All Star Weekend* was about the joy of working with other wrestlers, the joy of tagging again and having fun, Battle of Los Angeles is about the joy of working the audience, about connecting with the crowd and all the crazy improvised chaos and satisfaction wrestling can hold.

Kevin and Generico have made their way through the brackets to face each other in the finals, to the delirious anticipation of the audience. In earlier matches, there have been glimpses of a small boy wearing a blue shirt in the audience. As the final match begins at midnight, the camera (and Kevin) spot him again—but now the child is on his father's shoulders and has put on a Generico mask. The mask is sized for an adult, making the child look like an El Generico bobblehead. Kevin powerbombs Generico onto the apron and climbs onto a chair to confront the child eye-to-eye, who watches him with wary dislike, leaning away as far as he can. He's not freaking out but is clearly convinced that Kevin is a threat and is treating him as such. The luchador mask turns his gaze unblinking, solemn and owlish as Kevin demands "Are you watching?" and prepares to hurt Generico. When Generico makes a sudden rally and kicks Kevin in the face instead, the child on his father's shoulders clenches his fists in that abrupt involuntary motion of every enthralled wrestling fan: *Get him!*

The whole first half of the match is pitched to that corner and that kid, weaving his responses into the narrative, making him part of the story. The top rope moves happen from the turnbuckle nearest him. Kevin positions his submissions so that Generico has to reach toward the child to break the hold. I'd say they're playing to an audience of one, but the child is no longer really the "audience," he's become a character as well in that most magical alchemy of wrestling.

After a neckbreaker, Kevin drops Generico to the mat, then ignores him to pivot and glare at the child, as if the kid is his true enemy and Generico merely a conduit for his spirit right now. And in a lot of ways that's what El Generico had become at this point, especially in PWG: a transparent glass, a filament that channels the audience's energy into light.

The crowd comes up with various laughing, ironic chants about this standoff between Kevin and the tiny Generico doppelganger, but there's very little ironic or winking about this match, this small story, this struggle over the spirit of a child and whether it's indomitable enough to be the force that lifts Generico to victory.

And it is!

It takes three Helluva Kicks, a brainbuster, and then a fourth Helluva Kick/brainbuster combo on the apron, but Generico eventually defeats Kevin, and the child comes down from his father's shoulders to pound the mat and then to be brought into the ring by Generico in triumph. Generico encourages him to flip off Kevin, who lashes out and smashes the Battle of Los Angeles trophy before retreating in sullen defeat, leaving Generico and his small copy to share the comically destroyed trophy and a hug. Generico then asks for the mic, apologizes for his "shit English," and announces to the audience, "You are PWG! You are El Generico! You make this special!"

"You are El Generico" may be "shit English," but it's a perfect encapsulation of the El Generico character. The man behind the mask (who is also the man behind Sami Zayn, that more transparent mask) is one of the greatest in the world at crafting a character that expresses the soul of the audience. Whether IWS's feral guttersnipe underdog, ROH's spirit of wronged retribution, or PWG's pure-hearted defender of orphans, El Generico always incarnated the best instincts of the audience. It's the reason people remember the character so fondly, even decades later. It's the reason fans have insisted on keeping his memory alive, even as they love and celebrate Sami Zayn. *Battle of Los Angeles 2011* is a masterclass in one of the deepest satisfactions of wrestling—collaborating with the audience, making them part of the story.

Steen Wolf

Through the summer and fall of 2011, Kevin continued to do brief run-ins in Ring of Honor, making life hell for the top brass, to the fans' anarchic glee. He ended up in weird cheesy promos with lawyers which violated his aesthetic sense so violently he winces recounting them years later,[9] but the audience didn't care, they just wanted him back. Corino and Jacobs stood in his way, playing their role as the repentant violence addicts. Again, it's a bizarre narrative disjunction, the narrative babyfaces being against violence—on a wrestling show! —and the apparent heel being a chaos whirlwind of gleeful mayhem, spitting defiance at the people in power. It's hard to believe Jim Cornette somehow forgot the dynamic that made Steve Austin one of the most popular wrestlers in history, but Kevin certainly did not. Every time he barged into a Ring of Honor show it was a gust of fresh air, and the fans needed him back like they needed oxygen. Meanwhile, El Generico continued to lurk around the edges of Kevin's comeback story. He had matches with both Corino and Jacobs, matches that suffered the typical lack of energy that plagues matches between two babyfaces, especially when everyone was just waiting for Kevin to run in and interfere, blowing the roof off.

Eventually Corino, still eager to redeem himself, asked Cornette to give him a match against Kevin at *Final Battle*. If he wins Kevin will leave ROH alone. If he loses Kevin gets his job back. But that's in December. Before that, Kevin met El Generico in PWG once more, at the show called *Steen Wolf*, in October.

This time it's a ladder match for the PWG world title, so the stakes are as high as they can get. Where *All Star Weekend* was about the connections between two tag teams and *Battle of Los Angeles* was about the connections with the audience, *Steen Wolf* is pure concentrated focus on each other and the title. It's a ferocious match, both emotionally and physically, crystal-sharp and lacerating. Probably one of their greatest.

The match starts with referee Rick Knox calling for the bell and then getting the hell out of the ring as the champion Kevin and Generico glare at each other. Generico spits at Kevin, Kevin blows snot on Generico, they punch each other for a while and then Generico hurls himself over the ropes at Kevin with a desperate urgency.

"Whoever booked this is a *dick*," Chuck Taylor says on commentary as they start pulling out ladders.

"We certainly hope nobody dies!" Excalibur (who booked this) adds cheerfully.

The match is an exercise in brutal inventiveness. The violence starts, ironically, when Kevin looks down at Generico writhing on the mat after a move, then nudges a ladder with sarcastically finicky precision to topple it onto the luchador's body. As the match progresses, ladders become weapons in every way imaginable—rammed into stomachs, smashed over backs, cracked into chins. Kevin batters and bruises and stands on Generico, and then there is a moment of wrestling dark magic. As his former tag team partner lies suffering on the mat, Kevin wanders over to a corner. He stands there for a second, staring down at Generico, expressionless.

He reaches out his hand as if for a tag.

Confused and dazed, Generico looks up and for an instant he sees Kevin, his friend and tag partner Kevin, standing at the turnbuckle with his hand outstretched like so many times across so many years. Without thinking, he lunges forward to make that hot tag so Kevin can save him from the awful beating his monstrous opponent is giving him.

The second their hands touch, he realizes his mistake and desperately scrambles to get away, crawling across the ring on wobbly limbs. Kevin follows him, hand still extended in a cruel parody of offered help, his face blank. He balls up his fist and punches Generico in the face, and the match charges on. The action now has escalated to the two of them being suplexed into ladders, back dropped into ladders, kicked through ladders, Michinoku driven onto ladders. Generico's bare back is criss-crossed with threads of scarlet and his white mask ties are dabbled in blood where they've touched his back.

Kevin finally gives Generico a brainbuster on the turnbuckle and

Generico tumbles to the outside to lie motionless. Kevin starts to make the climb up to grab his title back ("Please, get the belt and end this fucking match," Chuck Taylor begs him from the commentary table) and it almost seems within reach when the Young Bucks show up to attack Kevin. They pummel Kevin's bad knee ruthlessly with chairs as the furious crowd yells "Fuck the Young Bucks" over and over, and then they disappear. Generico emerges from the floor to boggle at the carnage as if he's just arrived with pizzas to find an apartment in flames, then starts to climb the ladder himself. When Kevin tries to stop him, he receives an amazingly horrible-looking sunset flip off the ladder onto other ladders, the back of his head smacking into the unyielding metal. He lies motionless as Generico climbs the ladder and pulls down the title—and the ventilation grate it was attached to, for good measure. He's showered with decades' worth of grime and dust, but he has the title in hand, he's defeated Kevin and become the PWG champion once more.

The Young Bucks show up again before Generico can celebrate and beat him up as well (just so they're not playing favorites), then challenge Kevin to a match, mocking him for not having a partner. A couple of extremely optimistic souls try to start an olé chant, but before that can gain traction the lights go out and Super Dragon appears in the ring to attack the Bucks and become Kevin's tag partner. They'll go on to win the titles later that year, but for now Super Dragon simply leaves the ring to Kevin and bewildered new champion Generico.

Kevin and Generico stare at each other for a long time, and after that match not one soul in Reseda calls for them to hug it out. Generico tauntingly lifts the title between them, and Kevin gets the mic. "I may not be happy with the results, but I'll tell you one thing: I knew," he says, pointing to the destroyed ceiling, "we'd tear the fucking roof down."

So Kevin finally makes it through this awful year with a lot of help. We see one kind of help at *All Star Weekend*, the connections with other wrestlers like Tozawa and Ricochet. At *Battle of Los Angeles* he's helped by the Reseda crowd, by the alchemy of creating art with the audience, making their reactions and emotions part of the match. And always, always he's helped by his connection to Generico and to the story they tell, in its purest and most ferociously concentrated form at *Steen Wolf*. All three of these aspects all come together in December in Hammerstein Ballroom again, when Kevin fights his old friend Steve Corino and special referee Jimmy Jacobs for the right to be admitted back to Ring of Honor. The crowd wants him back and they let him know it. Steve and Jimmy put up a good struggle but in the end Kevin is triumphant, as Jimmy is forced to do the three-count that gives Kevin back his job. Magnanimous as always in victory, Kevin starts to take a measure of revenge on Jimmy and everyone else in his way, a dervish of madness. As he faces down Jim Cornette, Generico runs in to try and stop him, only to be met with a package piledriver off the apron and through a table.

They lie there, ending yet another *Final Battle* together, battered and broken. Last time they finished the year with Generico waving goodbye. This time, blood-soaked and laughing with triumph, Kevin grabs Generico's face and says something to him. The audience is screaming, commentary is yelling, so his words are totally inaudible and impossible to discern. But based on his lips, one possibility—and a good one—is that he's laughingly saying to Generico, "Forever, and ever, and ever."

VIEW FROM THE TOP
(2012)

Working Stiff

JUST A FEW MATCHES after Kevin beat Steve Corino to win back his place in Ring of Honor, world champion Davey Richards faces his former tag team partner of the American Wolves, Eddie Edwards, in the main event. Edwards, slowly being consumed by jealousy, loses the match. As he sits disconsolate in the ring, Richards begins to cut a promo. For months through the end of 2011, Richards has been finishing up shows and sending the fans home with what's called a "white-meat babyface" promo—pure of heart, courageous, gallant.

Boring.

Richards, who in reality had a sardonic, even cruel wit (remember that in their first ROH promo together in 2008, he started off calling Kevin "tons-of-fun" and "fat boy"), had been told by Jim Cornette to stay a traditionally honorable champion, upholding fair play and brotherhood. So by late 2011 the ROH audience has heard him finishing up shows with stout-hearted platitudes for months. They're sick of it. "Shut *up!*" an exasperated voice from the audience yells as he gets started, but he forges doggedly on about how he and Cornette had a talk before the show. "Jim Cornette reminded me that this is Ring of Honor, it's about sportsmanship," he says to a smattering of tepid applause. He talks about how tough Eddie is, what a great heart he has. Another wrestler might have been able to pull it off with authenticity, but from Richards it just sounds smarmy.* "When you find closure, your brother will always be waiting for you," he says to Edwards.

At which point theatrical, insincere sobs ring out over the speakers, interrupting his speech. "Thank you, Ring of Honor!" the voice blubbers, and the crowd goes insane as they recognize Kevin's astringent sarcasm cutting through the cloying insincerity. Kevin throws open the curtain to a howl of approval that nearly drowns out commentary groaning that "this son of a bitch is back." His face is still etched with dried blood from his match against Corino. "Shut up with your ass-kissing horseshit," he brusquely informs Richards as the crowd shrieks in delight. "You want honesty, Davey? The honesty is that if you step out of this ring and come down here I'm gonna take you apart, *motherfucker!*"

("I was told before I went out, 'whatever you do, don't say *fuck*,'" Kevin remembers later, half-chagrined and half-proud.)[1]

He announces that "what matters tonight is that Kevin Steen is back!" The fans agree with him, vehemently, and boil over with glee when he promises to take Richards' title from him.

So ends 2011 in Ring of Honor. In WWE, the current top title-holders are CM Punk and Daniel Bryan, two former Ring of Honor champions. Kevin Steen, back from his long exile, is gunning for the belt they both held before they left for WWE.

In the feud with Richards, Kevin could do no wrong—at least in the fans' minds. He did plenty wrong according to the official voices of Ring of Honor as he clawed his way toward that top title. Kevin and Cornette traded scathing, barbed promos brimming over with that most prized wrestling commodity, sincerity. They clearly meant every vitriolic thing they said, and the audience loved it. In later shoot interviews, Kevin somewhat reluctantly has admitted that he and Cornette

---

* Richards absolutely meant every positive word he said about Edwards here—but being able to express your true feelings and *sound* sincere while doing it can actually be a challenge.

worked really well together, that they had finally learned how to channel their resentments and disdain into a storyline.[2]

In the ring, when wrestlers don't hold back and their blows are meant to land, even to hurt, it's called "working stiff," and a match where both wrestlers are working stiff has an extra edge of urgency and authenticity to it. It's the same with promo work. Do wrestlers stay safely behind the fiction of their characters and their constructed feud, or do they say things to each other that are viscerally wounding, that cut into truly raw nerves?

An entirely illusory feud can be fun, but it's the ones where the wrestlers tap into their real conflicts, transmuting them into fiction, that are the most riveting. Kevin was working stiff not just with Cornette, but with Richards, mocking him for being Cornette's "boy," a bland apple-polisher, an ass-kisser who had the right look but no personality. The insults welled up from an honest source in Kevin's soul, and in an ideal feud, Richards would have come back with his own caustic and authentic opinions about Kevin's look, his wrestling style, his attitude.

Unfortunately, Richards was the babyface, and Cornette believed babyfaces should be courageous, stalwart and stoic. "He never got to have a good comeback because Jim wouldn't let him," Kevin has admitted ruefully.[3] He had to stick to the script, a flimsy shield against Kevin's vicious broadsword attacks. On the mic, Kevin jeered that Cornette had "neutered" him, and it was real enough that Richards seethed behind the babyface mask while mouthing his pious platitudes.

Kevin was coming for him with the stiffest of promo work, gunning for that title.

But first he had to go through every wrestler Cornette could throw in his way, which meant most of the ROH babyfaces.

Including El Generico.

You're Jesus Now

From January to May 2012, Kevin scratched and clawed his way toward a title match with Davey Richards. He beat Kenny King, Adam

Cole, Jimmy Jacobs, Eddie Edwards, Kyle O'Reilly, BJ Whitmer. He mocked and kicked and spat and bled, he profaned every single bit of the Code of Honor. Richards cut valiant promos, respected the audience, fought clean and fair.

And the fans loved Kevin.

No matter who he was fighting, they wanted him to win, cheered him with all the bloodlust and chaos in their souls. When he faced down Jimmy Jacobs, still the repentant addict-to-violence, and manipulated him into using his old villainous weapon of a metal spike, the audience loved him for it. Jacobs stared wildly at the spike in his hand, at Kevin's blood-smeared and laughing face, and the audience rejoiced in the intuitive understanding that he was tempting Jacobs back to the dark side. Kevin at this point was the avatar of the fans' longing to see stuffiness and convention blown to smithereens. They loved him not despite his contempt and crudeness but because of it.

Meanwhile, El Generico was "recovering" from Kevin piledriving him through a table, although his recovery technique apparently involved having matches in Japan, Hungary, Russia, Germany, Denmark and Finland in quick succession. He was wandering the world like always, sailing far afield, while Kevin honed in on the top title in ROH with fanatic intensity. Generico's first 2012 appearance in Ring of Honor didn't happen until March, when he was put up against Kevin at *Showdown in the Sun*, the latest to try and stop Kevin's violent rampage across the roster. The Fort Lauderdale crowd is delighted to have Generico back; they cheer and sing.

And then Kevin's music hits.

Kevin always lists Showdown in the Sun as one of his favorite matches against El Generico. Part of his satisfaction with the match comes from a moment backstage, just before Kevin's music hits, when Jim Cornette calls out to him, "Tear it up, Kevin!" Buzzing with adrenaline and the anticipation of fighting Generico in front of a Ring of Honor audience for the first time in over a year, Kevin swings around and announces, "Pay attention, I always do!" and bursts through the curtain, as the audience erupts in a howl of ecstasy that shakes the venue and shoves Kevin's popularity right into Cornette's face. Undeniable.[4]

VIEW FROM THE TOP

The howling clamor continues almost without pause all the way through the match. The audience loves both wrestlers but in very different ways. At this point Generico's appearances in Ring of Honor have been sparse and fleeting, he's like a beloved migratory bird that comes and goes, whose heart isn't quite with them as wholly as Kevin's is. Their love for Generico is platonic, pure, chaste. Their love for Kevin is none of those things. It's visceral, yearning, practically erotic. They switch between chanting for Kevin, singing for Generico, and screaming at the top of their lungs for both of them, until at one point half of the crowd is pounding on the barricade and stamping their feet, chanting "Steen! Steen! Steen!" while the other half is singing Generico's song. The rhythm and the melody come together, the one that hits the guts and the one that makes the spirit soar, becoming whole and complete for one breathless moment.

On commentary, Steve Corino—his character still in recovery as an evil addict—is notably subdued. The camera catches him looking thoughtfully at Kevin in silence now and then. This is the time that Corino is thinking of when years later he sighs in amazement and recalls, "Kevin could burn down a houseful of puppies, and he's not gonna get booed."[5]

The finish of the match isn't clean—Jimmy Jacobs comes to the ring, looking like he's going to help Generico, then falls violently off the evil wagon by hitting Generico with his spike and helping Kevin win. That does get some scattered boos from the Ring of Honor audience, who generally reject interference in finishes, but most of them don't care. Whatever it takes to get Kevin to the top, they'll embrace it.

When Kevin and Sami get to the back after the match, Sami says in amazement, "What the fuck, dude? I've been gone for four months and you come out and you're Jesus now!" Deeply gratified, Kevin answers "I am Jesus, thank you!"[6]

On message boards and social media at about this time, Ring of Honor fans were mystified that El Generico was getting so few bookings with Ring of Honor. "You're stupid for not pushing one of the best wrestlers currently alive," one fan scolded the company after Showdown in the Sun. "You'll be sorry once EVOLVE and Dragongate USA scoop him up for the east coast bookings."[7] The attitude was accurate, but his prediction was laughably modest. What he and most other fans didn't know—but Kevin and Sami did—was that Canyon Ceman, WWE's talent scout, had been in the audience that night in Fort Lauderdale. After he witnessed their match and the reaction from the audience, WWE contacted Sami and started tentative negotiations toward a WWE contract.[8] The negotiations stalled out in the middle of 2012 because rival wrestling promotion TNA was embroiled in a lawsuit with WWE and WWE refused to sign any wrestler who had worked with TNA until the lawsuit was settled. Sami's "work" for TNA was limited to two dark matches in 2011, but that was enough to leave him in limbo, waiting for the lawsuit to be concluded before he could sign paperwork.[9] It was increasingly clear to Kevin and Sami that any match together might be their last—not just in ROH, not just in PWG, but their last ever.

Because practically no one thought it was possible Kevin would ever make it to WWE.

Vince McMahon's preference for jacked-up bodybuilder physiques was infamous, his dislike of wrestlers who wanted to control the details of their careers legendary. Very few people looked at Kevin in 2012 and thought "That is a future WWE world champion." So as the year progressed, Kevin and Sami were facing, once again, the reality that this might be the end of their partnership. In 2003 it had been because young Kevin was going to get that WWE tryout thanks to Rougeau and walk away from IWS and Sami. In 2012 it was Sami's turn to hear the siren's song of WWE, but this time it was no illusion, and there was no way he was going to turn his back on it.

Champion

In May 2012, Kevin finally wrests the Ring of Honor title from Davey Richards in Toronto. The preference of the Canadian crowd is clear from the moment they shower Kevin with a cascade of colored streamers and bonk Richards in the face with a couple of rolls of toilet paper. The audience, feeling the momentum of the story gathering at their back, sings "olé" to Kevin—usually a mockery, but it feels like support on this evening—and jeers "you can't beat him!" at Richards.

Kevin suffers, his old wounded knee giving out time and time again, keeping him from locking in the sharpshooter, causing him to wail in anguish when Richards targets it. But in the end, he finally hits that package piledriver and puts Richards down for the count.

Jimmy Jacobs joins him in the ring to wrap himself around the new champion like a koala with a particularly beloved eucalyptus tree. Steve Corino, who has been sitting silently on commentary, leaves the desk to confront Kevin for a dramatic moment before giving him a huge hug, abandoning his "recovery" and embracing Suffering, Chaos, Ugliness and Mayhem again, to the audience's joy. Owner Cary Silkin, who has handed over the title to every new ROH champion, refuses to hand it over to Kevin, leaving in disgust. "Evil lives here in Ring of Honor," Kevin Kelly intones morosely, but Toronto is filled with fondness and love for their life-embracing evil champion. Kevin grabs the mic, yells "I don't need a speech! I'm Kevin fucking Steen!" and continues to celebrate with Jacobs and Corino.

S.C.U.M. became the name of their faction which ruled ROH with anarchic glee, Kevin as their ringleader. He was at the very top of Ring of Honor, and El Generico was nowhere to be seen on any of the upcoming ROH cards. Before Kevin's match with Richards, El Generico tweeted in his typical broken-but-eloquent English, "He is evil & forever my enemy, but [Kevin] is tough & most deserve person to hold #ROH champion. I will not be far."[10] To most fans, it must have seemed as if Kevin had left Generico far behind, that he had achieved the summit of the mountain while his former tag partner was wandering further and further from the goal.

Kevin and Sami knew otherwise.

From his spot at the very top of Ring of Honor, the place he'd scratched and clawed to finally reach, Kevin could see what most couldn't. Sami wasn't failing to conquer ROH, he was getting ready to begin the assault on one of the loftiest peaks in the world, the one they had spent a decade planning to scale together. He was on his way to the base camp, while Kevin—whose Ring of Honor contract wouldn't run out for another fifteen months—couldn't even dream of joining him for another year, and that's if WWE ever even gave him a look. The champion was alone at the top of the indie mountain on barren stone high above the treeline, the air almost too thin to breathe. Watching Sami off in the distance, moving on without him.

"I will not be far," El Generico says. It's a spoken threat with a hidden encouragement.

This Ends Now

Kevin's time as ROH champion was a wild rampage, his stated goal the destruction of the entire promotion of which he was the champion. The vibe of his reign is perfectly captured in a backstage promo cut after he defended the title against Roderick Strong. Standing in front of a Ring of Honor banner, he smiles wryly and announces, "Ring of Honor... is an illusion." He taps the bold black and red logo behind him. "They have this banner, and they think us standing in front of it fools people." He grabs the banner and tears it from the wall, revealing the bare cinder blocks beneath it. "But the illusions end with me."

He commands the camera to pan around the room he's in, slowly revealing shoddy lockers, a trash can, a chair with a roll of duct tape on it, and a single bleak shower stall with a forlorn clear plastic curtain. "Once I finish this promo I'm going to strip naked—*naked!* Do you understand? *Naked!*" he repeats, reveling in the viewer's assumed discomfort, "and jump in the shower." It all flawlessly encapsulates Kevin's strengths as a character—his awareness of the illusions of wrestling and his intolerance of them. "From now on, Ring of Honor is all about *being genuine.* And I am the most genuine person one can meet," he says, somehow making this sound like a threat, before concluding, "Jim Cornette, things will just keep getting worse... until it ends." In June, Kevin probably thought that this storyline would end with "Wrestling's Worst Nightmare," as his entrance graphics dubbed him, dethroned and defeated, the heel conquered by Cornette's chosen one.

As it would turn out, Cornette would be dethroned before Kevin.

All through the summer, Kevin was lobbying to have a match with El Generico at *Final Battle 2012*. Final Battle is ROH's last show of the year, the climax, and he desperately wanted to have that main event title match with El Generico, to give closure to their time in Ring of

Honor. "We *needed* that match," he says when he remembers it, a weight of yearning frustration on that *needed*.[11] Jim Cornette, though, was unwilling to give the main event of the last show of the year to someone who was no longer under contract to Ring of Honor, someone who was clearly moving on. For his part, Sami still refused to communicate directly with Cornette because he disliked him so much, leaving Kevin to do all the negotiations, which only increased Cornette's annoyance and reluctance.[12] It was a struggle that lasted through the fall, through Corino and Jacobs winning the tag titles together, through Kevin's bitter feud with Jay Lethal which most notably saw him spitting in Lethal's mother's face at ringside, through the beginnings of his feud with Michael Elgin. His matches with Lethal and Elgin earned the highest ratings he would ever receive from Dave Meltzer pre-WWE, but for Kevin the payoff was the moment when, after beating Elgin, he received a mysterious box. As he started to open it, the audience noise spiked in anticipation, as if they knew what was going to be inside simply from the way Kevin held it and opened it. Reaching in, he took out a familiar black-and red mask, staring into its emptily-accusing eyeholes like Hamlet lifting Yorick's skull as the crowd went mad.

Cornette had finally capitulated and booked Kevin and El Generico for a ladder match in the main event of Final Battle.

It was one of Cornette's final acts as the Ring of Honor booker. Even before Kevin lifted the mask from the box, he had stepped down as booker and been replaced by Hunter "Delirious" Johnston. Kevin and Sami get their main-event title match, Cornette is gone from ROH, and things are looking up for Kevin—except for that nagging knowledge that Sami will soon be moving on, that this is their swan song in Ring of Honor.

The day before *Final Battle 2012*, Kevin's son comes down with the flu. Kevin leaves home and heads to New York City, and then the inevitable happens. By the time he gets to the venue, he's sick himself, vomiting regularly. But there's no rescheduling for something like this, no second chance for an ending for Kevin and his greatest foe, his dearest rival. So Kevin heads out for what he knows will be his last match ever with El Generico in Ring of Honor, possibly their last match ever anywhere.

Unsurprisingly, it's a vicious match, full of brutal spots as they both try to scale the heights and secure gold one last time. Kevin and Generico batter at each other with a grim, bleak relish as Generico tries to take away from Kevin his proof of superiority and Kevin desperately tries to hold him off. Kevin throws Generico into so many different barricades that it feels like every person in the first couple of rows ends up with a chance to touch and cheer on Generico for what they don't know will be the last time—a final gift from the pair to their unwitting fans.

As it turns out, even the flu can become part of the story, because Kevin spends a lot of the match looking almost existentially nauseated. He's exhausted, he's going on sheer spite and cussedness. You get the impression Generico would have to kill him to get that title off him, and now and then you almost feel like it's a possibility. One of the best moments in the match is when Generico clocks him with a ladder and Kevin, reeling, starts to fall—but finds the wherewithal to flip him off as he drops, his upraised middle fingers somehow defiant and pathetic at the same time.

It's hilarious but it is also perfect for who Kevin is: unable to let it go, even as he falters. But Generico's an avenging spirit and he can't stop either, and so as they fight they slowly manage to assemble—seemingly without any real plan—a contraption of ladders that reaches almost to the title. Scrambling up it together, they finally reach a stalemate, swaying precariously on their makeshift perch, a point where they can do nothing but stare at each other while the crowd chants *please don't die* and the Ring of Honor Championship hangs shining above their heads.

"I hate you!" Kevin yells, desperate and frantic as they scrabble at each other, and finally manages to kick him between the legs as he did three years ago at the beginning of this rivalry. As Generico buckles, Kevin grabs him and folds him up in preparation for the package piledriver. *"This ends now,"* he howls, the last words Kevin ever says to El Generico in Ring of Honor, and piledrives him through both ladders.

Generico drops as if dead and lies there, unmoving, as Kevin scrambles up the ladder and unhooks his title. The still-reigning champion barely takes a second to celebrate before he starts to hurry back down the ladder, tossing the title down before him to the mat so he can get down faster.

(The match has gone on for 28 minutes at this point; the PPV is almost out of airtime).

Kevin poses on the turnbuckle with his title, triumphant for the crowd—and then he stops and looks back at Generico, still motionless in the middle of the ring. He gets down off the turnbuckle and drops the belt, then staggers to where Generico lies. There's a tense, awful pause.

And then Kevin helps Generico to his feet.

Finally, closure.

He doesn't hug him, he doesn't even shake his hand, he doesn't show any kind of affection—this isn't some kind of curtain call where the wrestlers break character. In fact it's vitally important that everyone is still in character. Because when Kevin helps Generico stand, when he reaches out and Generico accepts that moment of connection, they move past their feud, past the bitterness and the hatred and the pain. Just a little bit, just enough to give closure. Just enough to let both of them move on. Jim Cornette is gone, and Kevin has laid his rivalry with Generico to rest; it's not a happy ending, but there's some hope to it. Maybe, maybe things will be better for him in this new Ring of Honor that he reigns over as champion. It's closure, it's an ending, it's a moment.

It didn't happen.

Well, it *happened*, there in that ring on that night. But the only reason that anyone who wasn't there knows it happened is that Kevin talks about it during his ROH shoot interview. Because there at the end of their match, their time finally, literally runs out. The broadcast ends before Kevin helps Generico to his feet, and the moment is not included on the DVD. The only people who witness it are the people in attendance that night. For everyone else, it may as well have not happened. When Kevin talks about it, he details it just as I described it—how there's no handshake, how it means that maybe Ring of Honor can be different for Kevin now.

When you know what's missing, the last seconds of the show look different. Looking at them again, it's clear that Kevin, exhausted and sick, is staggering around shoving ladders out of the way specifically to get the ring clear and ready for the final tableau with his former friend, his most tenacious enemy. He's trying to clear away the debris, to untangle four years' worth of story and bring it down to one quiet moment that will give the fans—and them—a sense of closure and the ability to move on.

He's still getting everything into place as the camera fades to black, the moment lost, the closure gone, the story forever not quite finished.

Luckily for Kevin and Sami, they still had PWG.

NOTHING WITHOUT YOU
(2012-2013)

This is Ours

EL GENERICO HAD ONLY five matches in Ring of Honor in 2012, but it's not because he wasn't wrestling much. All told, he had matches in about 25 different promotions that year, from Japan to Russia, Quebec to Italy. He was criss-crossing the globe, saying farewell to the many different audiences around the world who had loved the masked luchador as his contract with WWE grew closer and closer to being inked. He had final matches with a huge variety of old friends and foes —Big Van Walter (the future Gunther) in RevPro, Akira Tozawa in Dragongate USA, Kota Ibushi and Kenny Omega in DDT Pro, the future Evil Uno and Stu Grayson in EVOLVE, Sara Del Rey in CHIKARA.

And over and over again, he came back to Pro Wrestling Guerilla, the first US promotion that took him seriously and his last chance for closure in his decade-long history with Kevin.

In September of 2012, at PWG's *Battle of Los Angeles* tournament, a variety of different pressure points start to converge. On night one, Brian Cage interferes with Kevin's tournament match, costing him the win. Kevin returns the favor on night two, jumping in to cost Cage his own match. Cage, infuriated, starts to beat Kevin up, and his allies the Young Bucks run in and attack Kevin as well. Then the crowd pops like mad when Rick Knox, the fan-favorite referee, runs out to try and settle things down. As Kevin rolls out of the ring, Cage and the Bucks shift their focus to Knox, who is saved in turn by El Generico.

At this point Knox, goaded beyond bearing by years of Young Bucks' shenanigans, grabs a mic and challenges the Bucks and Cage to a match that very night, enlisting Generico to help him. Generico is willing, but the match would be three on two and Knox isn't even a wrestler. So Knox turns to the last member of this standoff: Kevin Steen, standing on the apron and looking surprisingly hesitant. Almost uncertain.

This is in the middle of his ROH Championship run, near the end of his intense backstage campaign to wrestle El Generico in the main event of *Final Battle* and get an ending to that branch of their story. The character of Kevin is still in no place to work with El Generico. After a long hesitation, filled with the entreaties of Knox and the crowd, the doubtful but almost-hopeful tension in Generico, Kevin flips his former partner off and walks away laughing as everyone boos and Generico's shoulders slump.

When the match comes along, Knox and Generico are up against Nick Jackson, Matt Jackson, and Brian Cage. It's two against three on paper, but in reality the situation is even worse, as Knox isn't an active wrestler. Plus Brian Cage is—well, his nickname is "The Fucking Machine," and he's gigantic and jacked, he looks he's got at least two other wrestlers worth of muscle stuffed into his skin, so it feels more like five on one at this point.

The match is, not surprisingly, a total slaughter of El Generico. Generico respects Knox and is willing to tag him in against the Bucks, where he does actually hold his own moderately well. But he's less willing to let Knox face off against the monster Cage, so he insists on staying in the ring and not tagging out. Meanwhile, the Bucks continue to be agonizing gadflies, interfering and triple-teaming the luchador while Knox and the audience suffer sympathetic anguish. By the time Generico realizes he's in way over his head and he *has* to tag out, he's too battered to make it back to his corner. When it looks like he finally might make it there after all, one of the Bucks yanks Knox off the apron to the floor, out of the match. Now there's no one at all for Generico to tag in and he has no choice but to keep getting pummeled. All is lost.

And then Kevin comes charging out of the locker room to the ring.

The crowd gasps in mingled hope and horror, unsure if he might just join Cage and the Bucks to destroy Generico. But as Kevin pauses, looking down at the fallen Knox and up at the action in the ring, the crowd starts to realize that this might not be a disaster after all. They remember that Kevin has plenty of immediate reason to hate Cage and the Bucks, and a desperate chant of "Help, Steen, Help!" breaks out as he jumps up onto the apron and—unbelievably—holds out his hand for Generico to make the tag, just as he did so many times in the past, before he threw it all away.

Dazed with pain, struggling to get away from his tormentors, Generico lurches toward the outstretched hand—and stops dead as he realizes whose hand it is. There's an incredible tableau of pure coiled tension in that moment, all of it centered on the gap between Kevin's outreached hand and Generico's faltering fingers, the space between Kevin's resolute expression and Generico's open-mouthed shock. It seems to stretch on forever, a timeless moment of doubt and hope, until the luchador lurches forward and tags in Kevin for the first time in almost three years.

In comes Kevin, the consummate wrecking ball once more, and bowls over the Bucks as they plead and beg for mercy. The match ends when Kevin gets Matt Jackson wrapped up for a package piledriver. He looks behind him and realizes Generico is in position for a brainbuster. They exchange a fraught look and then perform their finisher, the first Assembly Line in almost three years, in front of a delirious and disbelieving Reseda crowd. Knox gets the actual pin, and Kevin and Generico stare at each other for a long moment before Kevin flips him off again as Generico starts to extend his hand. Generico quickly turns his extended hand into his own raised middle finger, and Kevin bursts out laughing and leaves. It's far from a reconciliation. But it's something.

Specifically, it's a realization by Kevin and Sami that time is running out.

Around this time—it's strange that we don't have a precise date for such a pivotal moment, but we don't—Kevin and Sami met in a restaurant in Montreal, and Sami laid a sheaf of papers on the table between them. It was Sami's WWE contract, ready to be signed. Sami wanted Kevin to be there when he put his name on the paperwork because, as far as he was concerned, this wasn't a contract for one person, this was for both of them. *"This is ours,"* he said as he put ink to paper, an assertion of faith that Kevin would be there with him soon.[1] It was a moment that one day, Kevin would use in-character to explain his resentment, his hatred and jealousy: Sami taunting him with his failure, mocking him that he was being left behind. The reality, of course, was more complex. Sami meant it as encouragement, as an affirmation, and certainly the non-character Kevin knew that. But when Sami says, looking back, "I think that stung him," that's not false either. "I am nowhere near," Kevin remembers thinking. "That's not happening for me. I'm still under contract with Ring of Honor for two years. I've never talked to WWE. I don't even know if they know my name."[2] In the absolute dreamland fantasy best-case scenario, where Kevin's ROH contract ended and WWE signed him the very next day, Sami would still have had nearly two years in WWE without him, and Kevin was sure Sami would be near the top of the card then, while Kevin would have to start at the bottom. They'd be eternally out of sync. Kevin would never catch up.

As always, they poured that bittersweet reality into narrative, trying to use the power of story to somehow make it right, make them equal, make them whole. Their attempt in Ring of Honor, at *Final Battle 2012*, was only partially successful. Kevin was so far above El Generico in the promotional power structure at that point, Generico so clearly on his way out, that a reconciliation was impossible. If it was going to happen, it had to be in PWG. And it had to be soon.

Nothing Without You

On January 12, 2013, PWG holds the Dynamite Duumvirate Tag Team Title Tournament (DDT4), their annual tag team tournament. El Generico starts off on the card but has to withdraw due to injury. At the last minute, however, word comes out that he's been signed with WWE. He's allowed to fulfill any last contracts, and it's announced that his appearance at DDT4 is on again—and that he'll be teaming up with Kevin.

So this is it: they've lifted each other to greater and greater heights for a decade, and now Generico is poised to make that final leap. If there's going to be an end to their story, it will have to be here. Their whole career together has been a long complicated tangle of teamwork and betrayal, a Gordian knot of emotions spanning years, seemingly impossible to untie, and now they only have one day and three matches at most to reach a conclusion. Can they work together? Can they somehow rely on each other one last time, here at the end of all things for El Generico?

It doesn't seem likely at first.

The first match of the tournament for Steen and Generico is against Mark and Jay Briscoe. The brothers had made it to PWG only sporadically, and this would be their last-ever match in the promotion. It's clear they're here to say goodbye to their old enemy, El Generico.

Kevin and the Briscoes come out first to their respective entrance songs, and Generico's separate entrance is greeted with so many streamers that the start of the match is delayed. Kevin waits in a corner, staring into space, refusing to look at anyone. Generico gazes at him, not even responding to the ring announcer calling his name, and every line of his expressive body emotes hopelessness.

He holds out his hand, and the crowd calls for them to hug it out, but it can't possibly be that easy. Kevin shoves Generico out of the ring to start the match, which features nine tags between them in eleven minutes, a nearly constant back-and-forth which is where the real story of the match is. They start with blind tags, made without each other's consent, usually more angry slaps than proper tags, aggression rather than cooperation. They progress, slowly and reluctantly, to a tag that's still not reached for but at least grudgingly allowed, and then to Generico actually offering his hand, and Kevin tagging him—though he ignores the outstretched hand and whacks his shoulder instead.

It's shortly after that something truly shifts. When Kevin is about to get leveled by Jay Brisco, Generico suddenly leaps forward, shoves him out of the way, and catches Jay in a drop toe hold. It's the opening of one of their traditional tag moves, in which Generico holds the opponent to the mat with the weight of his prone body for Kevin's somersault leg drop or senton. It's a move they did hundreds of times together.

There's an awful pause as Generico, lying on the mat almost entirely vulnerable, stares up at his old friend. Kevin could kick him in the head, could spit at him, could walk away.

Instead, he completes the move.

The crowd cheers in delight, and shortly after cheers again when they make their first true tag of the tournament, in which Kevin slaps Generico's hand. It's brusque and perfunctory, but it's an actual tag. A man's voice in the crowd calls out, "Are you friends again?" There's laughter, but that's what they want, what they're hoping for. And when a few more not-unfriendly tags get made, they almost start to think maybe they're going to get it.

Not yet.

Because while Kevin has Mark in a submission hold, Generico gets shoved into him and they both go sprawling. The audience groans, because they know how this goes— miscommunications, misunderstandings, and misery. Shortly after, Kevin grabs Jay Briscoe in a rear choke hold. Kevin's back is against the turnbuckle, Jay held helpless in place. Sensing an opportunity, Generico goes for his yakuza kick, and the Reseda crowd starts yelling "No! No!" at him, knowing what's coming. Indeed, Jay gets out of the way, and Generico manages to pull up just in time to avoid kicking Kevin in the face, but the damage is done, the fragile detente is broken. They start shoving each other and the crowd noise sinks into despair, then rises in panic as the Briscoes get Generico into position for their finishing move. Generico manages to roll one of the brothers up for the win, dodging disaster and getting into the second round of the tournament—but without using their own finisher, without any true reconciliation.

Generico holds out his hand, but Kevin—still angry about the near-kick—spits at him in a fury and leaves him alone in the ring. The mood is grim, but as long as there's another match, it's not the end. There's still some hope.

The second match of the night (Kevin and Generico wrestle three matches this night—and remember, Generico originally pulled out of this show because he was injured) is against Future Shock, Adam Cole and Kyle O'Reilly. Again, Kevin and Generico come out separately to their own music. Again, Kevin will not meet Generico's eyes. Again, Generico keeps looking at him—though he does manage to lift one arm in a half-hearted acknowledgement as his name is called this time.

The first match had a progression from hostile tags to neutral tags, nine tags in all. This match has only one tag in it, because Kevin has an intense grudge against Adam Cole, who took the PWG world championship off him a month ago. As a result, he starts attacking Cole immediately and won't let up until he eventually gets in over his head. Battered and bruised, he cannot get back to his corner where Generico waits, holding out his hand with increasing urgency. This leads to a long sequence where the eventual tag is thwarted over and over as Reseda's desire for it grows—again and again Kevin's lunges are interrupted, or Generico is yanked off the apron at the worst possible time, or it's just not quite enough to get there. There's even a moment where Kevin starts to crawl blindly toward the wrong corner while the crowd screams in frustration and longing, until finally he comes to his senses. He turns to stare at Generico's flailing hand, scrubs his face as if in disbelief, then finally lurches forward to complete the tag, the *hot* tag, the one they've driven the audience into a fever pitch yearning for.

And that's the only tag of the match, the only one necessary. Generico finally comes in, to the joy of the audience, and eventually Kevin joins him and gets Adam Cole wrapped up for a package piledriver. He looks over his shoulder and realizes Generico is in just the right position for their old team finishing move. Their eyes lock for a moment, and then, once again, Kevin chooses to work with Generico as a team. He piledrives Cole and passes him to Generico for what will turn out to be the very last Assembly Line, ceding the pin to Generico as the crowd jumps up in delight.

Kevin and Generico have now made it through a match without overt conflict. They've achieved a hot tag. They've even won with their old finishing move. They've basically moved, across two matches, from enemies to an actual tag team again. But when Generico holds out his hand again, Kevin rejects it once more and walks away. There's only one match left, and it's the final against the tag team champions, Nick and Matt Jackson.

The Young Bucks! The team that Kevin and Generico fought just before Kevin turned on Generico, the team that attacked both of them at the end of their vicious match at Steen Wolf, the team that caused them, for a fleeting moment, to team up again a few months ago. The team that's triggered so many of their most awful and hopeful moments is now the last team they will ever face together, for a final victory or an ultimate loss.

As this last match starts, Kevin's music hits, but this time he doesn't come out. It plays again, and still no Kevin. There's a pause, and then Generico's theme music starts and they come out together. They come out as a team.

The Young Bucks attack them before they even finish getting in the ring, cutting right to the chase and forestalling any questions about how well Kevin and Generico's alliance is doing. As the dust clears, Generico is the legal man at first. As in the previous match, there's only one tag between them, a hot tag ten minutes in—there's no need for any other tags. Everything has already built to this and things are as hot as they're going to get.

The climax of the match revolves around three specific moments in the final five minutes after that hot tag, each of which shifts the final chapter of the story toward its ending. Here's something no words can truly capture: the sense of terrible urgency in each of these moments. It's wrestling—there's only one take, there's only one chance, and each moment is clearly essential to completing the story. All four wrestlers execute every move as if it's the most important thing they've ever done, and the crowd is caught up in that urgency, hanging on every instant.

The first emotional beat occurs just after the hot tag, as Generico lies on the floor outside the ring and Kevin struggles alone against the Bucks. He manages to knock them both onto the outside, but they yank his legs out from under him so that he crashes to his hands and knees at the edge of the ring.

Outnumbered, vulnerable, he yells, his voice cracking in desperation, "Help me, Generico! Help me, help me!"

Back in 2009, Kevin explained that he turned on Generico because he was an addiction, a crutch, a dependency that needed to be broken. Now in 2013, on his hands and knees Kevin begs the man he betrayed to help him, begs the person he insisted was holding his career back and making him weak to come to his aid.

And El Generico, without hesitation, comes flying into the ring to save him.

He uses Kevin as support, leaping on his back to launch himself upward, to soar one more time over the ropes of Reseda. He wipes out the Bucks, and the match continues. But something has shifted in Kevin, between the two of them. Something's different.

The second moment takes place when the Bucks have managed to get the upper hand once more. Generico has just kicked out of More Bang for Your Buck, the Bucks' finisher, and the referee has gotten knocked out, but Kevin barely seems to notice. He's crawling across the ring to Generico's side.

Inch by laborious inch he drags himself across the ring to reach his old friend, his most bitter foe. As the Bucks laugh and taunt the crowd, he puts his head close to Generico's and they talk together, too low to be heard, a conversation none of us are privy to. But whatever it is, it's a moment, a resolution, strangely private in such a public place. When Kevin stands up, the Bucks point out that he should be happy they've destroyed Generico, and they suggest that he simply walk away and let them finish the job—or maybe even join them in the beatdown.

Kevin responds by spitting in their faces, standing by Generico even though he can barely keep his footing, wavering on his feet, demanding they go through him first. In three matches they've managed to move from enemies to reluctant allies to being *partners* once more, a speed run of the last ten years. It's a gallop, but somehow they manage to keep it from feeling rushed. Surely they would have preferred to spend another decade slowly coming back together, but this tournament is all they have, here as the character of El Generico wavers on the brink of non-existence.

The final moment in the match comes after Generico delivers his very last brainbuster off the top turnbuckle to Nick Jackson, who bounces like a helpless rag doll across the ring, coming to rest in a heap. It's a move almost no one has ever been able to kick out of, so when Generico goes for the pin Reseda goes wild—but there's no ref, because the Bucks knocked him unconscious earlier. Referee Rick Knox eventually shows up to make the count, and once again a win looks certain—but Matt pulls Knox out of the ring to stop the count. Knox superkicks Matt and jumps back in the ring, but it's too late, now Nick can and does kick out of the pin attempt.

Kevin seems almost to levitate with fury, like he cannot believe this bullshit. He stalks over to Generico and shakes him then cuffs his face. The energy in Reseda falters into unease and at least three distinct voices cry out "No!" in anguish, as though Kevin has struck them instead of Generico. Are they going to fall apart again? Did they come so far only to find out that they can't actually do it, that when it matters they can't take the pressure?

Kevin screams at the disconsolate Generico: "LET'S KILL THESE MOTHERFUCKERS!"

Generico leaps to his feet revitalized, and Reseda erupts in joy again at the furious, anarchic glee of it, the commitment to cooperative ass-kicking. It's a vow of re-commitment, a pledge to just keep fighting together. In any fair fictional world, they should have gone on to win the PWG tag team titles one more time, even if it meant Generico would have to vacate it immediately. The crowd is hoping for it.

And it's not that wrestling isn't fair—at its base, no matter how often it messes it up, wrestling is all about fairness—but in this case the titles aren't the point, so although Kevin manages eventually to package piledrive Matt Jackson, as he goes to roll Matt over to Generico for the brainbuster to finish the finishing move Matt groggily manages to roll up Generico while Kevin's back is turned and get the pin to retain their titles.

The audience is horrified. Kevin is horrified. Rick Knox kicks the turnbuckles, furious at having to count out Generico for the last time. The Young Bucks evaporate like dew, gone almost without the camera even seeing them leave. And Generico—miserable, apologetic—holds out his hand to Kevin one last time.

El Generico has no real character arc in this tournament. He is what he is, here at the end of his existence. He's held out his hand over and over, willing to work with Kevin. Not much has changed in Generico. All of the change has been in Kevin and in how they relate to each other. This is the fourth time Generico has extended his hand this evening. The first time, the audience called for them to hug it out, but this time, after three rejections, no one is so presumptuous. They make an amazing, garbled, seething noise of desperation, and then a lone man's voice cuts across the babble with a hollered "Shake, Steen, shake!" Reseda picks up the chant, begging Kevin to take Generico's hand as an equal, just one more time. Kevin looks at Generico's hand, and he clearly wants to, but then he shakes his head and turns away as the crowd noise wilts into heartbreak and boos. He walks past Generico and leaves the ring, walking toward the back.

In 2003, Kevin and El Generico had their first singles match in front of a handful of people, and they thought it was their last because

Kevin was about to leave for WWE. That night so long ago, Generico offered his hand and Kevin ignored it to walk away, but ended up choosing to turn his back on the mirage of WWE success and stay with Generico. This time it's no mirage. There's a real contract that was signed on the table between them. But it's Generico that's really leaving, and Sami will not be turning back to stay with him. This moment, the very last time Kevin is ever in the ring with El Generico, is a callback to that first match—not because anyone will make that connection, but because it's important for both of them to reference it. That's part of what keeps their characters compelling over the decades, that they do things not so fans will catch their clever references but because it's what would be resonant to their characters.

And to the real people animating them.

When Kevin suddenly wheels around and gets back into the ring, the crowd bursts into a buzzing babble of sound. A woman screams once, the sound caught between hope and a horrible certainty that she is going to watch Generico die right here with her own eyes, as Kevin charges straight at him.

You know how in an action movie, the film will go utterly silent for a split-second just before a huge explosion? Reseda goes, for one heartbeat, that kind of completely still. I don't think a soul there is breathing. If wild tigers were released into American Legion Post #308 in that moment, the audience would have patted their muzzles and shushed them, their eyes on the ring. If an angel of the Lord appeared above the ring, next to the mirrorball, and announced that this was the Rapture and all here were about to be accepted bodily into Paradise this very instant, they may well have asked for just one more minute, just sixty more seconds here in Reseda.

When Kevin throws his arms around Generico, knocking him back into the turnbuckle with the force of his hug, Reseda bursts into cheering as joyous as if they've witnessed a victory more precious than any title win.

They hug, the streamers—carefully saved across three matches by the very most hopeful of fans—fly. Kevin is openly weeping in his friend's arms. All of this night's work, all of this urgent desperate work, was in part to give Kevin-the-character and Kevin-the-real-person a chance to fully inhabit the same space for a moment, so that both of them are feeling the same thing and none of it is false or untrue, to either the character or the man.

During their feud, in 2010, Kevin stood on the ramp and screamed at a horrified El Generico, "You're *nothing* without me!"

Both Generico and Kevin have feared that they can be nothing without each other. They've beaten each other bloody to prove it untrue, to *make* it untrue. But in Reseda in 2013, Kevin takes the mic, points at Generico, and says, "Wherever you end up, wherever you're going, whatever happens to you, please know: I would be nothing without you."

His tearful voice cracks on the "nothing," and then he gets out of the ring and joins the crowd pounding on the mat as Generico stands in the ring alone, clearly in tears himself.

And here we are, full circle. The first time we saw El Generico and Kevin in the same place, way back in 2003, Kevin was in the audience, throwing his hands up in delight at an Asai moonsault, like any one of us. Here he is again now, standing outside the ring among the crowd to say goodbye, El Generico's biggest fan at the beginning and at the end.

The locker room clears out and the ring fills with wrestlers, beaming and crying and cheering for Generico, on the way to achieving the goals and the dreams that he and Kevin used to talk about in the long drives up and down the St. Lawrence River. A few wrestlers—B-Boy, Eddie Edwards, Roderick Strong—go over and give Kevin a hug, as if aware that he needs some extra support right now.

The others lift Generico up on their shoulders, and Kevin retreats to a corner, mostly out of camera range, to watch.

It seems like everyone is there for him—and you know, if you still despise the Young Bucks, if you still resent them for their many undeniable crimes against physics and psychology, consider this some small measure of punishment: that at this moment of farewell, they are probably sitting in a locker room alone, because someone had to defeat El Generico one last time.

Generico gives a short speech, his accent wavering wildly between Montreal and Tijuana, cracking under the strain of too many emotions at once, thanking everyone. Surrounded by his fellow wrestlers and the loving, grieving crowd, he says to them, "You deserve the truth." Everyone immediately goes quiet as he goes on, "For a long time, I come here and I don't tell you the truth about me. I wear a mask. You don't know my face, you don't know who I am! So now, I'm going to tell you the truth." Reseda is silent in startled anticipation: is he going to unmask? Is he going to give them the gift of who he really is, here at the end?

Generico looks at them and says: "My name... is El Generico."

He takes a deep breath, then lets it out in a sigh, as though he's bared his inner soul, while the fans break into laughter at what seems to be an anticlimax. And then you can hear that laughter hitch a little, and shift, and deepen into joyous applause. It's as if they've reached out their hands for Mardi Gras beads and found themselves holding ropes of diamonds instead. *This is the truth. El Generico is real, and every time you cheered him or suffered for him, that was real.* El Generico, the Generic Luchador, was one of the greatest characters ever created in wrestling, and he stays solid and real right up to the end.

It's not just the audience who appreciates this gift. The wrestlers around him light up with delight as his words sink in. Adam Cole rises in ovation, Stu Grayson kneels down to pound the mat in glee, Jay Briscoe embraces Roderick Strong and pumps his fist in the air.

You deserve the truth, says El Generico, and gives the fans packed into that American Legion hall not the boring mundane truth, but the real truth of the heart, and that's all we ever ask of wrestling.

Then he looks over at the corner Kevin is in and says, "Wherever I go—"

It's clearly meant to be an echo of Kevin's last words to him, but he breaks off and says in distress, "Oh no," and has to take a moment to compose himself before trying again, echoing Kevin's speech to him earlier. "Wherever I go, whatever I do, this has been the best time in my life." Reseda cheers, everyone cries, and they say farewell to the luchador.

So that's the end of Kevin and Generico's story, a decade-long story that grew out of random encounters and cobbled-together matches to become one of the greatest stories in wrestling. It's a story about friendship and ambition, about the struggle to balance dependence and independence as human beings, about the hope that we can become better than what we are, and the fear that we won't. In the end, it's about how we're stronger together, how it takes courage both to support and to allow ourselves to be supported. In the end, two men from Montreal created a story with the message, *If we are nothing without each other, that means that with each other, we can be anything.*

But now they would be without each other once more. Kevin's Ring of Honor contract wouldn't be finished until 2014. Nobody from WWE had ever contacted him, ever shown a glimmer of interest in him. And the man who was not yet Sami Zayn was walking into a deeply uncertain future. Nobody in that American Legion Hall knew what would happen to El Generico on the other side of the veil that cuts off WWE from the larger wrestling world. Not even the man behind the mask knew what the future held for him.

But both of them were determined that whatever it was, somehow, someday, Kevin would share it.

SEPARATION
(2013)

Disjunction

HERE WE ENTER UNCHARTED WATERS.

From 2003 to 2013, Kevin and Sami (who was, of course, not yet Sami) were in the ring together—as allies or as enemies—nearly every single week. Rarely seriously injured at this early stage, they traveled together nearly everywhere, shared nearly every experience. A measure of how utterly intertwined their lives were is found in Kevin's 2013 interview with Jimmy Jacobs, where Jimmy tells a story about Sami scouring a motel, a group of Quebecois wrestlers in tow, looking for someone willing to let them crash in their room. Jimmy laughs when remembering how the Ring of Honor wrestlers had hid in the bushes to avoid the earnest and over-familiar Canadian, watching from the shadows giggling as he went from door to door in a vain quest to find a place to sleep.

Listening, Kevin's brow creases. "But I must have been with him!" he says, the implication clear that he never would have forgotten such an incident—or never would have allowed it to happen in the first place. "Was it in New Jersey? Is that possible? Because he did one show without me."[1] They were so inseparable ("joined at the hip," as Jim Cornette described them) that Kevin finds it easier to remember the shows they *didn't* share. For a decade they were a unit, pushing each other, teasing each other, looking out for each other. In those ten years, the longest they went without a match together was from Dec. 18, 2010 at *Final Battle*, where Kevin lost his Ring of Honor job, to May 27 2011 at PWG's *All Star Weekend 8*, where Kevin teamed up with Akira Tozawa to fight El Generico and Ricochet. That had been 160 days.

After Jan. 12, 2013, when Kevin said farewell to El Generico, they wouldn't share the ring again for 729 days.

So here the narrative becomes, for a time, disjointed. The two went their separate ways, the former luchador entering the hermetically-sealed WWE system which cut him off from Kevin both as a character and—to some extent—in reality as well, as he moved to Florida. But both of them worked tirelessly through those days to stay connected, in very different ways.

"Tell 'Em Dream Said Sami Zayn"

The WWE world that not-yet-Sami-Zayn walked into was quite different from what it is today, what it would evolve into over the years. Aside from a scattering of names, WWE in 2013 was not interested in investing time and energy on established "indie" wrestlers who had already made a name for themselves, who would need to be re-trained to fit the WWE in-ring and promo style. Notoriously, most established wrestlers had to give up their previous name and take on a new name, one that WWE could own. Chris Hero had become Kassius Ohno, Tyler Black had become Seth Rollins, Pac had become Adrian Neville.

El Generico would have to become someone else.

The luchador appeared one time in WWE, accompanying another wrestler to ringside in his mask and sparkly cape at an untelevised, unrecorded house show. Only a few hasty photographs caught this glimpse of the Generic Luchador, the last time he was ever seen. Sami cut a promo in promo class laying El Generico to rest, then got on his bike to go back to his apartment and found himself crying tears of grief and loss all the way there.[2] But the luchador's time was over. Even if

WWE hadn't wanted a new name they could own, the visuals of a Syrian-Canadian playing a fake-Mexican luchador were awkward at best. The days of wrestlers pretending to belong to groups they didn't —Ghanaian-Americans playing Jamaicans, Samoans playing Japanese —were coming to an end. And WWE wanted people who could cut promos, who could explain their actions and their motivations with words.

He was going to have to unmask, to be a version of himself closer to reality.

He probably wasn't pleased with this situation. Sami has always guarded his privacy fiercely, to the point where many fans had no idea he had a wife and child before the build to *Elimination Chamber* in 2023. The mask had granted him near-total anonymity, and after a decade of privacy, he struggled with finding a new self. He couldn't even seem to come up with a name. Unsure what WWE would package him as, he made different lists of names: Irish names in case they couldn't see past his pale skin and red hair, French names because he's from Quebec, Arabic names in case they decided to lean into him being Syrian-Canadian. He took his lists of names around to the people in charge of these decisions, and they rejected every one of them.

He started over again, re-building a list of new names, but there was one Arabic name on the first list that he decided to put back on the new list as well, just because he liked it.

He took his new list around and every name on it got rejected again.

While he struggled with his name, he started to wrestle at house shows, teaming with Kassius Ohno against the Wyatt Family. Since he hadn't been able to come up with an acceptable ring name, he was forced to wrestle under his legal name, which couldn't have been ideal. He made a third list of names, and for some reason put that Arabic name on it a third time.

A third time, they were all rejected.[3]

At this point, still nameless and probably pretty frustrated, he met with the head of Creative, Dusty Rhodes—the American Dream—and mentioned to him that he was having a hard time settling on a name.

"Which one do you like?" Dusty said.

SEPARATION

He replied that well, he kind of liked this name, the one he kept moving onto new lists even though it was constantly rejected. Apparently it was a stubborn name, a scrappy name, a name that refused to be forgotten even when Creative had nothing for it.

Dusty read the name out loud. "Sami Zayn," he said, testing how it sounded. "Sami Zayn," he said again, waving his hands as if picturing the name on a marquee, on a *WrestleMania* Titantron. "I like that. That's the name. You tell 'em Dream said Sami Zayn, that's the name."[4]

"*You tell 'em Dream said.*"

So he finally had a name. He had a character—a world traveler, a journeyman, an idealist in a friendly flat cap who was just a little too enthusiastic, a little too quick to make himself at home. A transparent mask as opposed to the opaque red and black luchador's mask.

All he needed now was a debut.

Weekend Escapades

Meanwhile, Kevin was setting into motion a full-scale offense, the indie wrestling equivalent of storming the Bastille. If it were true that, as Kevin suspected, no one in WWE was even aware of his existence, it was his responsibility to change that. So he embarked on a campaign to raise his profile and generate buzz. If his matches hadn't caught WWE's eye, he'd force them to notice him in other ways. He did a barrage of shoot interviews, talking about his history, his matches, his wrestling philosophy. They got his name out there, worked to counter the negative image of him created by others,* and were a chance to prove that he would mesh well with the WWE corporate style. Jeff

---

* Jim Cornette was always especially happy to trash-talk Kevin, and Davey Richards had gotten some measure of revenge for being muzzled during their feud by filming a shoot interview where he complained about Kevin's attitude, physique, and lack of in-ring ability.

Schwartz, a long-time Ring of Honor fan, remembers hearing him say "moments are more important than matches" in one interview and at that instant knowing "oh, he's done with Ring of Honor, he wants to go to WWE, and that's all he wants."[5] Schwartz's intuition was right. Kevin was setting off on a quest to get to where Sami was, and these shoot interviews were his career retrospective and audition tapes combined.

He also started conducting shoot interviews of his own. On weekends after wrestling shows he would set up a signboard with "The Kevin Steen Show" on it in pasted-on stenciled letters, perch a Kane mask on the sign to glower down at him and his interviewee, and sit down with another wrestler to talk for a couple of hours. They were free-wheeling informal sessions with a wide variety of friends and colleagues, interviewer and interviewee alike usually exhausted and punch-drunk, sharing stories. Adam Cole remembers his training school duct-taping him to the ring post and chopping him until his chest looked like ground meat. Johnny Gargano reminisces about dressing up as Shawn Michaels for Halloween as a little kid and looking like a male stripper. Cliff Compton regales the camera with a story of going to a Guns and Roses concert with an awkward redhead who he sometimes calls El Generico, sometimes Sami, and sometimes Rami.

Over the course of a year, from 2013 to 2014, the letters on his signboard curled and ripped with wear. Kevin interviewed wrestlers from all different points in their careers, his questions always circling around the same themes. *How do you feel about your life? Would you do things differently? Can you be content with where you are now? And if you never get **there**, can you live with that?* Rising young wrestlers on track to the top: *How are you going to get there?* Wrestlers who got tryouts or made it to Developmental but no farther: *What do you think went wrong?* Former WWE superstars back on the indie circuit: *Do you have regrets?* Kevin was looking for answers—and not just from his guests.

Can you get to the top, and if you try and fail, can you live with yourself?

Kevin's first guest on the Kevin Steen Show was Michael Elgin, freshly back from a WWE tryout that came to nothing. Kevin listens intently as Elgin describes having to line up to do moves, to cut

SEPARATION

promos one by one. Elgin mentions that Jim Ross criticized people with tattoos, and Kevin shoots the prominent tattoos on his forearms a comically distraught look: *damn, one strike already.* He's still laughing when Elgin remembers how Dusty Rhodes asked him if he was married, if he had kids, if it would be hard for them to relocate to Florida, if his parents would mind him moving so far away. Kevin's laughter congeals as he listens, his smile going stiff and awkward as Elgin ruthlessly works Kevin's weak point, his devotion to his family. Sami had worried that Kevin's dedication to his family might end up costing him, and for Kevin, hearing Elgin's description of his conversation with the American Dream must have felt like agonizing proof that those fears were well-founded.

At the end of this first show, Kevin turns to the camera, suddenly formal. "I would like to make an announcement, actually," he says. "I am going to announce to the world and whoever watches this—which I hope is not that many people, because I don't want it to bite me in the ass if it doesn't happen—I'm really gonna try to get in shape. Starting, like… now." He's enlisted Elgin and Tommaso Ciampa to try and push him to get in better shape, he says. It's clear he's decided that his weight is what might keep him from getting to WWE, and he's determined to do something about that. This is a promise—to himself and to whoever might be watching this video, this not-quite-audition-tape sent out into the void—that he's going to do what it takes to overcome that obstacle and make it to the top.

In the ROH ring, Kevin's fortunes seemed to turn. With Cornette gone, he found he didn't want to destroy Ring of Honor quite so much anymore, using his very real relief to shift his character in a new direction. "I care about this company," he announced, sounding slightly surprised himself. "I'm proud to be Ring of Honor world champion!" He granted Jay Lethal a title shot as a thank-you gift for Lethal's storyline-injuring Cornette so badly that he had to retire, and in early March of 2013 faced off against him. When Jimmy Jacobs interferes, spike in hand, Kevin pushes him away, yelling "Get the fuck out of here!" Lethal kicks out of the package piledriver, Kevin's usual finisher, and as they brawl on the top turnbuckle Kevin, in desperation, suddenly does El Generico's finisher, the brainbuster from the top turnbuckle.

It's not a great brainbuster—Lethal barely clips the turnbuckle, and you can see Kevin grimace with annoyance at himself as he goes for the cover—but it keeps Lethal down for the count. The symbolism is clear: Kevin's future is not with S.C.U.M., but with the spirit of the luchador that's pulling him forward to victory. The crowd spontaneously starts to sing "Olé," as if Kevin's triumph is also Generico's.

If this isn't a clear enough sign, he finds himself sidelined a moment later when his faction is joined by Cliff Compton, Rhett Titus, Jimmy Rave and Matt Hardy. The ring fills with a wild assortment of wrestlers running in to attack or join S.C.U.M, a maelstrom of violence, but Kevin seems bewildered and disconnected. He rolls out of the ring, standing off to the side as Steve Corino re-dedicates the enlarged faction to the death and destruction of ROH. He's out of sync, out of step, and after he loses the championship a month later to Jay Briscoe, it's no surprise when Corino kicks him out of the faction altogether and appoints Hardy the leader.

Kevin's lost his faction, he's lost his title, he's lost the thirst for revenge that got him to the top of Ring of Honor. He's in narrative free-fall from the top of that mountain, and even he doesn't know where he's going. He hasn't gotten in better shape. There's still no sign that WWE is interested in him.

And Sami Zayn is about to make his debut in WWE.

"We're Gonna Get to Know Each Other Pretty Well"

Watching old *NXT* episodes years later is often a surreal experience. Characters you've come to know like old friends show up, but they're usually just a bit *off* in some ways. It's like watching very skilled cosplayers working from a detailed description of a character they've never seen, struggling to embody a still-hypothetical image.

Sami Zayn is, from his first appearance, remarkably close to his final form. His first NXT TV appearance is a backstage promo with Renee Young, where one can see his sleeve jittering into the frame as she introduces him, vibrating with eagerness to get started.

Jarringly, his voice in this interview is ever-so-slightly off, maybe a half-pitch too high. It is, in fact, so very close that it's weird, the

SEPARATION

Uncanny Valley of Sami Zaynness. But by the time he actually appears in Full Sail, a week later, things have settled into place. Some of that is probably because he's wrestling, because Sami seems like the kind of wrestler who finds his sense of self in the ring more than in promos, and the more he wrestles the more solid and real he becomes.

He faces Curt Hawkins in his debut match. Hawkins is at this point a former WWE tag team champion showing up in NXT for some easy pickings.

Instead, he gets Sami Zayn.

On the episode that airs on May 22, 2013, Sami enters Full Sail for the first time with an unusual expression on his face, something caught between pride and self-consciousness, as though (for some reason) he's not used to people seeing his face as he comes to the ring.

"Hello, it is me, and my face!" his raised eyebrows telegraph, and a smattering of Olé chants break out as he comes to the ring to take on Hawkins.

The match is short, a scant four minutes and fourteen seconds, and the end is a happy surprise when Sami Zayn pins Hawkins clean. The audience is gratified, already half in love, though not entirely won over. Sami pauses on his way up the ramp and looks out at their applause—happy but not delirious—and he announces: "We're gonna get to know each other pretty well!"

He's right—and sooner than Full Sail expects, too. Because in the very next match, Antonio Cesaro, recent US champion, shows up. He makes short work of his opponent and launches into a rant about the inferior quality of wrestlers in NXT and the lack of actual competition. His character at this time is given to switching into one of the variety of languages Cesaro is fluent in, the time-honored method of gathering heat, and tonight is no exception, as soon he breaks into German and harangues the audience angrily.

A polite but insistent voice from the ramp interrupts him. It's Sami Zayn, who has taken some offense to being described as an inferior wrestler and decided to face this jerk down.

"Maybe you don't need to look too far for some competition," Sami suggests. Cesaro points at him, incredulous, and Sami smiles and says "You wanna fight?" in slangy Syrian Arabic.

Cesaro looks blank. Sami feigns surprise: "You speak a bunch of languages, right?" He turns to the audience and says laughingly to them, "Oh, I guess he doesn't speak Arabic. Let's change this, here." Then he says—in French—"You speak French, right? You can understand what I'm saying?" As Cesaro nods, Sami switches back to English and says "Maybe you'll understand this: if it's competition you want, it's competition you're gonna get, homeboy." Incensed and offended, Cesaro invites him into the ring. Sami bounds in and the match begins.

What an amazing choice, to have a wrestler who has spoken exactly zero languages fluently in public for over a decade come out and speak three languages fluently in his first promo in front of an audience, as a babyface at a time when speaking another language than English was reserved almost entirely for heels. And how the fans aware of ROH and PWG, the ones who knew that El Generico and Claudio Castagnoli had created fantastic matches in those promotions, must have thrilled to see this interaction and intuit where Sami's trajectory was heading. For those who had never seen Sami in action, it must have looked like he was about to get annihilated.

Instead, seven and a half minutes in, Sami gets a rollup on the startled Cesaro and the bell rings.

Sami is overjoyed, the crowd is ecstatic. Horrified at being defeated by this debuting "unknown," Cesaro beats him down while Full Sail yells in anger. Sami's first feud in WWE is on in earnest.

Weekend Escapades

A month after Sami's dramatic NXT debut, Kevin kicks off the next prong in his assault on WWE. He starts posting a series of "life on the road" videos to Youtube, called *Kevin's Weekend Escapades*. They're fun, slightly goofy looks at life as a professional wrestler, full of wrestlers hanging out, bored and jittery and killing time. Most episodes begin with a dashboard shot of Kevin behind the wheel of his car, usually exhausted in the early dawn, mumbling about where he's going this weekend. It's as if he's used to having someone with him on these

SEPARATION

long, boring drives, distracting him, and he doesn't quite know what to do with himself anymore.

The *Weekend Escapades* are immensely popular—despite the careless and casual tone, they're deftly edited and paced, giving us glimpses of a relatable, likable Kevin Steen. There's also a strange touch of magical realism to the videos—under the relentless mundanity of the hotel rooms and Dennys and endless highways lurk hints of a continuing narrative, because Kevin Steen breathes narrative like oxygen and suffocates without it. Give him a supposed slice-of-life video series and the next thing you know there are themes and motifs popping up. When he goes to the Highspots headquarters, he wanders through the warehouse and comes across a Generico t-shirt on a shelf. "Huh!" he says, nudging it. "Whatever happened to him?" Then he strolls on, whistling.

In another episode, he's driving to yet another wrestling show. He's late, and he points out that he got in the habit of being late from traveling with El Generico. "I don't know how he's doing these days, with the orphans," he says. "I don't know if he's on time for the orphans." From there the show progresses as usual: bored wrestlers hanging out, Eddie Edwards showing up to say "Hi Eddie," a long discussion of Adam Cole's grotesquely inflamed elbow. After the show, Kevin is hanging out with some wrestlers in a parking lot, the same as usual, when things take a sudden left turn into the surreal.

As the wrestlers chat, Kevin's attention is suddenly drawn to a couple of people walking by the car he's in. They're wearing luchador masks, one of them a very familiar red and black. "Is that... Generico?" Kevin says, his voice wavering slightly.

"It looks like it," the other wrestlers exclaim as Kevin jumps out of the car. "It has to be! It has to be him!"

He grabs the luchador in shock and rips his mask off to reveal—well, we don't know what El Generico looked like, but Kevin doesn't seem to recognize the person beneath, who stares at him and then bolts off into the night, leaving Kevin holding Generico's empty mask, confusion in his eyes. The lighting and video quality are so poor it's almost impossible to get a good look at the man's face, but in the next scene, in the car driving home, Kevin notes, "I got to meet Curt

Hawkins, as you were able to witness." Which would seem to imply that was Hawkins wearing the Generico mask... Hawkins, who was, of course, Sami Zayn's first opponent at Full Sail.

It's a startling intrusion of fiction into the mundanity of the videos, a sudden slip from the casual chatter about daily life into a deliberately choreographed, scripted moment. That's always been one of Kevin's greatest strengths, his ability to seem utterly genuine, grounded and real while the wackiness and illogic of wrestling go on around him.

The ghost of El Generico is haunting Kevin. Meanwhile, Sami Zayn has continued his climb.

Two Out of Three Falls

Sami's feud with Cesaro was one of the best things in NXT in 2013. The two of them played off each other beautifully, with Cesaro the urbane, unflappable, contemptuous powerhouse, and Sami the earnest, stubborn gadfly that will not just let it go and admit Cesaro is superior.

Their feud culminates in a Two Out of Three Falls match which is an eye-opener about what both Sami Zayn and NXT can be. It's perfectly paced—Sami comes out hot and wins the first fall fast, followed by an agonizing sequence where Cesaro slowly crushes the breath out of him, grinding him in a chinlock submission until Sami has no choice but to tap out, even as Cesaro refuses to relinquish the hold. The match showcases one of Sami's greatest strengths as a wrestler: his ability to portray suffering in ways that are hyper-realistic, emotionally involving and heart-rending. Cesaro's flawless strength and skill work perfectly with Sami's rubbery-legged, wild desperation. They both look amazing, and when Sami almost manages to get that last pin, only to be snatched out of the air and tossed into oblivion by Cesaro, hearts break all over Full Sail. The crowd chants "match of the year!" and it's clearly one for the history books, even though Cesaro remains contemptuous and Sami will keep demanding his respect for months until the feud reaches its true climax the next year in 2014. It's immediately obvious that this is a match that will seal the image of Sami Zayn in people's minds and start to shift the image of NXT from developmental to the NXT it eventually will become.

SEPARATION

When Sami first debuted without his mask, fans on forums like Reddit had been dismayed and contemptuous. Comments ranged from "I KNEW they were going to screw it up" to "NO! NO! NO! :(this makes me sick!" to "Please just be a bad dream. I'll wake up anytime soon, and all will be fine." Here and there someone disagreed ("WWE saw past the gimmick and wanted the actual person. He's so talented why limit him to just his indy gimmick?") but on the whole there had been a resounding rejection of the very concept of Sami Zayn.[6] By the summer of 2013, however, people were starting to think that maybe there was something to this earnest Canadian wrestler after all.

"What Are You Doing That's Not Working?"

Far from Full Sail, far from WWE, Kevin was on the road, shooting his Weekend Escapades, and being torn in two by hope and doubt. "I'd go from thinking maybe it wouldn't happen to *knowing* that it would eventually happen. I'd have days where I'd be like 'This might not happen, you gotta accept it,' to the next day I'd be like 'No, this is happening.' For about a couple months I couldn't watch it anymore. Because I felt like, I guess, I was getting passed by."[7]

It wasn't exactly anger he seemed to be feeling, but something more internal, more bewildered than enraged. He would look in the mirror and ask himself, "What are you doing that's not working, why haven't they come to me?"[8] His efforts to lose weight had come to nothing. Would his goals and dreams do the same? It was in this state of mind, full of mixed resolve and despair, that he came to PWG's *Battle of Los Angeles* in August 2013.

The tournament caused chatter immediately, because William Regal, the former wrestler heavily involved in WWE's developmental process, was spotted standing at the backstage curtain at the Reseda American Legion Post. The Internet erupted with speculation about which indie wrestlers he could be there to look at. Backstage, the wrestlers were as excited and as unsure. Kevin had a match with Johnny Gargano, and they decided that this was no time to play it safe. They played every single spot to the corner where they knew Regal was watching, ignoring the camera completely to emote toward the backstage curtain. Kevin executed every move as if he were yelling "I HEAR YOU'RE LOOKING FOR SOMEONE TO TORTURE YOUR SCRAPPY, PURE OF HEART BABYFACE" at the top of his lungs, and by the time he finally tapped out to Gargano's submission, they both looked like a million bucks.

Later that evening, watching the Young Bucks teaming up with Adam Cole, he was struck by how much fun they all seemed to be having, and on impulse asked PWG booker Excalibur if he could turn heel and join his old enemies. Bemused but game, Excalibur okayed it, and Kevin leapt up from commentary to attack Candice LeRae and join Cole and the Bucks, creating the faction they called Mount Rushmore —a faction based largely on wearing a lot of fringe, not taking themselves too seriously, and having a lot of fun. The sense of exhilarated resignation from Kevin was palpable: he'd taken his best shot in front of William Regal, and if that wasn't enough, at least he was going to start having some fun.

On Reddit, a post about Regal's appearance got sixty-eight excited responses combing through the card, trying to guess who WWE might be interested in.[9]

Not one person guessed Kevin might be on Regal's radar.

Kevin himself doesn't seem to have thought it likely that Regal had any intention of giving him a look. He was just hoping to possibly pull Regal's attention away from the wrestlers he was scouting, to perform brilliantly enough to merit a flash of interest. "Oh my God," he remembers thinking, "If I can just get him to *look at me…*"[10]

Kevin tells the story again on his official WWE DVD, *Fight Owens Fight*. He remembers the urgency, the desperation of that match. How lucky he had been to have caught Regal's eye! What a happy coincidence that he had been on the card.

The camera cuts to Triple H, who's laughing. He shakes his head in disbelief.

"Why do you think Regal *went?*" he asks.

OUR EVOLUTION
(2014)

A New Year

KEVIN UPLOADED a new episode of his *Weekend Escapades* web series on January 1, 2014, covering the end of one year and the beginning of the next. It features the usual shenanigans: Kevin blearily explaining his next few shows in the pre-dawn dimness, filming Colt Cabana taking a shower, wandering around Chicago in the dark, admiring the Christmas lights of Muncie, Indiana. Near the end of the video Kevin, sitting in his parked car back in Montreal, notes that he's recording this on New Year's Eve to thank everyone for making his 2013 great. As he talks, there's a sudden rapping on his car window. "Ugh," he says in annoyance, rolling down the window.

"Excuse me," says a polite voice from outside the car, still offscreen. "Hi, thank you. Do you know where I can catch the 161?"

Kevin shoots the viewer a deadpan incredulous look and swivels the camera to reveal a bearded figure in a flat cap, fidgeting in the cold. It's nobody Kevin Steen has ever interacted with.

"Oh, you're.... rolling up the window," Sami Zayn points out in mild surprise a moment later. "You're rolling up—" His voice gets cut off as the window closes and he's forced to pull his fingers away to avoid them getting caught.

"Get the fuck away from my car!" Kevin bellows as Sami bobs apologetically outside, then flips him off for good measure. Sami waves as if oblivious to the rudeness and wanders off. Kevin turns back to the camera, only to have the guy suddenly pop back into the frame, his mouth open to ask more questions. "NO!" Kevin screams, and Sami finally retreats. Kevin looks back at the camera and snarls, "fucking *douchebag*," but even before the insult is out of his mouth he starts laughing, brimming over with delight at the world, at this new year, at this random red-headed idiot that he's never met suddenly showing up in his life and refusing to go away. It's not just a small gift for the fans who helped him get through 2013. It's also an implied promise for 2014.

I'm starting the year with Sami Zayn, and I intend to finish it with him as well.

Kevin had reason to be in good spirits. A few days after PWG's *Battle of Los Angeles* back in August, where he and Johnny Gargano had put on their best show for William Regal, Kevin got the call from WWE he'd been waiting for.[1] Sami had spent all of 2013 praising Kevin to whoever in management would listen. "As soon as I got my foot in the door, thought that I had the ears of the right people and earned their trust," he remembers, "Kevin was the first person I said they needed to look at. . . . I was really pulling for him. He was my guy, you know what I mean?"[2] But it was that match with Gargano which finally got Kevin the tryout offer he'd been fighting for. He was heading to Orlando in March 2014, just before *WrestleMania 30*, to see if he could impress enough to get a contract.

It was by no means a sure thing. The locker room culture in NXT was starting to shift toward a place more friendly to indie wrestlers, but in late 2013-early 2014 the reception was chilly at best. The trainers were often careful to make clear to wrestlers who had experience outside of WWE that they would be treated exactly the same as the weightlifters, body builders, and football players being brought in to learn how to wrestle. This might have been a good idea in theory. In practice, it meant wrestlers with decades of experience were put to work doing rudimentary back bumps and forward rolls for mind-numbing hours. And WWE notoriously preferred wrestlers with a muscular (not to say steroidal) look, so there was concern that Kevin might not be able to get people to look past his physique. Even the path to that tryout was littered with potential land mines. In December 2013 he was a guest on the Stone Cold Steve Austin podcast.[3] Kevin— who had idolized Austin as a teen, to the point where his bedroom walls were literally papered over with Stone Cold posters[4]—has not said how he felt upon hearing Austin say "This cat can work his ass off" and "This kid's pretty special," but his voice on the podcast is a shade higher than usual, his words a little quicker than normal. He starts off with the story of him and El Generico meeting Austin in an airport in 2005, prompting Austin to ask "Let's talk about Generico, how's he feeling these days?"

"He's actually retired," Kevin says, "but now there's this wrestler in NXT called Sami Zayn who seems to be doing pretty good."

Austin, somehow, does not seem to be catching on. "That's really young to be retired," he says, concerned, and you can practically hear Kevin break into a cold sweat, faced with the dilemma of breaking the cherished wall between Sami Zayn and El Generico or appearing to dare to rib the legendary wrestler. His tryout is in a few months, but if he alienates Austin he might well find himself done before he even begins. He decides to play it straight, noting that El Generico and Sami Zayn are both twenty-nine ("they actually share a birthday, weirdly enough") and that the orphanage needed the luchador, but because he inspired Sami his spirit lives on. Austin continues to be concerned for poor Generico, and it's unclear if he is in turn ribbing Kevin, but whatever the situation, he seems to have approved of how Kevin handled it. The two stay in touch—a future behind-the-scenes documentary catches Kevin getting an encouraging text from the Texas Rattlesnake —and the podcast will one day lead to a *WrestleMania* main event.

But that's getting ahead of the story and we don't want to skip ahead, because 2014 is where Sami's story hits one of its highest points.

ArRival

By early 2014, Sami had been pestering Cesaro for months of *NXT* broadcasts to face him again. He beat Cesaro on his debut night in May

2013, and since then Cesaro had defeated him twice in singles matches, including their amazing two-out-of-three-falls match. Cesaro had nothing but contempt for the scrappy underdog who didn't seem to know when to give up, but Sami kept demanding yet another rematch, determined to beat Cesaro and force him to respect him at last. Finally, Cesaro agreed to one more match, on the condition that if Sami lost, he would accept defeat and stop bothering him. Sami agreed, and the match was set.

In February 2014, NXT had their first live event, *ArRival*. It was the first live broadcast ever on the newly-launched WWE Network. It was a momentous test and a huge risk, and the wrestlers they tapped to open up this landmark event were Sami Zayn and Cesaro, finishing up their nearly year-long feud. Sami and Cesaro take that responsibility and deliver magnificently, in a match that's one of the best in either of their careers.

Sami struggles, scratches and claws through the whole match. He's clearly overmatched by Cesaro from the very beginning—in fact, he might be at an even bigger disadvantage now, because this time Cesaro is ready with counters for his flashiest moves, stopping the underdog in his tracks.

He works Sami's knee, brutalizing him over and over with kicks and merciless submissions, but Sami simply refuses to admit defeat and just keeps pushing, pushing, pushing. It's one of the most classic of all wrestling stories, and it's rarely been told better—the sneering ubermensch versus the resolute everyman. Sami will not submit, he will not stay down, and as the match progresses you can see Cesaro go from contemptuous to wryly frustrated to finally almost awed at the depth of Sami's need to be respected, his imperious refusal to give up.

In many wrestling matches, there's a moment where the issues and conflicts of the story are resolved before the action moves into the finish. Sami's WWE matches often have these moments where the narrative crystallizes, and here against Cesaro, it's when Cesaro has knocked Sami to the mat and looms above him, demanding that he stay down. Sami struggles to his feet, and Cesaro knocks him down again. Again he yells "Stay down!"—but this time *his voice cracks*. Sami drags himself to his feet, just to get knocked down again. "Stay down!

OUR EVOLUTION

Stay down!" Cesaro keeps saying, his voice going from commanding to almost begging. Sami shoves his fist to the mat to brace himself, to push himself to his feet one more time, and when the camera cuts to Cesaro you can see the horrified realization dawning—in his face, in the very way he stands—that he no longer *wants* to keep destroying Sami. And this is how Sami Zayn at his very best triumphs—not by a simple win, but by resisting, and resisting, and resisting, until something breaks through: in his opponent's heart or in his own or in ours. Sami's won the fight that matters in this moment, although he doesn't know it, not yet.

Sami rallies and charges at him again, and the match moves on through a flurry of wild offense and counters, until Cesaro delivers a massive European uppercut to the exhausted, wobbling Sami, then pins him—and Sami kicks out *at one*. He hardly seems aware he's done it, he's almost out cold, but Cesaro is aware: more than aware, he's appalled. There's something close to fear on his face. He leaps forward and hits his finisher on Sami and finally keeps him down long enough to pin him. The crowd applauds, a bit sadly. Sami, barely conscious, manages to prop his back against the ropes. He sits there, struggling to catch his breath, as Cesaro leaves the ring—and then Cesaro turns around and comes back to confront him.

Sami stares up at him, and you can see he wants to summon the strength to get up and fight again, but he clearly has nothing left, either physically or emotionally. He's lost, he's failed to force Cesaro to respect him. He's looking despair in the eye and refusing to flinch.

And then Cesaro drags him to his feet and hugs him as an equal, as a peer.

It's an incredibly satisfying, hard-won moment, and one that has long-term impact on both wrestlers' characters. The feud and the match firmly establish Sami Zayn's personality, both the strengths and the flaws: tenacious to the point of obsession, willing to go to any lengths to wrench the respect he knows he deserves from other wrestlers, from the fans, from the entire world. For his part, Cesaro's character ends up shifting face for a time, largely due to the momentum from this match and his willingness to admit defeat in the midst of victory and embrace Sami.

The first Network special is a success, and it's in part because Sami and Cesaro came through and kicked it off right. Backstage exclusive videos show Triple H congratulating a still-tearful, almost overwhelmed-looking Sami.

It's a great beginning for the Network and for Sami's 2014.

Tryout

Kevin does his last in-depth non-WWE shoot interview at around the same time. The tone of this interview feels different from earlier ones: more reflective, more reminiscent. He tells stories about life on the road with El Generico and mulls over puzzling booking choices in his career, stating his opinions on a variety of issues rather like an elder statesman aware that he'll be departing the stage soon.[5]

Near the end of the video, the interviewer asks him if it's true he's got a tryout with WWE in March. Kevin hesitates, and the voice behind the camera, guessing the reason for his reticence, reassures him that the video won't be released until after that date. Kevin blurts out "It's true," then stops and says "can you *guarantee* me this won't come out until after March, please?"

The producer interjects that yes, he can promise that, and Kevin relaxes and begins to talk about his upcoming tryout with barely contained excitement. The interviewer responds to this information with his excitement much more contained. He points out the American Wolves had appeared on NXT programming for only one week, and that the rumor was WWE would not be hiring any more indie wrestlers. "Do you feel discouraged about your chances?" he asks.

Kevin answers before he's even done with the sentence, speaking over him to say "No. No. Why would they pay for somebody to come in to do this tryout if they have no intention whatsoever of hiring them?" The interviewer presses him, asking what Kevin will do if they require him to do physical drills. Will he be able to keep up?

"Yes," Kevin says.

But what if they tell you you can't wear a t-shirt, the interviewer wants to know, referencing the old story of CM Punk and Kevin's clash in Ring of Honor.*

"I'm not going to wear a t-shirt," Kevin laughs. "I'm not an idiot."

What if they change your name. What if they change your whole character.

Kevin shrugs. "I've been doing this for a long time. Something new will probably feel great. It might be scary, if it happens, but how exciting, you know what I mean? All I want is to be able to go there and say that I gave it my all. And if it doesn't work, I can look at myself in the mirror for the rest of my life. That's what I want."

So that's where Kevin was mentally when he flew down to Florida in March 2014 to walk into the Performance Center for his WWE tryout. They put him through grueling physical drills, so demanding that he ran to the bathroom and "explod[ed] in tears" during a break.[6]

But he got through the drills, and finally, *finally*, they had him cut a promo. This was his chance to shine, and the topic he chose was Sami Zayn and their friendship.[7] He told the story of when Sami signed his WWE contract in front of him, of watching the ink slowly dry on the paper between them, and how that had ruined his life. "I want to make it here for the most valid, genuine reason of them all," he said, "Because I'm *jealous*!" On the last word, his face twisted with rage and his voice shattered into a shriek before he visibly regained control of himself. Laughing slightly, unnervingly, he said "Oh, but I'm here now." Years before, he had screamed a vow to "rain a hell" on Ring of Honor that would make everyone regret ever offering him a contract. At his WWE tryout, more quietly but with equal venom, he swore to have his revenge on everyone who was signed before him, and ended with an ominously calm "and Sami Zayn, my *old friend*, I'm coming for you... first." It was a masterful performance, one that revealed just how deep and well-formed Kevin's character already was, how complete his motivations were. It also tied him inextricably to Sami. It was undeniable, and Kevin sensed it immediately.

---

* Somewhat ironically, Punk had just walked out of WWE that January and refused to return, leading to his eventual firing. He would not be seen in a WWE ring for almost a decade.

"When I was done, I knew I was hired."[8]

It seems WWE knew it as well. From that date, Kevin seems to have been assured his hiring was a lock. Of course, he couldn't sign the contract yet because he was still under contract with Ring of Honor until August. But the Kevin Steen Shows recorded in New Orleans the week of *WrestleMania 30* have a dramatically different tone than the ones that had gone before. These are effervescent, almost giddy. Kevin is bubbling over with energy and his guests—Johnny Gargano, Cliff Compton, the Young Bucks—are glowing with happiness for him. The Bucks are his very last guests, and they wrap up the show by asking Kevin "Can we get a Too Sweet to end this thing?" putting up the hand signal of their faction at the time, the Bullet Club. "I'm not even in the Bullet Club," Kevin says, laughing as they touch hands. Nick Jackson smiles at his old friend on his way to WWE. "Of course you are," he says fondly.[9]

Kevin attended *WrestleMania 30* that same weekend. He was there in the audience when Cesaro won the Andre the Giant Battle Royal, he was watching when Daniel Bryan created one of the greatest moments in wrestling history. "I have to have those moments," Kevin thought as he watched the crowd leap to their feet for Cesaro's victory, a wave of jubilation rippling up the stands. "I have to have this."[10] There in the crowd, Kevin swore to himself that it would be the last *WrestleMania* he would ever attend as a spectator. From now on, he would either be in the spotlight or not there at all.

Sami had spent the weekend doing matches for *WrestleMania Axxess* and was watching from the tunnel as Daniel Bryan won his implausible, unforgettable main event, the indie underdog WWE could not deny.[11] Kevin and Sami were watching the action from the sidelines, but they were inching closer and closer to their goal, to the dream of that main event.

My Name is El Generico

The spring and summer of 2014 had the feeling of a threshold, a cusp, an event horizon. A point of no return looming.

In May, Kevin's second child Elodie was born. It was a difficult pregnancy. For a while Karina was in the hospital, her life at risk, and Kevin sat by her bed holding his son and wondering if he was going to get signed to WWE just as he found himself a widower and single father. When Karina was out of danger, he went on a farewell tour around the country, losing his last matches in a giant range of promotions. He lost to AJ Styles, Trent Seven, Marty Scurll, the Dudley Boyz, Matt Menard, tying up loose ends, saying his goodbyes to promotions, to wrestlers, to fans. NXT at this time was a mystery. The days of wrestlers keeping their names and identities were going to start soon, but Kevin didn't know that, and he certainly didn't know he'd be part of the wave that pushed that door open at last. For all he knew, he'd end up a Siberian lumberjack, or a circus lion-tamer, or a time-traveler from 1910. His name might be any sort of create-a-wrestler hash: Morcant Davis or Donovan MacQueen or Jesse Simon. The one thing he definitely won't be is Kevin Steen. So this was a farewell, less all-encompassing than El Generico's but with equal finality.

Kevin's final matches in Ring of Honor and Pro Wrestling Guerrilla, one week apart in July, both start with the audience hurling so many streamers at him that he decides to roll around in them, coming up with his limbs flailing like a rainbow Abominable Snowman.

The biggest difference between the two matches is his opponents. In ROH he faces Steve Corino, his former mentor, factionmate, and rival; in PWG it's young up-and-comer Trevor Lee. He defeats Corino but is beaten by Lee, and when the Reseda crowd chants "bullshit" he grabs the mic and chides them: "What just happened here, Trevor Lee beating me... that's not bullshit, that's the future." He puts away the past but puts over the future, each match serving a different purpose and type of closure.

Each match is full of callbacks and references. The ROH match against Corino is of course already the capstone of his time there, the denouement to his feuds and his faction with Corino and Jimmy Jacobs, SCUM. He even throws in an allusion to Colt Cabana, doing his jaunty arm-swing before a hip strike in the corner. In PWG he comes to the ring in the Mt. Rushmore gear he wore with the Young Bucks, all neon and tassels. All of his past allies are there with him in spirit as he says goodbye.

But most of all, of course, he references El Generico.

In the Ring of Honor match, the ring announcer lists off the many former ROH greats that Kevin now goes to join beyond the promotion: Austin Aries, Sarah Del Rey, Claudio Castagnoli, Colt Cabana, Eddie Edwards, Tyler Black, Samoa Joe, C.M. Punk, Bryan Danielson. El Generico is saved for last, and when the crowd hears the name they've been waiting for, they immediately start singing. For his part, Kevin gestures to the camera, telling the operator to close in on his wrist tape, where he's written "Olé," in much the same way he always wrote his grandfathers' initials on his wrist tape before he got them tattooed on his knuckles. He carries the luchador with him, here at the end.

Early in the match, he makes this even more clear. After scanning the crowd, he takes a moment to call out to a person wearing a Generico mask, asking them to hand it over to him. When they do, he puts it on and proceeds to wrestle as El Generico, as if wearing the mask has granted him access to the luchador's spirit. He does Generico's signature kick with the uncanny accuracy of someone who has watched the move countless times, right down to the buoyant little starting hop. After executing it, he raises his finger in the air and the crowd goes nuts at his summoning of his rival and friend back from Tijuana or Florida or the grave to be there with them.

Generico once told a PWG crowd, "You are El Generico," and there's always been a weird magical feeling that the luchador's spirit lives in anyone who believes in him.

By that standard, there's almost no one in the world more worthy of being El Generico than Kevin.

The theme continues even more explicitly at the end of his PWG match, where Kevin picks up the mic and starts his final address with "To be honest, and to tell you all the truth... My name... is El Generico."

They're the same words El Generico said in his farewell speech at PWG, a year and a half ago. Kevin smiles, the audience laughs and sighs at the memory; he's poking a little bit of fun at Generico's earnest goodbye, but at the same time he's not. At the same time, when he says "My name is El Generico," it's just kind of true. El Generico evolved into a sort of collaborative creation, the boundaries of his heroism defined by the shape of Kevin's villainy.

So this, really, is El Generico's final goodbye.

Kevin leans into that, explaining that he got a call from Generico, panicked because the orphans were out of control, begging Kevin to come help him. So Kevin is packing up his family and uprooting everything to go and be with Generico again. It's a perfect melding of the story and the reality, true and false at the same time like the best of wrestling.

And so Kevin leaves Reseda for the last time,* goes back to Montreal, packs everything up and drives to Florida to sign his contract and start training with WWE.

Almost There

Kevin posts one last video in his *Weekend Escapades* series, recording his family's vacation in Florida, with trips to Disney World and Gatorland. It includes a reference to that earlier video in which a red-headed stranger asked a hostile Kevin for directions in Montreal. This time it's Kevin who's lost and asks for directions from a passer-by. Kevin stares at the person giving him directions, then reaches out almost tentatively to touch his arm. "Hey, we... we know each other," he says.

"I don't think I know you," the stranger says blankly.

"Yeah, we definitely know each other."

Sami Zayn stares at him without a flicker of recognition and asks what his name is. When Kevin tells him, he says with solemn deadpan, "I don't know any Kevins." He walks away, though not before taking a moment to quietly reassure Kevin that his destination is nearby.

"You're almost there," he says.

Kevin declares him a "douchebag" once again and the vignette ends with this scene and its note of surreal truth—because maybe Sami doesn't know him.

---

* When the Reseda American Legion Hall is scheduled for demolition in 2021, WWE will air an episode of RideAlong that shows Kevin stopping by with Mustafa Ali and Apollo Crews to walk in and take one last look at the debris-strewn floor of the place where he created so many stunning matches. It's a poignant farewell.

Indeed, at this precise moment—August 2014—Sami and Kevin's paths seemed to be only fleetingly intersecting. Sami was already having dark matches with the main roster and it looked like he'd move up to *Raw* or *Smackdown*. And if that happened, the chances were good that Kevin and Sami might never interact at all in WWE, because Kevin had been told that he was unlikely to ever graduate from developmental, that his career would probably peak and end in NXT. An unidentified someone at the Performance Center informed Kevin, "I was specifically told to let you know that we are going to hire you, but don't get your hopes up for *Raw* and *Smackdown*."[12]

Fans who loved them both, who had followed their careers since Ring of Honor or before, were gripped with anxiety. Was Kevin too late? Would they be forever out of sync now, Sami always further ahead, always a few rungs higher? Kevin and Sami themselves must have wondered the same as Kevin reported to the Performance Center in Orlando, ready to see what WWE would make of him.

"You've Got to Be You"

For Kevin's first WWE photoshoot he was told to "wear your gear." Simple enough, right? But for Kevin the issue was fraught with years of uncertainty. "This is the voice of God. You're a wrestler. Don't wear a shirt," CM Punk had announced over the PA back in 2007, and the gibe had followed him for years. "I'm not going to wear a shirt," he had told that interviewer in March. "I'm not an idiot." So he spent thousands of dollars on new singlets and brought them to the Performance Center. Trying them on, he stared at himself in the mirror and thought, "I look ridiculous. I wouldn't pay to see this guy."[13]

He was still glaring at his reflection when wrestler Enzo Amore wandered by and said, confused, "What are you doing?"

"I'm a wrestler," Kevin responded, in a conscious or unconscious echo of CM Punk's old sneer.

"No, where are your shorts and your shirt and stuff?" Amore insisted. "You've got to be you."

He was right, and Kevin knew it. He switched back into his shorts and shirt. Then he realized he couldn't wear a Guns n' Roses shirt in official material, so he turned it inside out. Finding himself in a blank black shirt and shorts and frantic to get something distinctive into the pictures, he borrowed a paintbrush from Finn Bálor as Finn painted his face for his own photoshoot, dipped it in white paint, and scrawled "Fight" on the shirt. There was no name, because he didn't know what his name was going to be, so just "Fight" would have to do. You can still see the shirt in a few shots in his earliest entrance video, the challenge written there before his name existed.

Soon enough, it was time for Kevin to get his new name. They batted around a lot of possibilities, from "Keller Stevens" to "Steven Keen," but at the last second, Triple H suggested they go with something more personally meaningful to Kevin, rather than trying to capture the sound of his original name.

Since arriving at the Performance Center, Kevin had relentlessly focused on how important his family is to him, so he decided to take his son's name, Owen, and adapted it into a last name. Since his son is already named after one of his favorite wrestlers, Owen Hart, this means the name captures two of the most relatable parts of his personality: his love of his family and his love of wrestling. Then they wrangled over what to make his new first name for a while, until Triple H finally shrugged and said "Why not just keep 'Kevin' and be KO?"

And so Kevin Owens was born.

R-Evolution

As Kevin makes preparations and decisions, as he moves his family south and starts to train with the other new WWE members, as he meets and immediately becomes fast friends with Finn Bálor, Sami Zayn is busy building his defining storyline in NXT, the capstone of his time there. Through the summer and fall of 2014, he's been gunning for the championship currently held by his good friend (both inside and outside of the fiction) Adrian Neville.[*] Neville is a decent guy, but

---

[*] Neville, "The Man That Gravity Forgot," is the once and future Pac—here less of a Bastard than he would one day become, but you can see the seeds of that character in his interactions with Sami.

he has an edge that NXT Sami seems to lack—he's willing to bend the rules, to push the boundaries of what's acceptable in order to win. In a four-way title match against Sami he yanks the referee out of the ring so he can't give Sami the three-count—technically not cheating, because there are no disqualifications in a multi-man match, but it's shady at best. When Sami calls him out for it and high-mindedly says he would never use such techniques, Neville retorts, "Sami, that's why you will *never* be NXT champion." He informs Sami that he lacks the killer instinct, the ruthlessness necessary to win the big one. Sami is stung by this—and also touched with self-doubt. He announces that he is embarking on a Road to Redemption, where he faces down people he's lost to in the past to prove to Neville (and himself) that he deserves another shot. He defeats Titus O'Neill, Tyson Kidd, and Tyler Breeze, joy and growing confidence radiating from him with each win, and the regulars at the Full Sail arena are entirely won over by him.

Eventually Neville gives him another shot at the title, only to take advantage of Sami's compassion. When Neville sustains a minor injury,[14] Sami stops pressing the attack and bends over him in concern, only to have Neville quickly roll him up for the win, then fondly ruffle his hair in apology as Sami sits on the mat, disconsolate. In the wake of this crushing defeat, Sami demands one last title shot from his friend, vowing that if he doesn't win he'll leave NXT forever. It's a threat with extra impact in NXT, because it's clear Sami is about to move up to the main roster. Would he leave without ever touching gold, or would his NXT run end with him as champion? His final match with Neville, his final shot, was set for December 11, 2014, at the show called *TakeOver: R-Evolution*.

Kevin debuts in WWE at that same show, his first match and what is possibly Sami's last match in NXT happening on the same night, to the anguish of those who already love them. He's in the opening match against C.J. Parker (the future Juice Robinson). The main event is of course the climax of Sami Zayn's Road to Redemption storyline, Sami and Kevin bookending the show. They'll be providing the explosive punctuation at the end, but the Full Sail crowd and the people watching on the WWE Network don't know that yet.

When Kevin's music hits and he walks out in front of a WWE audience for the very first time, as he lets himself fully take in the fact that he's about to have his first match in the promotion he's always had his aim set on, the camera closes in on his face. His eyes are full of wonder, close to tears. He's all business by the time he gets to the ring, setting aside his awe with a neck-roll and shrug and preparing to prove himself.

Which he does, although not in the way he planned.

He has time for only one dramatic spot, a somersault plancha over the ropes that leaves the audience gasping, before Parker delivers a palm strike to his face that shatters his nose.

It's an awful injury. With less luck, there's a chance it could have been fatal—a startling reminder that some of the most dangerous moments in wrestling can happen with some of the least flashy moves. Parker doesn't emerge unscathed either, as Kevin's nasal bone slices almost all the way through his palm like a knife. Blood starts pouring from Kevin's nose, splattering his face and hands. The camera's gaze tries to wince away from the carnage as much as possible, but two minutes into his first match in the most famously family-friendly, PG-rated, blood-averse promotion in the world, Kevin's face is drenched with his own blood like some kind of horror-movie serial killer. Despite the match being cut short and Kevin abruptly getting the win, it's an electrifying debut, Kevin's pale and gore-smeared victorious face an indelible image.

As the show winds on through the Lucha Dragons defending their tag team titles, through Baron Corbin squashing Tye Dillinger in 41 seconds, through Charlotte staving off Sasha Banks in her first major title shot, there's a brief backstage segment showing Sami in the locker room, psyching himself up for his match. The camera moves to reveal Kevin sitting across the room staring at him,* and he and Sami lock eyes for a long, silent moment before Sami stands up and leaves the room. It's the first time they've ever appeared on WWE television

---

* Kevin is miraculously unscathed despite being covered in blood only twenty minutes ago, his injury accidentally revealing that the vignette was shot much earlier, but no matter.

together, and although commentary doesn't mention it, the ambivalent weight of their long relationship is already clear in that fraught look.

Sami and Neville's match is perfect, the kind of match one shows to a friend to teach them how beautiful wrestling can be. Neville's character is perfectly calibrated, because the real conflict in this match is not between Neville and Sami but between Sami and his own self-doubt. There's almost no personal animus between the two friends, so Neville's cool fondness and utter lack of faith in Sami ("We all know you can't win the big one," he says over and over with condescending affection) makes clear that the struggle isn't merely between two individuals, it's Sami and his ideals versus the world-weary pragmatic cynicism that Neville stands for. "This is where I go wrong every time, when I try to *do the right thing*," Sami had seethed at Neville at their last promo together, "be the good guy, Sami's gotta *be the good guy* and *show respect*." He had slapped Neville's patronizing face in fury, then stared wildly around the ring for something tangible to fight, baffled and furious, tearing at his own hair with the hand that had struck his friend. Now he comes to the ring angry at Neville, angry at the world of wrestling which so rarely rewards the good, angry at the world in general which even more rarely rewards the good. And finally, of course, worst and deepest of all, angry at himself and afraid that Neville is right. There's a deeper story winding under the one-year story they're telling here, with echoes of El Generico the comedy act who was "too happy to be a wrestler," El Generico who never "won the big one" in Ring of Honor. Sami is emotionally and spiritually frayed, right on the knife's edge, desperate to prove that he belongs here in WWE, that he hasn't said goodbye to the luchador forever for nothing.

The match is fast paced and incredibly good—Sami and Neville had been meeting each other in the ring for a decade, and the base story of the match is that they know each other so well and are so well-matched that it's difficult for either one to get the upper hand. Someone's going to have to dig in and find some extra inspiration, that killer edge that Neville claims Sami doesn't have, and when Neville finds himself about to be on the receiving end of Sami's finishing move, he yanks the referee into the way of Sami's kick and rolls out of the ring while Sami checks on the unconscious man.

As Sami shows compassion to the referee, Neville grabs his title and gets back into the ring, preparing to whack Sami with it. Sami, however, sees it coming and manages to deflect the blow, knocking Neville down and kicking the title out of his hands.

Thus Sami finds himself standing alone with the title at his feet. If he just picks up that belt and uses it to hit Neville, that could be the edge he needs to win. And why not do it? The ref is out, and specifically out because of Neville's underhanded actions. Neville just tried to cheat and hit him with that very title. Sami would be entirely justified in making sure his career is saved by giving Neville a taste of his own vicious medicine.

He slowly picks up the title, then pauses, irresolute.

And the audience acts.

In interviews, Kevin has said that one of Sami's gifts is unerringly knowing how an audience will react before the match even starts.[15] Given a situation where a babyface wrestler has been driven to the brink and has the chance to cheat, audiences will almost always cheer for the rules to be broken, for propriety to be thrown out the window and chaotic violence to reign supreme in the service of revenge or of justice. But NXT was shot week after week in the same venue, the Full Sail arena, and this audience had watched Sami's struggles evolve bit by bit across the whole year. They had come to love Sami's character more than they loved mayhem and violence, and there's very little in this world that wrestling fans love more than some good mayhem and violence.

Full Sail explodes, nearly every member of the audience passionately begging Sami not to do it. They keep desperately making the "no" sign, yelling as Sami argues with himself, pacing, preparing himself to be as vicious as he needs to be to win. They don't want that. They want him to win the right way, the way that's true to himself. Sami's head lifts as their pleas penetrate his self-doubt, and his shoulders straighten. "Fuck this. Fuck this!" he announces,* rejecting the

---

* The Network originally merely bleeped out his profanity. When the footage moved to

whole idea that you have to choose between morals and victory, and he goes to put down the title. The audience's "no" chants start to shift to cheers of relief and support—and Neville jumps up and gets him into a quick rollup pin.

Full Sail explodes into a keening wail of horror. People throw their hands in front of their eyes, because they know how this goes, they were shown it three weeks ago. Sami has been too honorable, too fair, and now he's going to lose again. But it's worse than that, this time. This time his career is on the line, and this time, the audience is complicit in his defeat. They begged him not to fight dirty, they implored him to not just win but to win well, to win the brightest possible victory, because they love him and wanted him to be true to himself. Now they know that Sami is going to lose, that they will lose him, and it will be their fault. For precisely two seconds, as the miraculously-revived ref's hand hits the mat like a horrified heartbeat, they are in utter despair.

So when Sami kicks out, the audience comes to its feet in joy and relief and wonder. Sami himself seems unable to believe it wasn't a three count, but once he realizes it wasn't, it's only a matter of seconds until he sets up his finisher and pins Neville for the victory and the title. At the end of his Road to Redemption, he is redeemed—and so is the audience's faith in him. Everyone's hands are in the air. The camera pans across tear-streaked faces transfigured by joy as they sing to him, the Olé chant cast out toward him like bright streamers.

The locker room clears out to come celebrate in the ring with him, but before anyone else can reach the ring Kevin comes charging down the ramp, putting on a burst of speed to make sure he gets to Sami before anyone else, that he's the first to share in this very first WWE title win. Sami steps backward as Kevin gets into the ring, his face suddenly uncertain and uneasy, but Kevin barrels straight into an embrace that knocks him backwards into the turnbuckle—deliberately or not, this first hug between Kevin and Sami echoing Kevin and El Generico's very last hug. The force of Kevin's hug has ripped the

---

Peacock, they excised the line entirely and in the process lost the actual moment Sami's character passes its last test, destroying the pacing of the match's end. Alas.

stitches across the bridge of his broken nose open, and blood starts running down his face again, dripping onto Sami's shoulder. He's crying. Sami is crying. Sami kisses his forehead over and over, and Kevin raises his friend's hand with a fierce shout of joy.

The rest of the locker room lifts Sami up on their shoulders, celebrating. Kevin retreats, leaving the center of the ring to the new champion. He watches from the corner as Sami lifts his title in triumph, and fans who knew their history must have felt a pang of regret at seeing him relegated to the side with Sami in the center. Obviously they're totally out of sync, obviously Sami's star is in ascendance, rocketing skyward trailing glory as Kevin just arrives on the scene and begins the slow process of working his way up the card. It took Sami a year and a half from his arrival in NXT to reach these heights, a year and a half of feuds with the Wyatt Family and Corey Graves and Leo Kruger. This moment of shared happiness was a kindness, a small gift before Sami soars out of sight to the main roster and leaves Kevin behind again, possibly forever.

Or so they thought.

Sami and Neville embrace to tearful applause, the ring clears out and Sami is left alone with the audience for a few moments more. He starts to leave the ring, then sits on the apron, gazing down at the glowing gold of his title and wiping away tears. As he does, Kevin comes down the ramp and embraces him again, bumping foreheads and then wrapping his arms around him. They whisper to each other, both of them smiling with joy at this shared moment. They've made it, the playful title of the show is theirs, R-Evolution, both a *revolution* and *our evolution* to the next stage of their characters. The closing copyright logo appears on the screen, all rights reserved as Kevin lifts Sami's hand one more time. Sami puts his arm around Kevin and they start to walk to the back.

The TV viewer is waiting for the fade to black when Kevin abruptly pivots, grabbing Sami's neck and hurling him backwards onto the ramp.

The crowd groans. Their aghast faces blur in the background of the shot as Kevin hoists Sami up and powerbombs him onto the apron.

Kevin powerbombs Sami into the ring apron.

Sami writhes in pain on the floor as the camera pans to Kevin, eyes gone dead and devoid of warmth, blood trickling from the bridge of his nose as he stares down at the broken body of his friend. Around the world, longtime Ring of Honor fans are yelping in mingled horror and delight, because Sami and Kevin are not out of sync at all, Kevin is not making any long climb to the pinnacle, he is vaulting to the top in one violent leap. Their story in WWE has begun.

Our evolution indeed.

RIVAL
(2015)

Authenticity

WITH KEVIN and Sami both in WWE, their story morphs into something much more sleek and streamlined. Once they're sealed off in the WWE bubble, there's no more piecing together a story from matches scattered across a handful of promotions. Everything happens in one place, in one storyline. The disadvantage of that continuity is that there are months, even years, where they barely interact, long stretches where their shared story is on hiatus, limited to a few notes written in the margins of their individual stories. In addition, the wealth of shoot interviews Kevin gave from 2012 to 2014 came to an end when he entered WWE, and he stopped speaking much about backstage politics or personal conflicts. With one dramatic exception, Kevin and Sami's story in WWE remains resolutely in front of the curtains from 2015 on, and any discussion of the real people's thoughts or feelings must remain largely speculation.

At the beginning of 2015, Daniel Bryan had just come back after an injury forced him to vacate the titles he won at *WrestleMania 30* the previous year. Sting had just appeared in WWE for the first time. Seth Rollins had betrayed his Shield brothers and was working for the Authority, carrying his Money in the Bank briefcase and getting ready for one of the most memorable cash-ins of all time. Wade "Bad News" Barrett was Intercontinental champion. Ryback was getting loud "feed me more" chants. Rusev was the US champion, but John Cena was starting a feud with him that would eventually lead to him overthrowing Rusev at WrestleMania. Nikki Bella was the penultimate Divas champion, although nobody knew the title would soon disappear.

And Sami Zayn was NXT champion.

The Underdog from the Underground walked into the show as champion for the first time in early January, cutting a promo that started with him running impulsively through the crowd as they cheered and sang, and ended with him comparing the wrestler-audience relationships to collaborating in a band and quoting Barry Manilow ("We write the songs that make the whole world sing!")

On the main roster, Roman Reigns was about to deliver—the very next day!—one of the most agonizing promos of his career, awkwardly reciting a script that required him to tell Seth Rollins "you're full of suffering succotash, son." With his blue contact lenses and stilted references to ancient cartoons, Reigns in early 2015 was clearly a fictional character created by old white men, reading words written by old white men. Sami Zayn's Barry Manilow line, on the other hand, *worked* —because with his bright yellow polo shirt, his polite old-man flat cap, and his gentle self-awareness ("here's the cheesy part," he had noted wryly before he started his passionate musical metaphor), he felt authentic in a way Reigns did not, could not at the time.

Kevin Owens felt authentic, too, though in a very different way. He referred to himself as "a prizefighter," in NXT to make money so he could be a good provider to his family. But behind his dead eyes the audience could always glimpse the shrieking jealousy that he had let slip in his tryout promo, his ravening need to revenge himself on the people like Neville and Sami who had made it to WWE before him, and who were likely to go on to the main roster without him.

After Kevin ambushed Sami once again, Sami demanded a match with his former friend. "Do whatever it is you have to do," he begged NXT General Manager William Regal, "just *give him to me.*" Regal was reluctant to reward Kevin's behavior, but granted it when Sami agreed to a non-title match. And so they met for the contract signing in late January. This feud, covering the early part of 2015, has some of the best promo work of the pair's career, presenting both of them as complicated, interesting people who also happen to be inextricably a part of each other's past, present, and future. And it starts with the first moment they both talk in a WWE ring at this contract signing.

"He *is Not the Prize*"

William Regal stands between them as they lock eyes across the table, across the fateful contract. Sami's eyes are full of hurt anger. Kevin's eyes are empty of emotion. Sami signs the contract, and Regal slides it over to Kevin, who looks at Sami, his fingers drumming on the table his only motion. Sami picks up the microphone and addresses Kevin.

"There's a microphone in front of you there, Kevin. You just gonna look at me?" Kevin remains silent. "That's good, just stare at me like that, that's good. Act like the last twelve years didn't exist." He goes on to talk about their history, their coming up together, his voice breaking with emotion. It's a great speech even if you don't know their former selves, and an astonishing image if you do—a complete and deliberate role reversal, Kevin silent while his friend fills the space between them with eloquence. "Everything we did out there, whether it was friends or as enemies tearing each other apart, it was all about ending up *here*," Sami says. They stare at each other across the table, like and totally unlike the way they will stare at each other across a *WrestleMania* ring ten years later. When he's done swearing vengeance, Kevin picks up the pen, looks at the contract, puts the pen down. He picks up the microphone and addresses, not Sami, but Regal.

"This," he says, pointing down at the contract, his voice flat, "says *non-title match.*"

The crowd gasps, grasping the implications immediately, the insult to Sami (I don't care about you, only the title). Kevin carefully unpacks those implications. "What I did at *TakeOver* wasn't personal, it was business. I fight for a prize, and *he* is not the prize," he says, pointing at Sami, his eyes still on the General Manager.

Infuriated, Sami demands that Regal change the contract to a title match, and the General Manager reluctantly does so. Kevin's face remains impassive as he signs the contract, then tosses it disdainfully back on the table and contemptuously flicks the pen into Sami's face. Regal holds Sami back as Kevin strolls out, and the ink dries on the contract for their first match together in WWE.

TakeOver: Rival

On Feb. 11, the two of them stand across a WWE ring from each other for the first time in their lives. There's a long pause as they look at each other, taking a moment to let the crowd noise peak and plateau.

It was all about ending up here.

Sami is full of avenging rage through the match, while Kevin is at his most viciously efficient. When Kevin takes a powder at the beginning, rolling out and laughing on the ramp rather than face Sami's righteous ire, Sami eventually comes flying over the ropes at him, transporting the crowd and horrifying his foe. When they get back into the ring, Kevin starts off trying to dismantle Sami, who takes his moves at his wobbly-legged best. He swoons backwards, his body an arc of pain, when Kevin chops him. He staggers, legs unsteady, in the face of Kevin's onslaught. When Kevin hurls him into a turnbuckle for an Irish whip, Sami's body contorts like a tesseract, an Escher painting of agony. Wrestling tells stories about anguish, and Sami Zayn is its Scheherazade of suffering.

The audience had started at *Fight Owens Fight* chants, then progressed to the Olé chant. Kevin starts chest-chopping Sami outside the ring, up against the barricades, and Sami wilts across them in pain as Kevin steps cooly onto the stairs and lifts an arm high in the air, mocking the vanished El Generico's traditional salute. The audience's chants shift to a mix of angry boos and a counter-balancing bloodthirsty *Kill Owens Kill*. When they get back in the ring, Kevin crawls on all fours like an animal to grab Sami into a headlock, wrenching him until the referee asks Sami if he wants to quit ("No, no, no" Sami gasps around Kevin's choking elbow).

When Sami rallies, coming up into a clothesline that bowls Kevin over, the crowd goes wild, cheering him on. He gets Kevin in position to do El Generico's old finishing move, the brainbuster from the top turnbuckle. Kevin muscles his way out of it in a panic, and like every other time Sami has teased the move, commentary doesn't mention it, but those who loved El Generico saw and knew. The tide of the fight has shifted in Sami's direction once again.

They brawl back outside the ring and Kevin goes for the powerbomb on the ring apron, the same move that shattered Sami for a month at his betrayal. This time Sami has the wherewithal to grab at the ropes, clawing his way out of the move. He does an Arabian press, a moonsault-adjacent move that has him basically bounce off the top rope using his thighs and throwing himself into a backflip that wipes out Kevin. As he tumbles through the move, the back of his head connects with the ramp.

And just like that, the momentum shifts again, and with finality. Commentary points out that he banged his head, and Sami climbs back into the ring with extra-wobbly steps, his eyes unfocused, his fury dissipated into a fog. He starts to do a Helluva Kick to Kevin in the far corner, but wavers, stopping, confused for just a second. By the time he finishes the move, Kevin is ready and meets him in the middle of the ring to snatch him into a pop-up powerbomb, tossing him in the air and then hurling him on his back to the mat. Sami kicks out, but he's disoriented, woozy. The referee starts to check on him, and Kevin's face fills with cunning glee as he realizes what's happened, what an advantage he suddenly has.

He jumps forward to start punching at Sami, pummeling his face and the back of his head. The air is going out of the audience, replaced by a mix of worry that Sami's legitimately injured and a dawning knowledge of the end. The referee keeps warning Kevin off, and Kevin keeps coming back and striking at Sami's head with fists and elbows.

A few faces in the crowd are laughing. More are crying.

The trainers and medical staff come out to check on Sami, who is increasingly dazed. Kevin shoves them aside to deliver two more powerbombs to Sami, and Sami *still* manages to lift one shoulder, clearly by instinct. The trainer checks on Sami, carefully and deliberately taking Sami's lax hand where the camera can see that Sami is not returning the squeeze, that he isn't giving the trainer the "secret signal" reassurance that he isn't concussed.

Kevin hurls the trainers aside and delivers another powerbomb to Sami, whose head hits the mat, his limbs all going limp. Another powerbomb, and the trainers on the outside of the ring start yelling at the referee to stop the match. The referee walks to the corner of the rings and speaks to the timekeeper and the bell-ringer, then makes the signal. The match is stopped, and Kevin has won the NXT title from Sami Zayn exactly two months to the day after his debut.

It takes a moment for the reality to sink in, and as it does, the crowd makes a confused howling noise, shredded between glee and despair. As the trainers bend over the semi-conscious Sami, Kevin curls up around his first WWE title, kissing and licking it. He climbs to the top turnbuckle and points at his family, and for a moment his face crumples into an emotion that leaves him looking very young until he wrenches it back into sadism. Grinning evilly, he moves until he's standing right behind Sami, still being tended to, and lifts his shining title over Sami's crumpled form. The show ends on this tableau. Within the fiction it's the new champion gloating and triumphant. Outside of the fiction it's Kevin making sure that Sami is there forever in this moment, his first victory inextricably linked to Sami's loss. The flip sides to the coin, the winner and the loser, the darkness and the light.

Asterisk

In the aftermath of his title loss, Sami disappears from Full Sail for about two months. He goes to Abu Dhabi to do some PR work for WWE, he goes back to Montreal to "lick his little wounds" as Kevin will refer to it later. He records a video to be played on NXT in which he's walking the snowy streets of Montreal at 2AM, his eyes dark and sorrowful. "Today is March 1, 2015, and today marks my thirteen-year anniversary in this industry," he says. "And for the first time in thirteen years I feel like I'm not mentally prepared to be there right now." To this point in WWE history, champions have always moved up to the main roster after losing their titles, though often not until they get a rematch, which they inevitably lose. It's always a bittersweet loss, because it's a farewell mixed with joy as a favorite moves from developmental to the most high-profile rosters in the world. The NXT fans were waiting patiently for that rematch. Maybe Sami would win the title back and stay with them a while longer? But even if it were to be goodbye forever, there would be happiness beneath the grief.

While Sami is walking the pre-dawn streets of Montreal, Kevin is running roughshod over the NXT roster, making life hell for everyone, never letting anyone forget he beat Sami Zayn. At WrestleMania that April, the NXT champion does signings. In a clip that appears on *NXT TV*, he holds up a children's book of WWE wrestlers someone has asked him to sign. "I'm not in this," he says, opening it to the page featuring a cartoonishly muscular illustration of Sami. "Sami Zayn is in this, and he's as big as Ryback!" he points out. Indeed, on the opposing page there's a cartoon version of the hulking Ryback, about the same size as Sami. Despite his loudly-telegraphed annoyance at this sign that Sami is headed for the main roster and he is not, Kevin deigns to sign the book, adding a little stick figure doodle of himself holding up the NXT title and smiling.

Sami comes back after WrestleMania week gunning for Kevin, for his title, and for revenge. After Sami attacks Kevin out of nowhere, they confront each other once more on April 29, with Kevin demanding he have a chance to fight Sami again. Regal makes the match for the championship at the next *TakeOver, Unstoppable,* for May 20, but Kevin laughingly says it's certainly not going to be a title match, that Sami hasn't earned it yet. "I'll fight him at *TakeOver,* but there's no way—no *way*—I'm putting the title on the line."

Three months ago, they had been in exactly this same position, reversed: Sami the title holder, Kevin the challenger, a non-title match made. Three months ago, Kevin manipulated Sami into changing it to a title match, and this time it's Sami's turn to return the favor. "You need this match," he says to Kevin, "and it's got nothing to do with what happened last week. I think it's got a lot more to do with what's happened over the last twelve years. Let's face it, Kev," he says, smirking, "anything you've done in your career has had my name next to it." The crowd needles Kevin with a prolonged "ooooooooh" and Kevin twitches as Sami goes on, "You finally made it, you finally got the Kevin—" there's a microsecond pause as he reminds himself to say the correct last name, "—Owens Show, but they're not just talking about Kevin Owens, are they? They're talking about what Kevin Owens *did* to Sami Zayn."

His eyes blaze as he winds up to deliver the thesis of their career together. "Anything you've ever done, and anything you ever *will* do will always have an asterisk with my name attached! And that drives you crazy, doesn't it?" Kevin has turned away, pacing angrily. "I guess you could say that Kevin Owens has been living in Sami Zayn's shadow!" As Kevin swivels back and forth like a caged tiger, Sami prepares his finishing blow, the final echo. "I'll give you that chance to get out of my shadow, but here's the thing, Kev: I fight for a prize. And *you* are not the prize. That NXT Championship is the prize."

Kevin's stoic dead-eyed look shatters into jealous fury, and as he lifts the microphone to respond, the audience busts, unprompted, into an Olé chant. "Fine! But you think the first time was bad? You have *no* idea," he snarls at Sami. The rematch is set for May 20. But before then, less than a week after telling Kevin he'll always be in his shadow, Sami has another major match, a date with destiny. A main roster debut.

Open Challenge

A month ago at *WrestleMania*, US Champion Rusev had discovered that even coming to the ring in a tank was no defense against the insurmountable John Cena, who at the time was so consistently triumphant that the phrase "Cena wins LOL" was coined to express how inevitable his wins were. The new champion then started having an "open challenge" every week, accepting all comers. By May he had defeated Dean Ambrose, Stardust, Bad News Barrett and Kane. On May 4, Monday Night Raw was in the Bell Centre in Montreal, and when Cena says his ritualistic "The John Cena US Open Challenge officially starts now. You want some? *Come get some!*" he's greeted by the strident guitar-squeal of Bret Hart's music.

The crowd jumps to their feet as the Canadian legend makes his way to the ring and takes the mic. "I came here tonight to introduce to you a hometown boy from Montreal, Canada!" The crowd roar almost drowns out his words as he explains to a somewhat-baffled looking Cena that this is "one of NXT's hottest, biggest superstars." An Olé chant starts to ripple around the arena, and when Hart says "Let's give it up for Sami Zayn" sound fills the Bell Centre like a palpable thing, pulsating with joy.

Sami's music hits and he comes down the ramp, buffeted by a wall of deafening cheers. Nobody backstage has confirmed it to him, but it seems likely this is his official debut on the main roster, and they're pulling out all the stops to do it right. He's been introduced by his childhood idol, one of the greatest of all time, and his first match is going be against one of the very top wrestlers in WWE today in front of his adoring home crowd. The fact that he's going to lose—because there's no way someone fresh out of NXT is going to beat John Cena—is beside the point. The fanfare, the joy, the excitement is the point.

And what of NXT champion Kevin Owens, who's been explicitly told that where he is now is likely to be as high as he goes, that there's little chance he'll ever follow Sami to the main roster? After *WrestleMania* weekend, he'd pitched the idea of facing John Cena in Montreal to Creative.[1] "If not me, then at least Sami," he'd begged, and they'd agreed this was a good idea—and then chosen Sami instead of him. He's watching *Raw* with Karina at home, "kinda pissed off," in his own words. When Bret Hart comes out to introduce Sami, Kevin says out loud, "Come *on* man, are you kidding me?" As Sami pauses on the ring steps and prepares to throw his arms in the air to acknowledge the crowd's thunderous love, Kevin must feel as if once again they're sliding fatally out of sync, that one of them is about to soar upward and leave the other one far behind.

And he's absolutely right.

But not in the way he expects.

UNSTOPPABLE
(2015)

Underdog

INJURIES ARE the wild cards of wrestling narrative. One slip, one move taken at slightly the wrong angle, one body part simply giving out after years of punishment, and months of storytelling can be derailed completely. The momentum of a story means it must barrel on without the injured wrestler, with someone else taking that place.

In 2019, Mustafa Ali suffers an injury and can't compete in a key gauntlet match before *Elimination Chamber*. He's replaced with veteran Kofi Kingston, and the crowd's positive reaction to Kingston leads to one of the greatest feel-good moments in wrestling, his winning the WWE Championship at *WrestleMania*.

In 2017, Finn Bálor wins the Universal Championship in his first title match on the main roster. But he's injured in the process and is forced to relinquish the title the very next day, leaving a vacancy that needs to be filled. So WWE books a four-way championship match between Roman Reigns, Seth Rollins, and— But that's a story for another chapter.

In 2015, Sami Zayn stands on the ring steps, the roar of joy from the Montreal crowd like a living thing all around him. He's just been introduced by the legendary Bret Hart. He's about to take on the juggernaut John Cena in his debut on the main roster. He throws his arms in the air to acknowledge the love of the crowd.

And he feels something *pop* in his left shoulder.[1]

The camera has cut back to focus on Hart and Cena, but on the edge of the screen you can see Sami grab his shoulder, his expression worried. At home, watching, Kevin sees it happen and instantly understands. "Oh," he says, "his shoulder just gave out."[2] But it happened so quickly Sami himself is not sure if he imagined it. It seemed to pop right back into place. He hopes maybe he imagined it. There is of course no way he is going to back down from a match in his hometown against John Cena. He thinks maybe it's okay.

About a minute into the match, Cena suplexes him and Sami realizes it is very much not okay. His arm is dangling, numb and useless. He struggles forward, hitting his taunting little backflip off the ropes into the center of the ring as Cena gathers himself outside after a move, but as he lands he wobbles, his balance thrown off by the dead weight of his left arm. Soon it's obvious something is badly wrong, and Cena eventually insists on stopping the match to have the trainer check on Sami. "I'm gonna keep going," Sami informs the trainer, "just stand by."

He and Cena seamlessly work the injury into the story of the match. It was always going to tell the story of how the NXT underdog won the respect of the powerful veteran, but now Cena plays up being reluctant to fight and worsen Sami's injury, hesitating and pantomiming that he thinks they should call off the match. Sami lunges forward with a snarl of pain and anger that is probably not feigned, swatting away Cena's condescending hand.

The match goes for ten minutes of action as the Montreal audience screams their hearts out. Sami's face is clenched in pain and determination as he does his spectacular moves—the Blue Thunder Bomb, the diving DDT through the corner ropes—all of which require him to put pressure on that torn shoulder. The outcome is never really in question, and after Sami is finally pinned he crawls awkwardly to the corner, pressing his face to the turnbuckle and weeping in frustration. The crowd roars its approval as Cena approaches and holds out his hand, pulling Sami to his feet and raising his uninjured hand in respect. It's a dramatic debut, but Sami doesn't look happy as Cena rolls out of the ring and leaves him to the adulation of the fans. His eyes are bright with pain, fury, and disappointment. "Fuck," the camera catches him saying inaudibly, but with bitter emphasis. *"Fuck."* He knows that any plans to bring him up to the main roster are on indefinite delay now.

And he still has his rematch with Kevin to get through at *Unstoppable*.

"I'm The One Who Hurt You"

The final episode of *NXT* before *Unstoppable* shows a video of Sami backstage after his match with Cena, his arm taped up and his face weary, talking about the injury and saying he still intends to fight Kevin. When they come back to Full Sail, Sami comes out with energy, swinging his arm to the "Let's go!" in his theme song, which would seem hopeful until one remembers that 2015 *NXT* is pre-taped, so all of this was shot *before* his match with Cena. When he demands Kevin face him, Kevin comes to the ring slowly, the title on his shoulder.

Once again Sami does all the speaking while Kevin stands in silence, his face an impassive mask. Sami asks his former friend, once again, to tell him *why* he attacked him. "Everything you're saying about providing for your family, I know there's an element of truth to it, but I'm not buying it."

When Kevin says nothing, Sami probes harder. "Is it just jealousy? Just simple jealousy because I got here first?" He studies Kevin's face carefully, and the camera shows us the tiny changes in expression that hint at the depths of Kevin's emotions behind the stoic facade as Sami goes on. "Do you think somehow if I didn't get here and I didn't pave the way for us—for guys like us—that you maybe wouldn't have got here or something?" There's another wrinkle, that fear of dependency, the worry that he would be *nothing without him*. There's the slightest wince behind Kevin's eyes.

"Is it worse than that, is it more personal than that?" Sami cocks his head like something has just occurred to him. "Is this about your son?" Kevin's eyes narrow dangerously, but Sami is charging on. "I just thought it was cute, is it a big deal to you? That he'd rather wear a Sami Zayn shirt to school than a KO shirt? That he runs around the house with a Sami Zayn wristband?" The crowd leans into a melodramatic "oooooooh" at this extra layer of personal, not just professional, jealousy being added. Kevin lifts the mic to respond, then simply turns and leaves the ring. He's on the ramp when Sami yells after him, "After all this time, you have nothing for me? You have nothing to say?"

Kevin stops with his back still to Sami. Without turning around, he lifts the mic and says,

"Everything you just said is completely irrelevant." (Meaning, of course, that it was all true). He explains that he knows Sami's hurt, that he's the one who hurt him at their last match, that he's about to do it again, and that this time Sami won't be coming back. The camera shows his face as he says the lines, so they weren't dubbed in after Sami's injury, and it seems to have been a lucky/tragic coincidence that they fit so well with Sami's current physical condition. Then he walks away without looking back, leaving Sami looking baffled—and worried.

And with reason.

"You Want Some?

Two weeks after Sami's *Raw* match, two days before *Unstoppable*, US champion John Cena is issuing his next open challenge in Richmond, Virginia. This time it's Kevin's growling guitars that answer him. There's no rapturous reaction from this crowd, many of them don't seem to know the NXT champion slowly making his way to the ring, but Cena looks wary.

A few days before, Kevin had been at an NXT show in Philadelphia and had received a note from the people in charge of travel telling him to skip going home and go instead to Richmond, where he'd be on Raw. "Oh, *now* they're going to have me answer the open challenge," he'd thought ruefully, "in *Richmond, Virginia.*"[3] He'd gone to check, and Triple H had informed him this wasn't just one match, he was getting called up. "You're starting on *Raw* Monday, full time." And more than that:

"You're starting something with John Cena."

Kevin was stunned into silence, "I just couldn't process it, in a way. I was just like 'okay.'" He was not only getting called up a mere six months after arriving, he was entering into a high-profile feud with the very face of the company. Sworn to silence, he told only his wife and Finn Bálor, who had become an inseparable friend backstage in NXT. Landing in Richmond, he bought his very first suit and showed up backstage at *Raw*.

His first meeting with Vince McMahon was a memorable one. Kevin asked, since he was to tell no one why he was here, what he was supposed to say if anyone asked. McMahon said "Oh," thought for a moment, and suggested, "why don't you tell them to go fuck themselves?"

And with these words of advice Kevin was dismissed to change into his gear and sit in catering.

As he sat, Seth Rollins noticed him and came over to sit next to him, asking why he was there. Kevin quickly weighed his options. He was sworn to secrecy and had been told he could tell Seth to go fuck himself. On the *other* hand, he couldn't help but remember the many times Seth had informed him he would never get a look from WWE unless he got in better shape.

"I'm debuting," he said.

"Get *out*," Seth said in disbelief. He cut off a piece of steak and lifted it toward his mouth. "So, what are you doing?"

"Well," said Kevin, "I'm starting something with Cena."

Seth hurled his knife and fork—the bite of steak still impaled on it—into the air and stared at him in blank shock. It was unthinkable. It was impossible.

It was happening.

Kevin strolls to the ring, his face studiously blank and unimpressed. He's finally where he deserves to be, where he always knew he would be. He doesn't feel nervous at all as he gets into the ring and stands face-to-face with the sixteen-time world champion. But then out of nowhere he has a sudden spasm of stress-induced derealization. "For some reason suddenly it felt like everything was *so close.*"[4] The hard cam, the audience, Cena himself—Kevin knows they are all feet or yards away, yet for a nauseating instant it feels like everything is mere inches from his face, distorted as if through a demented magnifying glass.

He lifts the microphone and the feeling passes, he's back in his element.

"I would introduce myself, but you know exactly who I am, don't you?"

Some of the Richmond crowd howls in acknowledgement, but Cena pauses to officially introduce "NXT champion, Kevin Owens."

Kevin grins toothily and thanks him for the introduction. "I know you feel responsible for the injury Sami suffered two weeks ago," he informs Cena. "But I'm here to ease your mind. The truth is Sami was injured before he ever accepted your little challenge. I know that because I'm the one who injured him." He promises to finish Sami for good ("this Wednesday night at *NXT TakeOver* on the WWE Network").

Cena takes offense at his callous attitude. "Young man," he says, stepping closer, "as one champion to another, allow me to bestow on you some veteran advice."

Kevin cuts him off. "Whoa whoa, wait wait wait," he says, dumbfounded and sarcastic. "*Veteran advice?* Are you kidding me?" He points out that he's been wrestling as long as Cena has. "You don't get to give me advice, *ever.*"

"Fine, then I'll give you a warning," Cena snaps, calling him a "scared kid" who's "crapping his pants" right now. He tells Kevin he shouldn't take Sami lightly, then reminds him that Kevin is there for an open challenge. "You want some?" The audience joins in the refrain as Kevin paces angrily, *"come get some."*

Visibly furious, Kevin raises his NXT title. "I already have a prize and it's the NXT Championship." Rejecting the challenge to a chorus of boos, he adds, "You and I, we are going to fight someday, but it's going to be on my terms, not yours. And if you think you've got me figured out, you're gonna realize—"

He cuts off mid-sentence to kick Cena in the gut. Cena collapses, the US title goes flying, and Kevin hurls him into the ropes and then into a pop-up powerbomb. Cena lies sprawled on the mat as Kevin picks up the US title, drops it next to him, then lifts his own NXT Championship, raises his boot, and places it squarely on Cena's red-white-and-blue title. About 75% of the crowd boos. The remainder starts a rumbling "Fight Owens Fight!" chant. He leans over and waves his hand in front of his face, mocking Cena's "You Can't See Me" taunt.

It's a spectacular moment, an assertion of dominance, a statement that cannot be ignored. Even more, his rejection of the open challenge makes clear that this is not a one-off, that this is an arrival and the start of a feud with an icon of the WWE. Kevin's little son Owen, a huge Cena fan, is watching the show clutching his John Cena stuffed Wrestle Buddy, and Karina captures his utter amazement on video: "Oh my God! He's fighting *John Cena?"* he yells, his voice cracking into a squeal of joy.

In his living room, Sami—who was not on the tiny list of people Kevin told about this—is flabbergasted, suspects he's hallucinating. "Am I really seeing Kevin in the ring with John Cena right now?"[5]

When Kevin got to the back Vince McMahon, Stephanie McMahon, and Triple H all broke into applause. Jimmy Jacobs, his old friend and enemy from the Scrub Room days in ROH, was there working as a writer and was openly in tears. The match between Kevin and Cena was set for *Elimination Chamber*, the next big show. His first match on the main roster was going to be at a pay-per-view against John Cena.

Sami, sitting at home facing the cold reality of surgery, made a video for WWE to post. "I wish I could say I was just happy for him," he said. "But we're at that pretty complicated point in our relationship where happiness is not the only thing I'm going to feel when I see something like that. I'd be lying if I said there wasn't a tinge of jealousy, a little bit of anxiety due to the uncertainty of the situation for myself and for him, and for whatever's going to happen between us in the future."[6] In just a few weeks, the balance had shifted dramatically. The jealousy was Sami's to feel now.

The anxiety and uncertainty, however, they both shared.

A Classic Three-Act Dramatic Structure

The match at *Unstoppable* between Kevin and Sami is thirteen minutes long—not a remarkably long match except for the fact that one of the participants is wrestling on a shattered shoulder. They're coming on immediately after one of the defining matches of the women's division at this time: Sasha Banks and Becky Lynch have just had a bout that sealed Becky as an indomitable underdog babyface, leaving her in the ring in tears after her loss only to have the audience break into her theme song, serenading their love to her.* Kevin and Sami both know that this will be their last match together for the foreseeable future. Kevin is off to the main roster, Sami is off to surgery.

---

* Kevin has terrible luck at TakeOvers in 2015. In August, he and Finn Bálor will have to put on a championship match immediately after Sasha Banks versus Bayley, widely considered one of the greatest women's matches of all time.

Kevin's reaction to that knowledge—both inside and outside the story—is the theme of the match.

It's common for wrestling matches to break down into roughly three "acts." A typical match begins with an enraged babyface having the upper hand, moves into a second act where the heel turns the tables and makes the face suffer, and ends with a third act that brings the themes to the front and resolves them. Within this basic structure, of course, there are endless variations, and Sami's matches often use this formula as a base. In fact, among a group of wrestlers playing video games from 2017, Sami starts expounding on how his loss is merely part of "a classic three-act dramatic structure," as the other wrestlers look as though they've often heard Sami talk about dramatic structure in the past.[7]

The first act of the *Unstoppable* match begins in traditional fashion, with Sami's righteous rage propelling him past his shoulder injury toward vengeance. Kevin basically falls apart in the face of this fury. He rolls out of the ring to get away from it but is immediately distracted by a chorus of "John Cena sucks" chants and doesn't see Sami roaring after him to jump him. The crowd switches immediately to an Olé chant as Kevin literally crawls on the floor to try and get away from Sami. "If you ask Kevin Owens, he'll say it's *not personal*," Byron Saxton says sarcastically on commentary as they brawl out into the crowd and then back to the ring.

In the ring, the second part of the match unfolds. Kevin ends up lying on the mat, holding out an imploring hand and begging Sami to stay back. There are a flurry of moves, many of them countered or avoided, which makes sense both in the story (they know each other so well) and outside the story (Sami's shoulder is so torn up that the Blue Thunder Bomb and tornado DDT from the top ropes that he does perform must be agonizing, so every other avoided move spares him some pain). Kevin once again dodges out of the ring and Sami follows him, suplexing him onto the floor and then trying to Helluva Kick him against the ringpost. Kevin counters the Helluva Kick, grabbing Sami out of the kick and into an extremely cautious powerbomb against the apron, so gentle it borders on being suspicious. It still must hurt like hell, and when Sami slumps onto the floor there's a look of something close to relief on his face for a moment. The hard sections of the match are over, the parts where Sami has to actually use his shoulders.

All that remains is the final act.

The referees check on Sami, but they barely get started before Kevin is pushing them aside to straddle Sami, punching him in the head. The referees shove him away and go back to checking on Sami. The camera zooms in close to Kevin's face as he stands at the ring steps. He's breathing heavily, his eyes wild, not furious but something closer to distraught. He charges back in again to start punching Sami, and again the refs push him back. Kevin seems to be in a daze, almost a fugue state, unable to accept what's happening. He swarms back at Sami and is rebuffed once more by the referees.

Back when El Generico retired in 2013, the events of the night lined up to make it possible for Kevin-the-character and Kevin-the-real-person to be feeling the same thing. This night at Unstoppable is similar, but with a twist: here the character and the real person are having the same reaction, but with different underlying emotions. Both Kevins are stunned, almost anguished at the idea that this match with Sami has to end. The beating keeps being prolonged because neither the character nor the real person wants to accept that it's over.

The trainers have come to check on Sami, joining the referees to cluster around him. Kevin's face is bereft, entranced by violence and loss. "Owens is cold and vicious," commentary says as the trainers try to ease Sami up to a sitting position, but ironically it's now that Kevin's cool dead-eyed stoicism is completely shattered, replaced not by anger but by a kind of desperate ferocity, a refusal to be separated from his enemy and friend.

He wades back in, sending trainers and referees scattering in his wake. Seizing the semi-conscious Sami like a cat with a mouse, he drags him back into the ring. He's not even going for a pin. He no longer seems to realize this is a match instead of a fight to the death. He prepares to powerbomb Sami's limp body again and the referees gather around him, pleading with him to have mercy.

Into this dramatic tableau appears General Manager William Regal, incandescent with fury. He confronts Kevin, demanding he stand down. "I'll strip you of the title!" he yells. "There'll be no match against Cena!"

Kevin seems to return to his senses at this reminder that he's got bigger prospects than Sami. He backs off... but only for a second, before turning back almost involuntarily to attack Sami once more, all pretense of being a pragmatic and steely Prizefighter who fights for a prize ("and he is not the prize") obliterated in that moment. Sami is more important than his title, than his main roster prospects, than anything.

Regal tries to stop him, only to get headbutted for his pains. Wild-eyed, Kevin rolls out of the ring and grabs a chair, the solution to so many of his interpersonal problems with El Generico. He swings it at the referees then stands over Sami as they bail from the ring. He raises the chair and there is a microsecond's pause, as if he's waiting for something. When nothing happens, he grits his teeth, unable to wait longer and risk the whole scene looking foolish, and brings the chair down squarely on Sami's injured shoulder.

Deep bass music rings out as the chair is on its downswing, announcing the presence of a new player just a belated fraction of a second later, but the chair connects and Sami's mouth winces in a distinct "ouch." But the audience is not paying much attention to Sami, because the former ROH, former TNA champion Samoa Joe has arrived on the scene to face down Kevin. He's wearing a "Samoa Joe" t-shirt as he strides down the ramp, which is an extra shock—the first indie wrestler to keep his name on entering NXT and not become "Island Jim" or some such. He and Kevin go toe-to-toe, staring at each other, a confrontation that hasn't happened since a very young Kevin faced Joe in 2004 back in Montreal. Kevin—potentially remembering that back then Joe kicked him in the face until it was a swollen mess—retreats, his eyes shifting uneasily. The crowd starts to chant "this is awesome." Sami, being checked on by the trainers, likely doesn't feel the same. But the match is over, Sami and Kevin's time in NXT has come to an end, they will never face each other again on the black-and-gold brand.

Aftermath

Sami's shoulder operation is soon after the match. It's the first time he's ever had surgery for an injury. *NXT* airs a vignette showing him being wheeled into the operating room on a gurney, his sinews and tendons bare and bloody on the medical monitor, his groggy thumbs-up from his post-op bed.

Kevin goes on to *Elimination Chamber* and faces John Cena. To everyone's utter astonishment, he beats Cena clean in a match that showcases both his high-flying moves and his brutality. Dudes in the audience wearing KO shirts high-five each other in amazed joy as his music plays. The cameras catch him backstage after the match, openly crying, thanking his parents and his wife for supporting him through all the hard times to get to this, "the greatest night of my career, there's no doubt about that." He looks into the camera, suddenly calm despite his tear-stained face. "I beat John Cena in my first match in WWE. I don't think it gets much better than that. And I'm just getting started."

TIME HEALS ALL WOUNDS
(2015-2016)

New Goals

IN JULY 2015, a rehabbing Sami Zayn shows up at NXT to talk to the fans. He's in a bright yellow polo shirt, his left arm in a black sling—an ironic bit of color coordination for the black and gold brand. "As corny as it may sound," he says, "I just wanted to take this opportunity to tell you guys that I haven't forgotten about you. And by the sounds of it," he goes on as the audience applauds and chants, "you haven't forgotten about me either." He tells them that while 2014 had been the best year of his career, 2015 has been the worst. "And it looks like it's going to stay that way, because I probably won't be back by the end of the year." The crowd groans and Sami grins wryly. "But I ain't finished! I got goals! My *goal* is to be able to find a comfortable position to sleep in. My *goal* is to be able to lift my arm above ninety degrees."

Long ago, in car rides through the Montreal winter, Sami and Kevin had talked about how making it to WWE was a goal and not a dream. Now Sami's rueful echo of those lofty goals seems painfully deliberate, especially when he concludes, "My *goal* is to come back better than ever and take back *my* NXT Championship. And as far as goals and motivations go, there's no better motivation than revenge, is there?"

He addresses the camera, his rival on the other side of it, on the other side of the barrier between NXT and the main roster. "Kevin, you might think you've got me in your rear view. You're on *Raw* every Monday, every week, and I'm sitting at home, laid up." He smiles fiercely. "But I meant every word I said when I said that your career since day one has been linked to me. Everything you've done for the last twelve years has been about you and me! And that's how it's gonna stay for the next twelve years!" Like so many of their promos to each other, it's a threat and a promise at the same time. "So guess what? Time heals all wounds, and time is gonna heal this wound, and when it does, Kevin, watch your ass, because I am coming for you!"

Sami's words resonated with the Full Sail audience because 2015 had indeed been a hard year, both inside the fiction and in reality. In June the legendary Dusty Rhodes, the mentor to a generation of WWE talent, had died, leaving the wrestling world heartbroken and grieving. At the ten-bell salute in NXT, champion Kevin Owens can be seen openly sobbing on the ramp. In July he lost the NXT Championship to Finn Bálor, beginning the first of two title runs that eventually secured him the spot of longest-reigning champion. The loss was bittersweet, as his meteoric rise meant he never got to spend much time in NXT, which he has often mentioned with regret.

On the other hand, Kevin was tearing it up on the main roster while Sami was at home working on lifting his arm above his head. His feud with John Cena stretched through the summer, continuing the theme of Kevin's jealousy: just as Kevin hated Sami in part because his son wore his t-shirt instead of Kevin's, he resented that while he was on the road struggling to make a living, his son came to worship John Cena. "John Cena became the hero to my son that I never got the chance to be!" When Cena informed him that for all his contempt for Cena's catchphrases ("Hustle, loyalty, respect!" "Never give up!") no one embodied them better than Kevin himself in his refusal to be denied, it clearly galled Kevin unbearably.* He didn't manage to win

---

* In the long run, Kevin's own babyface catchphrase, "Just keep fighting," is both a deliberate co-option of Cena's platitudes and a wry acknowledgement of the truth of Cena's observation so many years ago.

the US title from Cena, but by the end of the feud he was a force to be reckoned with.

The first wrestler to have to reckon with him was "the big guy," Ryback, of the "feed me more" chants. He had won the Intercontinental Championship after Daniel Bryan had been forced to relinquish it and retire, and Kevin came gunning for it right away.

The Intercontinental was Owen Hart's belt, the belt that, as a kid, Kevin had always competed for when he wrestled his pillow and imagined himself in WWE. When he won it in September at Night of Champions (with some help from a well-timed eye rake) his joy was so pure and palpable that he was forced to hide his face to avoid breaking his heelish persona. He had only been on the main roster for four months.

He was winning over the audience as well with his swagger and humor. "I've been called out of shape, I've been called a slob—you just called me a dirtbag!" he notes to Cena. "Well, this out of shape slob dirtbag just *beat you!*" At his title match with Finn in Tokyo, a young Japanese woman formally hands him a bouquet of flowers which he churlishly chucks out of the ring to a cascade of boos from the normally polite Tokyo crowd.

He became famous for his quips while his opponents were trapped in chinlocks, from the straightforward (a screamed "I hate this country and everything in it!" in Japan with his elbow locked around Finn's neck) to the witty (informing Jimmy Uso that he shouldn't have picked a fight with him, as "I actually like you!" he yells, wrenching Jimmy around, "especially on *Total Divas!*") One begins to suspect that his intent may actually be to make other wrestlers break into giggles, and he succeeds more than once.

At *Tribute to the Troops* in 2015, he gets Ryback into a chinlock and begins to serenade the soldiers with a belted-out "O Canada," warbling until Ryback's grimace of pain is barely hiding that he's laughing helplessly. At a house show while wrestling Roman Reigns, he puts Reigns into a chinlock and strikes up a conversation with a heckler, starting by noting "I make more in a week than you do all year," then adjusting his "punishing" grip on Reigns and calmly itemizing his income. "So, I got 35K just in royalties," he explains as Reigns has to lift his hands to cover up his laughter.

People were loving to hate him, which in wrestling is the same as loving him.

Making Me Zany

Meanwhile, Sami was impatiently waiting for his shoulder to heal and neither of them were letting fans forget it was all about the two of them. At the San Diego Comic Con in July, new NXT champion Finn, Charlotte Flair, Sami and Kevin appeared on a panel to discuss their new action figures.[1] The entire panel was conducted fully in-character, with Kevin sarcastically cheering when Sami said he was free of his sling and melodramatically moaning "awwwww" when he said his rehab was far from over. A fan asked a question about El Generico, only to have Sami say he couldn't speak for the luchador and wasn't sure what he would say if he were there. Kevin leaned forward and drawled, glancing over at Sami, "If he were here, he'd say you were pathetic." When asked what he thought his legacy would be in ten years, Kevin said, "I think it's gonna be a legacy of chaos and destruction, mostly." He paused. "But... I think what I want to be remembered most for is that I got on *Raw* on a regular basis before Sami Zayn." He gestured dismissively in Sami's direction without looking at him and took a defiant swig of water, while Sami lifted his hands with a long-suffering look on his face.

With Ryback out of the way and Sami "in his rear view," Kevin spent November and December feuding with Dean Ambrose. After beating Kevin for the Intercontinental title in December, Ambrose leaned into his epithet of "The Lunatic Fringe," noting in a backstage interview that "Kevin Owens' master plan is to drive me crazy! Drive me loony! Drive me up the wall!" He pauses for an instant, then adds with a sly look at interviewer Renee Young, "Make me *zany*!"

The wording might have been a coincidence. But considering Sami Zayn had just had his first match back three days earlier, it seems unlikely.

Sami was back, yes, but still not on the main roster. Instead, he was

TIME HEALS ALL WOUNDS

wrestling in NXT, on their first-ever international tour through the UK. Kevin started to act increasingly unhinged—ostensibly because he had lost his cherished first main roster title. But those who kept track of both of them might well have noticed that his violence and simmering rage seemed to be escalating along with the rising chances that Sami might be showing up to get his revenge as well.

Two thousand fifteen ticked over into 2016. Ambrose challenged Kevin to a last man standing match at the *Royal Rumble* for the Intercontinental title. Through the build to the Rumble, Sami continued touring with NXT as it expanded its reach and prestige, until on Jan. 14, they came to Milwaukee, Wisconsin, for the first time. Bayley defended her NXT title against Nia Jax, Finn Bálor defeated Baron Corbin and Apollo Crews, and Sami fought Tommaso Ciampa.

When he'd appeared on the Kevin Steen Show back in 2013, Ciampa had said one of his dreams was to fight El Generico, and Kevin had chuckled and said he'd have to go to Mexico to do that.[2] Ciampa never did find El Generico to fight him, but in Milwaukee he got to fight Sami Zayn, and that would probably have to do. After the match Sami grabbed the mic and talked about how great Ciampa was and how much he loved Milwaukee, noting that "someone" had once told him Milwaukee was one of his favorite towns to work in.

And Kevin's music hit.

Kevin hasn't been seen in NXT since August 2015, five months prior, so the crowd erupts in shocked delight as Kevin himself strolls out to confront Sami. He reminds Sami that the "someone" who had talked about his love for Milwaukee was himself, but after seeing how much they love a "pumpkin-headed piece of garbage" like Sami,[*] he's changed his mind. Apparently, he has come all the way to Milwaukee on his day off to let his former friend know that "I'm looking you dead in the eye right now and I'm telling you, you are a pathetic piece of trash." As Sami stares, then seethes, he declares himself untouchable. "You know why you're not going to hit me? Because last Monday night I was personally hand-picked by the chairman of this company,

---

[*] A jab at the fact that Sami had buzz-cut his hair recently. Kevin tends to complain whenever Sami's hair is shorter or longer than he prefers it.

Vincent Kennedy McMahon, to main event *Monday Night Raw* against the WWE world heavyweight champion." He boasts that he's been main eventing for months while Sami's been injured, bragging about how he's totally left Sami behind (in a typical irony of wrestling, he has come all this way on his day off to make clear just how little Sami means to him). "This company needs me, and Vincent Kennedy McMahon probably doesn't even know who you are," he sneers. Turning away from Sami, he gestures outward, threatening to drag him out of the ring and "rip him limb from limb" before, inevitably and satisfyingly, turning around and right into a Helluva Kick from Sami that sends him scrambling to the back.

The message was clear: Kevin and Sami weren't done with each other, not by a long shot. And the *Royal Rumble* was just nine days away.

Rumble

Kevin and Ambrose's last man standing match at the Royal Rumble is a wild romp of chairs and tables, the two men hurling everything they had at each other. "I hate you!" Kevin screams at one point, and Ambrose answers matter-of-factly, "I hate you, too." The match ends when Ambrose throws Kevin off the turnbuckle through two tables stacked on top of each other, creating a narratively satisfying *crunch* and leaving Kevin sprawled in the wreckage, unable to rise in time for the ten count. He's failed to regain the Intercontinental title.

Later that night, thirty minutes into the *Royal Rumble*, the crowd counts down to number eighteen and Kevin's music hits. A roar goes up from the audience as Kevin limps laboriously to the ring. He has a burst of energy as he enters the ring and comes face-to-face with AJ Styles, a surprise entrant into the Rumble in his WWE debut. The last time these two met was two years prior, in a Philadelphia armory wrestling for Tommy Dreamer's House of Hardcore, and now they trade kicks and blows with gusto until Kevin gets the best of the Phenomenal One, yells "Welcome to the WWE!" and hurls him over the ropes to the disapproval of the audience.

He doesn't get much time to gloat, however, as number nineteen is

TIME HEALS ALL WOUNDS

Dean Ambrose, who comes to the ring wincing and battered but ready to continue to scrap it up with his nemesis. The two of them battle around the ring, dodging the other remaining participants: Chris Jericho, Neville, Stardust, and two hulking members of the Wyatt Family, Luke Harper and Braun Strowman. Kevin and Stardust are briefly teaming up to manhandle Neville as the next countdown to twenty ends, and Sami Zayn's music rings out.

Kevin stares up the ramp, aghast, as Sami enters the arena and the crowd swells with excitement. Sami pauses, just looking at his friend and rival for a moment, getting ready to be in a main-roster ring together for the very first time. Kevin's chest is heaving and his eyes are as huge as if he's seen a ghost. He grabs his hair, pulling and twisting his face up into a cartoon mask of horror, as Sami starts to break into a run. The camera cuts back to Sami but you can faintly hear, under the music and the crowd hubbub, Kevin's howls of anguish.

The story will never be over between these two.

Sami slides into the ring and comes up swinging directly into Kevin's welcoming punches, the two of them instantly locking together like magnets, hockey-brawling as the crowd erupts in screams. Sami gets the best of Kevin, but is briefly distracted by Stardust and Kevin jumps him from behind. "Go back to NXT!" he yells, winding up to throw him out of the match, but Sami reverses the move and uses Kevin's rage-filled momentum against him, tossing him over the top rope, just as the crowd starts singing "Olé" for Sami. Kevin rolls to a stop against the barricade, face frozen in shock, hands arrested in midair, motionless.

Unfortunately, Sami has little time to savor this comeuppance. The next entrant into the Rumble is Erick Rowan, another member of the Wyatt Family. Harper, Strowman, and Rowan go on a tear together, and Braun Strowman dumps Sami unceremoniously out of the ring. It's the first but far from the last time that Sami or Kevin will face off against the Monster Among Men, and the results will rarely work out well for them.

The Story is Never Over

Oddly, Sami did not immediately come up to the main roster after his appearance at the *Royal Rumble*. Instead, for the next nearly three months he continued to appear in NXT despite having no clear storyline there until it grew worrisomely close to WrestleMania season. The reason behind the hesitation eventually became clear in March, when Japanese legend Shinsuke Nakamura appeared on the Full Sail monitors to challenge Sami to a match at the *NXT TakeOver* before *WrestleMania*—the beginning of another association that would thread throughout Sami's career.

Shortly before that challenge, Kevin had won his Intercontinental title back from Ambrose. He was cheerfully tormenting Neville on Raw, preparing to powerbomb him on the apron—the same move he had used on Sami so many times—when Sami's music hit to announce his presence. The camera zoomed in on Kevin's expression, his jaw dropping and fear filling his eyes as Sami charged to the rescue. They locked up with the same eager flurry of fists as commentary gleefully noted, "Your past is back to haunt you, Kevin!" Kicked in the head by Neville, thrown over the ropes again by Sami, Kevin grabbed his beloved title and retreated. It was clear Sami was about to have a momentous *WrestleMania* weekend, welcoming Nakamura to WWE and being in the Intercontinental title match in the same weekend.

Interviewed backstage after *Raw*, Sami talked about how painful it had been to be injured and watch Kevin main eventing, winning titles, moving on without him. But he was on the main roster for good now and had no intention of letting Kevin slip ahead of him again. Almost smiling, he drove home the point for anyone who didn't yet understand their dynamic.

"The one thing I can tell you for sure is that when it comes to Sami Zayn and Kevin Owens, that story is *never* over."

PAYBACK
(2016)

The Road to WrestleMania

SAMI SHOWED up on *Raw* to attack Kevin in early March 2016. By Smackdown later that week he was a guest on Miz TV. When The Miz asks Sami to tell the fans about himself he starts off with "Well, I've been doing this for a long time, fourteen years—"

Miz cuts him off, literally yelling "Cut! Cut, cut, cut," as Sami looks bemused. "Can we move it along? Fast forward to your relationship with Kevin Owens."

Sami lifts his eyebrows along with the mic. "All right. To make a long story short, the history with Kevin and I goes back thirteen years."

It's the second sentence he's spoken on TV, and it's to set firmly in place the fact that he and Kevin have a shared history that cannot be untangled from each other. He lays out the depth of their friendship, explaining the only reason they made it to where they are today was "we relied on each other. Whether it was as tag team partners, as opponents, as enemies or as friends, our names have been linked together since *day one*."

Miz, of course, smarmily notes that "like every story, there's always two sides," and invites Kevin to join them. Kevin appears, Intercontinental title slung over his shoulder and mic in hand, to inform Sami there was nothing personal about his attacks. On the other hand, Sami attacking him at the *Royal Rumble* and on *Raw* was extremely personal. "The bottom line here is, *I'm* the victim," he says as the crowd boos lustily. "I said I'm the victim!" he snaps at them, eliciting more boos.

Sami tells him he's going to take his title, "and I'm gonna do it... at *WrestleMania*!" he says, doing his very first sign-point as Kevin fumes. But it's not time yet for the two of them to have a singles match on the grandest stage of them all. As the weeks go by, other wrestlers are drawn into the title scene: first Miz, then Stardust, Dolph Ziggler, Sin Cara, and Zack Ryder, until it's a chaotic seven-man ladder match.

As the weeks tick on toward *WrestleMania*, Sami goes on a winning streak. He and Neville beat Kevin and The Miz in his first Smackdown match. He fights Stardust at Roadblock and wins his first-ever PPV singles match. He beats The Miz in his first match on Raw, with some accidental help by a distraction from Kevin. In a six-man tag on the next *Raw*, Stardust and The Miz get so annoyed when Kevin refuses to tag in and fight Sami that they walk out, which leads to Sami getting his first-ever pin of Kevin in WWE.

And so we reach Kevin and Sami's first *WrestleMania*.

Farewell

Sami is pulling double-duty this weekend, wrestling Shinsuke Nakamura two days before *WrestleMania*. It's Nakamura's debut match and Sami's farewell match and the very first time they've ever wrestled each other. When the head of the Performance Center suggests to Sami the two of them spar in the ring a little bit to get a feel for each other, Sami quickly says he'd rather they not. He soon finds out Nakamura had already said the exact same thing.[1] Both of them were eager to experience each other for the first time in the heat of the match, as fluid and unscripted as possible. It's a level of spontaneity only the best wrestlers in the world can pull off well, but when it works, it's magic.

That night in Dallas, it's magic.

It's like watching water and fire woven together, an elemental dance that creates energy in its wake. It's a welcome and a farewell, a match that needs no video package or commentary to understand. For the first time, a "Fight Forever" chant is heard on a WWE broadcast, by a crowd carried away with emotion. At the end, the victorious Nakamura is smiling through his own blood, and Sami is sitting in the corner of the ring with his head hanging down, wrung out. Nakamura approaches him and holds out his hand. Sami stares up at him and doesn't move. Nakamura, realizing, sinks to one knee to reach out to Sami as an equal. After a long moment, Sami pulls himself to his feet without assistance. Nakamura rises with him, and only then does Sami shake his hand and allow himself to be gathered into an embrace. As he walks away, he turns to wave goodbye to the NXT audience one last time, to say farewell to the ring where Sami Zayn was born, created through the loving alchemy of a wrestler and the fans who believed in him.

As of 2024, Kevin has gone back to NXT for segments and even a WarGames match.

Sami has never wrestled in NXT again.

"Motherfucker, Come On!"

Two days later, Sami Zayn is standing in the ring on the grandest stage of them all, *WrestleMania*. He had been shocked to hear 80,000 people singing his song as he came out, but he's gotten his emotions mostly under control as the other wrestlers came to the ring. In the end, he reminds himself, it's just a ring like any other. It's just a match, he's done thousands of those. It's just—

Kevin's music hits, the growling guitars calling an answering *roar* from almost a hundred thousand throats, and Sami sees the Intercontinental Champion, who is also his friend Kevin, coming down the ramp to fight him at the showcase of the immortals. His hair stands on end like an electric current has run through him, and he starts screaming at the top of his lungs, transported with rapture, urging Kevin to the ring: "Yeah, motherfucker! Come on!"[2] Fortunately for him, the camera isn't on him as he swears, it's watching Kevin coming down the ramp, his eyes locked on the ring and the title suspended above it. He's screaming back at Sami in a frenzy of emotion.

When the bell rings to start the match, everyone immediately bails out of the ring but Kevin. He throws out his chest and poses, but everyone has busied themselves grabbing the ladders scattered around the ring. Sami is the first to slide a ladder into the ring, coming in after it, grabbing one end and straightening up, only to find that Kevin has grabbed the other end.

They come face to face.

Two years before, Kevin had attended *WrestleMania* as a spectator and watched the fans standing up in a wave in response to Cesaro's win and thought "I have to have moments like that." Now as he and Sami stare at each other from either end of the ladder, the audience ripples to its feet behind them, jumping up in acknowledgement of this moment. In unison, Sami and Kevin toss the ladder away and hurl themselves at each other, their hatred outweighing any desire for a title, until the other wrestlers join in and the match is on in earnest.

People fall from ladders and fall onto ladders, a carnival of nonstop acrobatic violence that draws gasps from the audience. Over and over again, Sami and Kevin thwart each other. Sami starts to set up a ladder and is interrupted by Kevin. The ladder falls to the ropes and Kevin back drops Sami, flipping him in the air to come crashing down onto the ladder like El Generico did so many times. Unlike the flimsy aluminum ladders of PWG and ROH, these ladders have no give in them, and Sami bounces like a rag doll to the mat. Sin Cara drops from a ladder to the ropes into a flip to the outside. Ryder does an elbow drop from the top of a ladder onto The Miz. And over and over again, Kevin and Sami find their way to each other. Kevin does a frog splash to Sami as he's draped across a ladder, both of them writhing in pain in the aftermath. In the home stretch of the match, Kevin gets to the top of the ladder, his fingers brushing his precious title, only to have Sami come charging up the other side of the ladder. They start a hockey fight at the top of the ladder, teetering precariously with their arms flailing until Kevin gouges Sami's eyes with his thumb. Sami, however, drags Kevin down with him and suplexes him brutally onto another ladder, where he lies unmoving. Sami scrambles up the ladder, but The Miz knocks him off, only to finally be unseated by the victorious Ryder.

Sami has cost Kevin his title, and anyone who thinks Kevin will take this well has their delusions shattered the very next night on *Raw*, when Sami gets put into a match to potentially become number one contender for the title just won by Roman Reigns, only to have Kevin attack him backstage. When the officials try to separate them, yelling at Kevin "that's enough!" he responds "That's enough? No way!" and powerbombs Sami through a table, leaving him broken in a pile of debris.

The score was most definitely not settled.

I Wouldn't Change a Thing

It was clear their path was taking them to *Payback* and to their first singles PPV match on the main roster. For weeks they circled each other warily, criss-crossing paths with Dean Ambrose and Chris Jericho, also embroiled in their own personal feud. On April 19, *Smackdown* came to London where Kevin and Jericho teamed up against Ambrose and Sami. It would be a standard PPV-building tag except for the fact that Kevin and Jericho turned out to have immense chemistry, both of them playing self-aggrandizing heels to perfection. Overjoyed after their win, Kevin impulsively and with no warning leaped into Jericho's arms on the ramp, sending Jericho staggering under his weight. At the top of the ramp, Kevin hollered at Jericho, "You're the GOAT!"

Misunderstanding the acronym, a bemused Jericho yelled back "Well, you're the... the donkey!"

"Fine, whatever, I don't care!" Kevin bellowed, raising their hands high. *"Canada!"*

In the back, Vince McMahon was roaring with laughter.[3] His amusement at their improvisational humor would bear fruit by the end of the year, but on the way to *Payback*, Kevin and Sami were focused on each other.

"I put him on the shelf," Kevin brags in the hype video for their match, taking credit for the injury that left Sami out for seven months.

"It was me, nobody else." Elsewhere in the video, Sami remembers hearing that Kevin had been called up to the main roster as he was recovering from his shoulder surgery. "He took my debut," Sami's voice says over footage of him with his eyes closed on his hospital bed, brow creased with pain both emotional and physical. "It felt like getting kicked in the stomach. It stung. It really stung."

The video concludes with Sami saying, "It's still a race. It all comes down to the desire to be the best. Neither of us are going to advance our careers until this score is settled." They're at a standstill, locked together in hatred, hindering each other from advancing.

And yet there's still an undercurrent of sadness, of a wish for reconciliation—at least on Sami's part. In an interview during the *Payback* kickoff show he's given questions submitted by fans. "Do you have any regrets about your relationship with Kevin Owens?" one asks. "I mean, if it were up to me, we'd be getting along right now, you know? This would be a Cinderella story and we'd both be in WWE together and just enjoying this." Threading the needle between fiction and reality in that deft way wrestlers can, he went on, "But I don't know if I regret anything, because the truth is, if we changed any of it, who's to say we'd be here right now? So I wish things were different, but I wouldn't change a thing at the same time." It's an answer that doesn't close doors about any future alliance. But for now, they're still both looking for closure. Maybe *Payback* can provide it.

On May 1, 2016, Kevin Owens and Sami Zayn met for the first time one-on-one on the main roster of WWE. As they circle each other, the Chicago crowd starts to sing Olé. Kevin stops dead. "Is that for *you?*" he says, his eyes shining with sarcastic glee. Sami smiles at him, in the WWE ring together, surrounded by waves of sound "They're all chanting Olé!" Kevin gushes. He clasps his hands together, bouncing. "That's so *nice!*" At the last word, the real joy in his face outshines the sarcasm for just a second, his love for this song that Sami has always shared with him, his delight that they're in this ring together at last. Then he twists his face into a scowl. "But it won't matter! They can chant Olé all night long, you're gonna have to—"

Fed up at last, Sami punches him in the face, and they launch into a hockey brawl as the audience roars its approval. Sami starts off with the upper hand, fueled by righteous rage, hurling Kevin out of the ring and following him by flying over the ropes and smashing into him. He pounds the announce table in an excess of adrenaline as Kevin crawls away and the cheering washes over him.

After throwing Kevin into the barricade a few times to thrill the excited fans, he gets his enemy back into the ring and does a perfect Generico-esque heel kick. Kevin cowers against the ropes, raising up a pleading hand to stall Sami off, but Sami will have none of it, swooping down to punch at him.

The momentum shifts when Kevin manages to get him out of the ring and hurl him shoulder-first into the stairs, the same stairs he hurt that shoulder on originally. As Sami writhes in pain, Kevin rolls into the ring and executes a courtly bow, soaking up the boos.

Leaving the ring to grab Sami, he loudly informs the referee, "I'm bringing him in!" then announces, "no I'm not!" and throws him back into the stairs. The crowd is aflame with rage as Kevin pulls him back into the ring. "Is that all you got? I thought you'd get *payback!*" he mocks his struggling rival, emphasizing the name of the show with a sardonic lilt. He wrenches Sami into a chinlock, his arm squeezing Sami's face into tormented distortion.

The torture comes to an end as Sami digs deep for inspiration, drawing power from the audience and his own rage. He comes off the mat with a clothesline that flips Kevin a full 360 degrees, and when Kevin comes to his feet, it's clear that playtime is over. He now realizes he's possibly bitten off more than he can chew.

The energy shifts into high gear as they each start pulling out their most powerful moves. Sami drives Kevin's neck into the mat with a Michinoku Driver. He grabs his flailing foe's shirt and pulls him back into a blue thunderbomb. Kevin whacks Sami's neck into his knee with a pumphandle neckbreaker. He crushes Sami with a frog splash off the turnbuckle, and when Sami kicks out, the recoil of the kickout and his own horror topples him over, his face frozen in disbelief.

"You're done!" he screams at Sami, and throws him into the ropes in preparation for the pop-up powerbomb, his finisher at the time. Sami counters with a kick and a suplex, but Kevin comes up out of the suplex and turns Sami inside out with a clothesline. They're both panting, desperate, unable to get the upper hand. On commentary, Michael Cole says "We talk about this being the first pay-per-view of the new era, and here are two of the reasons why!" Sami counters another pop-up-powerbomb into a rollup pin, and when Kevin kicks out he goes for the tornado DDT off the turnbuckle, but Kevin counters that, bringing Sami's back down hard against his knee.

They're both spent, unable for the moment to stand. They roll slowly to the apron and lie there facing each other. Kevin glares at him, his face twisted with hatred. He manages to get to his knees and grabs Sami's ear. "You should stay down!" he says—the first time this phrase appears, one which will haunt their feuds in the future. Sami rises with him, trading punches back and forth that escalate slowly from exhausted swipes into another full-on hockey brawl there on the apron. Kevin buckles Sami over and gets his head between his legs.

The Chicago crowd knows their history, knows this is the starting position for Kevin Steen's package piledriver, a move he's never done in WWE, and roar in response, a roar that turns into a triumphant shriek as Sami flips Kevin over his head and drops him onto the apron on his back.

Outside the ring, Kevin staggers close to the announce table. There's blood in his beard. Sami realizes he's in the right position and does his spectacular diving DDT through the corner of the ring, sending Kevin skidding across the floor, arms and legs splayed.

A daredevil sequence.

Chicago starts singing Olé again.

The end comes quickly after that. They drag themselves back into the ring, where Sami gets ready to do a Helluva Kick, but Kevin greets him with a superkick to the face. He manages to get off a pop-up powerbomb, then falls across Sami's inert body, unable to move himself. The pin is almost accidental, but it counts. The crowd seethes and mutters, but Kevin has denied Sami his payback.

Kevin Owens is the Better Man

After he's declared the winner and his hand raised, Kevin hauls Sami to his feet, cuffs him across the face, then throws him out of the ring like garbage. He demands Byron Saxton come to the ring and interview him on the spot. As Saxton stands confused, he puts his hand to Saxton's ear and whispers in the loudest *sotto voce* ever, "Ask me about beating Sami Zayn, *now!*" Saxton asks if he thinks it's over between them and Kevin notes that's *not* what he told Saxton to ask him, but that's okay, "I beat Sami Zayn! Kevin Owens is the better man!" He rededicates himself to winning back the Intercontinental Championship, in such an expansive mood that he decides to join Cole, Saxton and JBL on commentary for the next match.

The next match, by the sheerest of lucky coincidences, happens to be the Intercontinental title match. The Miz, who beat Zack Ryder for the title the day after WrestleMania, is fighting Cesaro. Kevin is witty and caustic on commentary, buttering up JBL, insulting Saxton and Cole. As Miz and Cesaro battle, he's reading Twitter comments. "This one says 'I could watch Kevin and Sami fight every day,' well that's nice, but you're not gonna see it, 'cause he's *done*." He's clearly in a great mood since disposing of his nemesis and is in the middle of saying he can't believe Cole is still employed when he breaks off into a startled yelp. "What? What?"

Sami comes sailing into view, flying at Kevin over the commentary table like a demented red panda, a blur of furious arms and legs. They start brawling around the ring, leaping onto the apron. The referee hurries over to reprimand them, and as a result misses the fact that Miz is tapping out to Cesaro's sharpshooter submission hold. Cesaro, frustrated, knocks them off the apron, and The Miz takes advantage of this distraction to get the roll-up pin and retain his championship.

Six years before, Kevin had betrayed El Generico and then beaten him in what seemed to be their blow-off match, only to have the luchador come back on the attack with renewed ferocity. In 2010 and in 2016 the message was the same.

You think this is over?
It's just beginning.

BATTLEGROUND
(2016)

A Brush with Destiny

FOR THE FIRST half of 2016, Kevin and Sami were narratively locked together, inseparable. They shared the ring on six of the seven PPVs in that span, one long unbroken story arc that reached closure only in July. It became their defining feud, the one that set the tone for everything that came after: a tale full of bitterness, resentment, and obsession that somehow—implausibly—ends on a transcendent note.

After *Payback*, Kevin and Sami have clearly not found any peace. The next night on *Raw*, Kevin starts the show by confronting the new general managers—Shane and Stephanie McMahon, forced by their father to run Raw together—pointing out he had never gotten a rematch for the Intercontinental title he lost at *WrestleMania*, and demanding an opportunity. He's interrupted by Cesaro, still angry about Kevin and Sami's interference the night before, demanding another title shot himself. Shane, following wrestling logic, books the two of them in a match together.

Miz sits in on commentary and eventually can't resist interfering in the match, leading to a no-contest decision. Cesaro finds himself outnumbered against the two heels, and Sami runs in to help. In the ensuing chaos, Miz's title—the classic Intercontinental title with its snowy white strap—gets abandoned on the mat.

Sami spots it.

As Miz, Cesaro, and Kevin lie sprawling, he crosses the mat and stoops over it, long fingers hovering near the leather and gold, almost hesitating to touch it. The crowd ignites. They can feel the weight of fate behind this moment, they *know* in that instant that this is the first title Sami will win on the main roster. Hearing them, Sami smiles and picks it up, lifting it above his head, limned by the crowd's love and the call of destiny.

It will take him almost four years to fulfill that destiny, but it will be fulfilled.

A Tag Team Victory

Sami, Kevin, Cesaro and Miz end up booked in a four-way title match at *Extreme Rules* later in May. On the go-home show before the PPV, Sami and Cesaro have a match. They're the two babyfaces in this feud, respectful of each other since their epic matches in NXT, but there's a tension as well. Sami's focus on Kevin has already cost Cesaro a victory, and Cesaro suspects (rightly, as it turns out) that he will end up collateral damage in his friend's blood feud with Kevin.

Indeed, Miz is on commentary, and soon he and Kevin start brawling into the ring, nullifying the match. General Manager Shane McMahon appears to book the traditional go-home match. "Tonight, you guys are gonna get your aggression out on each other in tag team form." He tells them it will be Sami and Cesaro versus Kevin and Miz, an announcement that none of them are happy with ("He's the worst one!" Kevin yells). Then co-General Manager Stephanie McMahon comes out to shake things up a bit, suggesting they cross the alliances, making it Cesaro and Miz versus Kevin and Sami.

Kevin breaks into indignant squawking. Sami is dumbfounded. But Shane and Stephanie agree this seems more fun, the crowd breaks into jubilant "yes" chants, and the match is official.

Sami and Kevin's first tag match in WWE.

Which they *win*.

It's a messy, petty, spiteful match, full of hilarious bickering and one-upmanship on both sides. It ends with Kevin hauling Cesaro out of the ring and hurling him into a barricade, giving Sami the space to Helluva Kick Miz and get the pin. Sami barely has time to get his hand raised before he's eating a superkick to the face by his own tag team partner. "I won, too!" Kevin tells the referee, holding out his hand to be raised in turn as Sami lies sprawled on the mat and wiping the sweat off his brow to flick it contemptuously onto Sami. It's not the most auspicious first win for a tag team, but here's a tiny detail that could easily be missed in all the hubbub:

After Kevin threw Cesaro into the barricade, as Sami got into position for the Helluva Kick, the camera caught a glimpse of Kevin going to his knees on the floor outside the ring, putting his face up to the apron so that the camera and the fans couldn't see his expression as he watched Sami hit the finisher for their first shared victory in WWE.

Obsession

The match on May 22 at *Extreme Rules* is a highlight of the card, a fast-paced affair between the four veterans that leaves the crowd on their feet. Sami literally kicks it off, rushing forward at the bell to Helluva Kick Kevin in the face. In the end, Sami manages to Helluva Kick Cesaro and it looks like victory is in his grasp, but Kevin grabs his feet and drags him out of the ring to break up the pin. Furious, Sami forgets the match and the fallen Cesaro entirely to chase after Kevin, and The Miz slips back into the ring with an opportunistic pin on Cesaro to retain his title. Sami jumps back into the ring, his face frozen in chagrin and dismay, realizing his own thirst for revenge has cost him the title.

Slowly, that righteous anger was morphing into something more negative, something that was starting to cost Kevin and Sami alike. In 2010, Kevin and El Generico had ended up locked in a vengeful hatred, unable to break free, each focused on tearing the other apart until even their friends and allies gave up on them and walked away. Now in 2016 the same thing was happening to Kevin and Sami.

After their failure to capture the Intercontinental title, they quickly found themselves in the field for the Money in the Bank ladder match. If one of them could just climb a ladder and grab that briefcase, the top of the card would open up for him. But over and over again, they couldn't get past each other. Cesaro, who had also moved from the Intercontinental picture to the Money in the Bank race, provided the exasperated voice of sanity as he had to deal with Sami's increasingly blinkered vision.

One show during the build-up featured Cesaro teaming with Sami again, against the *ad hoc* and reluctant team of Kevin and Alberto Del Rio. When Kevin ditches Del Rio and walks to the back, Sami stares after him and then—after a quick apology to the flabbergasted Cesaro —jumps down to pursue him. "This is a *tag match*, you idiots!" Cesaro bellows after them, only to turn around and walk right into a DDT by Del Rio. From then on, the match is basically a singles match between Cesaro and Del Rio, with Kevin and Sami running in and out of the match at intervals, intent only on each other, until Kevin manages to pin Cesaro and steal a win. Climbing onto one of the ladders set up along the ramp, he blows a taunting kiss to Sami, who pounds the mat in frustration while the long-suffering Cesaro struggles to process what has just happened to him.

Money in the Bank, the June PPV, is no different. Kevin and Sami lock up into a hockey brawl the instant the bell rings as commentary asks "will they distract each other?" To no one's surprise, the answer is yes, although their distraction doesn't keep them from constructing a raucous ladder match full of bumps with Del Rio, Cesaro, Dean Ambrose, and Chris Jericho. This is the match that Jericho remembers with laughter as the time Sami walked into the locker room and told everyone how the match was going to go, as well as the match where Kevin and Sami kept suggesting wilder and wilder spots that Jericho kept vetoing. Despite the vetoes, Kevin and Sami contrive to slam each other into ladders wherever possible. At one point Sami does a Michinoku driver to Kevin on a ladder lying sideways on the mat, leaving Kevin on his back on the side of the ladder, his head hanging off the end and nearly touching the mat, a ninety-degree angle of agony. There's a showcase spot with two ladders set up side-by-side under the briefcase, four men on one ladder and two on the other, a seething mass of muscled humanity trying to reach that briefcase. There's one moment where Sami is all alone on top of a ladder. The camera cuts to a close-up of his shining hopeful face, one hand reaching out, just able to brush the corner of the case, which sends it swinging off into space away from him with a majestic slowness before he's interrupted and pulled back down the ladder.

In the end it's Dean Ambrose that's holding the briefcase, there on top of the ladder. He cashes in later that very evening to unseat Seth Rollins.

Kevin and Sami are right back where they began, at the base of the ladder looking up. In each other's way.

On *Raw* the next night, they got another chance to settle the score, their second singles match on the main roster. On the pre-show, an exasperated Sami talked about how they had cost each other the Rumble, the Intercontinental Championship, the Money in the Bank briefcase. ""The relationship between Kevin Owens and I has now reached the point of an obsession," he concluded. "My career is never going to move forward until I can put this rivalry to rest. So tonight, that's what I'm going to do. I'm going to end this story." Ambitious words from a man who once claimed that this story would never be over, but surely once Sami won the match with a surprise rollup, that would certainly be the end of the—

No, of course not. Kevin attacked Sami on the ramp after the match and things broke down into a brawl that ranged through the arena, Sami leaping off boxes at Kevin, Kevin sobbing "I hate you!" at the top of his lungs. Eventually it took six referees to break it up, three black-and-white striped bodies each holding Sami and Kevin in place as they raged and spit defiance at each other.

There was a brand split and a draft brewing, but at this point the boundaries between *Raw* and *Smackdown* were at their most porous, so Sami showed up that week on *Smackdown* as well to challenge former champion Seth Rollins to a match. Rollins laughingly told Sami he was surprised "your master, Kevin Owens, let you off your leash for a couple of hours." Indeed, the tether between the two was almost palpable—but the only "master" was the anger and hatred holding them back from focusing on higher goals.

On June 27, Chris Jericho has a segment of his talk show, "The Highlight Reel," in which he decides to interview Sami and Kevin, who he describes as "hell-bent at ruining their own careers." As Sami and Kevin stand and glower wordlessly at each other, Jericho reminds them (and the audience) that Sami was the best man at Kevin's wedding, taunting Sami with Kevin's past betrayal until Sami cuts him off, saying he came out here to put an end to their feud so that they can both finally move on. "My career isn't going anywhere until this is over and guess what, Kev, neither is yours," he says, suggesting a final showdown at *Battleground* in July.

Kevin, after insisting he was always the better friend because he *never* held it against Sami that Sami signed with WWE first and left him behind, while Sami irrationally holds a grudge for Kevin beating him for the title, agrees to a match. "You wanna go one more time at *Battleground*? You got it."

As they stand and stare at each other across the great chasm of their differences, Jericho trash-talks Sami, condescends to Kevin, and announces that they both are lucky to even be in the same ring as himself, the legendary Chris Jericho. While he talks, Kevin and Sami slowly shift their stares from each other to him. Wrapping up, he tilts back his head and closes his eyes in self-adulation, and as he does Kevin and Sami—simultaneously, spontaneously, with no communication between them—kick him in the face.

Sami's kick is a big boot while Kevin's is a superkick, and because of the follow-through momentum, they finish the assault with their backs to each other. As Jericho crumples to the mat, Kevin and Sami both turn slowly and make eye contact, their expressions carefully neutral in response to this moment of perfect teamwork. After a long pause, Kevin is the first to leave, brushing past Sami to walk away, leaving Sami looking after him with a complex mix of anger, sadness, and perplexity on his face.

Battleground

Battleground is held July 24, 2016, in Washington, DC. The show is also notable for being the only triple threat ever between the members of the Shield, so there were two deeply personal rivalries on the card.*

Sami comes right at Kevin with a Helluva Kick the instant the bell rings, but Kevin rolls out of the ring to dodge him. As Sami pursues, Byron Saxton on commentary explains the dynamics of the match: "See, sometimes we have a hard time getting over an ex-boyfriend or girlfriend—"

He's forced to cut the thought short as Sami levels a punch at Kevin and they are off in earnest. The crowd launches into noisy and relatively equal dueling chants as they fight back into the ring and there are the first of many counters between the two, with Sami going for a tornado DDT and Kevin shoving him at the apex on the turnbuckle so Sami crotches himself on the ropes. He then cannonballs Sami as he tries to recover in the corner, almost bowling over the referee, and unloads a series of punches, chops, and kicks, leaving Sami writhing in pain.

The Olé chant breaks out.

Kevin stops his assault to acknowledge it, saying "Oh, that's *cute!*" while standing squarely on Sami's hand as Sami struggles and shoves at him. Sami manages to get to a sitting position, only to take a couple of sharp kicks to the back. Kevin goes for a third kick, but he stops short just to enjoy Sami's anticipatory flinch, then puts him in a chinlock.

Chinlocks are often used in wrestling as "rest holds," a chance for the wrestlers to catch their breath and get any updates they need from the referee. As such they can naturally be a bit boring sometimes. This one, however, manages to be the most dynamic chinlock ever. Sami squirms, he struggles, he grabs at Kevin's hair, he nearly manages to get to his feet and Kevin pulls him back down again and bites at his fingers to boot. Kevin informs the referee that Sami wants to give up.

The ref, unconvinced, asks Sami "Do you want to give up?"

"Yes he does!" snaps Kevin.

---

* After Ambrose won by pinning Roman Reigns, the Smackdown roster came out to celebrate the win and Jimmy and Jey Uso lifted Ambrose up on their shoulders, a sight that might have burned itself into the future Tribal Chief's memory.

"No!" wheezes Sami, gasping and choking and trying to shimmy out of the hold.

Kevin is indignant. "Yes, you do!"

Sami finally manages to get to his feet, jumping up into a clothesline that knocks Kevin over, and the action is on again.

Eventually, Kevin drags Sami out of the ring and tries to powerbomb him onto the apron, but Sami grabs the ropes and pulls himself out of the move, onto the apron. He goes to do the Arabian Press, springboarding off the ropes backwards onto Kevin—

And something goes wrong.

It happens in a split-second, so fast the naked eye can hardly make sense of it in real-time. Sami under-rotates and instead of arcing back toward Kevin he drops straight down toward the apron headfirst. Kevin instantly leaps forward, pushing at Sami to change his trajectory just enough so he comes down on his shoulder rather than his neck. Sami's feet come down squarely on Kevin's back and they both go sprawling. When they get to their feet the shoulder impact becomes part of the match, so seamlessly and completely that people will later insist it must have been a pre-planned spot.[1]

Kevin takes advantage of Sami's mistake and its connection to the injury that left him out for so many months, shoving him shoulder-first into the ringpost to both highlight and aggravate any damage. As they get back into the ring Sami grabs Kevin into a Blue Thunderbomb, but —again stressing that banged-up shoulder—he can't lock in the pin well enough to keep Kevin from kicking out. He shakes his arm, trying to get the numbness out of it, powering through the pain. Kevin then gets him into a crossface submission—not his usual submission hold, but it allows him to stretch out Sami's arm, putting further pressure on that shoulder. "Give up! Give up!" he yells, but Sami manages to extend one long leg to the ropes and break the hold.

The pace picks up, both of them pulling out more and more spectacular moves as they grow more desperate to finally put the other away. Kevin clotheslines Sami against the turnbuckle, sending his limbs flying. Sami does a brainbuster to Kevin on the apron, leaving commentary gasping. Sami tries to leap through the corner ropes to

DDT Kevin, but Kevin superkicks him halfway through the move, throwing him back into the ring for a cannonball and a frog splash.

A "fight forever" chant breaks out. It's the second time that chant has been heard in WWE. It's the second time Sami has heard it this year.

The pace becomes blistering, a sequence of moves and near-falls that pulls the crowd from their chairs for a standing ovation during one of the brief breaks in the action. Sami charges at Kevin for a Helluva Kick but runs straight into a pop-up powerbomb. Kevin's finishing move. The audience catches its breath as Sami lies motionless, then explodes again as Sami gets one foot just barely to the ropes at the last second, stopping the count.

There's a sudden sense of stillness, a kind of narrative hush. Kevin jumps to his feet in disbelief and horror. Sami has pulled himself to his knees and is swaying, half-conscious. There is a feeling that this is it, the decisive moment.

Kevin and Sami, the real people behind the characters, haven't planned exactly what they're going to say at this moment. They're waiting to see how their characters feel when they reach this point, "the culmination of all those years."[2]

"Why?" Kevin howls at Sami. "Why won't you stay down?" He slaps him across the face.

Sami reaches out toward him woozily. Kevin bats his faltering hand aside. "Don't make me do this! Stay down!" It's an intriguing choice of words, revealing that maybe at some level Kevin doesn't want to be attacking Sami, that he might actually want to stop and break the cycle, but can't figure out how. He slaps Sami across the face again.

This time Sami starts to smile up at him and beckons tauntingly: *Come on, keep it coming, I'm not done yet.*

Kevin grabs his own hair, yanking, goaded past all endurance. "Stay down!" he commands one more time, with one more slap.

And this time, Sami comes roaring up off his knees with an answering slap that connects so hard it almost knocks Kevin out.[3] Kevin staggers backwards, shaking his head, wounded, then comes charging forward with a bellow of rage. Sami meets him mid-charge, suplexing him into the corner, then yanking him into another suplex that leaves Kevin up against the far turnbuckle, almost out on his feet.

Sami puts his back up against the turnbuckle and looks across the ring at Kevin, breathing heavily. He takes a moment and his breathing stills. He closes his eyes. He rushes forward into a Helluva Kick. Kevin falls forward into his arms, out cold, and Sami holds him and looks down at him.

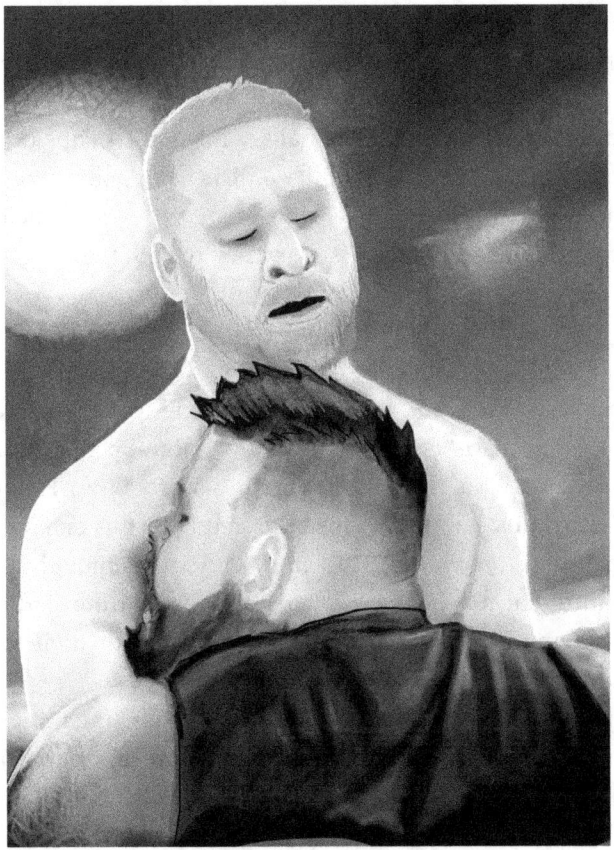

Physical poetry.

He holds him for ten full seconds, though it feels like much longer. It's a moment charged with emotions, none of them easily put into words. It's the kind of moment that human beings created dance, or song, or wrestling for, where the physicality of the act expresses more than any scratching pen, any clattering keyboard, any chattering voice. It's a moment they will return to time and again in future matches, adding new layers and new nuances every time.

For ten seconds, Sami looks down at Kevin's vulnerable unconscious face, and an impossible range of emotions go across his own.

Then, with equal parts gentleness and resolution, he pushes Kevin back into the corner. He grabs his best friend and worst enemy by the chin, lifting his face to look into it one more time, then runs back to the far corner, turns, and delivers the second Helluva Kick, the one that will stop this chapter of their story and finish the cycle of bitterness and revenge.

Kevin falls forward and Sami falls with him, collapsing into the three count. The bell rings. Kevin lies still as Sami goes to his knees in tears that slowly transform into a smile of joy and relief as he hears the audience cheering. It's done. He's free. They're both free.

Destiny Again

Just before *Battleground*, WWE had a draft designed to put a stricter brand split into place. Sami was chosen by Raw in the third round. Kevin was chosen in the fourth round, also to Raw. This decision puzzled many fans, because with a bitter feud like this one, wouldn't it make more sense to split them up after? Other fans thought that there was a chance that maybe, *maybe,* with the closure from Battleground, Kevin and Sami could move into a new chapter of their story, one where they could slowly come to work together.

Kevin's reaction to the draft, of course, was howling indignation at being drafted later than Sami. Sami's reaction to the news had been wry laughter. "Destiny keeps pulling us together," he said.

This time, however, destiny was going to swerve everybody.

THIS IS OURS
(2016-2017)

Universal

IN 2016, WWE tried out a new style of documentary. The idea of the "365" series was to document one full year of a wrestler's career, and Kevin Owens was picked to be the first subject of the new format. For a complete year, from *SummerSlam 2016* to *SummerSlam 2017*, a camera crew followed Kevin even more closely than usual, capturing all the details of those three hundred sixty-five days. As it turns out, they happened to pick one of the most turbulent and dramatic years of Kevin's career. Momentous events swept Kevin up like a boat in a flood, in which he—and Sami as well—struggled to maintain any kind of control of their careers. The results included indelible moments and shocking reversals of fortune, not just in front of the audiences but also backstage, witnessed by the relentless documentary cameras.

This first full year of Kevin and Sami's time on the main roster established a pattern that has generally borne true across the years: they tend to have extremely high-profile *WrestleMania* matches, followed by relatively lackluster *SummerSlams*. In 2016 they were in a *WrestleMania* title match together, where Kevin walked in as champion. By *SummerSlam*, however, their momentum had cooled off considerably, despite their emotional and acclaimed feud. Sami found himself on the kickoff show, teaming with Neville to fight the Dudley Boyz. Kevin's comedic alliance with Chris Jericho landed the two of them a spot on the SummerSlam card proper, fighting Enzo Amore and Big Cass, but there was no doubt both Kevin and Sami wanted more prestigious spots on the card.[1]

One person they could both be happy for, however, was their mutual friend Finn Bálor, who had recently arrived on the main roster and was steadily climbing the card. At *SummerSlam* Bálor and Seth Rollins fought each other to see who would be the inaugural Universal Champion, a title unveiled by recently-appointed *Raw* General Manager Mick Foley. Bálor emerged victorious but at a heavy cost.

In the middle of the match, Rollins had thrown Bálor into a barricade and Bálor's shoulder had given way. He'd kept fighting, feeling his shoulder pop back in and out of place, and said to himself, "oh, you're not going to be wrestling, not for a long time."[2]

The night after *SummerSlam*, the first Universal Champion came to the ring with his arm in a sling and sorrowfully handed his title back to Foley, less than 24 hours after he had won it. He was eventually diagnosed with a torn labrum, torn bicep, torn pectoral, and a broken socket after a surgery that took six hours to complete[3] and faced a long and agonizing rehabilitation.

Which left WWE with a shiny new world title and no one to hold it.

They acted quickly. The same night Bálor relinquished the title, there were matches to determine the participants in a fatal four-way match for a new champion. Big Cass defeated Rusev. Roman Reigns defeated Chris Jericho, despite Kevin's best efforts to help his friend. Seth Rollins beat Sami. And Kevin beat Neville, Sami's tag partner from the night before.

On August 29, 2016, in Houston, Kevin, Reigns, Rollins, and Big Cass met in a fatal four-way elimination match. Crucially, in this type of match wrestlers are eliminated as they get pinned, with the winner being the last wrestler unpinned.

Also crucially, there are no disqualifications in this kind of match.

After eliminating Big Cass, Kevin was managing to hold his own against Reigns and Rollins. It was assumed—by fans on the Internet, by the Houston crowd—that either Reigns or Rollins would be the winner, and they weren't terribly pleased with either option. When Triple H, the COO of WWE, shows up after a long hiatus and lays out Reigns, it's clear that he's here to hand the victory to Rollins, who he's coddled and protected ever since Rollins betrayed his Shield brothers. Triple H shoves the exhausted Rollins into the ring to pin Reigns, to the jaded boos of the audience. Then he rolls Kevin into the ring and props him up. Seth walks toward them, smirking.

And the match, the path of WWE, and Kevin's career all take a sharp left turn.

A shocking twist.

"The Cerebral Assassin" Triple H swings around and attacks Seth with the air of a father who's done spoiling his entitled child. Sitting in the corner of the ring, Kevin watches this with his jaw dropped. Triple H gives him a level look, nods, and delivers the Pedigree, his finishing move, to Seth. The crowd goes insane. Kevin looks utterly dumbfounded. He scurries over to Seth's body and pins him, staring up at Triple H the whole time. His face is flushed, his eyes wide. The bell rings. He's just become a top champion in WWE.

The cameras catch him after the match, coming backstage with his new championship. They show him thanking Triple H, getting a hug from Mick Foley. He walks over to where Vince McMahon is monitoring the show to get the boss's opinion on the match, and McMahon embraces him, smiling.

The cameras also catch the very first person he walks up to after he comes through the curtain, which is Sami Zayn.

Sami's mind has gone totally blank under the onslaught of memories and emotions brought on by seeing Kevin win the highest rank in WWE.[4] Kevin wraps him up in his arms, both of them starting to cry, and mumbles into his shoulder, *"This is ours."* It's a vow, a declaration, a deliberate callback to the moment when Sami signed his WWE contract in front of him, years ago.

And it's just as bittersweet, just as meaningful and hollow at the same time, because you can't truly share a contract or a title, not really. But over the next six months, Sami is woven into Kevin's story as much as possible, in ways both large and small. They have three singles matches in that time, and each one uses Kevin and Sami's history to underscore the themes of the current canon, ranging from triumph to despair, from friendship to betrayal.

Match 1: *"I Am the Universal Champion"*

The very next week on *Raw*, Sami is being interviewed backstage. He admits to feeling "directionless" since beating Kevin at Battleground, noting that it "stings" that Kevin is now the Universal champion, that he's feeling "a little bit of jealousy."

On cue, Kevin swaggers into the scene, title slung over his shoulder. "It's funny," he smirks, "just a couple of years ago it felt like *I* was trying to catch up to *you*. You got signed to WWE first. You won the NXT title first. A couple of months ago you even got drafted to *Raw* before I did." He hoists the title. "But *this* has always been the finish line, hasn't it? And guess what, Sami. I won the race."

Sami rolls his eyes as Kevin charges on, "You know what this means," he says, pointing to the title. "This means that I am better than you. Even at your best, the only time you've had success is when I was backing you up. And now I'm WWE Universal champion and you?" He pauses, dead-eyed. "Are *nothing.*"

Sami scoffs and shoots back, "You know as well as I do that the race between you and me? It's not over, and it never, *ever* will be." Kevin's sneering smile slips away as Sami informs him that when Sami wins the Universal title, he'll do it on his own terms, not by having someone hand it to him.

And so the first time Kevin comes to the ring as Universal champion, that night, it's to fight Sami.

It's a non-title match—Sami never gets a title match against Kevin during this run—but he kisses the title lingeringly, showing off for Sami before handing it over. It's a solid 13-minute match that starts with the traditional hockey fight flying hands. Sami takes a beautiful dive over the ropes, executes a perfect Blue Thunderbomb, does his barricade moonsault. For his part, Kevin throws Sami into barricades, clotheslines him repeatedly, and crushes him with a corner cannonball.

At one point he demands, as he did at *Battleground*, that Sami "stay down," adding "*I* am the WWE Universal champion!" The disjunction between the backstage "this is ours" could hardly be more dramatic—and yet, at the same time, the fact that Sami is his inaugural match as champion means something, it connects Sami to the title, it stitches him into the story. When Sami surges up and slaps him again, it's the public version of the backstage embrace, in the bizarro wrestling world where hatred in front of the cameras is so often the mirror image of love behind them.

The balance of the match shifts when Sami comes down on the ankle he tweaked the week before against Rollins. Hobbling, stumbling, he still snaps "do not stop this match" at the referee that checks on him. But eventually he limps directly into a superkick, then a pop-up powerbomb, and it's over.

Kevin comes up out of the pin bellowing "Yeah!" at the top of his exulting lungs. He demands his title back and is embracing it fervently when Roman Reigns' music hits and he finds himself face-to-face with Reigns, out for blood after being cheated out of the title Kevin carries. As Kevin slowly retreats, Chris Jericho comes to the ring as well to back up his friend. The scene is set. Kevin will be feuding with both Reigns and Rollins in the months to come, with Jericho as his wingman.

Match 2: "That's Why I'm the Champ"

Kevin and Jericho are comedy gold together, able to take anything and make it hilarious. They're able to get the mere word "it" over with the fans by becoming muddled about what exactly the "it" was that a person was going to get when they were "going to get it," to the point where audiences are hanging on Jericho's phrases, giggling into his dramatic pauses, ready to explode when he gets to the "it." They ping off each other in oddball, delightful ways, as when Jericho informs Mick Foley that Kevin is "the longest-reigning WWE Universal champion," with Kevin nodding into the silence and adding solemnly, "Seven days." Between them they improvise a barrage of hilarious bits. When Jericho starts putting people on "his list" for slights and offenses, it soon becomes a literal list that Jericho carries around with him, a clipboard with "The List of Jericho" printed on the back in cursive font. Jericho, always a genius for delivering lines in satisfyingly meme-like ways, hones it to perfection: when a wrestler, interviewer, fan, camera operator, entire city, or anyone else annoys him, he fixes them with a steely eye, clicks his pen menacingly, pauses to let anticipation build, and barks *"You just made the list!"* to a delighted gale of laughter from the audience. Kevin is always at his side, pointing out who should be on the list, sometimes peering at it and correcting his spelling *sotto voce*.

But it's not all sunshine and roses for the duo. There's a constant tension between them as well, because they each know the other is a treacherous backstabber. Early on, they talk about possibly becoming tag team champions together, and as they rhapsodize about how great it would be, Kevin calls them "Team Kevin and Chris" while Jericho calls them "Team Chris and Kevin," not pointedly or passive-aggressively but as if they're unaware they're revealing their real priorities. Jericho saves Kevin's title over and over again—handing him brass knuckles, slipping him the key during a cage match, attacking opponents disguised in a luchador's mask—but at the same time he keeps accepting matches for Kevin, putting that precious title at risk. At key moments, Kevin abandons Jericho to a furious Reigns or Rollins, saving his own skin. For months they teeter on the precipice of a split, always coming back together with exaggerated pronouncements of eternal fidelity. As 2016 starts to wind down, the fans can sense that the most logical conclusion to all of this, the most satisfying ending, would be Kevin and Jericho in a match for the Universal title at *WrestleMania*.

And where is Sami while Kevin savors his new best friend and their utterly unbreakable bond?

For a few weeks after losing to Kevin, Sami feuds with Jericho. Jericho has him on his talk show and Sami plays the role of Cassandra, telling Jericho that "the truth about Kevin is he doesn't care about the fans, he doesn't care about you, he only cares about Kevin Owens." This earns him a cell phone to the side of the head and a PPV match with Jericho in September at *Clash of Champions*, which he loses. Shortly after that, he catches the attention of Braun Strowman.

The former member of the Wyatt Family, known as the "Gift of Destruction" and "The Abominable Strowman" at this time, is a 6'8" bully who has been demanding GM Mick Foley give him some *real* competition every week, only to annihilate whatever unfortunate has a match against him. After a few weeks of watching Strowman torment others, Sami eventually storms to the ring as Strowman is threatening Foley, facing him down. This leads to Sami's first storyline on the main roster not related to Kevin, a confrontation that showcases both his bravery and his tendency toward self-destructive obsession.

In November at *Survivor Series*, he's pitted against *Smackdown*'s The Miz for the Intercontinental Championship, the title that slipped through his hands earlier in the year because of his single-minded focus on Kevin. This time he has The Miz in a submission hold and it looks like he might win when Miz's wife Maryse rings the bell, tricking Sami into thinking Miz has tapped out so he releases the hold and ends up rolled up for the loss. As punishment for that loss, Stephanie McMahon puts him in a match with Strowman where he gets beaten so savagely that Mick Foley insists on calling off the match and giving the win to Strowman. A "backstage exclusive" video shows a dazed-looking Sami sitting on the floor as medical staff and a shaken Foley hover, worried, over him. "Am I bleeding?" he mumbles, pawing glassy-eyed at his bloody mouth.

Strowman returns to gloating that no one can defeat him, bragging no one could even last two minutes against him. When Sami demands a rematch to prove himself, Foley refuses. "Sometimes in life, you have people who need to be saved from themselves," he says. "This is a matchup that you cannot win!" Sami had spoken, while in NXT, about how Mick Foley was a huge influence on his wrestling, how he admired his "sacrificial" style of wrestling, how he would "give every fiber of his being. You could tell there was that passion that drove him."[5] Now, rejected by his hero, he lashes out, telling Foley he's given up his ideals, that he would never have let someone stop him from tackling even the greatest obstacle, that he's a hypocrite, storming off as Foley warns him, "Let it go!"

It's in the middle of this feud that Sami and Kevin have their next singles match.

The match furthers both of their stories. Sami is, as always, a reminder of Kevin's bone-deep perfidy. He and Jericho's friendship has started to become more and more rocky and unstable, and Jericho has even started to eye his "best friend"'s Universal title. For Sami, the match serves to reinforce the idea that he never gives up, even when it's clear he's defeated. This time they both pull out moves that send them over the ropes, Kevin with his rare somersault plancha that Sami follows up with a soaring tope. There's a moment where Sami has Kevin up on the turnbuckle, in position for what commentary says might be a superplex, but longtime El Generico fans know is the right position for his turnbuckle brainbuster, the finisher Sami had never done in WWE. Kevin knows it as well, and there's a burst of panicked energy as he fights his way out of it and counters it.

In the thick of the fight, Kevin yells after a move, "That's why I'm the champ and you're not!" In the end, Kevin is near-exhaustion and manages to hit a pop-up powerbomb but then merely falls across Sami's body, a win granted more by gravity than by willpower. For his part, Sami's long legs still feebly kick, trying to get out of the pin, but it's no good.

The loss means Foley won't trust him in a match against Strowman until Sami in desperation threatens to leave and go to *Smackdown*. Eventually, won over by his passion, Foley puts him in a PPV match against Strowman, a timed match where Sami will win if he can simply last for ten minutes. Sami lasts the ten minutes, becoming one of the few wrestlers to ever beat Strowman. In fact, he's just Helluva Kicked Strowman and is about to make the pin when time runs out, leaving it an open question whether Sami could just possibly have beaten him straight-up.

On the same PPV card, Kevin battles Roman Reigns almost to a standstill, broken only by Chris Jericho coming out and attacking him. But of course Jericho's attack means Reigns is disqualified and Kevin is the winner—Jericho attacked Kevin in order to help him, in a play on the topsy-turvy logic of wrestling, and their friendship remains strong.

For now.

Festival of Friendship

Twenty sixteen ended with Sami defeating Strowman and Kevin retaining his championship with the help of Jericho. Their fortunes, however, would take a sudden sharp reversal from the very first show of 2017.

Infuriated by his loss to Sami, Braun Strowman demanded a rematch. Specifically, he insisted on a Last Man Standing stipulation, where the winner is whoever cannot rise to their feet at a ten-count. Sami fights with everything he has, even throwing himself bodily at Strowman to send them both hurtling off the stage and through a table at one point, but time was not on his side this match. Commentary calls him "valiant," the crowd cheers him in a frenzy, but eventually Strowman simply wears him down until he is no longer able to get to his feet. By the end, Strowman is interrupting the count to do his finisher to Sami again, prolonging the suffering to guarantee Sami can't rise. "Finally," Michael Cole sighs as Sami lies motionless and Mick Foley arrives with a stretcher, and even then Strowman knocks over the stretcher, picks up Sami's limp body and hurls him into a barricade one last time. "Ashes to ashes, dust to dust," he bellows, stomping off. Sami's feud with Strowman is basically over from here. Soon Strowman will be moving up the card to challenge Kevin for a match and feud with Roman Reigns.

On the same show, Kevin hosts the Kevin Owens Show, his talk show. Jericho is with him and announces he'll be in the *Royal Rumble*, to Kevin's horror. If Jericho wins, he'll get a shot at Kevin's title. "Don't get me wrong, we both deserve to be in the main event of *Wrestlemania*," he says, "but I don't want to fight my best friend!" The crowd very much wants to see him fight his best friend. Kevin and Jericho have been making the audience laugh and leaving them on the edges of their seats for months now. A title match at *WrestleMania* seems inevitable. Then Kevin's guest arrives on the show. It's Goldberg.

If this were a documentary, here is where the ominous foreshadowing music would start.

Bill Goldberg is fifty years old when he appears on the Kevin Owens Show. Once the highest-paid wrestler in WWE's rival promotion, WCW, he's famous for his year-and-a-half-long undefeated streak. Even at fifty, he's a grizzled mountain of muscle who can still pull off his two best-known moves—the spear and the jackhammer powerslam—in explosive fashion. He recently showed up in WWE for the first time in over a decade, inspired by a desire to have his ten-year-old son see him actually wrestle. Fresh off a feud with Brock Lesnar (whom he beat in one and a half minutes), he's on Kevin's show to announce his entrance into the Rumble—and to give Kevin's shiny title a nice long look.

Kevin—a tribalist WWE fan as a teen who always disliked Goldberg[6]—responds with furious bluster. "Wait, wait, wait, wait, wait, no no no, this is *my* show! I'm *Kevin Owens*, I'm the *Universal champion*, and *I don't care who you are!*" But soon Roman Reigns comes out to face down Goldberg, then Strowman arrives. Kevin, with Jericho, makes himself scarce, sidelined on his own show. The next week, Jericho (with a lot of help from Kevin) beats Roman Reigns for his first United States Championship. Kevin clearly is hoping that helping Jericho win a title will keep his increasingly avaricious friend from coming after the one on Kevin's shoulder.

The 2017 *Royal Rumble* was won by Randy Orton, taking that storyline to *Smackdown* and out of this narrative. On the *Raw* after the Rumble, Brock Lesnar, still smarting from his *SummerSlam* loss, challenged Goldberg to a rematch at *WrestleMania*. On the same show, Sami got a non-title match with Jericho and won, setting him up for a match for the US Championship. The road to *WrestleMania* seemed clear—if Sami were to beat Jericho for the title, Jericho would naturally turn his attention to Kevin's title, causing a rupture in their friendship. Sami's gain causing the loss of Kevin's friend *and* his title would be perfect poetic justice. Eagle-eyed fans soon noticed the venue for *Fastlane*, the last PPV stop before *WrestleMania*, was carrying an ad trumpeting a Zayn-Jericho match for the US title at the show.[7] The storyline for Kevin and Jericho to fight each other on the grandest stage of them all for a top title was picking up momentum.

And then all of the wheels start to fall off.

Goldberg accepts Lesnar's challenge for a match at *WrestleMania* but decides to also challenge Kevin for his title at *Fastlane*. Jericho accepts on Kevin's behalf, to Kevin's dismay. Then Sami abruptly gets his title match with Jericho on that *Raw*, not at *Fastlane*. And he loses.

Something is going wrong. It seems unlikely Kevin is going to defeat Goldberg just before Goldberg has a huge match against Lesnar. And indeed, Jericho, who had been told just a few days before that he and Kevin would be fighting for the Universal title at *WrestleMania*, suddenly finds out backstage this is no longer the case.[8] The Universal title is going to move to Goldberg at *Fastlane* so that the Goldberg-Lesnar fight has the luster of a title match connected to it, and the title is connected with names considered bigger and more marquee. Kevin and Jericho will instead be feuding over the US Championship.

Jericho, who has never won a world championship as a babyface, is crushed. Kevin and Sami have never talked openly about their reactions, but it's a good guess that they weren't happy. Kevin is losing his chance at a main event at *WrestleMania*. Sami, bumped downward by the ripple effect of this decision, has lost a chance at his first singles title on the main roster.

Despite this, Kevin and Jericho forge ahead with a segment they've been planning for months, the moment when their friendship finally implodes. And even through their bitter disappointment at the change in stakes, they create one of the most memorable segments in wrestling history, the Festival of Friendship.

It takes place in Las Vegas on February 13. Jericho has announced that he wants to throw a huge extravaganza to celebrate his eternal friendship with Kevin Owens. There's thunderous pyro, spotlights, and a line of gaudy Vegas showgirls. Jericho comes to the ring wearing a truly astonishing suit of spangled silver with a matching top hat, sparkling like a disco ball. He's carrying the List of Jericho with him in case anyone needs to be put on it. Kevin follows him to the ring, looking dubious. Jericho gives him gifts "to prove what you mean to me," including an abstract statue of two embracing figures. "We are intertwined, man! Best friends forever!" He also gives him a piece of original art, a parody of Michelangelo's "Creation of Adam," with a scarf-wearing Jericho as the first man and Kevin as God, reaching out from a cloud for the hot tag of friendship. Kevin is baffled by both gifts, so Jericho quickly gives his third gift: a performance by "Friendship the Magician," who produces scarves from his mouth and conjures up a rose. Kevin points out that his son can do better magic tricks and Jericho quickly agrees. He picks up the List of Jericho and the crowd buzz lifts in delight and anticipation. "Friendship the Magician… you just made the list!"

Jericho's final gift is supposedly a beatdown of Goldberg. Jericho calls him to the ring, where "you're gonna get…"

"IT!" the audience choruses gleefully. Goldberg's music hits, but Jericho's gift is actually the comedic parody wrestler Gillberg. Kevin beats up Gillberg in a rage. He's visibly furious at Jericho, who suddenly calls a halt to everything and shifts register from comedic to serious. "I gotta tell you, listen, I've had such a great time working with you, being your partner. It's made this last year in the WWE one of my favorite years in my career." It's clear that Chris Irvine, the man behind the garish Chris Jericho, means it. "It's been a joy. You've made my job here and my time here in WWE a better place, and I wanted to thank you for that."

Kevin is touched. He tells Jericho that actually, he has a gift for him as well. He hands Jericho a box. Looking into it, Jericho finds a new list. The crowd cheers as Jericho lifts it from the box… and then Jericho looks down and says in a perfect tone of bewilderment, "How come my name's on this?"

He lifts the list from the box, which lets the camera see what he cannot, that on the back is written "The List of KO."

Kevin waits just long enough for the crowd's cheers to shift into gasps of realization, and then he attacks, destroying the set and Jericho along with it, launching them toward their match for the US title at *WrestleMania*.

It's a flawless segment, a roller coaster ride of humor and horror, a perfect farewell to the partnership.

Match 3: *This is Your World Now*

The week after the Festival of Friendship, on the go-home show for *Fastlane*, Kevin has a match with Sami Zayn. On his way to the ring, Sami is ambushed by Samoa Joe, who's recently been hired as an enforcer for the nefarious Triple H. As Kevin watches impassively, all sense of friendship burned out of his soul, Joe throws Sami into the ring posts, screaming "this is your world now!" into his suffering face. Sami refuses to forgo the match with Kevin, but he's so badly hurt that it's nothing but a squash, a one-minute affair in which he's barely conscious for two clotheslines, a cannonball, a pop-up powerbomb, and the win.

Back in September, the first time Kevin entered the ring as champion was against Sami. Six months later, he leaves the ring as champion for the very last time against Sami. The two matches are bookends for the title that Kevin has said belongs to both of them. At *Fastlane*, Kevin gets distracted by Jericho, and Goldberg hits him with a spear and a Jackhammer to defeat him in twenty-two seconds. Sami gets choked out by Samoa Joe, left with no clear path for a *WrestleMania* match.

This is your world now.

In March, on the way to *WrestleMania*, WWE has a house show in Montreal. Kevin and Sami are the main event. After the match, Sami calls out to Kevin as he staggers up the ramp, and Kevin stops to listen. Sami addresses the Montreal audience, saying "I don't like Kevin Owens, that's not a secret, right? But it sounds to me like a lot of you people *do* like Kevin Owens!" He pauses to let Kevin hear the ovation of the crowd. "And listen, I may not like you. I don't. I haven't for a very long time. But after what we just went through... I have to say that I do respect you." He turns back to the audience. "Whether you like him or not, you have to respect the fact that for the last nine months, the guy on top of WWE, the Universal Champion, was a Quebecois! Here is a guy who represented *chez nous*! So I might not like you, but me, and these people, in this ring... I give you respect."[9]

Kevin wipes his eyes. The crowd noise grows, washing over him, and his breath hitches and he scrubs at his face, his shoulders shaking. In the "365" special that comes out later in 2017, he'll talk about how he couldn't enjoy any of his Universal title run because he was too stressed and worried about making it perfect. Now it's over, and it wasn't at all perfect, and he isn't going to defend the title at *WrestleMania*. He's upset and discouraged and worried about his place in the company.

But for a moment in Montreal, he's reminded that his place in some hearts is assured.

HELL IN A CELL
(2017)

"Get Out of My Life!"

IN THE BUILD to *WrestleMania 33*, Kevin and Sami crossed paths a couple more times. The night after losing his title to Goldberg, Kevin angrily informs Chris Jericho that they were *never* really best friends. "You know who *was*, at one time, my best friend? Sami Zayn! And yeah, I stabbed him in the back! And I would do it again, and again, and again!" As they start to brawl, Samoa Joe joins in, and his presence (and maybe Kevin's reminder of his past misdeeds) summon Sami to wade into the fray as well, leading to a match between them. It's a short match, one that Kevin wins handily, looking strong on the way to *WrestleMania*. Sami does finally manage to get some measure of revenge on the last show before *WrestleMania*, where he announces he's entering the Andre the Giant Battle Royal only to be told by Stephanie McMahon that if he beats Kevin that night, he can be in the battle royal, and if he doesn't beat Kevin, he's fired.

The fight lasts twelve minutes, and since it's a no-DQ match, they take advantage of the stipulation to fight out into the crowd, starting with Kevin shoving Sami off a barricade mid-moonsault, tumbling wildly out among the fans. Sami leaps off the stage into a tope, bowling Kevin over. Back in the ring, Kevin, desperate at the opportunity to get Sami fired, grabs Sami and wails "Just *go away!* Get out of my *liiiiife!*" Eventually, Jericho and Samoa Joe will get involved, which will distract Kevin enough that Sami will get his first singles win in five matches with Kevin. Ironically, despite Kevin's plea, 2017 will end with the two of them more entangled than they have ever been on the main roster.

Are We Good?

There's an alternate timeline where Kevin Owens and Chris Jericho main event WrestleMania 33 *fighting for the Universal title, while Sami defends* his recently-won US title.

In this timeline, however, Goldberg and Brock Lesnar are fighting for the Universal title at *WrestleMania.* Kevin and Jericho are battling over the US title, and Sami is on the preshow, in the Andre the Giant Battle Royal. Kevin, Jericho, and Sami all come into the event in Orlando with chips on their shoulders, determined to prove they should have been higher on the card. The camera crew still doggedly following Kevin for the "365" documentary catches him pulling up to a car carrying AJ Styles, both of them on the way to the venue.

"Are you ready to show them why we both should have been in *WrestleMania* main events?" he says to Styles, then catches sight of Charlotte Flair and Becky Lynch in the back seat. All four of them have lost titles in the last three months. "We'll all be champs again," he says, and all three in the other car respond in unison, a ritualistic chorus, "One day!"

"Let's fuck shit up tonight!" Kevin says, laughing.

At the venue, Kevin and Jericho are annoyed to discover they've been put second on the card. It's a thankless position. The crowd's energy will be high for the very first match, so opening the show is a coveted spot. After that, however, the energy will ebb as people settle in for a long night, and getting them involved again will be a huge challenge. Jericho is so upset about this—"that's a fucking insult!" he rages—that he starts to make plans to leave WWE, plans that will eventually lead to him becoming AEW's first champion.[1]

Sami is on the pre-show, in a 33-man battle royal. He manages to

HELL IN A CELL

get some measure of payback on Braun Strowman when he spearheads a group effort to lift up the gigantic Strowman and push him over the top rope, but he doesn't win.

Kevin and Jericho's match is Kevin's first singles match at *WrestleMania*. Eager to overcome the inertia of the audience, he decides to pull out a few of his more dazzling moves from the top ropes, like a frog splash and a senton. Vince McMahon's philosophy is generally that heels shouldn't do any flashy moves, but Kevin decides it's worth bending that rule to try and get the crowd fired up for the end of this eight-month story between him and Jericho, the culmination of all their work. It's a risk, but it will be worth it if they can create a great match.

It's a good match, including a fantastic moment where Kevin breaks a pin by getting one index finger to the ropes at the absolute last second. The camera closes up on that single extended fingertip, an echo of the Creation of Man parody Jericho gave Kevin at the Festival of Friendship. In the end, Kevin's hardened heart wins the day. He beats Jericho and takes his title, retreating up the ramp, red-faced and gloating. Triumphant.

Jericho makes his way backstage to go through Gorilla, getting a cursory thumbs-up from McMahon as he passes through. The "365" camera follows Kevin as he goes from frontstage to backstage and witnesses his mood evaporate into anxiety and a sense of growing dread. "How do you feel?" says the person behind the documentary camera as Kevin removes his wrist tape backstage, his eyes scanning the air as though frantically reviewing the match in his mind. "I don't wanna talk right now," Kevin says in a rush and stands up and walks away.

The camera cuts to him backstage a while later, approaching McMahon with a studied casualness as the head of WWE stares at a bank of monitors, directing the tag title match. "Are we good?" Kevin says.

Without turning his head or looking up from the monitor, McMahon says "No."

The syllable is pointedly curt. Kevin says "No?" in a tone of stunned disbelief, rocking back like he's been slapped. Then he goes utterly still as it sinks in. He stands there in awkward, horrified silence as McMahon ignores him completely. It's clear McMahon is not finished with him, that there is a dressing-down to be had. Kevin stands motionless. Waiting.

Eventually the camera mercifully stops recording.

"Vince did not like the match. It wasn't what he was looking for. He wasn't happy about it at all," Kevin remembers in the "365" special. Chris Jericho's second-hand account of the criticism is more blunt. According to him, Kevin later told him McMahon had called it "the worst match in *WrestleMania* history" and informed Kevin "you're fat, you're out of shape, you do too many moves, and you're just not a good heel."[2] Jericho, used to McMahon's style, told Kevin "you're going through the Vince boot camp, just stick with it and you'll do okay." Kevin remembers the confrontation "made me question myself as a performer, made me question my place in WWE."[3] As Jericho put it more simply, Kevin was "very fucking sad."[4]

The next few months would be one of the most difficult times Kevin and Sami ever experienced in WWE.

Superstar Shakeup

Smackdown at the time was billed as the "Land of Opportunity," run by Daniel Bryan and Shane McMahon. Bryan—friends with both Kevin and Sami since their days on the indies together—was still struggling with the aftermath of his injury and retirement, constantly seeking to have himself medically cleared to wrestle once more, suffering at being so close to the ring but unable to be part of the action. Shane was being written as "the good McMahon" in contrast to his evil father and sister. Both of them were soon to become an important part of Kevin and Sami's story, because shortly after *WrestleMania*, WWE has a "Superstar Shakeup"—a re-arrangement of talent short of a full-on draft—and Kevin is moved to *Smackdown*.

He shows up in a suit, his hair and beard cut short, swaggering and calling himself "The Face of America." Despite his bluster, the change in look is a sign that he's still struggling after his disastrous *WrestleMania*, discouraged at being moved to Smackdown, often considered the secondary WWE brand. "I was trying to find myself, after *Wrestle-*

Mania, after that match, I tried to kind of change things about my personality or my character or whatever, and even the way I wrestled, to be more in line with what the company needed me to be or the show needed me to be, but it was hard because I wasn't finding it."[5] His character's cheer at his new beginning is shattered just a few minutes after his arrival when Sami Zayn's music hits. "This cannot be happening! You cannot be real!" Kevin howls as the newest *Smackdown* superstar strides grinning down the ramp and is almost immediately put into a triple threat match with AJ Styles and Baron Corbin to determine who has the next crack at Kevin's title.

It's a promising beginning for Sami, but he is pinned by Styles, who immediately guns for Kevin. The very next week Sami is put into another number one contender's match, this one for the top WWE title. Again he is pinned by the winner, Jinder Mahal, on his way to dethroning Randy Orton. A backstage video shows Sami sweaty and miserable in defeat. "It's the same story all over again," he says with a mix of sadness and fury, gritting his teeth. "A *second place finish* every time." In an interview a few weeks later on "Talking Smack," the post-*Smackdown* interview show, Sami says "It's been a very rough week for me, honestly. If I'm being totally honest." He looks tired, and although it's impossible to say for certain what's character work and what's reality on "Talking Smack," it certainly fits with Kevin looking back and saying "those couple months were really rough."[6]

Kevin spends May, June, and July feuding with Styles and Jericho, who has also pursued him to *Smackdown*. He and Sami both end up in the Money in the Bank ladder match in June—another chance at a title shot for Sami. It's another match that crackles with their chemistry, including a resonant little nod to the Battleground spot where Kevin kicks Sami in the crotch, then cradles his head gently as Sami falls forward in agony before tossing him backwards again. In the end, it's Baron Corbin who wins the briefcase, although his cash-in will ultimately fail. Another chance at a chance gone by for Sami.

Drifting

From there both Kevin and Sami enter a period that feels static, almost stagnant, stretching through the summer of 2017. Kevin loses the title to Styles in a non-televised match at Madison Square Garden. He wins it back a couple of weeks later at *Battleground*, in an awkward and possibly botched ending where the referee does a bizarrely slow count as Styles and Owens seem to struggle to get into the correct position. The "365" documentary, which largely glosses over this painful summer, shows us a glimpse of Kevin backstage after the match in deep conversation with officials, his face creased in worry. "This match is not what we needed," he says to the camera afterwards, struggling to explain why he's unhappy despite winning a title without breaking the fiction. "It doesn't feel great to not have delivered what the company needed."

This possibly-mistaken title reign lasts only two days until the next *Smackdown*, where Styles recaptures it by pinning Jericho in a three-way match. It's Chris Jericho's last television appearance for WWE. Still furious about his *WrestleMania* slight, he's soon out and working for New Japan Pro Wrestling, where he meets up with Kevin's old friends the Young Bucks and begins the trajectory that leads him to AEW.

That two-day reign is the last time Kevin will hold a championship for more than six years.

As Kevin feuds with Styles over the US title, Sami drifts gently down the card. He's had three opportunities to win a chance at a title and has failed at each of them. Soon he's in an angle with Maria Kanellis, recently returned to WWE, and her husband Mike Bennett, debuting for the first time. Their gimmick is that they love each other so much that it's annoying. Mike even decides to take his wife's name and go by Mike Kanellis, a sure sign of villainy. Eventually their storylines will spiral (inevitably in this era of WWE) into humiliation and cuckoldry, but for now they feud with Sami simply because he tripped over something backstage and interrupted them while they were talking about their great love. It's not a lot for any of them to work with, but they do their best.

The glitchy ending of the Owens-Styles match at *Battleground* gets worked into their feud when Kevin gets a rematch with the new US champion in early August. After Kevin accidentally knocks out the referee, he makes the three-count for Styles, failing to see that Kevin got a shoulder up. Furious, Kevin storms backstage after the match to demand that General Manager Daniel Bryan and Commissioner Shane McMahon do something about the shoddy refereeing. Shane appoints himself special referee for yet another Kevin and Styles rematch at *SummerSlam*.

Kevin Owens "365": I Dunno

The *SummerSlam* match is classically "overbooked"—that is, complicated (usually unnecessarily), full of distractions, a match that isn't a pure showcase of the two wrestlers. The story of the match revolves, naturally, around Shane's presence as a guest referee. Kevin pulls Shane down on him as Styles does a springboard 450 splash, for example, then complains when Shane groggily fails to count a pin fast enough. Then Kevin breaks a submission by kicking Shane into Styles, and when Styles manages to lock it in again, Shane is still knocked out so he doesn't see Kevin tapping. Finally, Kevin delivers his pop-up powerbomb, pins Styles, and seems to have won his title back. He leaps to his feet, celebrating, but behind him Shane has jumped up and voided the count, just noticing that Styles got his foot on the ropes. Eventually, Kevin loses to Styles yet again and is furious, but his fury is starting to be transferred to Shane instead of Styles.

SummerSlam marks the end of the "365" documentary focused on Kevin, the end of a truly unpredictable year. It makes a surreal bookend to his disastrous WrestleMania. The camera follows Kevin backstage after the match as he goes up to Vince McMahon. "Was that alright?" he asks.

"It was exactly what we were looking for," McMahon responds.

Rather than make Kevin happy, this approval seems to almost make him more miserable. He didn't particularly like the match and is left confused about why the match he liked was *the worst WrestleMania match ever* and this match was *exactly what they were looking for*. "I don't know that I delivered in the way I should have," he says, sitting backstage. "Vince says I did so that should be good enough for me, right? But it's not. I dunno. Maybe that's what we should call this. *Kevin*

Owens 365: I Dunno. That's all I've got." His face is flushed, his eyes red. He seems deeply discouraged. "Right now it's hard to look in the future and think it'll be good," he says. "I get in my own head too much."

The entire documentary seems about to end on a note of despair, but at the last second the producer adds the title "30 Minutes Later." Kevin appears, phone in hand, grinning almost sheepishly. He's just received a text from his idol, "Stone Cold" Steve Austin, that says "Great job. I loved that match" and adds a thumbs up. "I'm fine," Kevin says, beaming. He fumbles the phone and drops it on the floor. "I'm fine," he says again, bending to retrieve it, and the documentary manages to end with a glimmer of hope.

Hell in a Cell is just around the corner in October, and Shane McMahon is famous for being willing to do crazy Hell in a Cell matches. Inevitably, people start to speculate that WWE might be heading toward Shane versus Kevin in the Cell. And they're right, but there will be a few wild swerves along the way.

Outshined and Eclipsed

Sami had nothing at *SummerSlam*. No match, no promo, no angle. Earlier in the summer he'd fumed about how it was a second-place finish every time, but by August he'd be lucky to get even that. He's started to feud with Aiden English in another low-mid-card program, and it's something of a surprise when his path suddenly crosses Kevin's again, right after *SummerSlam*. Kevin is on a rampage, furious about Shane's shoddy refereeing, and he demands not only a rematch but a chance to choose the referee. Shane grants this, with the condition that if Kevin loses, he'll never get another rematch with Styles.

Not surprisingly, after years of bad behavior Kevin can't seem to find anyone willing to help him out. In desperation, he turns to Sami, telling him that after all their years together as friends and enemies, Sami is the only one he can trust. Unexpectedly, Sami doesn't instantly reject him. Instead, he says that he's been thinking about the past and "it just feels like we've been fighting for so long, sometimes I forget what we're even fighting about."

Kevin's eyes light up and he seizes eagerly on Sami's words. "You know what, yes! I agree! You're right! I kind of feel the same way!" It's been over a year since Sami defeated Kevin at *Battleground* and put that chapter of their story to rest. A few weeks before this at a Montreal house show, they briefly teamed up to rescue local legend Pat Patterson. But Kevin manages to stomp out any possible embers of friendship when he goes on, "and I know you're not busy tonight, because the truth is since you've come to *Smackdown Live* you haven't really been doing much of anything." Sami's face, rather than being angry or defiant, goes oddly blank at these words. He doesn't contradict Kevin. "But tonight you can do something that *matters*," Kevin tells him. "You can do something that *counts*." He bustles off after telling Sami to "think about it."

Later that night, he hurries up to Sami, beaming and carrying a referee jersey. Sami looks at him and says, "I did what you told me to do. I thought about it. I thought about it real long and real hard." Kevin already knows where this is going and his smile slowly slides off his face. "And the more I thought about it, the more I thought about every rotten thing you've ever done to me, every time you stabbed me in the back." He wishes Kevin some sardonic luck and tosses the jersey back at him. Eventually Kevin is forced to ask Baron Corbin to be his guest referee, and when Corbin quits in exasperation mid-match, Shane McMahon dons the jersey, declares himself the ref, and is there to make the final count that means Kevin will get no more title opportunities.

The next week Kevin, still fuming about Shane's meddling in his life, puts himself on commentary for Sami's latest match with Aiden English. Working himself up into a fury about what he saw as "bad refereeing," he finally jumped into the ring and bullied the referee into giving him his jersey. Sami turned from fighting English to find Kevin in the middle of the ring wearing the striped shirt and announcing "I'm the ref now! I'm the ref!" Then he powerbombed Sami and left him for English to pin. The match was less than three minutes long, yet another discouraging loss for Sami.

Things keep heating up as *Hell in a Cell* looms. On the next show Kevin informs Shane his family would be better off if he were dead and Shane attacks Kevin, battering him until General Manager Bryan has to interfere and call him off. That same show Sami loses *again* to Aiden English in a mortifying ninety-second match.

In the wake of being assaulted by Shane, Kevin threatens to sue WWE. Using pro wrestling logic, he decides that means he'll be running the company soon. He explains to the audience there'll be a lot of people fired immediately, and the first person he'll fire is Sami Zayn. When Sami confronts him about it backstage, Kevin reminds him of a night long ago in Ohio, where they had been driving through a blizzard after performing in an armory for about forty-two people. "Remember the promise we made that night?" he says. "We promised we'd do anything in our power to get to WWE so we'd never have to do that again." Like their other backstage segment, it's a moment of something close to warmth, a moment where they're each reminded of the long history they share and how amazing it is that they're here, a moment that Kevin then tramples on by telling Sami that after he's fired, he has Kevin's permission to break that promise and go back to fighting in armories. Sami responds that he'd rather wrestle in armories than ever work for Kevin and stalks off.

That same night, Kevin confronts Vince McMahon, CEO and Chairman of the Board, in the ring. McMahon makes the Hell in a Cell match between his son and Kevin official, and Kevin tells him he'll accept the match if he's allowed to assault a McMahon with no consequences. When Vince agrees, assuming he means Shane, Kevin proceeds to assault him, head-butting the seventy-two-year-old square between the eyes. As blood starts to trickle down Vince's face, Kevin then punches, kicks, and frog splashes him to the amazed horror/delight of the crowd, earning him Shane's eternal enmity. Kevin is, of course, unrepentant. He makes a video explaining with a calm, mad intensity that if Shane thinks he can banish him to Hell he's badly mistaken. "For what I'm going to do to you, people like me don't go to Hell. No. People like me... go to Heaven."

Two weeks before *Hell in a Cell*, Kevin is bragging in the ring about his actions when Sami comes to the ring to face him. "What is wrong with you?" he asks, nearly vibrating with emotion. He's keyed-up, horrified. "I'm not out here to fight, I'm out here because you have lost complete control." He's trying to warn Kevin off of his path of vengeance, warning him against fighting Shane in the Cell.

Kevin just scoffs. "You're out here because once again I have completely and utterly outshined and eclipsed you, just like I've done for the last fifteen years of our lives." He ticks off his WWE achievements as rage tightens Sami's shoulders. "I've been Intercontinental champion *twice*. I've been Universal champion. I won the US title at *WrestleMania* while you watched from the back!" he laughs. "What have you ever done in your life that had as much impact as the impact my skull had on Vince McMahon's head?"

Sami fires back, biting off his words. "You're right. Since coming to WWE, you've done a lot more than I've done. But you've also taken every cheap shot, you've cut every corner, you've taken every reprehensible action to get to where you are. Right now? I'm not doing so great, I'll admit that. But my day will come! And when it comes, I will do it *my* way! I will do it the *right* way!" He rattles off Kevin's accomplishments again, then says the difference between them is that he can still look at himself in the mirror. He's furious, rigid with anger, brittle. When Bryan sets up a match between them for later that night, he's filled with fierce joy.

But to Sami's horror, Shane McMahon calls Bryan and tells him that he's on his way to the arena and he will deal with Kevin. Sami begs Bryan to keep Shane from interfering "Shane has his opportunity at Kevin at *Hell in a Cell* in two weeks. I would *love* to fight Kevin in a *Hell in a Cell* in two weeks, but I don't *have* that opportunity." He smacks his fist into his hand for emphasis, frustrated at all the opportunities he's lost. "I have Kevin tonight. Let me have tonight."

Bryan sighs and shrugs. He's known both Kevin and Sami for decades. He'll do his best.

The match starts with the traditional hockey brawl, fists flying. Kevin is particularly brutal, hammering Sami with punishing lariats and clotheslines. While Sami writhes on the mat in pain, Kevin crouches, staring holes into him, feral. As he slams Sami into the barricade, the camera cuts to Shane arriving at the arena, on his way to interfere. Sami starts to rally. He does a beautiful tornado DDT and the crowd goes nuts for him, chanting and cheering. He follows it up with a Blue Thunder Bomb—Kevin howls in panic at the apex of the move —but when he tries to do his through-the-corner-ropes DDT Kevin counters it, kicking him in the face. Grabbing his dazed foe, he powerbombs him onto the apron, the same move he did years ago when he betrayed Sami in NXT.

Sami collapses as if his back is broken and the referee quickly calls the match off. Sami cries out in pain and frustration and Kevin starts forward at the sound, one hand outstretched. The ref warns him off, but it's not exactly clear he was going to attack Sami. He looks confused, almost as dazed as Sami. He reaches down and grabs at Sami's beard and face in something that's part assault and part caress, then retreats to sit on the announce desk as the medical staff comes out to check on Sami, his eyes vacant. As Sami is being helped out, something sparks behind Kevin's eyes again and he runs to attack Sami from behind, bowling him over onto the ramp, then going to grab a chair, his weapon of choice against both Sami and El Generico. He's getting ready to destroy Sami with the chair when Shane McMahon's music hits.

As Shane charges down the ramp, Kevin shoves Sami into his path and makes his getaway through the crowd. How does Sami feel being treated as cannon fodder in Kevin's feud with Shane? He doesn't say explicitly, but the next week, the last show before Hell in a Cell, he approaches Shane to offer his help. Shane doesn't know what evil Kevin is capable of, he says, his eyes blazing.

Shane isn't interested. He dismisses Sami, saying with frosty politeness, "Please, with all due respect, you take care of you and I'll take care of me. Thank you, though." As he walks away, Sami nods pensively to himself.

Hell in a Cell

Hell in a Cell matches are always played up as life-changing. This one will be no exception. Shane has made this a falls-count-anywhere stipulation, which means they can range out of and onto the Cell, which of course they eventually do, battling across the unsteady chainlink surface of the structure. At one point Kevin has the opportunity to

HELL IN A CELL

leap off the top of the Cell, but he takes a long look down at the dizzying fall and—wiser than daredevil Shane—decides to retreat. He and Shane fight their way down the outside wall of the Cell until Shane kicks him loose and Kevin falls from halfway up, crashing through the Spanish announce table. Shane climbs down as the medics check on Kevin who appears to be out cold. He could just cover him. Instead, clearly remembering Kevin's assault on his father, he makes a fateful decision. He sets Kevin on the other announce table, climbs back up to the top of the Cell and stands there on the edge, looking down to where Kevin lies, helpless. The crowd is shrieking, everyone's eyes riveted to the lone figure on the edge. He crosses himself. He steps off the Cell and plummets the twenty feet to the table.

But Kevin's not there.

To the rescue.

Shane crashes through the Kevin-less table like a sandbag to lie motionless. The camera swings crazily, looking for Kevin. It spots him lying on the floor nearby, then swivels up.

It stops abruptly on Sami in a black hoodie, pale with shock, staring at Kevin.

Pandemonium. The playback shows what almost no one saw: Sami on the sidelines, leaping forward at the moment Shane stepped off the Cell to grab Kevin and pull him out of danger. Everyone in the arena is screaming. Sami seems almost paralyzed, but suddenly shakes it off to leap forward, grab Kevin and drag his inert body on top of Shane's. He yells at the referee to make the count. The bell rings. Kevin's beaten *Smackdown* Commissioner Shane McMahon.

Kevin pushes himself up enough to stare groggily at Sami. He's clearly completely flabbergasted to discover his oldest enemy and oldest friend has saved him. Sami barely seems to see him. His glassy gaze is turned inward. He puts his back up against the fencing of the Cell and shudders sharply all over, one time, as if something inside him is shattering.

Sami Zayn won't be a babyface again for over half a decade.

KEVIN'S HEAVEN
(2017-2018)

J.J. MCGEE

Guardian Angel

ON THE FIRST *Smackdown* after *Hell in a Cell*, Kevin comes to the ring alone. He's in high spirits, glowing with happiness, illuminated from within by joy. He's here to tell everyone about the miracle that happened at *Hell in a Cell*. According to him, as he lay on the table helplessly awaiting Shane's plunge, he had a near-death experience. His soul ascended into white light and he found himself at the gates of a cartoon-perfect Heaven, complete with pearly gates and a Saint Peter, who informed him that while Heaven would love to welcome him, the world needed Kevin Owens. Saint Peter had sent him back to his body, but not before assigning him a personal guardian angel, Sami Zayn. His eyes shine as he explains, "As I re-entered my body, that's when I realized my new purpose, and that's to turn *Smackdown Live* into my very own personal paradise. And here we are, all gathered here tonight... in Kevin's Heaven." Just a few weeks ago he'd promised Shane McMahon that people like him went to Heaven, and he has been vindicated by apparently divine fiat. "Without further ado, let me introduce to you..." He takes a deep breath, bellowing the words from his chest, from his heart. "My *best friend* and *guardian angel, Sami Zayn!*"

Sami makes his way to the ring, grinning. Before he can say anything, though, Kevin says "I think you need to explain to everybody that I had no idea you were going to come out Sunday night at *Hell in a Cell*, that I had no idea you were going to do that, that I had no idea why you chose to pull me away from certain destruction." He looks surprised, questioning, almost uncertain. "I need to tell you from the bottom of my heart... Sami. *Thank you.*" His voice shakes. His chest is heaving with emotion.

Sami's smile is stretched brightly across his face. Where Kevin's voice is warm, Sami's is all sharp edges. "Actually," he says, "you powerbombing me on the apron a few weeks ago is what started opening my eyes to *everything*." His violent epiphany at Kevin's hands was that his righteousness had gotten him nowhere. "I tried to be the good guy and do everything the right way," he chides the audience, "I put all of your hopes and dreams and morals and beliefs and ideals and your values and I put it all on my shoulder and I embarked on a long and arduous journey, and it brought me all the way to..." He scrunches up his face, a cynical muppet. "...to mediocrity. Meanwhile, Kevin Owens, my counterpart, became the Intercontinental champion. He became the Universal champion. He became the United States champion. But that's okay, because *I* get to *sleep at night*," he says, sarcasm dripping off his words.

For Sami, *Hell in a Cell* was a night not of miracles, but of revelations. He had come in hopes of helping Shane anyway, even though Shane had brushed him off, even though Shane had never given him the time of day. But when he saw Shane give up the chance to pin Kevin and instead aim to destroy him, he had been unable to stand by any longer. "I saved my brother because it was the right thing to do. I saved my brother because Shane McMahon had become an absolute psychopath!"

He doesn't say it explicitly, but it's easy to read between the lines and see the seeds of his seemingly-abrupt alignment shift. He found himself leaping forward to save Kevin instinctively. But his moral compass—rigid, righteous, already overloaded with disappointment and despair—had been unable to take the weight of realizing he'd saved the man who had just been bragging about how he'd totally eclipsed him. If he'd chosen Kevin over Shane, that must therefore mean that he accepted Kevin's worldview. "Kevin, for the longest time I thought I despised you," he says. "Now I realize I just despised the fact that you were right." Kevin nods solemnly at this capitulation. He's wanted for years to hear Sami admit that Kevin was better than him. Now Sami is literally thanking him for opening his eyes to reality. Truly, this is Kevin's Heaven.

They embrace. Sami's smile is crystalline, bright and brittle. He's gleefully happy, delighted to be aligned with Kevin once more, but there's an emptiness behind his eyes that Kevin doesn't seem able to see.

When General Manager Daniel Bryan calls Sami out next week to scold him, Sami responds with a manic cheer that he simply got tired of caring about the fans' needs and hopes and desires. According to Sami, their love should have lifted him to the top, and instead it weighed him down, burdened him. He points at Bryan, baring his teeth in an angry grin. "They are the reason *you* were in the main event of *WrestleMania!*" he says. "But they *never* did it for me."

Sami notes there are similarities between the two of them, the classic underdogs. "We both are talented in-ring performers," he says, then pauses for a long painful moment before scoffing, "Well, I still am." The crowd has been cheering Sami, wanting to believe in the power of friendship, but having their hero's forced retirement thrown in their face is too much, and the cheers shift to boos. Sami chastises the audience, saying that Bryan's retirement "broke my heart, more than it broke any of yours," that he'd spent his whole career trying to catch up to Bryan, one of the greatest wrestlers of all time, but now Bryan is a broken man who can no longer wrestle.

Bryan goes pale with anger and anguish and leaves the ring. As Kevin mocks him with the memory of his retirement, saying "walking out of this arena is the best thing you've got nowadays," Bryan says he's going to find "a couple of dudes to punch you in the face."

Thus begins a strange program in which different active wrestlers —Nakamura, Styles, Orton—end up in matches with Kevin and Sami, but that's not where the real feud lies. The real conflict is between the two Canadians and Shane and Bryan, the Commissioner and the General Manager. They constantly need proxy wrestlers because Shane isn't a full-time wrestler, and (as Kevin and Sami have just reminded everyone) Daniel Bryan tragically cannot wrestle.

No Me, Only We

Kevin's Heaven is all he's longed for, at first. He and Sami are exuberantly overjoyed, constantly hugging each other, dancing, filled with delight. As an alliance, Kevin and Chris Jericho had disagreed about whether it was *Team Chris and Kevin* or *Team Kevin and Chris*. For the first few months of Sami and Kevin's alliance there is no such friction. When Sami says that Smackdown is *Team Kevin and Sami*, Kevin quickly corrects him, saying it's *Team Sami and Kevin*. When Sami says that this is now the *Kevin and Sami Show,* Kevin leans toward him to fervently declare that no, it's the *Sami and Kevin Show*. The two cut hilarious backstage promos in which Kevin sets up the basic situation —mocking a Christmas display, terrorizing a backstage interviewer, selling an injury—then watches in rapt adoration as Sami takes over, riffing on the theme, tossing it back and forth between them.* Kevin is expansive, euphoric that Sami has "finally seen the light," as he puts it. Sami bounces and struts and skanks, spaghetti-limbed, around Kevin, and there is no light behind his eyes.

They sow chaos all autumn, terrorizing the Smackdown roster and taunting Shane and Bryan. They interfere in the Survivor Series match in November to attack Shane, giving Raw the victory in "brand supremacy." Infuriated, Shane tries to retaliate, his vendetta against them deepening every week. Bryan is torn between his frustration at Kevin and Sami and his long friendship with them, trying to play peacemaker when he can. Kevin and Sami remind him of their history, play on his sympathies, flatter and cajole him, even setting up a "Yep Movement" in homage to Bryan's "Yes Movement." Bryan hates his role as authority figure on the sidelines. He's trying to be fair and impartial, but everyone else keeps making this harder and harder.

At December's *Clash of Champions* PPV, Shane books Kevin and Sami versus Nakamura and Orton with the stipulation that if Kevin and Sami lose, they'll be fired from WWE. Then—as constantly happens in this feud—he goes further, a step too far, and appoints himself the special referee for the match. Bryan decides to counteract this by making himself a second special referee. This goes about as well as you might imagine a match with two referees, each with a different agenda, might go. Bryan and Shane squabble and bicker about slow counts and fast counts until they finally decide to divide the ring in half. At the climax of the match, Sami manages to roll Orton up into a pin on Shane's side of the ring, and Shane goes to make the

---

* Until this turn, Sami was a lifelong babyface, with the exception of a few months here and there where he acted more heelish specifically to be in a partnership with Kevin—a "unicorn" as Edge and Christian laughingly call him on their podcast. He responds by saying he never expected to turn heel, that he thought he'd be one of the rare wrestlers who stays babyface their whole career. And he's never had to speak as a heel, so this is entirely new ground for him. The segments are fun, but they're also Kevin walking him through how to cut a heel promo.

count—and stops at two, his fist hovering above the mat, refusing to make the final count and allow Sami and Kevin to keep their jobs. Sami stares up at him, his cynicism suddenly stripped away into wide-eyed shock as all of his mistrust of Shane is validated. Bryan argues vehemently with Shane, and in the resulting chaos Sami avoids an RKO from Orton and rolls him up again, this time on Bryan's side of the ring, where Bryan makes a fast count and declares Kevin and Sami the winners, their jobs safe.

Backstage in the locker room, Kevin and Sami dance with joy, spraying champagne everywhere. Kevin yells "You did it! You covered him!" and Sami shoots back "No! There is no *me*, there is only *we!*" Truly, this is all Kevin has yearned for, a world where any of those *extremely* minor and unimportant betrayals in the past are forgiven and forgotten, the slate wiped clean, he and his friend in total blissful unity. Heaven.

Twenty seventeen ticks over into 2018. Shane and Bryan continue to squabble. Kevin and Sami continue to preen and play. Bryan, frustrated with Shane's vendetta, books both Sami and Kevin in non-title matches against WWE champion AJ Styles, which they both win when their buddy interferes. Exasperated, Styles tells Bryan he might as well book them in a two-on-one handicap match for the title at the *Royal Rumble*, and Bryan decides he can't hear sarcasm and does exactly that. If Kevin and Sami win, they will become the first ever co-champions in WWE.[*]

It's strange that somehow, Kevin and Sami's alliance managed to almost entirely skip the tag team division. They had spent exactly two weeks in November fighting established tag teams—two matches on *Smackdown* against the New Day, one match on the *Survivor Series* kickoff show against Breezango. In that span of time they had three title shots against the reigning champions, the Usos, but only at house

---

[*] Interestingly, Kevin and Jericho technically were United States co-champions during their alliance, when they won the title off Roman Reigns in a two-on-one handicap match. Before the match they had claimed they'd share the title, but Jericho made the pin and the idea of co-champions was quietly dropped. However, the theme of trying to become such an inseparable unit that you can share a title clearly is not a fluke in Kevin's career.

shows. Then abruptly they were back in the singles division, allied but not a tag team. Their first broadcast tag team title shot would not happen for another five years, at *WrestleMania*. So in 2018, winning Styles's title is their one chance to actually be champions together, to share an accomplishment. To truly be equals.

When they fail to capture the title—inevitably but awkwardly, due to a referee thinking a tag had been made and Styles therefore pinning the wrong man—that chance to be equal champions evaporates.

And this is where Kevin's Heaven starts to evaporate as well.

The One Who Wins the Titles

As Kevin and Sami complain to Bryan the next week, Bryan agrees that the referee was in error, though his decision is still final. However, he has decided they deserve another opportunity, he says in an unnervingly chipper voice. He's made a main event for the following week and the winner will face AJ Styles at *Fastlane*.

Sami's face lights up in anticipation of this new opportunity. In dramatic contrast, a shadow falls across Kevin's. As Bryan starts to announce the wrestlers in the match, Kevin whispers "No. Come on." He already knows what Bryan is about to do, and he already knows that his friendship with Sami as currently constructed, this jerry-rigged alliance based on the hollowing-out of Sami's soul, will not survive direct competition. But that's what Bryan has done, given them conflict in the guise of opportunity.

Things immediately start to fall apart. They don't even get through that show before starting to snipe at each other, jockeying for position. During their tag match against Nakamura and Styles, when they should be working together, Kevin gets frustrated that Sami is out of position for the tag. "You're supposed to be there when I need to tag you!" he complains.

Sami's eyebrows fly up and he immediately takes Kevin's statement at the wrong level, months of buried resentment pouring out. "I'm not there for you? I'm not there for you every single time? I wasn't there for you at *Hell in a Cell*? I've been there for you for *everything*, don't give me that!" He storms out, leaving Kevin to his fate, pausing on the ramp to yell back at his friend, "See how you do without your *guardian angel!*" Backstage he watches on the monitor as Kevin inevitably loses, tearing at his hair in mixed frustration and anger. When the interviewer asks if their friendship can survive this, Sami barks "This isn't about friendship! It's about opportunity! Kevin understands that, okay?" It's a cruel echo of Kevin's cold assertion back in NXT that his attacks on Sami weren't personal, they were business. Now that Sami has accepted Kevin's worldview, he understands that championships are the only way to measure worth. As Sami says, Kevin should understand this.

Their match to determine who gets to fight Styles at Fastlane is a disaster. Oh, it's a good match, of course. But the heart of the match, the moment where everything crystallizes, is when Kevin, increasingly desperate as he realizes Sami and he are equally matched, finally snaps. He yells at Sami to "stay down" like he did a year ago at *Battleground*. This time, however, he adds in a panic, *"I'm the one who wins the titles!"*

On his knees in front of Kevin, Sami's eyes go wide with hurt as he hears Kevin deny any equality in their relationship. He grits his teeth and surges to his feet to renew the fight, but never gets a chance to show his dominance because eventually Styles, on commentary, gets embroiled in the match and it's ruled a no-contest. Bryan puts both of them into a match with Styles at *Fastlane*.

The build-up to *Fastlane* is chaotic. Through a frankly Byzantine series of events that would take an entire chapter to unravel, more and more people keep getting added to the match until it's a messy six-person fight. Kevin tries to talk to Sami about the situation but is coldly rebuffed. "Let me explain something to you," Sami says. "There is no *we* in this championship match." Kevin flinches at how far they've come from Sami's ecstatic assertion that there was no *me* in their partnership, only *we*.

The next week, abruptly, he changes his tune. He comes to Kevin backstage and explains that he's remembered he owes Kevin for opening his eyes, for helping him get to where he is now. "You don't need another enemy. You need your guardian angel." Sami says he's always done what's right, "and doing what's right... is paying back my friend after all he's done for me."

"Are you serious?" Kevin almost whispers.

Sami nods. "I will lay down for you in the center of the ring," he promises.

You might expect Kevin to be thrilled about this. Surely this is the ultimate in Kevin's Heaven, Sami being willing to lie down (to *finally* "stay down") and let him be the one to win the title. But Kevin's expression is anything but happy as Sami lays out his plan. He starts off confused, then moves slowly to disbelief and distrust. When they were enemies, Kevin called Sami the only person he could trust. In this hollow parody of friendship he realizes this Sami is impossible to trust. And beneath the doubt there's sadness and a growing horror. *Maybe,* his expression hints, *maybe it would not be good if Sami actually did this. Maybe it would be bad if Sami were so broken as to give up.* "I... I don't know what to say," he murmurs. Sami grins his cheerful, empty grin, tells him he doesn't have to say anything, and pulls him in for a hug. Over Sami's shoulder, Kevin's eyes are almost mournful.

Backstage before the *Fastlane* match, Sami re-asserts that he'll lie down for Kevin. When Kevin seems uncertain, Sami beams at him. "It's still me!" he says brightly. "It's still your buddy, still your pal. It's..." He pauses and his smile sharpens as Kevin looks unnerved, *"it's your guardian angel."* The match is a frenzy of characters and storylines, six men in the match and Commissioner Shane McMahon hovering around the ring, attempting to foil his nemeses of Kevin and Sami. Through all the confusion, there's a moment where Kevin and Sami's relationship reaches its crisis point. They find themselves alone in the ring together. Kevin, uncharacteristically, does not demand Sami lie down. Instead, he puts up his fists, inviting Sami to brawl. "Come on!" he says.

Sami just shakes his head. "I'm a man of my word," he says solemnly, and lies down on the mat, spread-eagled like he's making a snow angel, waiting for the pin as the audience boos his capitulation.

Kevin doesn't make the pin. He wavers. He goes to one knee beside Sami, looking down at him, his lower lip quivering.

He reaches down and starts to drag Sami to his feet to keep fighting him as his equal.

Sami, who has of course been lying in wait for his ambush, immediately uses that moment of vulnerability to try and pin Kevin.

They both come to their feet in a blaze of mutual fury and a flurry of fists, pummeling at each other. Commentary doesn't mention that Kevin was trying to lift Sami to his feet. The moment goes by, largely unremarked on by the actual narrative, but it's an absolutely crucial instant of character development for Kevin, one that will continue to unfold and play out for literal years.

Later in the match, Kevin is about to pin Dolph Ziggler, but Shane McMahon leaps forward and pulls the referee out of the ring, breaking the count. Then Sami Helluva Kicks Kevin and is about to win the title when Shane grabs Sami and pulls him out of the ring. The Commissioner of the "Land of Opportunity" has cost them both the title.

Kevin and Sami's Hell

At the next show, Shane comes to the ring and recaps the long, tortuous history between him and the Canadians. He admits that he's often let his emotions get the best of him and says he's stepping down as Commissioner, but he's making one last match before he goes. Pointing out that Sami and Kevin seem to be having friction, he's booking them to fight each other at *WrestleMania*.

Maybe there's an alternate world where Sami and Kevin get that singles match at *WrestleMania* in 2018. Maybe they have a feud leading to the grandest stage of them all in which they get their conflicts out in the open and get closure on them. Kevin even says backstage earlier in the show that he'd love to teach Sami a lesson and "open his eyes up to the truth," words almost identical to the ones he would use years later when they actually get that singles match at the showcase of the immortals, in 2021. But as in 2017, they end up caught up in other events. In 2017, it was Goldberg's return.

In 2018, it's Daniel Bryan's.

Bryan had been trying to get cleared to wrestle since his forced retirement years ago. It doesn't seem a coincidence that since the

KEVIN'S HEAVEN

beginning of Sami and Kevin's alliance, they were embroiled in a proxy feud with Bryan, just in case the impossible happened and the General Manager actually achieved permission to wrestle.

Events start to move really quickly.

Kevin and Sami come out to mock Shane and then attack him in an extended vicious beatdown, setting their differences aside and putting their conflict on the back burner. The next week, literally hours before Smackdown, it's announced that against all odds, against all hope, Bryan has been cleared to wrestle again. When he shows up to announce the news, Sami and Kevin come out, rejoicing, to embrace him.

At which point Bryan fires them.

He's doing it in sorrow rather than anger, but he's implacable. They laid their hands on the Commissioner—even worse, as he points out, they did it after he'd announced he was stepping down. They'd gotten what they'd wanted, and in their obsession they'd insisted on taking it too far, just as Shane had done at *Hell in a Cell* when he'd stopped trying to pin Kevin and started trying to injure him. Sami has become what he hated, and Bryan is here to bear grieving witness to his fall.

So, inevitably, Kevin and Sami lash out at him and attack him in a prolonged, brutal beatdown.

Their assault on Shane had been gleeful and anarchic, but the tone is totally different this time. They're enraged, but also miserable, almost in tears, trapped in a hell of their own making. They stand close together over Bryan's crumpled body, touching foreheads, murmuring to each other as if they're desolate. This time, they know in their hearts they're in the wrong.

Bryan comes back the next week to formally challenge Kevin and Sami to a match, his first match back. "Where should I fight them?" he asks the crowd, and as one, a sea of hands lifts without prompting to point at the *WrestleMania* sign. Bryan takes Shane as his second, and adds the stipulation that if Kevin and Sami lose the match, they also lose their jobs.

The match at *WrestleMania* involves four people—Kevin and Sami against Bryan and Shane. The heart of the match, however, the deep wound of the conflict, is between Bryan and Sami, the two wrestlers who have mirrored and echoed each other for years. The relationship between Kevin and Sami is backgrounded. They attack Bryan and Shane during their introductions, so they don't even get an entrance of their own. They won't have a shared entrance until 2023.

The early attack on Bryan means that Shane has to fight alone for a while while Kevin and Sami taunt him. When Bryan leaps into the ring to break up a pin, Sami stares at him as if he's seen a ghost. At last, Bryan gets the tag and steps into the ring for the first time in years to face Sami, the crowd's ovation breaking around them like waves, both of them almost in tears. Sami batters angrily at him, yelling "Why did you have to break our hearts, Daniel?" Bryan weathers the storm of his rage, then straightens up and looks straight at Sami, his gaze level and filled with sorrow. Sami flinches backwards in the face of Bryan's judgment. From that moment on, his tapping-out at Bryan's hands is inevitable.

Sami and Bryan will face each other one-on-one at *WrestleMania* in two years, under very different circumstances. That battle will be fought not through the ovation of thousands, but in the eerie silence of an empty building. The themes, however, will be a continuation of this match.

I Need This, Okay?

In the wake of their loss, Kevin and Sami—subdued, diminished, banished from *Smackdown*—show up on *Raw* to beg for a position there. They're told there's a place for only one of them, and they'll have to fight each other for the spot.

So they've gone from fighting for a title to fighting just to keep their jobs. Sami aims a Helluva Kick right at Kevin's face as the bell rings, then laughingly apologizes, saying "Job's on the line!" Kevin shares a chuckle with him, then attacks him, and a deathly serious fight ensues. Sami is fierce and fervent but also enjoying the challenge. When he flies over the ropes to wipe out Kevin he comes up smiling. Family man Kevin, on the other hand, is nakedly desperate, snarling an echoed "job's on the line, buddy," over and over as he pummels at Sami. As the crowd sings Olé, Sami grabs Kevin into a Blue Thunder

KEVIN'S HEAVEN

Bomb, and you can hear Kevin shrieking "No! *No!*" as he's twirled around, barely kicking out. After crotching Sami in the middle of an attempted tornado DDT, Kevin keeps pinning Sami over and over, three times in quick succession, more frantic every time Sami kicks out.

The crowd starts chanting *Fight Owens Fight*.

Sami hits a Helluva Kick on Kevin, but Kevin manages to roll out of the ring and avoid the pin. Kevin hits a pop-up powerbomb, but exhaustion is setting in, and he falls out of the ring again, this time to his own detriment.

The crowd starts chanting *Both these guys. Both these guys*.

Finally, Kevin starts to climb the turnbuckle, preparing for a senton or frog splash. Looking down at Sami, his face red and his eyes wild, he yells "I need this, okay? I need it!" It's the nearest Kevin has ever come to sounding apologetic or regretful to Sami. But Sami's need is equal to his, and Kevin eats a kick in the face. As they struggle on the turnbuckle, Kevin does an avalanche fisherman's buster, and they both end up lying on the mat, battered and exhausted, unable to move.

The ref starts the ten count that will end the match as a no contest.

Sami crawls over to Kevin as the count reaches eight and starts trying to pull him down, or push himself up—the two actions amount to the same thing. But it's impossible, they're just too evenly matched. Sami can't hold Kevin down, and he can't use him to raise himself up. The count ends and they're both still on the mat, both of them out of a job.

Of course, General Manager Kurt Angle eventually gives them both jobs anyway. They're both on the same brand, their friendship still a tenuous and fractured thing, a narrative hole demanding a closure it will never really get. They drift slowly apart but never actually split. They enter separate truly woeful programs—Sami accusing military veteran Bobby Lashley of stolen valor and mocking his glurgy Instagram posts, Kevin getting flipped head-over-heels approximately sixty thousand times by Braun Strowman.

At *Backlash*, they have one more team-up, Kevin and Sami against Strowman and Lashley. After being battered by the two behemoths, Sami decides he's had enough. He bails, heading up the ramp. Kevin runs after Sami but not to abandon the match with him. He grabs

Sami, yelling "No! We stay and we fight together! You and me. You and me!" It's a surprising character shift for Kevin, this assertion that the two of them together could overcome this hulking shared obstacle. He even seems sincere, passionately certain that their alliance could actually triumph. For a moment Sami seems to consider it—then he grabs Kevin and throws him into the ring to face the two slabs of muscle on his own and take the pin.

Kevin never confronts Sami about this. They keep interacting sporadically, but they won't be in the ring together again for over a year.

Soon after this, Sami revealed he'd been fighting injured for the last eight months. His shoulder had never quite healed from the earlier surgery in 2015, and in compensating for it, he'd torn his *other* rotator cuff and now needs double shoulder surgery. He mentions being unable to lift the sheets off his body in the morning.[1]

Kevin limps along for a few more months. With Sami gone, he waxes eloquent on more than one occasion about how if only, if *only* his *best friend*, Sami Zayn, were here, he'd help him defeat Braun Strowman. It's a desperate self-delusion, a wilful attempt to stay in Kevin's Heaven with a fantasy version of his guardian angel who had no sense of *me*, only *we*, who never tricked him into getting pinned or abandoned him to be bludgeoned by monsters. Eventually, after a painful summer that includes getting hurled off a stage while trapped in a port-a-potty by Braun Strowman and losing (again, to Strowman) at SummerSlam in under two minutes, he gets double surgery on the nagging knee injuries he's been working through and also disappears from television for months. He later admits he needed the time off to recover mentally almost as much as physically.[2]

Kevin's Heaven took a hellish toll on both the characters and the real people behind them, their bodies and their souls. Closure for the events Sami's heel turn put in motion would have to wait through surgeries, separations, and a global pandemic.

THUNDERDOME
(2019-2020)

J.J. MCGEE

Invisible Orbits

TWENTY NINETEEN TO 2022 were difficult years for Kevin and Sami's shared story. They faced challenges that ranged from the individual (they both started off 2019 injured, then spent large amounts of time on separate brands) to the institutional (these years were the height of what might be called Late Stage Vince Booking, where storylines sometimes seemed to be raised and dropped arbitrarily), to the global (an international pandemic that made wrestling for a live audience impossible for over a year). The narrative cord connecting the two of them frayed and weakened. At times it almost vanished entirely.

Back in Chapter Six, I described their relationship as a sort of binary star system, each of their orbits shaped by the gravity of the other, even when the other isn't visible. This was one of those times that the influence they had on each other must often be inferred by the paths of their characters. Through it all, they held true to the orbits their characters had set each other on in their first doomed alliance and arrived, eventually, at a kind of closure.

This chapter will try to pull that slackened narrative line a little tighter and find the invisible arcs they traveled through these times of disaster. That means large amounts of time will sometimes be skimmed over, entire complex and interesting feuds summarized in a few sentences, in order to bring Sami and Kevin's story into sharper relief. This chapter will also rely more than usual on moments caught at house shows and not broadcast on television. Generally matches and material from untelevised events exist in a canonical gray area, but during this time Kevin and Sami had several interactions at such events that illuminate how they saw their characters and the ways they were still connected.

Change of Attitude

Kevin came back early in 2019 with a new attitude. It wasn't a dramatic shift—Kevin's sense of character continuity is far too strong for that—but was clear from his return vignette videos that show him being charmingly bad at bowling and talking about missing wrestling.

When he returned to the ring in February, he had started using the Stunner as his finishing move, with his idol Stone Cold Steve Austin's blessings. And the glimmerings of remorse he'd seemed to be feeling about Sami had crystallized into a clear sense of regret. When he came out to confront Daniel Bryan and his partner Rowan, Bryan taunted him with his lack of anyone to team with. "You don't have any friends left," Bryan sneered, and Kevin looked away as if angry—or ashamed.

"I used to have friends," Kevin responded. "I used to have backup. I've lost them all, and that's my fault." That was the heart of his alignment shift, his willingness to accept responsibility for his past actions, an assertion he will repeat over and over through the next set of years. He ended up helping out the New Day, down a member because Big E was briefly out injured. Kofi Kingston dubbed Kevin "Big O," and he and Xavier Woods, through the power of positivity, became the first people to truly trust and like Kevin in WWE. From early 2019 to at least 2024, Kevin would be a babyface, though there would be a couple of odd ethical bobbles along the way.

The first bobble came after Kingston won the world title from Daniel Bryan at *WrestleMania* that year. Almost immediately after that, Kevin abruptly superkicked Kingston in the middle of a match, powerbombed Woods on the apron, and came gunning for Kingston's title.

The non-storyline reason for the sudden shift was that Bryan was concussed and they needed someone to quickly step into his role as Kingston's first opponent.[1] Within the story, Kevin managed to make it work by apparently suffering some kind of psychotic break when Kingston took a kick meant for him, as if having a selfless friend was too much for him to bear.

And after feuding with Kingston and failing to capture his title, Kevin got to team up with Sami again.

Sami had come back later than Kevin, the week after *WrestleMania*. Neither of them had been on the card due to their injuries, the only WrestleMania they've both missed as of 2024. And where Kevin had come back with a changed heart, Sami had only grown more bitter and cynical. For four weeks after his return, he cut long, lacerating promos about how much he hated his job, hated the fans. He compared performing to being in prison, to being in hell. Tellingly, he even claimed total apathy about winning titles, saying "I'm not that interested right now" in going after one. Not wanting a title is the most unthinkable form of nihilism in wrestling, a sign that something is deeply wrong with a wrestler's psyche. Sami's character was on a downward spiral that wouldn't end for a long, long time.

This brief renewal of Kevin and Sami's alliance was even more doomed than the first. They feuded with the New Day for about a month, winning their first PPV match against them in June, but Kevin seemed puzzled by Sami's new vicious humorlessness. On the way up the ramp after their win, he stopped to mockingly gyrate his hips back at the New Day, one arm around Sami's shoulders. "Swivel, Sami, swivel!" he yelled at his friend, but Sami was too busy hollering abuse and challenges at their opponents to be playful.

This win led to Sami getting a match with Kingston, and it was here the real shift in Sami's demeanor became clear. He didn't do any of his high-flying, elegant moves. He was, in fact, more focused on hurting Kingston than actually winning. "Cover him, cover him, cover him!" Kevin called from the sidelines as Sami mocked Kingston and kicked at him. "You should really cover him," he finished, his sentence trailing off into uncertainty and something close to worry.

On Smackdown the same week, Kevin and Sami were wrestling as a team again, part of an eight-man tag match. Sami, far from being the canny strategist/coward he'd been in the past with Kevin, jumped ahead of the other wrestlers to tag himself in and threw himself straight at his opponent with no finesse, no skill, no moves, nothing but anger. On the apron, Kevin watched, frowning—more disappointed than angry, more baffled than enraged. As Sami got inevitably trounced, Kevin finally tilted his head in disgust, threw up his hands, and bailed on him. Soon after that, he'd go back to being a babyface again, with the only remnant of this little detour a long-term distrust between him and the members of the New Day.

Ironically, that summer Kevin entered a feud with Shane McMahon, this time with their alignments reversed—Kevin as a salt-of-the-earth face and Shane as a glory-hogging megalomaniac heel who Kevin finally forced to leave WWE (for a while, at least) while Kevin moved to *Raw*. After briefly going back to NXT in the fall to help out in the men's WarGames match, he started feuding on *Raw* with Seth Rollins, who had recently turned heel and started calling himself the "Messiah." The down-to-earth face and the wild-eyed fanatic were on a collision course for the 2020 *WrestleMania*.

In the meantime, Sami wasn't doing as well. In the wake of Kevin giving up on him, he drifted further into darkness. In his matches, he never bothered doing any actual moves, he just threw himself blindly at opponents, trying to hurt them. In quick succession, he lost to Rey Mysterio in five minutes, Aleister Black in six minutes, Samoa Joe in a crushing forty-five seconds. Fans hypothesized that he still wasn't healed from his injury, or that he was being told he was no longer allowed to use his more spectacular moves.

Whatever the backstage situation, however, the storyline reason for this slow and agonizing diminution was clear—Sami Zayn had lost faith in himself. He no longer believed in his skills, in his own heart. In August, after losing to Cedric Alexander in four minutes, Sami grabbed a chair and smashed it against—not Alexander, but the ring itself, battering at it in an agony of despair. It was as if the ring, as if wrestling itself, had betrayed him and become his enemy.

Then he stopped wrestling altogether.

Instead, he attached himself to Intercontinental champion Shinsuke Nakamura, who was also a heel at the time. Announcing that Nakamura had the soul of an artist but an inability to express himself, he proclaimed himself Nakamura's manager. Soon he had enlisted Cesaro to join them, creating what Sami called The Artist Collective. Nakamura and Cesaro were the wrestlers against whom Sami had fought some of his most beautiful and passionate matches. Now he was reduced to being the mouthpiece of wrestlers he had once created magic with, refusing to get in the ring himself. For all that he called himself "the Great Liberator," Sami had become a shadow of his former self.

Other wrestlers even pointed it out onscreen, a sign that it was a deliberate story point. The Miz said to Sami, "why don't you step into the ring and beat some respect into me?" and there was a flash of panic in Sami's eyes before he laughed, a moment where he seemed to realize he didn't even have confidence he could beat a former reality

TV star. Mustafa Ali jeered that Sami "doesn't even *compete* anymore, he's just a mouthpiece," and although Sami scoffed, months passed and he didn't prove Ali wrong.

The memory of him in 2016, lifting the Intercontinental title as the crowd roared its approval, became a goading anguish to his fans as he stood beside Nakamura with the title around his waist and never showed any interest in it. He even took responsibility for the redesign of the belt, presenting it as a gift to Nakamura in November 2019. Did his fingers linger on it just a trifle possessively as he handed it over? Anyone who wanted to see him wrestle again could only hope.

Through 2019, Kevin and Sami would cross paths now and then on untelevised house shows. Each time the same thing happened: they'd start off friendly, then Sami would run his mouth, and Kevin would give him a Stunner and leave him flopping on the mat. Sometimes he would urge Sami to listen to the fans cheering for them both. "I'm trying to help him, and he never shuts up!" he complained to the camera in Buenos Aires. It was the very faintest of continuities, but a consistent trajectory from their parting—Kevin aware that Sami needed help, trying (in the mad logic of wrestling) to bring him to his senses through violence, to force him into wrestling again.

If you're thinking that this setup looks familiar—Sami with his confidence shattered, attaching himself to a group of powerful wrestlers in the hopes of leeching some of their shine for himself, with Kevin in the wings willing to help if (when) they turned on him—it does seem possible that the rough structure of the Bloodline story began as a second shot at a story Sami started in 2019.

On December 9, Mojo Rawley mouths off to Kevin as he searches backstage for Seth Rollins' henchmen, and Kevin slaps him. Later in the show, to Kevin's bemusement, Rawley interrupts Kevin in the ring. Sami is at his side, claiming to be representing him. He tells Kevin he's gotten a manager's license so he can appear on either *Raw* or *Smackdown*, then pauses. "But you know me better than anyone, and you know I'm not a manager, right?" Kevin's face is scrunched up with a mix of disgust and worry. "I'm a *liberator*," Sami explains, and offers to help and guide Kevin. Before Kevin can respond, though, Rawley interrupts and earns himself a beating at Kevin's hands. Sami, wide-eyed but untouched by Kevin, retreats. It might have been a totally random segment (Sami never interacted with Rawley again). It *might* have been a reminder of their relationship in preparation for a future angle when Nakamura and Cesaro turned on Sami.

That week in Wuhan, China, a handful of people were developing coughs and pneumonia-like symptoms.

Countdown to Silence

Battling against Seth Rollins' Messiah and his plans to make everyone on *Raw* bow down to him, Kevin enlisted help from Samoa Joe and the Viking Raiders, despite admitting to Joe that he'd "done some pretty bad things to a lot of people in this company." That acknowledgement of his untrustworthy past would become a theme through 2020. At the same time on *Smackdown*, Braun Strowman, who you may remember as the monster that beat Sami until he couldn't stand up back in 2017, came gunning for Shinsuke Nakamura's Intercontinental title. Despite the best efforts of the Artist Collective, Strowman beat Nakamura on Jan. 31, 2020, to become the new champion.

That day, a seventh case was found in the United States of the disease that had become known as COVID-19. The day before, the World Health Organization had declared COVID-19 a Public Health Emergency of International Concern and said that "all countries should be prepared for containment."

As Kevin continued battling Seth and his gang of followers, he kept finding himself alone—sometimes because Joe or the Viking Raiders suffered fictional injuries, now and then because of unlucky legit injuries. Over and over he found himself with no one to rely on. Meanwhile on *Smackdown*, Nakamura sneak-attacked Strowman with Cesaro and Sami, goading him into a rematch.

On February 28, Strowman sneeringly said that he could take all three of them in a title match, and Sami quickly seized the opportunity to write exactly that into the contract, making it a three-on-one handicap match for *Elimination Chamber*. Cesaro and Nakamura then attacked Strowman, with the Great Liberator standing by watching.

But when Strowman got both of his compatriots in chokeholds, Sami suddenly leapt forward and Helluva Kicked him in the face.

It was clearly done totally on instinct. Sami himself seemed shocked to have found himself doing an actual wrestling move after five months of inaction. But when Cesaro and Nakamura recovered and restrained Strowman, Sami kicked him again, and this time there was a crafty glee in his expression, an awakening of a desire to win. A revival of ambition.

That same day, an elementary school in Oregon was closed when a staff member tested positive for COVID-19. The next day would see the first recorded U.S. death from the virus.

Elimination Chamber was held on March 8, 2020. Sami, Nakamura and Cesaro faced Braun Strowman for the Intercontinental Championship. At the climax of the match, Cesaro and Nakamura hoisted Strowman upside down while Sami Helluva Kicked him. Sami then waved Cesaro and Nakamura out of the ring and pinned Strowman, finally taking as his own the title he'd first touched almost three years ago.

Despite it being a handicap match, there was no question of sharing the title. Sami lifted it alone, his face alight with joy beneath his first title on the main roster. The Philadelphia crowd rained boos down on him, a chaotic welter of sound. It would be the last time Sami would hear a live audience's reaction for over a year. Three days later, the WHO declared COVID-19 an international pandemic. WWE was forced to tape Raw and Smackdown in the empty Performance Center with no audience. After insisting for weeks that *WrestleMania* would not be canceled, WWE eventually would have no choice but to hold it with no audience, in near-total silence.

The Pandemic Era had arrived.

Thunderdome

COVID-19 was of course terrible for every spectator event. But it was especially devastating to professional wrestling. Both competitive sports and theater could be done without a live audience, though the experience was surreal. But wrestling, like improv and stand-up comedy, is inherently collaborative. Wrestlers take cues from and adapt to the audience both at the micro level, while performing, and at the macro level, while planning out storylines. Without real-time feedback from fans, wrestling essentially becomes paralyzed, frozen in amber, unable to evolve or develop in the organic way it must. After an excruciating month of performances to an empty and silent arena, WWE tried to create the illusion of a live audience, first by using trainees to play the part of spectators, and then by creating the Thunderdome, a barrage of videoconferenced faces and piped-in sound. But it was only an illusion, not the actual living responses that are the lodestone pulling wrestling narratives forward. As a result, with a couple of notable exceptions like Roman Reigns becoming the Tribal Chief or Alexa Bliss allying with the Fiend, most WWE characters and storylines plateaued through 2020 and 2021, caught in a kind of holding pattern.

Most notably for Kevin and Sami's story, it was impossible for Sami to turn face in this era.

Sami's style of babyface feeds off the crowd's energy, a feedback loop of positive energy between performer and audience. In the silence of the Performance Center or the artificial chatter of the Thunderdome, there was no way to establish that loop. He could have started acting nicer, but for the narrative energy to truly make the turn, he needed a live audience. So if the story had in fact been leading toward a Bloodline-style face turn for Sami, his character was now frozen in place as a heel, waiting for the other half of the wrestling equation, the fans, to return.

WrestleMania 2020, executed in the very depths of the uncertainty of the early pandemic, was a unique document of the time. The Undertaker had his last match, against AJ Styles in a movie-set graveyard. John Cena and Bray Wyatt created their bizarre psychological-thriller cinematic match in the Firefly Funhouse. Drew McIntyre won the WWE Championship in total silence, a fact that would drive his character for years after.

Kevin and Seth Rollins used the eerie silence to stress the physicality of their match. As they dropped each other on aprons and hit each other with chairs and ring bells, the impacts of flesh against wood and metal rang out sickeningly loud against the hush. The sound of their gasps for air or their yelps and moans of pain, no longer concealed by the hubbub of thousands of voices, underlined the cost of wrestling in a stark new way. Kevin got a big character moment when Rollins attacked him with the ring bell and Kevin therefore won by DQ, but rejected that win and insisted on re-starting the match as a no-DQ match so he could get a true victory. When Kevin eventually leaped from the *WrestleMania* sign onto Rollins as he lay on a table,* the thudding impact had a finality that wasn't drowned out by any pop from an audience.

For his part, Sami had a match with the man he'd been chasing for a decade, Daniel Bryan. Sami had taken offense when Bryan had rejected his invitation to join the Artist Collective and was out to see him suffer. Bryan was determined to prove that Sami didn't deserve the title that he had won only with help from his allies. Sami and Bryan leaned into the silence of the arena as a chance to tear down Sami's psyche. Sami desperately dodged and ran from Bryan for the first half of the match, but when Bryan finally cornered him he found himself face-to-face with the implacable judgment of his idol. "You haven't earned anything!" Bryan informed him with a sharp cuff, kicking and beating him as Sami found himself helpless to respond, all of his beautiful wrestling moves locked away in his mind. In the silence, you could hear Sami start to snivel as Bryan's contempt flayed him, sobbing and then howling with pain both physical and mental as Bryan's kicks thudded against his heart. "You did this to yourself," Bryan informed him, more disappointed than angry, the words falling like stones into the silence of the Performance Center. Panicked and acting on sheer instinct, Sami eventually Helluva Kicked Bryan out of midair and got the win, seeming almost startled that he'd been able to tap back into his well of skill.

And then he disappeared from television for months, most likely because his wife was pregnant and he wanted to minimize her risk.

---

* A backstage documentary released later shows Kevin checking out the set before the match, looking at the giant sign and declaring, with a gleam in his eyes, "I'm gonna dive off that bitch!"

THUNDERDOME

The Intercontinental title was vacated and passed to AJ Styles and then Jeff Hardy. Sami eventually returned in August, his hair grown long and unkempt in quarantine, brandishing the title that he claimed he had never relinquished. The two titles were hung above the ring for Sami, Hardy and Styles to battle over.

Sami spent the first half of the match in a daredevil renaissance, doing long-vanished moves like his Arabian press moonsault and crashing through ladders at terminal velocity (backstage footage released later shows Kevin—not on the card, but backstage despite the strict COVID protocols—watching the monitors, the mask over his mouth and nose not hiding his wince as Sami smashes through steel to the floor). Eventually Sami remembered that there are smarter and less painful ways to win a match and defeated both Styles and Hardy though cleverness and cunning, handcuffing Hardy to a ladder by the hole for his ear gauge and then handcuffing Styles to the bottom rungs of the ladder, leaving him free to retrieve his title in front of a glassy sea of frowning LED faces. He would hold the title until late December 2020, and that loss to Big E would set him on a spiral of paranoia and conspiracy theories.

Kevin was on a very different kind of path. Through 2020, in the empty Performance Center and the glittering Thunderdome, Kevin was busy reminding everyone that his past continued to haunt him. In August he helped two wrestlers, Liv Morgan and Ruby Riott, reconcile their past and become friends again by explaining his own regrets to them. "I've done a lot of really crappy things to a lot of people. I've said a lot of crappy things. I've lost friendships," he explained. "And it's always because I thought it was better for my career. And right now I can stand in this ring and look at both of you and say *I don't know if it was really worth it.*" It's the most stark statement of regret Kevin has ever made about all his past misdeeds, and he kept hammering it home, repeating the theme in case anyone missed it. "I've done a lot of crappy things to a lot of people for my career to try to get to the top spot, the titles, all that stuff, right? I'm trying to take a different way there," he explained to a bewildered-looking Ric Flair at one point. On *Raw Talk* he jumped onto a table to announce "I've done a lot of really terrible things throughout my career to try to get my points across, to try and make my career go forward, and it *never felt right"*—an extraordinary statement in wrestling, where the heel form of a wrestler is so often treated as their most authentic self.

His opponents were happy to throw his past in his face. "You have a knack for betraying the people who rely on you," Aleister Black intoned from the darkness. After months on *Raw*, Kevin showed up unexpectedly on *Smackdown* to interview Alexa Bliss, newly-allied with the Fiend, and she informed him with wide-eyed innocence that "People change, Kevin. Don't you want to change? Be better?"

"Yes! I've been trying to change! I've said it before," Kevin reminded her. And he had—but only on *Raw*. With the draft looming, he was re-establishing the theme to the *Smackdown* audience, where he was about to be drafted. "I've done a lot of really terrible things throughout my career and I've tried to change and better myself and do things the right way." The Fiend, of course, found this desire for redemption intriguing, and Bray Wyatt showed up to lecture Kevin from the Funhouse about friendship, reassuring his puppets that the draft would never separate them. "Don't worry. Friends stick together through thick and thin, no matter which brand they're on," he said, glinting a knowing smile at Kevin standing unnerved in the ring. Then he led the whole Funhouse in a song about friendship, concluding with Ramblin' Rabbit singing "friends til death do us part" and immediately being eaten by Mercy the Buzzard. Sadly for anyone who wanted to see Bray Wyatt dig into Kevin's psyche, they were ships passing in the night as Kevin went to Smackdown and Wyatt to Raw, but it helped introduce the Smackdown audience to Kevin's quest for redemption, this loose end still dangling, never explicitly connected to Sami, but always there.

After the draft in October 2020, Kevin and Sami were back on the same brand. Yet somehow they managed to never quite interact—a choice that was not coincidental, as revealed by a deliberately teasing segment backstage where Kevin interacted with Daniel Bryan, then exited to the left of the screen a split-second before Sami arrived from the right to talk to Bryan. They were both busy that fall. Sami was dodging people trying to take his title, while Kevin was getting embroiled for the first time in Bloodline matters when he jokingly criticized Jey for becoming Reigns' subordinate. A full two years before he and Sami would work together to break Jey away from his cousin's control, Kevin ended up battling Reigns alone in a series of intense matches that lasted through the fall.

"Our Next Guest?!"

By the time of his second reign as Intercontinental champion, Sami was really clicking as a comedic heel. He was by turns put-upon, whiny, self-aggrandizing and self-pitying, and his rants about how everyone was out to get him were becoming increasingly unhinged and entertaining. Part of his work at the time included being one of the regular hosts of "Talking Smack," the after-show panel that interviewed various wrestlers.

In early November 2020, Sami takes intense offense when his co-host Kayla Braxton appears in a Halloween costume as "Sami Zayn," nattering about fair trade coffee in a Canadian accent. As he expresses his rage and umbrage (between choked bouts of laughter), Kevin suddenly wanders onto the set to offer Braxton some pointers ("you probably need to throw up your hands a lot more"). After Braxton flees Sami's anger, Kevin sits down in her seat and starts bantering with Sami. "I don't even know what you're doing here! I'm trying to run a show!" Sami cries in exasperation. They're both laughing, effervescent, almost bubbling over with glee. It's the first time they've shared a screen in almost a year, the first time since the pandemic started. Visibly trying to get back on track, Sami finally says, "we're just gonna keep it going, because actually our next guest—"

Kevin's face lights up at his pronoun choice. "*Our* next guest?!" he exclaims in incredulous delight, bursting into peals of laughter.

"*Apparently* you're hosting with me now!" Sami yells at him as Kevin keeps chortling. "I don't even know how this *happened!*" His outrage is only the thinnest of veneers over some other intense emotion, something closer to joy. They're both giddy, giggling, crackling with energy.

It's almost certain that they've heard the recent news that the next *WrestleMania* has been moved from its originally-planned location in

California to Florida.[2] Without a doubt they either have been told or have made the leap of logic the fans have all made to the likelihood that there will be a live audience for the show, the first time in over a year.

It's possible that, as they fall over themselves laughing together, they know what they'll be doing at that *WrestleMania*.

KARMA
(2021)

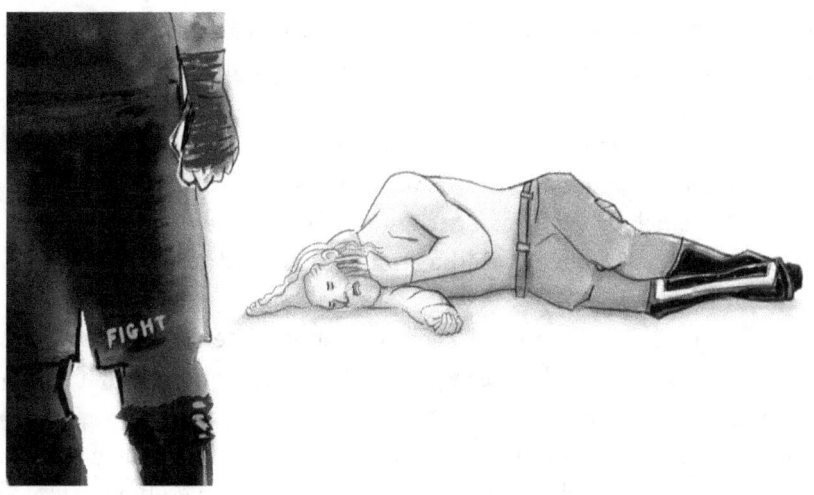

"Let's Do This Together!"

SOME OF THE greatest partnerships in wrestling, those pairs of friends with intertwined careers, have never had a one-on-one confrontation at *WrestleMania*. *WrestleMania* matches are a finite resource, and if the timing is a little off, it's just never going to happen. Christian and Edge, Triple H and Shawn Michaels, John Cena and

Randy Orton, the three members of the Shield—none of them have ever faced each other across the ring one-on-one at *WrestleMania*. When Kevin and Sami were just kids driving through the early darkness of a Montreal winter, surely that was one of their goals, but it must have been at that point where goals start to fade back into dreams, something you mention half-joking: *ah yes, the moment the two of us will stand across the ring at the Showcase of the Immortals, before tens of thousands of screaming fans.*

At the *Royal Rumble* in January, Kevin had a Last Man Standing match with Roman Reigns, the third in their series of vicious title-match brawls that cemented Reigns as a heel. Reigns threw Kevin off the LED displays and ran him over with a golf cart. Kevin countered with a swanton off a forklift. In the end, as usual, interference from the Bloodline cost Kevin the title. Because of the interference, General Manager Adam Pearce granted Kevin a spot at the Elimination Chamber match to determine Reigns' opponent at WrestleMania.

In the meantime, Sami—furious at losing the Intercontinental title to Big E, seething with conspiracy theories, increasingly wild-eyed and haggard—won himself a slot in the Elimination Chamber as well. By this point, he was "filming a documentary" about the injustices against him, which included having a "documentary film crew" following him around everywhere, much to the annoyance of commentary, referees, and other wrestlers.

Despite being on the same show for months, Kevin and Sami had continued to avoid each other with a deliberate carefulness that made clear it was not merely that people in charge had forgotten their connection. They hadn't interacted on TV in over a year, they hadn't been in the ring together for a year and a half. On the go-home *Smackdown* before *Elimination Chamber*, the requisite six-man tag between the participants was booked, the first time the two had been in a match *against* each other for nearly three years. Yet through a series of clever character touches—Kevin's babyface teammates very reasonably didn't trust him and were reluctant to tag him in, while cowardly Sami continued to dodge tags from the other heels whenever possible—the two of them didn't end up facing each other through the whole match. Only in the brawl that broke out after the match did Sami rush up behind Kevin and hurl him backwards into a suplex.

A few days later, at *Elimination Chamber*, the two of them are bristling with barely-concealed excitement. When Sami enters the Chamber, Kevin is already in his pod, and Sami stops to taunt him. "Come on. Get in here," Kevin responds, bouncing on the balls of his feet, eager to fight. "Get in here so we can get this started! Get in here, come on. Come on buddy, get in your pod. You talk too much!"

When Kevin's pod finally opens, Sami is already in the ring, and he grabs Kevin, imploring him. "Let's do this together!" he begs. "We have a history. They're not like us. They don't want me in this match, they don't want you in this match. We're not the poster boys! Let's do this together!" He rises up on his tippytoes with the force of his indignation. "Let's do this together, like old times!"

Two years ago Kevin had begged Sami to work with him, but in the Elimination Chamber there can be only one winner, and Kevin knows that perfectly well, so Sami's appeal breaks off into a squawk of alarm as Kevin hurls him against a pod. Eventually Kevin goes on to eliminate Sami from the match, only to have Jey Uso repeatedly slam his arm in the chamber door, incapacitating and then eliminating him. One more crime by the Bloodline against Kevin Owens.

A More Righteous Path

Desperate to have an ally, increasingly unmoored from reality, Sami turns (as Kevin had back in 2017) to the only person he felt he could trust. Cornering Kevin backstage on *Smackdown*, he begs for his support and explains that his documentary is going to be a gigantic hit. "It's gonna do *massive* numbers. I'm talking, like…" He pauses, then says words that will cause a ripple effect through WWE far beyond this feud, for the first time invoking the social media figure who would one day be US champion. "Like… *Logan Paul* numbers."

"Have you ever considered that whatever's happening, you're…" Kevin sounds almost hesitant in response, unwilling to jar his delusional friend too badly. "Kinda… twisting reality into whatever you need it to be… so it works for your story, fits your narrative?" Sami's confused and baffled head tilt indicates that no, he had never considered this. After losing his match later that night, Sami turns to Kevin on commentary, demanding he agree that the referee had been unfair. When Kevin tells him he has to let go of his grievances, Sami howls "I thought I could trust you!" and kicks Kevin squarely in the face.

Although both of them get angry at each other through this feud, at its base the conflict is more ideological than personal. Neither of them ever denies they still *want* to get along. Ranting after the show, Sami stammers wildly to his documentary crew that "I'm not gonna get into the fact that I kicked him and I didn't even *want* to kick—" before breaking off and repeating "I'm not gonna get into all of that!" For his part, on the next KO Show, Kevin informs the banks of glowing screens that "I really tried to make it clear to Sami Zayn that even though I don't believe in all his conspiracy theories, I still have his back, I'm still on his side."

When he calls out Sami to "ask him a question," Sami is sincerely, if derangedly, apologetic. Standing on the ramp, flanked by his documentary crew, he says, "If I'm being honest, it's just that this conspiracy stuff, it's been getting to my psyche, it really has. It's affected my mental state." He seems truly rattled, almost unnerved by himself, but unable to break out of his fantasy world. To make amends, he reassures Kevin that he can still, of course, be part of his documentary.

Kevin's face falls as Sami explains wildly that there'll be a red carpet premiere of the trailer next week, that the "global YouTube sensation" Logan Paul will be attending. "Then everyone will see!" Sami beams at him. "And yes, you can be a part of it," he reassures Kevin, all generosity itself. When Kevin says he doesn't care about the documentary, Sami loses his cool and starts screaming about how Kevin is part of the conspiracy against him, until Kevin finally yells at him to shut up. Sami's eyes go wide with alarm as Kevin corners him against the KO Show sign. "Kevin," he gabbles, "you're making a huge mistake, listen to me, listen to me, *listen to me*. It's not how we have to go about this, we need to be working together! Just listen to me, we need to be working together!"

But the time for working together is over—or is not yet here. "You and me," Kevin says. "One on one. At WrestleMania." He points at the sign, eyes fixed on Sami. "Yes or no?"

Sami's face goes through a truly remarkable set of expressions. He looks at the sign and for an instant there's a thwarted longing on his face, but fear wins out. He shakes his head in a panic until Kevin finally has to bully him into accepting the challenge that just about any other wrestler would leap at. The next week, when Sami's guest of honor, Logan Paul, actually *does* appear for the first time on WWE television, Kevin interrupts the uncomfortable spectacle of Sami fawning over a less-than-enthusiastic Paul to stunner Sami. Sami is enraged at this spoiling of his "premiere," and the conflict is joined in earnest.

On *Talking Smack*, Kevin explains that Sami is "one of the *best*. But the problem that I've had the last few months… This conspiracy theory stuff that he's harping about and this alternate reality that he seems to live in, it's taken him away from being one of the best." He explains to a baffled Paul Heyman that "Hopefully once it's all said and done, I'll have managed to beat some sense into him, and the old Sami will be back, and he can straighten things out and get back on a…" He pauses, looking for the right way to put it, "a more *righteous path*."

It's been too long, especially in the goldfish-attention-span WWE of 2021, for Kevin to hearken all the way back to 2017, to talk about how he himself put Sami's feet on his current path, leading him away from his righteous self into the brambles and thickets of mixed self-pity and self-loathing. But it's there, under his constant discussions of how he has failed his friends in the past, under his desperate desire to get the "old Sami" back. This is Kevin's chance at redemption, his opportunity to force Sami back into what he used to be.

When Sami first came back from injury, two years before this, Kevin had said over and over that he was going to "stun some sense into him." As the world started to emerge very tentatively from its pandemic shell, he was finally going to get the chance to make good on his old promise, on the grandest stage of them all.

Time is a Construct

WrestleMania 37 was the first time WWE had a show with an audience in over a year. The crowd capacity was limited, but the fervor of the fans was intense as they gathered to welcome their favorite wrestlers back to their shared world.

So of course, the start of the first night of the show was delayed.

Violent thunderstorms raked Central Florida that night, making it impossible to start the show for thirty agonizing minutes. As the fans crouched in the stands, lashed by wind and rain, the wrestlers and staff scrambled to fill the time. Backstage, Kevin stepped up and delivered an impromptu recap of his current feud with Sami for those who hadn't seen him detail it on *Talking Smack*, getting them ready for their match on Night 2. "The Sami Zayn that you guys see these days," he told the waiting audience, "it's not the Sami that I've known for two decades. It's not the Sami that you've all come to appreciate as a performer through his career in WWE!" The show finally went on and Drew McIntyre (who had just a month before lost the championship he carried through the worst of the pandemic) got to be the very first wrestler to come out and hear the applause of the audience as he tried to win his championship back in front of fans—and failed. Bad Bunny electrified the audience. Sasha Banks and Bianca Belair became the first black women to main event *WrestleMania* together. And Kevin and Sami waited for Night 2 and their match against each other.

When Sami comes out for their match that second night, the audience bursts into song with delight at seeing him, singing him to the ring, unabashed by his heelish mugging.* He introduces Logan Paul to be at ringside, buttering him up. The crowd already hates Paul and refuses to cheer for him even though he's more or less babyface as he takes his seat at commentary.

The howl that greets Kevin as he comes out seems to hit him like a physical thing. Overwhelmed, he spins around and goes roaring back up the ramp as if he barely knows where he is before heading back toward Sami in the ring.

The match starts with Kevin immediately pop-up powerbombing

---

* One assumes this is where it became obvious he was going to have to have a new theme song when audiences came back, as the slowed-down, remixed, unsingable version debuted shortly after live audiences returned.

Sami, but Sami rolls out of the ring, frantically dodging him. He manages to get Kevin down to the mat and straddles him, jabbing and punching down at him, but against his oldest foe he cannot rely on the cunning brute force he's used for years now. Eventually he pulls off the crispest Michinoku Driver ever, turning Kevin perpendicular to the mat and driving him down with clockwork precision. Kevin responds with a frog splash and a pumphandle neckbreaker, then starts what long-term fans will recognize as the setup for the package piledriver, his pre-WWE finisher. Sami fights free. His skin is scratched and abraded, his hair and eyes wild. He counters Kevin's stunner attempt into a blue thunderbomb, followed up with an exploder suplex, a half-and-half suplex, and a brainbuster in rapid succession, as if he can't help but reach deep into his bag of tricks against Kevin. He even teases the top-rope brainbuster, El Generico's old finishing move, though Kevin counters it as Sami had countered the package piledriver.

Finally, Kevin runs to the corner, probably planning on a cannonball, but Sami races right behind him, and when Kevin turns, he pivots right into Sami's Helluva Kick.

He falls forward heavily against Sami and Sami holds him up, replicating the *Battleground* ending from 2016, the moment that Sami put aside his hatred of Kevin to end their first feud.

But this is a very different Sami. He pauses as the audience sound rises and crests, then laughs and shakes his head. "This is because of *you*," he says bitterly to Kevin, propping him back up in the corner and running back to start the approach for the second Helluva Kick that will end him.

But this is a very different Kevin as well. He comes forward to meet Sami, superkicking him twice in the middle of the ring, and this time it's Sami that falls forward onto Kevin's heart, this time it's Kevin's turn to be the one who gazes at his foe with sorrow more than anger, resolute.

"*You* did this," he says almost gently to Sami, the same message Daniel Bryan delivered to him a year ago at the last *WrestleMania* in the hushed and horrible silence. Then he stunners Sami and pins him.

As the crowd cheers, Logan Paul—who has been watching the whole match with interest—jumps into the ring. He pats Sami on the shoulder. Then he comes up to Kevin. "That was awesome!" he enthuses.

Kevin just blinks at him, but Sami is horrified at this betrayal and confronts Paul. "You're my guest of honor! What are you doing? He's the enemy!" Paul has had enough and shoves Sami roughly to the mat. The crowd mutters angrily. Kevin is watching him, his eyes narrowed. As Sami throws up his hands, almost in tears, and leaves the ring, Paul lifts Kevin's hand in victory.

Kevin looks up at his hand, absolutely expressionless. A ripple of excited anticipation goes through the crowd, building as they watch Kevin fix his gaze on Paul like a snake on a slightly annoying bird. Paul, a natural-born showman, immediately starts effusively accepting the applause he assumes is meant for him, beaming at the audience right up until the moment that Kevin stunners him and leaves him a limp pile on the mat.

The cameras don't catch what Sami's reaction is to seeing Kevin lay out the man who had been mocking him. Backstage, when asked about his reaction to Kevin's actions, he seems bewildered. There's an odd half-smile on his face. "I don't know how to process any of this, if I'm being totally honest, because all of this seems a little surreal." He starts laughing incredulously. "It doesn't even feel real when I say these words out loud! Logan Paul pushed me, yeah? And then Kevin did give him a stunner, yes?" He describes it as "an out of body experience," like he was floating above it all, watching it unfold. "None of this feels real to me. Right now none of this feels like it's really happening." He laughs softly, his eyes distant. For a brief moment he seems almost like the Sami of old. After a long moment, the interviewer finally says "Well, thank you for your time." Sami's eyebrows go up in something like wonder. "Time," he intones. "Time… is a construct." He wanders off.

Karma

This brief flash of near-lucidity doesn't last, however. By the next *Smackdown*, Sami is back to insisting that he only lost because worrying about Logan Paul had distracted him, demanding a rematch. When he

KARMA

actually gets it, however, he runs away, leaving a frustrated Kevin to say backstage that "Being in the ring with Sami on that stage... I still didn't accomplish what I wanted to do, which was stun Sami back to reality." He vows that he'll stun Sami "over and over and over again, every week, every month, every *year* if I have to," until he can snap him back to his truer self. He's fought Sami and fought by his side for two decades, he says, and "I want to spend the next two decades fighting—and teaming up with—the Sami that *I've* known for the last twenty years, not this version."

Each of them doggedly fixed on their goals—Sami to prove the conspiracy against him, Kevin to stun Sami back to his senses—they circle each other for two full months, criss-crossing paths with Big E and Apollo Crews as they battle over the Intercontinental Championship. Kevin takes this opportunity to mend bridges with Big E, who is slow to trust him after his attacks on Kofi Kingston and Xavier Woods years ago. In a truly astonishing backstage video, he explains to the interviewer that he felt badly about his past actions and he hoped maybe teaming with Big E "could repair some of the damage that I did."

At this point, the camera pulls back to show Big E sitting a few feet away, smiling. "I've been here the whole time. Like, the whole time, from the beginning. I don't know if you didn't see me? It was a little weird."

Kevin sighs and turns to face Big E. "See, even though I *am* sorry, I have a hard time expressing those feelings directly to people." Big E nods sympathetically as Kevin explains that he knew E was there, and by talking to the interviewer, he'd hoped to make his regret clear. It's all very funny, but at the same time played totally straight, these two meaty men meeting to discuss their feelings, hoping they can somehow work together.

In the meantime, Sami becomes obsessed with "karma," with the idea that cosmic justice will make sure Kevin gets what's coming to him. "*I* didn't kick you," he screams after a sneak attack on Kevin, trembling with outrage from his disheveled hair to his tippy-toe feet, "*karma* kicked you!" After Crews's henchman punches Kevin's throat and leaves him gasping for breath in the ring, a backstage camera shows Sami gloating over the screen displaying Kevin's suffering. "Oh baby!" he explains in glee, caressing Kevin's agonized image and giving it a little kiss. It's the mirror-image version of Kevin's torments of El Generico, his relishing of the luchador's suffering.

At *Hell in a Cell* in June he and Kevin meet again. This time Kevin is still suffering the effects of that attack to his throat, struggling to breathe all the way through the match. At some point Sami's lip gets cut and Kevin ends up with Sami's blood daubed all over him. When Sami finally gets the pin, he collapses over Kevin laughing in a frantic exhaustion that's close to tears. "Karma!" he cries as Kevin lies defeated, wheezing. "Karma, baby! Karmic justice!" Backstage his eyes blaze with fervor as he expounds further. "It's divinity, it's divine, it's consciousness, it's love! There's an *order*, and it's true, and it's gonna save me. Karma will save me!" The next show finds him still euphoric. "The universe is a machine designed to deliver cosmic justice!" he explains backstage, his eyes wild. And he's right, of course, but not in the way he means it, because the fictional world of wrestling is indeed a storytelling machine that almost always delivers justice at the end of a storyline. Unfortunately for Sami, he doesn't seem to realize that karma is not on his side this time around.

When the interviewer breaks the news to Sami that he has another match against Kevin next week to qualify for the Money in the Bank ladder match, you can see all the gears in Sami's head grind to a horrified halt. *"What?"* he gasps.

Karma is not done with him yet.

Last Man Standing

They come into this final match tied. Kevin got the win at *WrestleMania*, Sami got the win at *Hell in a Cell*. It's a Last Man Standing match, one of the match stipulations with the most closure. Whoever can't rise to continue the match loses. Sami is desperate to prove that cosmic justice is on his side. Kevin is determined to get another match with Roman Reigns, the man who cheated him out of a title so many times, and this match with Sami is just one step on that path. This time it truly is nothing personal.

Kevin starts off on the attack, pummeling Sami to the mat and then hitting him with a cannonball. They battle out into the Thunderdome, past the flickering screens of faces. "Say hi to the WWE Universe!" Kevin says, smacking Sami into a few of them. He does a senton off the barricade onto Sami on the floor, but when he lays Sami out on the commentary table and goes back to the barricade for a frog splash, Sami rallies, seizes him, and sends him bouncing across the table to the floor. Kevin pulls himself up as the referee counts, wincing and favoring his back. As the match goes on, Kevin seems to grow, strangely, less and less angry. Grabbing Sami's head, he puts one foot against the back of Sami's knee to force him to kneel with his throat on the ropes, then sharply kicks the rope to drive it into Sami's throat, matching his injury Sami had been gloating over. Kevin isn't gloating. He's taking no joy in this. As Sami chokes and swipes at him in a blind and frantic fury, Kevin simply cuffs him across the face, knocking him down again. He follows him out of the ring as Sami scrabbles and scrambles, stalking him, as inexorable and unavoidable as... well, as karma.

As Sami lies writhing on the floor, Kevin looks down at him with a detached mix of pity and disgust.

"Stay down," he says, the same phrase he has said to Sami so many times. When he was a heel and Sami a face, he screamed it in frustration. When they were both heels, he implored Sami to know his place. This time, with him as the face that realizes his mistakes and Sami the heel, lost in darkness as one of those mistakes, there's no heat to it at all. "Just stay down."

But he knows it's going to take more than that, so we move into the next stage of the match, the rising action. Kevin sets up two tables, one on top of the other, outside the ring at the corner, but when he pulls Sami up to the turnbuckle Sami dodges and rallies, finding enough fresh energy to hurl himself out of the ring onto Kevin in a *tope con giro*. Now it's his turn to get Kevin up on a turnbuckle, teasing the beginning of that top-rope brainbuster one more time, but Kevin counters it into a fisherman buster suplex and sends him back down to the mat. This time when Kevin drags Sami up to the turnbuckles it looks, for one insane moment, like he's going to do his old finishing move, the package piledriver, off the turnbuckle. But Sami slips out of his grasp and shoves him off the turnbuckle and into the waiting stack of tables with a wild crunch that the mechanical din of the Thunderdome does no justice to.

Sami's laugh of triumph slowly turns to disbelief as Kevin struggles to his feet through the wreckage, managing to stand before the referee reaches ten. Frantic now, he sets up another table next to the announce desk and tries to throw Kevin from the stairs into it, but Kevin wrenches himself free. Sami suplexes him on the apron. He gets back up again. Sami Helluva Kicks him. He falls heavily on his side and lies still for a moment, then drags himself to his feet, his eyes fixed on Sami's. Not laughing, not angry. Just... impossible to defeat. Like karma.

Sami tears at his hair, then Helluva Kicks him again. This time Kevin falls forward, into the *Battleground* spot, lying in Sami's arms. Sami pushes him back up against the turnbuckle and explains to him "This is karma! For everything you've ever done!" He raises his arm in victory as Kevin falls on his face, then watches in horror as Kevin slowly rolls out of the ring and—and an instant before the ten count—props himself up against the ring in a standing position. It counts as standing for the match, at least. In desperation, Sami goes for one of his oldest moves, the dive through the corner ropes DDT, but Kevin kicks him halfway through and leaves him sprawled on the mat.

Not even waiting for the count, Kevin drags Sami back up and pop-up powerbombs him, then stunners him. Sami tumbles out of the ring to the floor and Kevin pursues him (like karma).

Spent, exhausted, Sami raises a hand to try and stave Kevin off. "Wait, wait, wait, wait," he begs wearily. "How did we get here, man?" He seems to be honestly unsure what the answer is. How *did* they find themselves here, neither hating the other, locked in combat that neither really wants? "How did we get here?" he repeats, wonderingly.

Kevin shakes his head. "Just karma," he says, and powerbombs Sami first through the announce table, then through the table Sami had set up earlier, and finally against the ring apron.

The referee counts to ten. The bell rings. Kevin gets back in the ring to look up at the Money in the Bank briefcase hanging overhead. He leaves Sami behind sobbing, curled in on himself.

After all these years, he's finally gotten Sami to *stay down*.

The Way to the Righteous Path

And yet, for all of Kevin's statements about stunning sense into Sami, for all of the talk of karma, Sami's path remains the same. Two weeks after this match, WWE leaves the Thunderdome. Yet even once the live audiences return, Sami remains bitter and conspiracy-riddled, deaf to their desire to love him. The out-of-story reason for this is probably that Sami was too valuable a heel at that point to turn face. Probably by August they were already discussing his match against Johnny Knoxville at the next *WrestleMania*, and he had to stay heel for that. But there's a perfectly valid in-story reason why none of Kevin's attempts to save Sami amounted to anything, something vital that Kevin, despite his regrets and repentance, had forgotten. Sami didn't turn heel, way back in 2017, because Kevin pushed him onto that path. No, he was *pulled forward* by Kevin's peril as Kevin lay helpless to Shane McMahon's plummeting form. In the same way, Kevin could never shove Sami back onto a "more righteous path."

The only way for Kevin to save Sami would be for Kevin to need saving himself.

INTERLUDE
(2021-2022)

A Promise of Redemption

IT'S NOVEMBER 2021, and backstage interviewer Sarah Schreiber is listening to Sami Zayn rant about the fact that he has just won a battle royal to earn a shot at Roman Reigns' title. "This is something we don't get very often in WWE. This is *redemption*," he breathes, beaming. "I promise you that when Sami Zayn finally takes on Roman Reigns, whenever that may be, I will finally have *redemption*." As he leaves, Schreiber tells the camera that "it'll be interesting to see what's next for Sami Zayn," only to have Sami pop angrily back into frame, yelling "no, no, no, no, no! It's gonna be *great*, not 'interesting!' It's gonna be *great*, it's gonna be *redemption*, it's gonna actually *mean something.*" He harangues the interviewer some more, then leaves with a cry of "Sami Zayn's redemption!"

It's a loaded choice, this constant repetition of *redemption*, with its echo of Sami's great storyline in NXT that was called his "Road to Redemption." For Sami, the word is always associated with the Underdog from the Underground, the version of him that claimed we were all in a band, making stories like music together. Ironically (or not) that very November Sami had finally rid himself of "Worlds Apart," the soaring entrance song that made everyone want to sing

INTERLUDE

along. Now his entrance started the same way as the old song before slowing down into a dreary sludge of fuzzy guitars, the first few bars lingering as if designed to taunt the post-pandemic audience yearning for connection. Redemption seemed the farthest it had ever been for Sami Zayn.

Rattlesnakes and Mousetraps

Shortly after their Last Man Standing match, Kevin had been drafted to *Raw*, and he and Sami had spent the fall of 2021 in various feuds on their separate brands. Sami had fought the Mysterios and played a role in Dominick's slow-growing dissatisfaction with his father. Kevin went through the second of his temporary heel turns since he'd become a face in 2019, sadly proving Big E's suspicion of him justified when he finally cracked under the strain of everyone's distrust and embraced being "a scumbag," in his words. He and Seth Rollins struck up an uneasy alliance based on equal amounts of exasperation and affection as the year wound down.

In early 2022, as *WrestleMania 38* drew closer, Kevin decided he really, really hated Texas.

WrestleMania was being held in Dallas, where Kevin's lifelong idol "Stone Cold" Steve Austin started his career, and Kevin's chortling trash-talking ("If North America was a human body, Texas would be its *ass!*") was an utterly transparent attempt to taunt Austin out of his 19-year retirement for one last match.

And Austin responded.

Unwilling to publicly commit to a match for fear he wouldn't be able to get into satisfactory shape, Austin insisted that officially he would only be a guest on Kevin's talk show. But in Kevin's promos and interviews at the time, the incandescent joy that seemed to leak from his every pore revealed that an actual match was very much on the table. And he had been hand-picked for the job. "Everyone was in agreement, from top to bottom, that it should be me. The quote I got was 'It wouldn't be done with anybody but you.'"[1] Quite an honor for the kid who had once wallpapered his bedroom in Stone Cold posters, who had thrown a mug through the wall of his house trying to create the iconic glass-breaking sound in his imaginary entrance. Now he'd be hearing it for real in front of sixty-five thousand people in the main event of *WrestleMania*.

While Kevin was preparing to fulfill an impossible teen-aged dream, Sami was facing a very different challenge. When Johnny Knoxville, the *Jackass* reality star known for his risky and hilarious stunts, decided to enter the 2022 *Royal Rumble*, Sami protested that he didn't deserve to be there, and at the Rumble itself he eliminated Knoxville. Shortly after that Sami won the Intercontinental title for the third time, off Shinsuke Nakamura—a short-lived run, as he lost it a mere two weeks later to Ricochet when Knoxville appeared and distracted him. Sami swore revenge on Knoxville, and the *WrestleMania* feud was on.

Unlike Kevin's lifelong love of Steve Austin, Sami had never been a *Jackass* fan. But he and Knoxville appear to have recognized each other as kindred spirits, masters of the art of self-annihilation for the enjoyment of others. As *WrestleMania* approached, their feud burst the boundaries of the wrestling bubble. Knoxville put Sami's phone number on an airplane banner and Sami spent a week of deep exasperation answering calls from stunned and disbelieving fans who called the number on a lark, not expecting to get the actual Sami Zayn. He appeared at the red carpet premiere of the *Jackass* movie, ranting wildly as the non-wrestling fans boggled, until he was chased off by a cattle-prod-wielding Knoxville. Andy Kaufman would have relished the spectacle.

That *WrestleMania* was a watershed for both Kevin and Sami. On night one, Kevin closed out the show with a full match with Steve Austin. He brawled out into the ecstatic audience with his hero, back-dropping him onto concrete, even dishing out a Stunner before he inevitably fell to the power of the Rattlesnake and lay vanquished, washed by waves of delight.

Both men shined on the big stage.

On the second night, Sami and Knoxville delivered one of the finest

INTERLUDE

comedic matches in wrestling history, a *tour de force* of stunts and gags wrapped around a story about a haughty jerk getting his comeuppance. Sami took a bowling ball to his crotch, got fireworks shot up his ass, and at the peak of the hilarity was bodyslammed by Knoxville's friend Wee Man in an homage to Hulk Hogan's epic bodyslam of Andre the Giant. In the end Sami lay in the ring defeated, trapped in a comically large mousetrap as Knoxville took his bows, laughter coruscating around them.

Two matches they both lost, matches with almost no "build," no titles, no stakes, just the pure joy of it all. In many ways, that *WrestleMania* was a pinnacle of both of their careers, proof that they could do anything asked of them and make it work, whether it was wrestling a 57-year-old legend with a previously broken neck or staging a spectacle with a group of non-wrestlers, a giant hand and a table covered with mousetraps.

At first glance, *WrestleMania 38* seems to be an anomaly for Kevin and Sami, two stand-alone matches that didn't tie in to any longer narrative. But aside from the backstage reality that both of them impressed important people with their performances (Roman Reigns had already stated his desire to work with Sami, but watching him with Knoxville made him even more certain),[2] the match with Knoxville was the gateway to something much bigger narratively as well. It provided the motivation Sami's character needed to finally launch into the storyline he'd been heading toward for months, perhaps for years, the story that had started with the Artist Collective in 2019 and been derailed by the pandemic.* As Sami puts it, "my stuff with Knoxville had to happen to kind of be the linchpin, the launching pad for the whole thing. I've been humiliated, and I need to recover. I need respect."[3] It's the story of how Sami Zayn realizes he's lost an

---

* There's a glimpse of what might have been another abortive attempt to tell this story in November 2021, where Sami briefly appeared with the faction Hit Row, attaching himself to them with the same incongruous awkwardness with which he would attach himself to the Bloodline after WrestleMania. This attempt at the story failed when Hit Row was unceremoniously let go just a few weeks later. It's right after that Sami's pitch is finally applied to the Bloodline, as mentioned in the ESPN story in the previous footnote.

essential part of himself, and how he finally finds his redemption and his soul again, by standing up to a powerful faction with Kevin at his side.

It's April 8, 2022, the week after *WrestleMania 38*, and the year-long story of Sami Zayn, Kevin Owens, and the Bloodline is about to kick off in earnest.

MIND GAMES AND WARGAMES
(2022)

For You, Big Uce

THE WEEK AFTER *WRESTLEMANIA 38*, Sami comes to General Manager Adam Pearce, distraught and indignant after his humiliating loss to Johnny Knoxville. "I have been reduced to a *laughingstock,*" he bristles. Pointing at the men's locker room door, he says "I want a match with the next person who walks through that door so that I can kick the crap out of them and get my respect back." When the door opens and Drew McIntyre comes out, Sami takes one look at the hulking Scottish Warrior and changes his tune, but it's too late. He ends up fighting McIntyre four shows in a row, constantly dodging combat, taking the countout loss rather than face his increasingly irate foe. In other words, the same weaselly heel tactics he's used for years.

But there's a difference this time around.

This time, he's visibly frustrated by his own cowardice. He struggles to try and psych himself up enough to enter the ring, talking angrily to himself, trying to get his frozen muscles to move forward instead of backwards. When his courage fails him and he flees up through the stands, surrounded by jeering fans, he looks back at the ring with something close to anguish on his face. He says he feels like he's lost the respect of the locker room. But even deeper than that, he's finally facing his own loss of self-respect, and it's flaying his soul alive. Five years ago he had faced Kevin's sneer and proudly told him that maybe he'd never been champion, but he could still look at himself in the mirror. A week later he'd joined Kevin in mocking that high-minded attitude, tossing away his ideals for pragmatism. Now it seems that maybe, just maybe, he misses being able to meet his own eyes in the mirror.

The third week, Sami's match with McIntyre is a lumberjack match. The ring will be surrounded by wrestlers to make sure he doesn't escape. In desperation, he finally plucks up all his audacity and takes a step that will change everything. He knocks on the Bloodline's door.

Inside that room are the members of the Bloodline circa 2022. There's the unctuous adviser Paul Heyman. There's happy-go-lucky Jimmy Uso, going along to get along. There's his brother, Jey Uso, outwardly broken down into a loyal minion, but always simmering with barely-controlled rage. And of course, there's Roman Reigns, the undisputed WWE Universal Champion, well into the most dominant title run of the modern era, a mob boss who can turn on the charm—and turn it off just as quickly.

The Usos are currently *Smackdown* tag team champions. Sami points out that he's seen McIntyre palling around with their next opponents, saying "some very disrespectful things about your entire family." He eagerly offers to let Roman know if he overhears any other useful information... if the Bloodline will just help him beat Drew McIntyre tonight. "I acknowledge you!" he says to Roman. "I need *you* to recognize me!"

The Usos and Heyman share a lot of "get a load of this jabronie" looks behind his back, but the Usos do indeed get involved in the match—although only to attack their current rivals, not really to help Sami. However, Sami takes this as a sign that indeed, he has a chance to join the Bloodline, and he redoubles his efforts to win them over. After that first meeting, all of his interactions are with the Usos or Heyman, but he does things like wear a Bloodline shirt to the ring, beaming at the camera and saying "For you, Big Uce!" to the absent Roman. He's constantly showing up and trying to get into the locker room as the Usos hide their contemptuous smiles behind their hands or an annoyed Heyman tells him yes, sure, the Tribal Chief admires him. It's pathetic, it's cringeworthy, it's a slow-motion car crash.

It's riveting.

The KO Show

Meanwhile, on *Raw*, the man who just main-evented *WrestleMania* with Steve Austin is on an oddly aimless trajectory. The night after *WrestleMania*, he kicks off a Byzantine and hilarious feud with a wrestler named Elias who has cut his hair, shaved his beard, and come back claiming to be his own younger brother "Ezekiel." In time-honored wrestling tradition, everyone accepts without question that he is a totally different wrestler, except for poor Kevin, who is reduced to spluttering outrage at the fact that he's the only person who can see the truth. For months he goes around the locker room trying to get someone, *anyone* to open their eyes.

And in May, he comes to *Smackdown* to have Sami as a guest on the Kevin Owens Show.

It's the first time they've interacted in almost a year, and once again they've come together assuming they can trust each other. Kevin is filled with faith that Sami will agree that Ezekiel and Elias are actually the same person. Sami is eager to hear that Kevin respects him as a fledgling member of the Bloodline. At first, they happily confirm each other's reality. "What you're doing for the Bloodline... you're unbelievable, you know that?" Kevin says. Sami responds that Elias and Ezekiel are clearly the same person, which moves Kevin so deeply that he gathers Sami into a hug, burying his head in Sami's shoulder, overcome with emotion. But of course, this state of affairs can't last. When Kevin tells Sami "I need you to drop everything you're doing on *Smackdown* and come to Raw and help me," Sami balks, telling Kevin the *Smackdown* locker room needs him, the Bloodline needs him.

Kevin's annoyance quickly starts to show. "That's the side of you I forgot, that naive, delusional side," he says. "Cut this out and listen to your *real* friends." Things quickly spiral downward from there. Furious, Sami tells Kevin he was just being nice, that Elias and Ezekiel are clearly *not* the same person, and they end up yelling insults ("Moron!"

"Liar!") at the top of their lungs at each other, until Sami says "Liar liar, pants on fire!" and Kevin points out that his pants are *clearly* not on fire. It's hilarious and juvenile.

And then suddenly, it's not.

Still angry, Kevin tells Sami that if it's true that he's such good friends with the Bloodline, they'll come out when Kevin tells them to prove it, right? An awful sadness starts to fill Sami's face as Kevin sweeps his arm wide and announces "Ladies and gentlemen, *the Bloodline!*"

Of course, no one comes out. No Bloodline music hits. Kevin mockingly says that he'll do it more loudly so they'll be sure to hear him. He belts it out again and Sami, his eyes suddenly dark and enormous in his stricken face, looks toward the ramp, hoping against hope. As he chews his lip in the awkward silence filled with the jeers of the audience, Kevin puts a hand on his shoulder.

"Sami," he says. "You know why they're not coming out? It's because the Bloodline couldn't care less about you." The mockery is gone, replaced with a pity that seems to cut Sami even more deeply. "I'm sorry," Kevin says, and he sounds sincerely sad.

Sami shakes off Kevin's hand and seems to shake off his own doubts as well. "Whatever, man," he manages to say, though his eyes are still hurt. "You don't know what you're talking about." He leaves the ring, and Kevin chases after him.

"Forget about all this!" Kevin says, grabbing his arm. "Just come to *Raw* with me!" Sami shoves him against the barricade in a burst of anger and stalks off. But the basic dynamics of the story are in place now, and Kevin—although his path will cross Sami's only rarely through the rest of 2022—is an integral part of it.

The Honorary Uce

After that disastrous KO Show, Kevin and Sami do not interact again for three months. Sami redoubles his cringeworthy efforts to join the Bloodline, fighting their foes and helping their cause. He dubs himself the "Honorary Uce," the Samoan term for "brother," and calls himself that at every opportunity. For these months, his interactions are entirely with Heyman and the Usos. Reigns is loftily above noticing Sami, hermetically sealed in the top-card bubble. Heyman, Jimmy and Jey tell the increasingly frantic Sami that the Tribal Chief appreciates him, he's just... too busy to meet him right now, all while hiding their smirks behind their hands. They constantly dangle the chance to truly be recognized as an "honorary Uce" before him, a carrot on a string that Sami chases wildly. Jimmy develops a tolerant affection for Sami, even creating a complex greeting handshake that they share, while Jey remains aloof and distrustful, glowering at him anytime something goes wrong. All of them are so obviously having fun with the angle— Jey especially has to visibly struggle against uncontrollable giggles at Sami's comedic flailing—that the crowd becomes more and more invested, more sympathetic to Sami's desperate need to be included. As Heyman will later note, the story is deliberately based on classic high school dynamics, the unpopular kid yearning to be included by the popular bullies.[1] Wrestling fans feel it in their very bones.

Over on *Raw*, events continue on their parallel path. In June, Gunther beats Ricochet (who himself beat Sami earlier in the year) for the Intercontinental Championship and begins his historical reign that will not end until 2024 at the hands of a very different Sami Zayn. Kevin, meanwhile, does not so much turn face as slowly relax back into being a babyface after the heelish blip caused by his feud with Steve Austin. By August he has won back the affection of the crowd entirely. When Drew McIntyre comes from *Smackdown* to *Raw* claiming he's "scouting the competition" for after he beats Roman in their upcoming title match, Kevin challenges him. He reminds everyone he and Sami fought each other at *Battleground* in 2016 in this arena and says he intends to challenge the winner of the McIntyre-Reigns match but he wants to fight McIntyre right now. When Jimmy and Jey Uso show up and interfere, causing a DQ after a grueling match that leaves McIntyre exhausted and diminished, Kevin leans over the ropes and calls out to the Usos, "Tell your Tribal Chief he owes me one."

That same week, *Smackdown* is in Montreal. The Usos can't make it, and to his delighted surprise, Sami finds himself summoned to an audience with Reigns. When Reigns asks him how things are going, Sami awkwardly blurts out that he's been having problems with Jey especially. Sami notes that even though he took a claymore kick from Drew to save Jey, Jey has remained hostile. "Does he even send me a text?" he says, growing more and more agitated. "Does he give me a call? He is so *ungrateful!*"

Then he freezes, realizing he's criticizing Roman's cousin, the one he calls his "right hand man." His face passes through horror and chagrin into a resigned grimace as Roman sits in silence. At the same time, something cold and calculating clicks into place behind the Tribal Chief's eyes. In this moment, he realizes he can use Sami to torment and humiliate Jey, who he has feared and despised ever since Jey defied him two years ago. He breaks into a sunny, disarming smile and tells the fidgeting Sami "You're right. He doesn't appreciate anything!" As Sami gasps in relief, Roman says "Why are you talking to *him?* You should be talking to *me!"*

Sami is exultant. At last, *at last* he is getting the respect he craves. But as he's getting ready to go to his match, Roman's face stills again. "One more thing before you go. You still cool with KO?"

Offscreen, the Montreal audience cheers as Sami says without thinking, "Kevin Owens? We're both from here, yeah, we go back forever."

"Well, just let him know I don't owe anybody. Anything. Ever," Roman says with significant emphasis.

Sami suddenly remembers that really, they've kind of drifted apart recently, they're hardly even in touch anymore, but Roman's point is made. Sami is surely thinking as long as he can avoid crossing Kevin's path, maybe everything will be okay. If he can just stay away from Kevin, maybe his tenuous connections to the Bloodline will finally become something more solid, maybe he can truly become the Honorary Uce he claims to be. If he can just dodge Kevin.

He doesn't even make it two weeks.

A Tableau with a Chair

On August 29, Sami and the Usos appear on *Raw*, breaking the (quite tenuous) brand separation to tell everyone *Smackdown* will be celebrating two years of the Tribal Chief as champion, and to remind everyone that the Bloodline runs both brands. Sami is awkwardly and charmingly goofing with the brothers, hyping up how great Roman and the Usos are, when Kevin's music hits.

As Kevin comes out, Jimmy glares at him, but Jey is scowling at the real problem which he knows is Sami. "Is this your boy right here?" he demands, causing Kevin to break into delighted chortles. "Am I your boy, Sami?" he asks.

Sami, whose face has the distinct expression of the loser kid who's finally making some headway with the cool kids only to have his fellow-loser friend show up, admits that uh, technically yes, Kevin is his "boy." Kevin then proceeds to berate Sami—for being stupid, yes, but specifically for being so stupid as to let the Bloodline convince him to forget "that you are one of the greatest in-ring performers *of all time*." A fair proportion of the crowd breaks into applause as Kevin urges Sami that "you should take a look in the mirror and re-assess things," and for a moment Sami's face is almost vulnerable, yearning for the love of the crowd and the support of his oldest friend.

But the gravitational tug of the Bloodline's coolness still wins out, and Sami leans across the ropes and sheepishly passes on Roman's message. This puts Kevin in a fighting mood, which results in him having a match with Jey.

The match is tight, but Jey is definitely getting the worst of it. Eventually he rolls out of the ring and grabs Jimmy and Sami, dragging them in for a conference. "Distract the ref," he tells Jimmy, then turns to Sami and says "Sami. Get a chair."

"What?" Sami says blankly.

"Get a chair!" Jey repeats more angrily.

"What chair? What chair?" Sami stammers. He's checked out, disassociating, trying to stay in some alternate world where this awful choice isn't barreling down on him. When Jey finally screams at him, Sami stumbles to grab a steel chair, returning to find Kevin on his knees, draped across the middle rope and Jimmy dutifully distracting the referee.

Sami lifts the chair. Jey holds Kevin helpless against the rope, his head out of the ring, open to the chairshot. Surely in this moment Sami remembers Kevin's vicious chairshot to El Generico's unprotected head, surely he tries to tell himself that Kevin has it coming. But he wavers. He raises the chair, then lowers it. Raises and lowers. Jey screams at him. The crowd screams the opposite at him. Kevin is struggling against Jey's grip, his throat pressed against the rope, not looking at Sami.

Sami's eyes go back and forth from Jey to Kevin, Kevin to Jey. He steps forward, steps back.

Finally Jimmy can no longer keep the referee distracted, and the moment has passed. Later Sami will rationalize, explaining that he was hesitating because he didn't want to risk the ref seeing him and thus getting Jey disqualified, but everyone—including Jimmy and Jey—knows that in the moment of crisis, Sami couldn't bring himself to hurt Kevin in order to help the Bloodline.

Acknowledgements

After this, Kevin goes back to *Raw* to feud with Austin Theory and have fun teaming up with Johnny Gargano. On *Smackdown*, Jimmy and Jey's brother Solo Sikoa shows up to help Roman beat McIntyre and then become the Bloodline's enforcer. By September, the Bloodline stands at five full members—Roman, Jey, Jimmy, Solo, Paul Heyman—with Sami nervously orbiting their constellation, yearning to be included.

A few weeks after Solo first shows up, Roman comes to *Smackdown* to make the traditional demand that Solo *acknowledge him*. Solo does so with no hesitation, and they embrace. As the Bloodline's music hits, Roman starts to leave the ring, and commentary starts to transition to the next segment, however, Sami grabs the mic. Jey snarls at him, but he nervously, stammeringly thanks the Bloodline for letting him be part of their family and says that he also wants to acknowledge the Tribal Chief.

There's a long, terrible silence as Heyman tells Roman he had no idea Sami would do this. Roman takes the mic and, as Jey paces back and forth angrily behind him, says "What are you talking for right now? Why are you saying anything right now? Why do you have our shirt on?" He's smiling, but it's a dangerous smile.

MIND GAMES AND WARGAMES

Sami looks down at his Bloodline shirt. Behind him, Heyman is covering his face with his hand. *"Take it off!"* screams Jey in a furious ecstasy. Roman points at Sami and demands he take off the shirt. The crowd—which has been chanting Sami's name—erupts into sad booing. Sami hesitates, misery etched on his face. Roman says "Jey," and before he can say anything else Jey leaps forward like a pit bull suddenly unchained, ripping Sami's shirt from his body with his bare hands. Sami doesn't resist, his face a study in shock and sorrow. He stands pale and half-naked in front of the Tribal Chief, hands raised in surrender, awaiting his doom. The audience moans with sympathy.

"I don't want to see you in that shirt *ever again*," Roman snarls. Sami's lips tremble. His eyes fill with tears. Jey is beside himself with joy, grinning behind Roman. "You ain't ever gonna wear it again," says Roman, "...because I got you a new one."

Swerve! He tosses a shirt to Sami, who unfolds it to reveal... a shirt with "Honorary Uce" printed on it. Sami's pain is magically transmuted to glory. Jey's smile drops away into shocked horror. Sami struggles into the shirt and throws his arms around Roman. After a moment in which we can see Roman calculating how much affection this fool needs to stay loyal, Roman returns the hug. Jey is visibly upset. Roman has used Sami to hurt Jey and put him in his place. It's a shockingly cruel and manipulative vignette, beautiful in its starkness.

From here, Sami is an honorary member of the Bloodline. As he dances and celebrates and makes them erupt in uncontrollable laughter that sometimes threatens their tough-guy images through September and October, there's a subtle shift in his relations with them. He's clearly no longer with the faction in a craven bid to shore up his own standing. He's all in on his newfound friends and truly cares about them.

Most notably, he starts to care about Jey.

Jey is still angry at him almost all the time, filled with traumatic rage and trust issues. But Sami starts to notice how Roman uses him to bully Jey—requiring Jey to answer to Sami, for example, or tauntingly telling Jey he might remove that "honorary" and make Sami a full Uce and member of the Bloodline.

Sami starts to grow uncomfortable, more and more sympathetic to

Jey. When Roman berates Jey and tells him to be more like Sami, Jimmy nods along, but Sami displays a complex mix of delight and unease. When Roman's music interrupts a promo, Sami casts a worried glance at Jey, knowing that Jey always bears the brunt of his cousin's bad moods.

It's incredibly gradual, nearly imperceptible, but Sami has started to shift from a cowardly lickspittle to a man who cares about other people. It's a trait he slammed the door shut on years ago, when he decided caring made him weak. Now, almost despite himself, he finds that door whispering open just the slightest crack.

In the meantime, there are hints that Roman is starting to realize he might have made a tactical error in recruiting Sami. The crowds are starting to cheer for Sami, to chant his name when they should be acknowledging the Tribal Chief. In these moments, Roman's eyes go sharp and cold. But so far, they're just hints.

Through October and November, Kevin and Sami stayed on parallel paths, touching only once—when Kevin came across Sami wearing his new Honorary Uce t-shirt backstage. He stopped and scoffed. "You need a new shirt, buddy," he said without rancor, and walked on, leaving Sami looking after him.

And then WWE started the build toward *Survivor Series: WarGames*.

WarGames

WarGames is a complex stipulation, a multi-person match in a double-ring enclosed by a steel cage in which wrestlers enter at set intervals. It's a perfect match for complex inter-factional conflict. In 2022, Seamus and the Brawling Brutes (Pete Dunne and Ridge Holland) were feuding with the Bloodline (Roman, Jimmy, Jey, Solo, and Sami) as it approached. At a two-man disadvantage, the babyface team recruited Sheamus's old friend and rival Drew McIntyre but were still down one man.

When Sami (after promising victory for the Bloodline at WarGames) loses to Dunne during the build to the match, the inevitable brawl breaks out between the two teams. Reigns strides to the ring to wade in.

MIND GAMES AND WARGAMES

Kevin Owens' music hits.

The fifth member of the babyface WarGames team comes to the ring and faces down Roman as the crowd chants "holy shit!" They throw hands, and Kevin manages to get Roman down into a corner, where he stomps on him over and over, then turns around—

Only to come face to face with a disheveled Sami in his Honorary Uce shirt.

A long "ooooooh" ripples through the audience as they stare at each other for a full twenty seconds, both of them uncertain, torn. When Roman breaks the standoff by Superman Punching Kevin, Sami flinches and staggers back exactly as if Roman has punched *him*.

The next week on the go-home show, as events spiral out of control, Sami tries to throw Jey the tag team belt to use as a weapon. Kevin jumps forward and stops him. "I'm not gonna let you do this!" he says, as the two of them struggle over the tag title.

Commentary takes this as Kevin's concern for his teammates, but more than that, it's a concern for Sami, an attempt to keep him from crossing a line. Years and years ago, fighting Neville in NXT during his Road to Redemption, he had a chance to hit Neville with the title and didn't, winning fair and clean instead. Now in 2022, Kevin's trying to keep him from crossing the line he refused to cross back then. Sami shoves him away, but Kevin's stalled enough for the referee to notice and make it impossible for Sami to interfere.

The question looms large over *WarGames*: will Sami be ruthless enough to ensure the Bloodline wins?

At the actual show, the women's WarGames match was the one with the crazy spots and high action. The men's match had its fair share of fun spots, but the heart of the match is the question of Sami's loyalties. Throughout the match, Sami and Jey miscommunicate and argue. But when Kevin actually pins Roman Reigns, Sami makes his first fateful decision. He leaps forward and catches the referee's hand out of the air, stalling the count.

For a long, horrible moment Kevin and Sami stare at each other. Sami's face is resolute and apologetic at the same time. Kevin's is blank —not angry, not disappointed, more resigned than anything.

A horrible moment.

They come to their feet, still staring at each other. "Is this your family?" Kevin demands, grabbing Roman's hair. "Is this your—"

He pivots as Jimmy tries to surprise him with a superkick, catching Jimmy's foot out of the air with both hands. But this has left him vulnerable, unable to block Sami when his friend, his rival, his brother drops to his knees and low-blows him.

Sami rises slowly to his feet, his face pale, as Kevin staggers to one corner of the ring. He moves like he's in a dream, or a nightmare. He kneels in front of Roman and they speak inaudibly for a moment. Roman nods, and Sami stands up and delivers the Helluva Kick to Kevin in the corner. Kevin falls forward into his embrace again and Sami looks down at his face. Then he lets Kevin drop to the mat with a thump of utter finality. He looks over to Jey Uso and steps aside, allowing Jey to deliver his frog splash and get the win and the glory.

The Bloodline is ascendant, thanks to Sami. Sami stares down at Kevin's fallen body, his mouth twitching. Roman rises to his feet. He opens his arms, and Sami steps over Kevin's body into the embrace of his Tribal Chief. The crowd cheers and boos, but then the cheers win out when Jey launches himself at Sami, wrapping him up in a hug, lifting him off his feet with the power of his emotion. The Bloodline lines up in triumph and the camera pans across them as they lift their hands in tribute. "I love all of you," Sami says fervently. "I love all of you."

He looks back over his shoulder at Kevin, crumpled on the mat, for just a second, then closes his eyes in pain and resolution, knowing he's closed the door on that friendship.

Roman's cold eyes take all of this in as the camera fades to black.

ROYAL RUMBLE
(2023)

The Opposite of Love

SAMI MADE his choice at *WarGames*, the Bloodline over Kevin. With all their long history, you might expect that Kevin would react to this with fury and violence, rekindling their feud once more. When Kevin comes out on *Raw* to confront the Bloodline, Sami clearly expects it, warning him not to do anything stupid like try to fight him. But Kevin has gone in a direction Sami never anticipated.

He's given up on Sami.

Oh, he's still feuding with the Bloodline, he still wants Roman's title. But as he explains to Sami from the ramp, he totally understands Sami's actions. "How many times throughout our careers have I done the exact same thing to you? I'm not mad at you, I can't blame you for it one bit. I'm not here to fight you, it's actually quite the opposite." Sami's face goes shuttered and wary as Kevin goes on, "For twenty years our names have been linked to one another, but man, after Saturday… I don't want to fight you. I don't want to team with you. I don't want to ride to shows with you. I'm just—" He shakes his head wearily. "I'm just done. I don't want anything to do with you."

Standing in the ring facing him, his new family arrayed behind him, Sami aims for "sneering bravado" and fails utterly, struggling to keep his face from crumpling at this exhausted renunciation. Clearly he never expected Kevin to just give up on him, to opt out of their glorious vicious cycle. "Fight forever" had always been a promise to care about each other, whether feuding or allying. For the first time in twenty years, he's in unfamiliar territory.

In the following weeks, when Kevin is brawling with the Bloodline, he targets Jimmy, Jey, or Solo. When he comes across Sami in the chaos of a scrum, he simply turns away from him to chase down one of the other Bloodline members, leaving Sami feeling a complicated mix of relief and chagrin. At one point Sami leaps into the ring to confront Kevin, a brightly feral smile of invitation on his face as he waits for the inevitable flying fists and hockey brawl between them. Instead, Kevin looks at him blankly and starts stripping the tape from his wrists. As Sami stares, Kevin raises his eyebrows and tilts his head, curious and polite as if greeting an uninteresting stranger. *Yes? Did you want something?* Sami is visibly crushed. There's never been a clearer example of the old saying "The opposite of love isn't hate, it's indifference." All those years, hate and love were two sides of the same coin for Kevin and Sami. Now Kevin has dropped the coin in the gutter and walked away, leaving Sami desolate.

Flashback to a Fall

Things aren't going so great in the Bloodline for Sami, either. He's finally won over Jey with his acts at *WarGames*, and since his fierce victory hug Jey has accepted Sami with the hunger of a man who's endured years of abuse and diminishment and finally found a person he can trust. Despite this (or more likely because of this), Roman's sharp and paranoid eyes have started to truly see Sami as a threat. There have been hints of it before this point, moments where Roman would be waiting for a town to acknowledge him, and when instead they started chanting for Sami his head would snap up and his icy gaze turn to the Honorary Uce. After *WarGames*, Sami has become a threat to Roman in at least three different ways: as Kevin's old friend, as Jey's new ally, and as a potential rival to Roman directly, even if Sami doesn't seem to realize it yet.

So Roman starts to put the screws to Sami.

"We got a problem," he announces shortly after telling Sami he might be able to become a full Uce, not just an honorary member of the Bloodline. "We got a *KO problem.*"

Sami's face goes from overjoyed to shocked as he realizes that he still hasn't done enough to resigned as it sinks in that he still has to prove himself, all in a span of seconds. He clenches his jaw, grits his teeth, and starts to denounce Kevin as malign and untrustworthy. "He continues to drag me down. He's a cancer, he betrays everyone in his life," he spits. "I mean, for crying out loud, *I'm his only friend!*"

The crowd murmurs and Roman's face goes dangerously still as Sami hastily reassures him that he got the tense wrong, that he *was* Kevin's only friend. *Was.*

Over and over Sami reviles Kevin—"His name has been tied to my name my entire career and I *can't get rid of him!*" he howls the next show as Roman smiles indulgently then gathers him into a warm hug, his dead eyes looking over Sami's shoulder into the camera as he mouths silent threats at Kevin. But it's increasingly clear that no matter how fond Jimmy, Jey, and even Paul Heyman have become of Sami, Roman's dislike and paranoia are looming.

Sami's relationship with Kevin is nothing but an excuse Roman is using to be a bully to this man who had been a laughingstock less than a year ago, who the crowds are now acknowledging organically, freely, with love. Outside the Bloodline locker room, Heyman warns Sami in hushed tones that crowds chanting for Sami while the Tribal Chief is standing right next to him are "not the right optics." Sami, of course, guilelessly asks Roman directly if the chants bother him, his brow furrowed with his desire to do the right thing. Behind Roman, the rest of the Bloodline react with a horror and chagrin that make clear that Roman's cool laughter in response is a very thin veneer. Sami is tiptoeing closer and closer to a very dangerous ledge, and when Roman challenges Kevin and John Cena to a tag match against him and Sami, Sami unwisely promises victory. When he takes the pin (from a businesslike Kevin, to add insult to injury) on the last *Smackdown* of the year, he puts one toe over the edge of that ledge.

On the first *Smackdown* of 2023, a Bloodline promo starts to veer out of control as Roman notes that Sami seems to be making a lot of decisions for the Bloodline lately when Roman isn't around. "Do you want to be me?" he asks Sami, seeming more baffled than angry at first. Sami laughs nervously at what he takes to be a rhetorical question, shaking his head as Roman presses on, "Do you want to be the Tribal Chief? Do you think you're me? Do you think you're me?" Then he lunges forward with a predator's abruptness, the mask splitting and shattering, to howl with bared teeth, *"Do you think you're me? Do you want to be the Tribal Chief? Do you want to run the Bloodline?"* Sami falls back, pale and shaking, before this onslaught. Behind them, Paul Heyman puts a hand over his mouth. Jey puts a hand on Jimmy's shoulder as if to warn him against interfering, although Jimmy shows no inclination to step forward. Solo Sikoa stares straight ahead, unmoved. Roman advances on Sami, still screaming, and Sami's back is up against the turnbuckle when he's saved.

He's saved by Kevin's music hitting.

Sami's expression trembles between relief and fear as Kevin comes out. His eyes flicker back and forth between Kevin and Roman, and you can almost see him wondering if Kevin has deliberately come out to rescue him. Kevin doesn't even look at Sami, though. "Your problem is not with Sami," he informs the fuming Tribal Chief. "Your problem is with me." He challenges Roman to a title match at the *Royal Rumble*, then announces he'll see Roman at the Rumble "and Sami, I'll see you whenever you decide to dig your balls out of Roman's pocket." Roman offers Sami a chance to prove his loyalty once again: fight Kevin in a one-on-one match the next week. Sami grits his teeth and accepts the challenge.

The match—which turned out to be Kevin and Sami's last match against each other for over two years—starts with commentary noting that Roman has told Sami they will not interfere in this match, that the Bloodline trusts him to get this job done. Sami comes out to his sludgy guitars, strutting as though it were his old theme song, pointing up at the "Honorary Uce" on the Titantron and pledging his fealty to Roman once more.

Kevin starts off with an insultingly polite and formal offered handshake, as if they were strangers following the old ROH code of honor.

When Sami kicks it away and follows it up soon after with a contemptuous slap, Kevin's stated desire to have nothing more to do with Sami falls away completely, and soon the two of them are scrapping it up as fervently as if they were nineteen years old and in Le Skratch in front of dozens of people. There are brainbusters, frog splashes, blue thunderbombs. Sami claws at Kevin's eyes. Kevin bites Sami's hands. As Kevin lies on the mat, Sami stomps on his face in a frenzy while Kevin screams "come on! Come on, bitch!" up at him. They end up on their knees in front of each other, trading stinging slaps that slowly raise them to their feet until they're hockey fighting again at last.

The years fall away. The Bloodline falls away. There's nothing left between them but the thrill of fighting each other.

Finally, as Kevin crawls exhausted to one corner, Sami finds himself at the other corner, in position for the Helluva Kick. Grinning with weary ferocity, he waits for Kevin to get to his feet so he can finally finish him, finally put him away, finally prove himself better—

And Jey, Jimmy, and Solo jump into the ring to attack Kevin.

The bell rings. Kevin has won by disqualification.

Sami looks as though he's woken up from a dream, as though he's had cold water thrown on him. He watches in stunned disbelief as the Bloodline stomps on Kevin, and you can see in his wide eyes the awful knowledge that they didn't trust him to win—no, worse, they didn't care if he won or lost, they didn't care if he proved himself better than Kevin. They just wanted Kevin battered before his match with Roman. The Bloodline tear at Kevin, oblivious to Sami's distress and his protests that he had this handled, assuming he'll share their glee. They drive Kevin onto the commentary table, and Solo leaps from the barricade to fall onto Kevin.

It's an echo of Hell in a Cell in 2017, the moment where Shane plummets towards Kevin lying helpless on the same table. And Sami responds the same way he did in 2017—he leaps forward involuntarily, hand outstretched in horror.* This time, however, he's far too slow, far

---

* The cameras don't catch Sami's futile attempt to save Kevin in the live broadcast, but in the recap the following week the replay of the moment is deliberately shown from another angle, one where you can glimpse his instinctive movement.

too late. As Solo celebrates in the wreckage over Kevin's body, the camera zooms toward Sami in exactly the same way it did in 2017. Sami has exactly the same expression of frozen horror on his face, as if his sense of self is crumbling. He wipes his mouth with a shaking hand as the Bloodline celebrate over Kevin, calling him over to join in the group pose.

As Sami raises his finger in the air, Kevin grabs feebly at his boot, clinging to him. Sami glances down and nervously shakes off his touch.

Tribal Court

Sami's tiny spark of rebelliousness has, of course, been noticed by the Tribal Chief, and the *Raw* before the Royal Rumble where he is to face Kevin, Roman announces there will be a Tribal Court held to determine Sami's guilt or innocence.

When the Bloodline comes out, Jey, Jimmy, Solo and Heyman are all wearing the scarlet *'ula*, the garlands of flowers worn at high occasions. Roman is wearing the *'ulafala* of crimson seed-pods that marks him as the Tribal Chief. Only Sami is bare of adornment, his face solemn and sad as he sits down in the ring to await his judgment.

The Tribal Court is one of the most riveting segments WWE has ever had. Each person plays their role to perfection, from Solo's silent executioner vibe to Jey's growing agitation to Heyman's over-the-top viciousness—he starts by wishing Sami were dead! Roman sits impassive as Heyman lays out the "evidence" against Sami, starting with fairly reasonable (video proof that Sami ran away from Drew McIntyre rather than help the Usos) but quickly spiraling out of control into wild paranoia, claiming to see secret hand signals, interpreting a slight shoulder-brush against Roman as an "assassination attempt."[*] The presentation style is hilarious, a parody of *Law and Order's* stark black-and-white captions and musical stings—but Sami's pale, miserable

---

[*] It's never stated explicitly, but based on Paul's reactions to the rest of the segment, his bombastic performance is probably meant to be deliberately ludicrous so that Sami can easily defend himself. He's lobbed Sami a softball.

face keeps it from ever becoming actually funny. The crowd is intensely behind Sami, and Roman is keenly aware of it, his lips twitching at every supportive chant.

When Heyman finishes his denunciation, Sami stands to defend himself. But instead of launching a counter-argument, he declares in a shaking voice of deep sincerity that he's terribly hurt by these accusations, that he loves and is faithful to the Bloodline, that "these people, they see it!" He gestures to the crowd to witness his fidelity, and they roar their support. He refuses to defend himself, throwing himself on the mercy of the Tribal Court, sitting back down with the set jaw of a condemned man.

There's no mercy in Roman Reigns.

Furious at Sami's lack of defense, he rants and raves and calls on Solo Sikoa. Solo steps forward to grab Sami, still seated, by his shoulder. He raises his hand to deliver the final blow. And then Sami is saved again—this time by Jey Uso.

The member of the Bloodline who resisted and resented Sami the longest leaps up and grabs Solo's arm, restraining him. The crowd shrieks with delight. Jey begs Roman to understand he means no disrespect, but he's put together his own presentation in defense of Sami. As the footage rolls, the audience sees Sami's unselfish actions from the last six months—-every time he took a kick or a chair in place of a Bloodline member, every distraction he created to help them win, his final sacrifice of his friendship to bring them victory at *WarGames*.

"Everybody knows I did not trust you," Jey says to Sami, whose eyes are shining with tears. "I despised you. But you saw the good in me the whole time and you never gave up on me. And that right there, that's what family do." Roman's shuttered gaze never shifts as he listens to Jey's glowing description of Sami as someone who builds people up instead of tearing them down. "Sami Zayn, I love you like a brother, Uce. One hundred," Jey goes on, then turns to address the audience. "If you want Sami Zayn to stay in the Bloodline, throw your ones to the sky."

Nearly every single person in the arena leaps to their feet, hands in the air in support of the Honorary Uce.

The camera cuts back to Sami, whose tearful expression has taken on undertones of a very real awe and joy. Because it's one thing to hear Jey say even sincere emotional lines from a script, and it's quite another to have the audience join in with all their heart. He's been a heel for five years and surely sometimes he wondered if the fans would ever be willing to embrace him as a babyface again after so long. But here they are, rising up for him in solemn delight, in the most serious of play that is the best of wrestling.

With all the appropriate dramatic pauses, Roman declares Sami "not guilty," then tacks on an ominous "*for now.*" Because Roman's match with Kevin at the *Royal Rumble* is less than a week away, and that will be Sami's final test.

Just Stay Down

January 28, 2023. The Alamodome was full of over forty thousand people, there to see the *Royal Rumble*. Cody Rhodes won his first Royal Rumble, while Intercontinental champion Gunther set a record for longest time in a 30-man Rumble. Bray Wyatt wrestled what no one at the time knew would be his last match. Rhea Ripley eliminated Liv Morgan to win the women's Rumble.

And in the main event, Kevin Owens took on Roman Reigns.

As the competitors are announced, Roman stands in his corner, Sami perched behind him on the turnbuckle. On the opposite turnbuckle Kevin sits, mirroring Sami. Kevin is picked out with a dazzling-white spotlight, Sami plunged into Roman's literal shadow. Kevin in the light, Sami in darkness.

As Kevin and Roman circle each other warily, the crowd starts a loud chant of "Sami Uso." Kevin chuckles, calling out to Roman, "I don't think they care about you!" as Sami beams sheepishly. The match is between Roman and Kevin, of course, but the real conflict is within the Honorary Uce, and Sami appears in nearly every camera shot of the match—sometimes foregrounded, sometimes in the background, but the camera is always keenly aware of where he is and what he's doing. Because the story of the match is all in Sami's face and Sami's reactions.

Back in 2013, in Kevin and El Generico's last match as a tag team, the story was entirely of Kevin's shift of heart. The luchador remained the same all the way through, while Kevin's character changed to finally meet him, there at the end of their story. This time in 2023, Kevin stays the same through the match: fiercely stubborn, gritty, proud. It's Sami that goes through a journey, and what a journey it is.

He starts the match squarely on Roman's side, cheering him, pumping his fist when Roman sends Kevin crashing into the turnbuckle with an Irish whip. But with each of Kevin's kickouts—and there are many of them—Sami's agitation and uneasiness grows. Kevin's fourth kickout is to the Superman punch, a move that has finished many of Roman's matches, and Sami is now shocked into disbelief. When Kevin next kicks out of Roman's spear, Sami starts to literally retch with nervousness on the sidelines.

When Kevin goes for a Stunner, Roman shoves him away and Kevin caroms into the ref, knocking him down and out, so that when he hits the pop-up powerbomb, there's no one there to do the count. The audience helpfully counts to ten for him, but eventually Kevin rolls to the ropes to look down at the fallen ref, nearly in tears of exasperation. He goes back over to Roman to pull him to his feet—and the Tribal Chief low-blows him, then screams at Sami to get a chair. After some stammering hesitation that causes Roman's eyes to grow even more icy, Sami does slide a chair to him, but the delay has given Kevin time to rally and hit a stunner, though in his weakened state it doesn't keep Roman down for the count. At his kick-out, Sami looks like he might faint, not so much from relief as from the sheer pressure of the situation. He's being put through an emotional wringer, and it's only going to get worse.

Roman comes up out of the pin and hits Kevin with a Superman punch, instantly followed up by a spear. It's a combination blow that nearly no one has ever kicked out of… but Kevin still does. Roman looks blankly stunned. The crowd is roaring. On the sidelines, Sami paces frantically.

In the clamoring din, Kevin rolls to the edge of the ring and falls heavily to the floor, crawling to the barricade to try and pull himself to his feet. Sami goes over to him, staring at him, his face white as if he's seen a ghost. Which in a way he has, because Kevin's refusal to give up, his utter inability to admit defeat in the face of a bully, is exactly what the fans had always loved about Sami. It's what *Kevin* has always loved about Sami, no matter how much he mocked it and tried to make Sami doubt himself. He was successful at that beyond his wildest dreams, leaving Sami trapped for half a decade as a hollow-souled craven coward, and now he's being the person Sami was before he listened to Kevin, showing Sami what he could be again.

Sami doesn't want to be shown this. It's causing him terrible agony. As Kevin struggles blindly to drag himself to his feet, scrabbling at the barricade, Sami pulls at his hair, looking down at Kevin with unwelcome pity.

Finally he leans forward and yells urgently at Kevin, "Just stay down!" The same phrase Kevin has thrown at him over and over across the years, that desperate plea to just give up, just stop fighting, just let me have this one thing. "Just stay down, what's *wrong* with you?" Sami cries out, and Kevin lurches toward him, falling to his knees, grabbing at his hand. Sami flinches away. "Just stay down, just end this, just *end this*," he begs in an anguished mix of pity and fury, and as Kevin stands up again Roman comes barreling from behind Sami to plunge into Kevin and spear him through the barricade.

Sami watches, shaking in horror, as Roman seizes his opponent and slams him backwards into the steel stairs, and then does it again. He rolls Kevin's limp body into the ring, but even now, *even now*, Kevin has enough fight left in him to swipe upward and cuff Roman across the face just once before the final brutal spear that folds him in half and leaves him motionless for the three-count.

Moment of Clarity

The match over, the whole Bloodline crowds into the ring to celebrate. Everyone is jovial, delighted at the destruction of one of Roman's most persistent enemies—except for Sami, still pale and shuddering and staring down at Kevin. They're all wearing the crimson flowers of the *'ula* around their necks. Jey has brought one for Sami, but as he goes to finally place it around his neck, Roman stops him, laughing, gesturing for them to finish with Kevin first.

A wild festival of violence follows. The Usos kick Kevin over and over. They set him up in the corner and Solo crushes him against the turnbuckle as Roman lays a heavy arm on Sami's shoulders, laughing. Sami wilts beneath that weight, watching the beatdown in silence. Heyman produces handcuffs and they cuff Kevin to the ropes for more superkicks that rock him left and right, semi-conscious, helpless. Roman calls for a chair, and when he lifts it to bring down on Kevin—

Sami steps between them.

Forty thousand people inhale in unison as Sami desperately explains to Roman that he doesn't have to do this, that Kevin is beaten, that this is beneath him. Roman stares at him for a long moment, then holds the chair out to him. It may be beneath the Tribal Chief, but it's not beneath Sami, apparently.

Sami hesitates, and Roman starts to snarl at him that there's no backing out now, that he belongs to the Bloodline. "You're ours! I care about you, I love you, I gave you everything. Go back to doing Jackass shit," he growls, contemptuously turning his back on Sami to taunt Kevin. Staring at Roman's vulnerable back, Sami lifts the chair, and forty thousand voices lift with it, a long ecstatic sound of anticipation that fades again as Sami lowers the chair, a conductor warming up his orchestra in preparation for the finale.

Sami looks down and makes eye contact with Kevin for the first and only time in the whole scene.

Roman turns. Seeing him hesitating, he peers more closely at Sami's face. "Are you *crying*?" he sneers in disgust, turning to his advisor to witness this weakness. "Paul, is he *crying*?" He shoves at Sami's tearful face with a contemptuous hand and turns his back on him again, going back to Kevin.

And this time, finally, Sami grits his teeth, steps forward, and whacks Roman in the back with it. The crowd erupts, a wild hurricane of sound with the wrestlers in the eye of the storm.

Roman falls forward into the ropes in an exact mirror image of the way he fell years ago when Seth turned on him, his face totally blank with shock.

Sami turns to the Usos and throws down the chair, saying he's sorry. Jey and Jimmy are incandescent with rage. Jimmy superkicks him and starts to punch him, joined in by Solo, goaded on by Roman who has recovered enough to bellow over and over in an almost unrecognizable voice something that sounds like "Kill all of them!"

A moment of clarity.

Suddenly everyone seems to realize at once that Jey is not joining in the beating. He's sitting on the turnbuckle, weeping, torn between betrayer and abuser. After giving Roman a tormented look, he leaves the ring and walks the long, long walk out of the arena, setting out on the path that would eventually lead him to the main event of *WrestleMania* in 2025, the crowd cheering wildly for him the whole time.

Completely out of his mind with rage at the first cracks in his empire, Roman grabs the chair and starts to beat Sami with it, over and over, the solid metal *thwacks* barely audible over the wall of roaring fury from the audience. Still handcuffed to the ropes, Kevin kicks vainly in Roman's direction, trying to stop the assault. Roman rips off the Honorary Uce shirt and stands over Sami's bare and bruised body. Jimmy hands him the flowered *'ula* that should have been Sami's.

As Roman goes to toss the garland on him, the crowd noise coalesces into a shockingly loud, full-throated FUCK YOU ROMAN chant, over and over. Roman's head snaps up, taking it in. Then—still staring out at the audience—he slowly begins to tear apart the flowers of the garland, taking his time, scattering the broken petals, red as drops of blood, across Sami's body. He leaves the ring, walking stiff-legged and outraged all the way to the back.

In his wake Kevin and Sami lie motionless in the ring, their bodies strewn with scarlet flowers like the aftermath of a funeral, or of a wedding.

THE FINAL CHAPTER
(2023)

Elimination Chamber, Montreal

AFTER THE *ROYAL RUMBLE*, after Sami sacrificed the respect of the Bloodline that he worked for a year to gain for Kevin, their friendship was rekindled and they swore to come after the Usos' tag team titles.

Well, hold up, let's not rush things. Because Sami and Kevin don't ever ignore the past for the sake of a quick pop or a mere one-year storyline. One year! Such short spans are for amateurs, come back when you've been developing the same characters and their relationship to each other for two decades.

So after his beating by the Bloodline at the *Royal Rumble*, Kevin goes missing for a while. Sami, full of a righteous fury he hasn't shown in years, challenges Roman for his title at *Elimination Chamber*, the next big show, which is in Montreal. As Sami defies Roman with all the fire in his soul, as Roman swears to humiliate and break Sami in front of everyone who loves him, as Jey vacillates and wavers and is torn between his family and his self-respect, Kevin is nowhere to be seen.

The *Smackdown* before *Elimination Chamber* is also in Montreal. When Sami's music hits, the crowd ignites. When the music continues through to the "let's go!" cry and the audience realizes he's gotten his babyface theme back to appear in front of them, they become incandescent. They go from singing "Worlds Apart" to singing "Olé" to chanting Sami's name to simply screaming in ecstasy, then loop back around to "Olé." Every time Sami merely *looks* at them, it's as if he's blowing on coals: the cheering blazes up again hotter than before. Sami breaks into tears. Eventually all he can do is say a few words of defiance in French and English rather than give any kind of promo, but the rapturous love of the audience speaks more loudly than any words.

When he does actually get a chance to talk freely in a backstage interview after the next *Raw*, we get a glimpse of what he might have said that night. He thanks the fans and adds "I haven't always been the best guy these last few years..." He stops and struggles for a moment, finally saying awkwardly and with honest surprise, "Oh, I'm getting weirdly emotional," before going on, "It means a lot that you've shown me this love after the past few years when I haven't always been at my best." The emotion that catches him off guard is a very real gratitude at the realization that the fans never stopped loving him, deep down, that they were so ready to pivot back into love after his heel run was prolonged by injuries and pandemics. There in Montreal that night, with his music and El Generico's mingling with the love of the audience, Sami Zayn finally becomes his truest self.

Unfortunately for Montreal, Sami's truest self is still not quite enough to knock off the Tribal Chief and his family. His match with Roman is exciting, perfectly-paced, and it was always somehow believable that Sami could actually pull it off—until the rest of the Bloodline gets involved. With the ref down, Heyman hands Roman a chair. Jey appears and steps dramatically between Roman and Sami. As Roman demands he use the chair on Sami and Jey hesitates, contemplating finally slamming it into Roman's back, Sami tries to spear Roman and spears Jey instead. Roman takes advantage of Sami's horror to repay him with a barrage of chair shots on Sami's increasingly limp body, then pins him as the ref decides to regain consciousness.

As the crowd deflates into deep melancholy, Jimmy shows up grinning to carry out Roman's wishes of a more severe beatdown. Roman paces, enjoying Jimmy's pummeling of Sami's unresisting form. The audience moans.

And Kevin's music hits.

Renewed energy surges into the crowd and they explode with delight as Kevin attacks Jimmy and Roman. Kevin grabs a chair and gets into the ring, though a brief attempt at assault by Heyman makes him drop the chair to stunner the Wise Man. As Heyman flails out of the ring, Kevin stands up to look at Roman in the corner. Behind him in the opposite corner, Sami has slowly pulled himself to his feet. Kevin looks at Roman, who has cost him so much so many times. He looks at the chair.

He turns and looks behind him at Sami, wavering in the corner.

The Montreal audience knows its cue. They start singing "Olé" with all their might, that song that was technically El Generico's but always truly belonged to both men.

An older Kevin would have pushed Sami aside to use the chair on Roman himself, getting some measure of revenge. Even a fairly recent version of Kevin might have grabbed the chair and demanded Sami use it himself. But this Kevin, the Kevin with gray in his beard and self-awareness in his eyes, steps backwards out of Sami's way so that Sami can cross the ring and Helluva Kick Roman to get some amount of catharsis for himself and the Montreal fans. Kevin rolls out of the ring and walks to the back without speaking to Sami, but Sami's eyes follow him the whole way with a mix of wonder and uncertainty and just a little bit of hope.

Brothers

Sami is, of course, crushed by losing to Roman. He feels terrible for disappointing the fans, guilty that he failed once more to carry their hopes and dreams to the top. But at the same time, he's careful to mention more than once that his match with Roman was not actually the climax of his story. Reflecting backstage after *Elimination Chamber*, he says thoughtfully that "tonight is like that last little lull in the movie before the third act, when things seem about as bad as they can get."

After the next *Raw*, he repeats the idea. "That this is not the end, and it's not a failure, and it's not where the story finishes makes me feel better." Most of Sami's matches through his career are structured in a classic style, where the babyface starts off strong in the first third, suffers a terrible setback in the second third, and then emerges to either victory or defeat in the last third. *This is not the final defeat*, he's saying. *It's just the second-act setback.*

When Sami comes out on the next *Raw* to thank the fans for their support and to apologize for not beating Roman, he moves that argument on-screen. "We are entering the final chapter," he says. "And the final chapter is not just about me."

He asks Kevin to come out so he can talk to him.

Kevin comes to the ring, his expression unreadable, nearly blank. "I want to say thank you, I guess," Sami says, his voice shaking. "I want to say I'm sorry." His voice cracks on the last word. Kevin is looking down at the ring, frowning slightly. His brows pinch together just a fraction. Sami says that after all the years, all the terrible things they've done to each other, he doesn't know if there's any coming back from that. "But for months and months you've said that there's only one thing you care about, and that's taking down the Bloodline." Kevin still isn't looking at him. He isn't rejecting him either. It's as if he's waiting for something. "You couldn't do it alone," Sami says. "And I couldn't really do it alone. I think there's only one way to get it done, and that's if we do it together."

The crowd goes crazy, but Kevin turns away for a second. When he turns back, it's clear that whatever he had been waiting for Sami to say, he hasn't heard it. He tells Sami that he didn't come out in Montreal to help him, that it had nothing to do with him. "I've been fighting the Bloodline for months on my own," he says. "And as far as I'm concerned, that's fine and that's the way I'm going to keep fighting them."

And that is indeed how things go for the next few weeks. Across *Raw* and *Smackdown*, Kevin and Sami keep fighting the Bloodline separately, and Sami keeps appealing to Kevin. "I don't know what else to do, what else to say," he says backstage to a withdrawn Kevin. "It's

THE FINAL CHAPTER

complicated, I get it. We don't have to be best friends again, we don't need to ride together, we don't even need to team! But we have the same objective now." Kevin, increasingly frustrated, snaps back that he's been fighting the Bloodline alone for months, and that Sami can go back to Roman and apologize, "but leave me out of it." And yet, there's a melancholy edge to his irritation. After Sami saves him from a beatdown and offers his hand, Kevin walks away without taking it... but he looks back over his shoulder at Sami in the ring three times as he walks away, and there's no anger in his face, just that same look like he's listening for something he hasn't heard yet.

Even when Jey finally decides to put family over friendship and self-respect and surprise-attacks Sami, Kevin does not appear to make the save. Instead, it's Cody Rhodes—winner of the Royal Rumble, Roman Reigns' *WrestleMania* opponent—who comes charging to the ring to help him. In the background of *Raw* the week after, Cody can be seen earnestly arguing with Kevin, and then on *Smackdown* he calls both Sami and Kevin to the ring, trying to negotiate some kind of peace between them.

Sami, his voice tight with frustration and desperation, begs Kevin to tell him what he needs to do to make an alliance possible. "If there's something you need to get off your chest, tell me! If you need to scream at me, do it!" He leans forward, chin out. "If you need to punch me in the face, do it! Do whatever you have to do so we can get back to working together!" He gestures at the audience, who scream back their support. "They want it! I want it! It's in your best interests, it's in my best interests!" Kevin looks tired, sad, disappointed all at once as Sami pleads with him to help take down the Bloodline. "We don't even need to do this as friends. We just need to work together—"

"—I know, I know!" Kevin snaps, finally goaded beyond endurance. "You've been saying it for weeks. You don't need a *friend*, you don't want a *friend*, you just need me to fight with you so that you, me and Cody can take down the Bloodline together. I get it, that's what's best for business, and we don't have to be friends, we don't need to be friends to do it. But man, why— why would I fight— why —" He stumbles over his words with the air of someone who realizes he's saying too much, he's revealing too much, but who can't stop. "Why would I fight for someone who doesn't even want to be my friend," he finishes in a rush.

Sami has gone pale with shock, his mouth fallen open. His expression is so aghast that it's clear it's never crossed his mind that Kevin might actually *want* to be his friend again, might feel snubbed by Sami's carefully neutral framing of this as a pragmatic decision. He watches blankly as Kevin awkwardly thanks Cody and leaves, staring after him with a complex mix of chagrin and surmise on his face.

"Well, there's no going back from that," Michael Cole says sadly as they fade out to commercial break. When they come back, Kevin is in the parking lot, heading toward his car. From offscreen we hear Sami yelling "Kevin! Kevin!" and he comes running up to grab Kevin's shoulder. "Forget about everything I said," Sami gasps, breathless from running through the arena. "Forget everything I said about the Bloodline, about fighting together. None of that stuff matters, okay?" Kevin's face has gone cautious, as though he might be hearing something longed-for, but isn't sure. Beneath the gray in his beard, he looks oddly young, and for a moment you can see twenty-year-old Kevin there, yearning for a friend to share his dreams and goals with.

"What you said in the ring—" Sami goes on, "you're wrong, okay? We *are* friends. We'll always be friends." It's suddenly clear the roughness in his voice is not from exertion but from tears. "We're not just friends, man, we're *brothers*. You understand that? *Brothers!* And if you never want to talk to me ever again… that's fine. I just want to let you know…" He holds his hands up, placating, almost embarrassed. "I love you, okay?" He blinks back tears. "That's it," he mutters. "That's it."

Kevin looks at him in silence for a second, then gets in his car and drives off without a word. Sami goes back to the arena to face Jey Uso on his own, resigned to going it alone. After a tense confrontation Jey attacks him, and Jimmy instantly shows up to join in on the beatdown. The crowd's response is muted, expectant. They're waiting and hoping, and when Kevin's music hits, they go mad with joy. They cheer wildly as he hands out stunners and pop-up powerbombs to the twins and

THE FINAL CHAPTER

undisputed tag team champions. Sami lies crumpled in the corner watching the Usos retreat, disbelief on his face. As he struggles to his feet the crowd noise rises with him until he and Kevin are facing each other, staring. Kevin crosses the ring to him, sweeping him up into a hug as the crowd erupts in delight. He's finally heard what he needs to hear, that Sami values their friendship over vengeance, over victories.

And so the stage is set, the grandest stage of them all. Kevin and Sami against the Usos. "The longest-reigning tag champions of all time!" Kevin explains next to a quietly jubilant Sami, both in their matching *WrestleMania* t-shirts. "The best team in WWE! And that was true *up until last week."*

Years and years ago, Kevin and El Generico debuted against the Briscoe Brothers in ROH. They broke up in 2009 and came back together in 2013 against Matt and Nick Jackson, the Young Bucks. And in 2023, once again the theme is brotherhood: brothers by birth versus brothers by choice. As of that year, a tag team match had only main-evented *WrestleMania* once. The tag team titles had never been on the line in the main event of *WrestleMania*.

Kevin Owens, Sami Zayn, and Jimmy and Jey Uso are about to make history.

Main Event

It's the first night of *WrestleMania 39*. April 1, 2023. Los Angeles. 80,000 people.

The Usos come to the ring to a live rap performance, carrying their four belts between them, the titles they have held for almost a thousand dominant days. Around their necks are the red and white flowered *'ulas* of their heritage.

Kevin and Sami enter to their usual theme songs. *Let's go*, Kevin mouths to Sami's music as his friend, brother, tag team partner comes out. They walk down the ramp empty-handed, wearing only their black hoodies over t-shirts. They have no special ornament beyond the golden PWG patches on their gear, a tribute to the Los Angeles promotion that gave them so much.

As the first Olé chants rise into the night sky, Sami faces down Jey Uso, the man who had stood up for him and called him brother.

Sami takes a vicious beating all through the first part of the match, pummeled by the Usos' kicks until he finally manages to tag out to Kevin. Wild with furious energy from watching Sami suffer, Kevin runs to the ringpost and does a senton out of the ring to the twins, then a frog splash out of the ring to Jimmy and another in the ring to Jey. When Sami comes back in, he does a version of the Usos splash to Jimmy, then a Blue Thunderbomb, but it's not quite enough. Wobbling and wavering from a myriad of superkicks, he finally goes down to another pin attempt, and this time Kevin has to dive in to break it up. Sami's eyes are glassy as the champions superkick him over and over in the head, yet he keeps kicking out.

Kevin drags Jimmy to the announce table and is teasing his old indie standard of the package piledriver on the table, but Jey comes to the rescue and they chokeslam Kevin through the table where he lies in the debris, unmoving.

Free from having to worry about Kevin, both Usos stalk Sami, who seems too dazed to even realize where he is. They do their finisher, the 1D, to him, hoisting him in the air and slamming him down. All the air goes out of the crowd. No one has ever kicked out of this finisher before.

Sami kicks out.

As the audience and commentary scream in disbelief, Jey fills with a berserker fury. "Why won't you quit?" he howls, dragging Sami by his beard and hair, slapping his face. "I called you my brother!" He backs across the ring, glaring at Sami, then runs forward and does a Helluva Kick to him. Sami falls forward onto him, and Jey taunts him: "You shoulda never left the Bloodline!"

Sami responds by suplexing Jey into the turnbuckle, leaving him sprawling. Blindly, he starts to crawl toward his corner. Kevin has managed to stagger there from the rubble of the announce table, arriving just in time to be there when Sami looks up at him in shock and wonder, just as El Generico looked up to find Kevin there to make the tag all those years ago in PWG, against hope, against reason.

One flying hot tag later, and Kevin is handing out pop-up power-

THE FINAL CHAPTER

bombs to both Jimmy and Jey. As Jimmy crawls to the far corner, Kevin yells for Sami to do his Helluva Kick, stepping forward to deliver a stunner to Jey at almost the same time, their paths crossing neatly. Jey kicks out of the stunner with a desperate energy, and for a moment all four just lie in the ring exhausted, waves of cheers and chants crashing all around them. Jimmy slowly crawls over to Jey's side. Kevin makes his way on his hands and knees toward Sami, who reaches out to him with an exhausted hand. Kevin puts an arm under Sami's shoulder and starts to stand.

Over and over again, across the years, Kevin has told Sami to *stay down*. When he was a heel and Sami was a face he screamed it in a fury. When they were both heels he blustered it, demanding. When he was a face and Sami a heel he said it with pity and resignation.

Now, with both of them babyfaces, both of them the best and most complete versions of themselves, he says to Sami, barely loud enough to be heard over the roar of the crowd, "Get up."

"Get up," he says again, here at the end of this impossible tandem journey. "We're almost there."

They come to their feet together as the Usos rise as well, and all four stare at each other, letting the crowd noise rise and crest around them like a tide. "Let's end this!" Kevin yells, and all four plunge forward with renewed energy, entering the final act of the final chapter.

There's another wild round of superkicks to both Sami and Kevin, and when Kevin is the legal man the Usos do their other finisher to him, stereo frog splashes. At this point the crowd can hardly get louder, yet they try when Kevin kicks out. Sami yanks Jimmy out of the ring and hurls him over the announce table then scrambles to his corner for the tag. Jey is in the far corner, dazed. It's come down to him and Sami and all the anguish between them.

Sami Helluva Kicks him once, and Jey falls forward into his arms. Sami looks down at him for a long time, pity in his face. "You did this," he says almost too softly to be heard, the same words Kevin said to him two years ago, and puts him back in position for the second kick.

Once again, Jey falls forward into Sami's arms. This time, as Sami hesitates, Jimmy jumps into the ring but is intercepted by Kevin with a stunner. Galvanized, Sami pushes Jey back against the turnbuckle and delivers a third Helluva Kick to the champion, and this time when Jey falls forward Sami goes to the mat with him and pins him. The referee counts one–two–three.

Sami and Kevin have just become tag team champions in the main event of *WrestleMania*.

The crowd explodes in joy. Kevin, who fell to his knees at the count, sits down heavily with his back against the ropes, tears on his face. One hand over his mouth, he stares around as if he's not sure where he is, looking terribly young. Sami drags himself to the far side of the ring and puts his back to the opposite ropes, so that they're facing each other across the ring.

For a moment, they just look at each other.

A lifetime passed in a single moment.

In that moment, all the events of the last twenty years seem to pass between them like a vast river. The icy car rides and the hot crowds, the setbacks and the triumphs, the grinding poverty and the contracts signed, the births of children and the deaths of friends, the injuries and arguments and promises and compromises, every single thing that lies between the covers of this book and so much more flows between

THE FINAL CHAPTER

them. And through it all echoes the question that has driven them and haunted them, the question both the characters and the very real people behind them have asked over and over again. *Can we be stronger together? Can we succeed together? Can we reach heights together that we never could separately?*

As they rise and embrace each other as champions, the answer is what it always has been, what it always will be.

Yes.

AFTERWORD

AND THAT'S where the narrative ended for Kevin Owens and Sami Zayn, a journey that brought them from the pool halls of Montreal to the main event of *WrestleMania*, a tale of friendship and betrayal, damnation and redemption and reconciliation. Here is where they finished the story, on the grandest stage of them all in Los Angeles, holding aloft four gleaming titles.

No, don't be ridiculous. You know better than that. You know the greatest sorrow and the deepest joy of wrestling is that there is never any finishing a story, that stories keep going from triumph to loss to triumph once more, as long as the characters in them draw breath. Here is only where we draw the line, where we choose to snip the thread and tie a bow and say: *well done.* In fact, in the time it has taken to finish this book, their story has already moved on past it. At *Wrestle-Mania 39* they answered the question *Are we stronger together?* Now they're asking new questions about the very nature of friendship and its value, their orbits on a collision course once more, heading for yet another spectacular explosion.

Sami and Kevin move forward into the future, through loss and separation, conflict and resolution, as they keep adding to the masterpiece that is their whole combined career, the increasingly complex and intricate tapestry that they have created together. They will weave

AFTERWORD

more and more threads into the pattern that has held green phantoms and tribal chiefs, young bucks and new days, American wolves and American nightmares and American dragons. With two brilliant threads running together through it all, sometimes parallel, sometimes crossing each other, sometimes tangled and sometimes smooth. Never ceasing, never finished. Because as Sami would tell you, the story isn't really over.

The story is never over.

CODA: THE STORYTELLERS
(2024)

Vibe Check

IT'S 2:30, and Sami Zayn is annoyed. "He's perpetually angry at me for my tardiness, but *actually* he's worse than I am," he says, hands sketching exasperation into the air.

We're waiting in a Zoom call for Kevin Owens to log in. Sami is in a red shirt, framed by a window that looks out into a wooded garden. I'm perched on the end of my childhood bed in the tiny attic room I grew up in, caught mid-family-visit by WWE suddenly giving permission for an interview after months of hedging on their part and seemingly hopeless effort by my publisher, Jonathan Snowden.

The WWE guy in charge had called me a half-hour previously to explain that there had been a change of plans. They had originally scheduled me to talk with Sami first, then with Kevin. Kevin, however, had felt strongly that they should be interviewed together. Sami had countered that he'd rather I talk to each of them separately. A compromise had been reached that I would start with them together, with the option to talk to them separately after the main interview.

Starting off with this disjunction has compounded my nerves, and I feel a bit rattled as I thank Sami for being willing to meet with me. I'm unnerved by their inability to agree about whether the interview is

CODA: THE STORYTELLERS

better as two solo interviews or as one team interview. The conflict is almost comically on-the-nose, the same question that has followed them from their start in Montreal through Ring of Honor and PWG and all the way through their time in WWE: are the two of them better as a unit, or as separate individuals?

At 2:36, Kevin enters the Zoom call. "Six minutes," Sami says. "That's not *too* bad."

"Shut up," Kevin says with the fondly weary tone of someone who has been needled about this for a decade. "You were late for four hours every time we've had to meet."

Sami rears back, indignant. "What did I say he's gonna do?" he demands of me in a tone of vindication. "What did I say he's gonna do? Point the finger at *me*, even though he's just as bad."

"I am not as bad as you. *Ever.*" The slightly-tardy Kevin is sitting in his car, wearing a Razor Ramon shirt with the phrase *Bad Guys Last Forever*. Tree branches and Florida-blue sky show through his sunroof. He grumbles a bit as Sami jibes at him. The interview hasn't even started yet, and they're already showing off the bickering they're famous for. But more on that later. For now I'm just sort of stunned to find myself here.

I'd met both of them at meet and greets for two or three awkwardly-stammering minutes at a time, but never both at once, and never at this length. I knew their story inside and out, backwards and forwards. I'd gathered up all the scraps and pieces of it I could find and tried to put it all together into a coherent narrative. But now I'm meeting the storytellers themselves, the people who have—part by accident, part very much by design—created a saga for their characters that spans the globe and over two decades.

I'm not really here to get facts from them, although over the course of the next ninety minutes I do get images that add texture to the tale. Here's a barely-twenty Sami in 2004, backstage at his first American show watching Super Dragon, Excalibur, B-Boy and Bobby Quance's match, turning to Kevin and saying "We're fucked, we can't keep up with this, this is great." Here's Jim Cornette in 2009 responding to Kevin's email laying out his year-long storyline with a laconic "I'll get back to you, but maybe don't make Generico such a little bitch." Here's

Sami in 2019, so filled with anxiety at finding himself a non-wrestling manager for Nakamura and Cesaro that he was driving everyone on the writing staff insane badgering them to tell him where his character was going, to the point where Vince McMahon hinted to Kevin that he was thinking about firing Sami and Kevin had to tell him he'd be making a huge mistake: "You want *more* people like him, not less."

But on the whole, the dates and events and story beats remain as I've put them down in the book (thank God). That's not the information I'm here to gather. I'm here to see what I can learn about their attitudes toward their art, their story, and each other. I'm here for a vibe check.

Pride and Passion

They started off bickering, but after that they only disagree about two things in the whole ninety minutes we talk. The first is a simple matter of dates—they're not sure in what month a match in 2010 took place. (I double-check later and surprisingly, it's Sami who's right).

The second is even more surprising, but I'll save that for later.

The quarrel over tardiness was affectionately heartfelt, but had almost the feel of a ritual, a performance for the interviewer. Kevin has mentioned in the past that their arguments have become a sort of schtick, an idea that he repeats today. "It's become an act," he says at one point. "We know people like it, so we just do it." I remember Eddie Edwards' groaning disagreement at the idea that people enjoyed their endless debates about how to call a match, but I hold my tongue, because both of them are in the middle of explaining the reason they argue so vehemently, and it's exactly the kind of thing I want to hear more about.

"They never understand *why* we're bickering," Sami says, "and the real reason is because it's about making it as good as it could possibly be." They paint a picture (supported by the howls of frustration from everyone who has ever had to work with them) of merciless perfectionism and pride—in themselves, in each other, in their work. It's a tendency that they admit could come off as arrogant.

"Other people take it as 'Oh, they just want it their way,'" Kevin

CODA: THE STORYTELLERS

says. "Well, maybe, but 99 percent of the time our way is better." His delivery is very I'm-just-stating-facts-here. "This sounds very cocky, and we only say this to each other, but... we're better than most." Sami breaks into a gleeful chortle and Kevin starts laughing as well, as if they've shared the most delightful secret with me.

It's pretty clear part of the reason they drive other wrestlers crazy is that each of them values the other's opinion over anyone else's. They argue so intensely because theirs are the ideas that matter. "Even if I'm arguing with him, his ideas are better than other people's, anyway," Kevin says. "Sometimes I know I won't win the battle with him, but I'll pick his ideas over anybody else's." He repeats a statement he's made elsewhere, that Sami has a preternatural ability to know how an audience will react to a match before they even enter the building. "When we're in a tag team, or anytime I'm in the match with him, I know it's an easy night."

For his part, Sami seems to hold Kevin's character work and long-term planning in some amount of awe. A lot of that goes back to their very different beginnings as wrestlers, and especially the fact that El Generico just kind of appeared by a fluke, at the time with no backstory, and of course Sami had no way to give the non-speaking character a backstory.

Talking about their early years, Sami says "I think Kevin did think more character based than me. I was much more like 'have the best match,' because everything was week to week." Caught up in the weekly grind of shows, young Sami "was just like, 'who am I wrestling this Friday? Who am I wrestling this Saturday?'" Meanwhile, stuck in Rougeau's school with a show every three or four months, Kevin had ample time to think about all the little details of his character, to try and find ways to add personality into the same rote match.

"Kevin, from earlier than I did, had much more of an idea of how he presents himself," Sami notes, and Kevin agrees. Recalling their first US match in CZW, the one where Sami was so worried that they "were fucked," and they ended up doing a mad bell-to-bell spotfest that had everyone chanting for them, Kevin says that "as good as the match was, the one thing I was excited about was at the end of the match, when Eddie shakes everyone's hand, and I spit in his face. When we called the match, I didn't care what I was doing, because I remembered I have that at the end. That's all that matters. So that shows the notion of where we were in terms of how we thought about wrestling at that time."

Their year-long feud in 2010 was, according to Sami, a "major turning point" in how he thought about wrestling storytelling. He remembers Kevin insisting in 2009 that they were stagnating, that their characters needed to evolve, and that—to Sami's horror—he thought they should break up the team. "Dude, what?" Sami had protested, still thinking week-to-week. "What are you saying? No! We're—we're doing well!"

"I'm telling you," Kevin replied, "If we do this, by next year we will main event *Final Battle*."

Doubtful at first, Sami had eventually come to see the genius of it and throw himself into it. "I didn't think in terms of a year-long story. Nobody did," he says with emphasis. He talks glowingly about Kevin's character work to set up the turn, how he started subtly selling his knee months in advance, how he "let himself go physically" ("It wasn't very difficult," Kevin breaks in, laughing), how he had planted stories about possibly having to retire with influential, high-profile fans.* "And once it was reported by Meltzer, it was like—" Sami pumps his fist in remembered triumph. "*Perfect.*"

In short, they're a prideful pair, with the only thing keeping them from flat-out arrogance is the fact that they insist it's not personal egos, but perfectionism that drives them. "I think that's what separates us from a lot of the lot is our pride in our work," Kevin says. "Not that other guys aren't proud, I just don't think they're *as* proud of what they put out."

He points toward Sami on the other screen. "More him than me. I do have it, but he really is on another level. It won't drive me crazy the way it would him. I think it comes down to pride in our work, and I've had to tell people that it's all rooted in passion and wanting to literally give everyone the best possible match." In the end, Kevin believes that "whatever drives people up the walls about Rami, it all comes from a

---

* Influential, high-profile fans take note: never completely trust this man.

place of passion, and he wants to give the best possible," and it seems pretty clear Sami feels the same way about Kevin.

Years of Support

Yeah, they've got a mound of chips on their shoulders. "There's not one place we walked into—except PWG—" Kevin quickly amends, "where people were welcoming and went *Yeah, these guys are great.* Everybody thought we were dumb kids and treated us as such."

But for all their pride, they also are keenly aware of how much support they've gotten along the way. As we talk, they pile up a list of people who helped them at different points. "Triple H saw us right away as top talent," Kevin notes. Similarly, he mentions that Cary Silkin, the owner of Ring of Honor, kept their feud from being abandoned when Jim Cornette wanted it gone: "Cary was the only reason we still got to do it."

When Sami hears Kevin say that, he counters, "The story was hot, it couldn't be denied at that point." He's more grateful for the wrestlers and staff that gave them support when things got really bad with Cornette. "People would come up to us and offer support in whispers like, 'Hey, man, I know they're doing this to you, but you guys have the best story. You guys are fucking killing it.' Stuff like that meant a lot to me, especially by [Shane] Hagadorn. He saw what was going on internally and he would kind of pull us aside and be like, 'Man, fuck that, what you guys are doing is the best thing.'" Kevin specifically mentions Hagadorn for his work on social media during their feud and Kevin's later solo work in ROH. "Shane Hagadorn was helping without us even knowing, is the funny part. He would do stuff like have accounts online to post things that would help the story. We didn't even know it was him, we only found out later."

And of course, they have glowing words for the support they got in that feud from Steve Corino and Colt Cabana. "They were crucial parts of the story. The story wouldn't have worked without them," Sami says. He laughs in disbelief when he remembers Corino telling him the feud was the most fun he'd ever had in his life. "I'm like, 'you were ECW champion!'" Going back much earlier, he talks about how Super

Dragon overcame his annoyance at being shown up by some kids from Montreal and welcomed them to PWG with open arms, even giving Sami advice on match pacing. I feel like the only limit to their gratitude was the time limit of the interview, because I know there are many names they would have mentioned (we didn't even touch on the Briscoe Brothers) given more time.

When I ask about Michael "Llakor" Ryan, the IWS publicist, they talk at length about how his write-ups made all the difference in creating actual stories out of an assortment of matches at a time when continuity and connection were hard to come by. Thanks to Ryan, "it wasn't just a card with seven matches, fourteen names," Kevin says. "He would give background to all these people that a lot of people reading the articles had no idea who they were, but they all had a sense of who they were once they were done reading it." Without any prompting from me, he immediately compares that to the work that Excalibur did for PWG, creating on-line summaries that spun the narrative threads to connect matches and give them meaning for the fans. "It was Excalibur's job to make the matches make sense or make them interesting in a story sense."

Sami was even more indebted to Ryan and Excalibur, because "El Generico just sort of showed up one day and then couldn't explain his background, couldn't make these things clear." With no ability to express his character or motivations, it was the work done by bookers and publicists that helped to turn Generico from a cartoon into, as Sami puts it, a folk legend. It was Excalibur who decided that El Generico's motivation was to raise money for an orphanage, the crucial bit of lore that lifted the character into icon status. Not all of the lore people gifted El Generico with stuck (Sami laughs remembering Ryan trying to convince him El Generico should spit like the Iron Sheik and his politely uncomfortable response: "I... I don't know. I don't know, man, I don't know, Michael."), but Sami had the intuitive ability to know which ones to hand on to the audience, which ones were the best and truest, to polish the character until it shone.

When I ask him if he wanted to bring that work with him to WWE, the answer is an emphatic *yes*. "I definitely fought hard for it because I had a lot of confidence in it," Sami says. "Even though it sounds silly on paper, like *El Generico?* Even on the indies it sounds like a stupid thing." I am struck speechless by this, so immersed in years of studying the luchador that I can't imagine the name being "silly." "I just had a lot of faith in it," Sami goes on as I collect my wits. "I kept fighting for it, and at a certain point he [Bill Demott, the head trainer at the time] was like, 'Don't you get it? *No.*'" He brings up the "super emotional" promo he mentioned once on Edge and Christian's show, where he said goodbye to El Generico and then biked home crying. "I'll have to try and find it," he says thoughtfully, and apparently I have a new piece of lost media I cannot rest until I see.

"But that's all good," he says now, this man who has become Sami Zayn, funny and altruistic and heroic as El Generico was, just in different ways. "I think it all worked out for the best. Even now, there have been so many times over the years where they wanted me to bring it back. Writers who were fans of El Generico back in the day have kind of mentioned like they had ideas."

Here Kevin cuts in. "I've tried," he says. "I've tried." He sounds sad.

Sami shakes his head. "I don't want to ever touch it, because it's a lot prettier sitting on a shelf, living in folklore and living in people's imaginations. It's like the Beatles. They existed at a very distinct time and place, and that's where they live forever. If they did reunite in the eighties and put out a new album in the eighties…"

"Yeah," Kevin says, "but McCartney still does his own shit, and it's pretty good. It's not the exact same, but it's pretty good."

"But what I'm saying—"

Kevin talks over Sami. "We need… We need a one-night comeback at least." But his voice is resigned. "I'll keep needling at you."

"I just don't know if it would be the *same*, that's what I'm getting at. And I—"

"That's what I'm *saying*," Kevin shoots back almost sharply. "It might not be the same, but it's still pretty good."

This is the only thing of substance they disagree on in the whole interview, and as it unfolds I sit in shock, trying not to show how totally they are upending all my assumptions. It had never crossed my mind that Kevin—*Kevin*, who for years has resolutely insisted El

Generico is dead, dead, *dead*—might be the one who yearns to have the luchador back, who apparently argues regularly for one last glimpse of him.

"I honestly also feel like the value that I have without the mask now has eclipsed any value I ever had with the mask," Sami counters. He seems upset, though not at Kevin. "I guess it's just sentiment. It's sentimental to me, and I'd rather let it live in our memories and in our hearts and just enjoy it for what it was, when it was. Do you know what I mean? I think— I don't know. It's very emotional. I'm even getting emotional talking about it," he says awkwardly, visibly uncomfortable. He talks about how the brainbuster on the turnbuckle he did to Gunther at *WrestleMania* in 2024 was a tribute to Generico. "I'm different now, you know, as a person, as a performer, as everything. I just feel like Generico was better off living in people's memories and in people's hearts than in reality, in a way, because that's always where it existed."

"You just don't want to cut your hair so the mask fits," Kevin says, laughing, and the tense emotion of the moment is defused into laughter. But it was very real, and this is where we reach one of the most interesting revelations of the interview:

Sami Zayn Is Still Working Through Stuff

Over and over again in the ninety minutes of the interview Sami keeps stopping to say some variation of *I never thought of that*.

"I'm just realizing as we're talking," he says about Ryan and Excalibur's influence.

"I didn't even realize how huge that was," he says about the importance of the orphanage to El Generico's character.

When picking apart what made their tag team dynamic great, he says "I'm just piecing it together now."

"I didn't even really think of it till now," he says of Cabana and Corino's selflessness in supporting their story for a full year.

It's possible that that's just the way he talks, that the kind of guy who suddenly wonders where all the graves are in England or starts talking about whether humans have free will often "just realizes" things mid-conversation. But for years as El Generico, caught in the nonstop grind of the indies ("Who am I wrestling this Friday? Who am I wrestling this Saturday?") he had no time to reflect on the character. He was creating it all on the fly, reacting intuitively to each new feud and match, unable to step back and see the big picture. Then he was plunged into WWE, forced to take on and master an entirely new persona and deal with new challenges with little to no support. During that same span of time, Kevin had literally hundreds of hours of shoot interviews to talk about his career, to process what it all meant. Sami has had almost none of that.

To add an extra wrinkle to all that, Sami's commitment to the legend of El Generico has meant he's incapable of talking about his ties to the character in all but the most elliptical way. "That wasn't me," he's said over and over to interviewers, gently but firmly. His dedication has elevated Generico to the status of a true folk hero, but at a price. I don't know if he'll ever have the time and space to look back on his bifurcated career and put it all together in a way that makes sense to him. I hope he does.

The Whole is Greater

In the end, and not surprisingly, I ran out of time before I ran out of things to ask about. Inexperienced with interviewing, unsure how to allocate my time, I never even got to a single question about their time in WWE. I had wanted to wrap up by asking whether they were satisfied with where their shared story had come to rest, there at Wrestle-Mania with the tag titles in their hands, and if it had seemed like closure. But after all my research and after talking to them, I already know the answer—and so do you, after reading this book. Of course they're not satisfied, because they're never satisfied, they're always trying to do it better, to get every detail just right. And of course it's not closure, because wrestling goes on, and their paths will always cross again. And then somehow—to their own surprise—they'll make it new and fresh and dramatic, this dynamic that has only gotten deeper and richer over the decades. So I didn't get an answer to that question, but it doesn't matter. Because at the very end, Sami answered the more important question, the one that was bothering me at the beginning of the interview.

"You know, I was... I was skeptical about doing it together." He's harking back to the beginning of the interview, and the fact that Kevin had wanted the three of us talking together and Sami had thought it would be better one-on-one. "But I actually see the benefit in it now, because there's so much I don't remember that he brings up, and vice versa." And there it is once again, the question answered once more. With these two, the whole is greater than the sum of its brilliant parts. The story is more complete when they're together.

NOTES

INTRODUCTION

1. Glasspiegel, Ryan. "WWE'S Kevin Owens Still Doesn't Have 'Full Grasp' of how Steve Austin Match Materialized." *New York Post*, 29 Dec. 2022. https://nypost.com/2022/12/29/wwes-kevin-owens-still-in-awe-of-his-steve-austin-match/

ORIGIN STORIES

1. *Talk Steen Talk: The Kevin Steen Shoot Interview.* Highspots, 2012.
2. "Johnny Gargano." *The Kevin Steen Show.* Highspots, 2013.
3. Cabana, Colt. "Kevin Steen." *The Art of Wrestling with Colt Cabana* 5 July 2011.
4. *Shoot Interview With Kevin Steen.* RF Video, 2014.
5. *Shoot Interview With Kevin Steen.* RF Video, 2014.
6. "KO Picks: Bret vs. Shawn." *Superstar Picks.* The WWE Network, 1 Oct. 2018)
7. Fordy, Tom. " 'I'M GETTING THERE' Sami Zayn on WrestleMania, Goldberg vs Brock Lesnar, the Montreal Screw Job and Hulk Hogan vs The Rock." *The Sun*, 7 Mar. 2017.
8. Austin, Steve. "Sami Zayn." *Steve Austin's Broken Skull Sessions.* 22 Jul. 2022.
9. WWE. "Sami Zayn's Elimination Chamber Vlog: Behind the Scenes of His War with Roman Reigns." 1 Oct. 2018. https://www.youtube.com/watch?v=e_mz4OPn_To
10. Ryan, Michael. "I Am El Generico's Father."*The W*, 1 Feb. 2005. https://the-w.com/thread.php?id=24405
11. Ryan, Michael. "I Am El Generico's Father." *PopOptiq*, 11 Jan. 2013. https://www.popoptiq.com/i-am-el-genericos-father/
12. POST Wrestling. "The Story of Sami Zayn with Pat Laprade | POST Interview." 17 Feb 2023. https://www.youtube.com/watch?v=VH6isAwLmvk
13. Technically the World Wrestling Federation (WWF) at the time, but soon to become WWE.
14. *Shoot Interview with Mr. Wrestling Kevin Steen.* Fortune Video Editing/OJ Productions, 2007.
15. *Talk Steen Talk: The Kevin Steen Shoot Interview.* Highspots, 2012.
16. Leroux, Yves. "A Fourth Generation of Rougeau Debuts." *Slam Wrestling*, 2 Jun. 2001. https://slamwrestling.net/index.php/2001/06/02/a-fourth-generation-of-rougeau-debuts/
17. *Fight Owens Fight: The Kevin Owens Story.* WWE, 2017.
18. Oliver, Greg. "Another Rougeau to Enter the Ring." *Slam Wrestling*, 18 May, 2001. https://slamwrestling.net/index.php/2001/05/18/another-rougeau-to-enter-the-ring/
19. Leroux, Yves. "A Fourth Generation of Rougeau Debuts." *Slam Wrestling*, 2 Jun. 2001. https://slamwrestling.net/index.php/2001/06/02/a-fourth-generation-of-rougeau-debuts/
20. Austin, Steve. "Kevin Steen." *The Steve Austin Show* [podcast]. 13 Dec. 2013.

NOTES

THREE WAY DANCE

1. Paradise City Ninjas. "Interview with Beef Wellington." *The Smart Marks*, 3 Aug. 2003. https://thesmartmarks.com/printer_1091.shtml
2. Not to be mistaken for Canadian wrestler *Biff* Wellington.
3. Melok, Bobby. "'Familiarity Breeds Contempt.': The Bitter History of Sami Zayn and Kevin Owens." WWE.com, 10 Mar 2016. https://www.wwe.com/article/sami-zayn-kevin-owens-history
4. Melok, Bobby. "'Familiarity Breeds Contempt.': The Bitter History of Sami Zayn and Kevin Owens." WWE.com, 10 Mar 2016. https://www.wwe.com/article/sami-zayn-kevin-owens-history
5. Melok, Bobby. "'Familiarity Breeds Contempt.': The Bitter History of Sami Zayn and Kevin Owens." WWE.com, 10 Mar 2016. https://www.wwe.com/article/sami-zayn-kevin-owens-history
6. *Shoot Interview with Mr. Wrestling Kevin Steen*. Fortune Video Editing/OJ Productions, 2007.
7. *Talk Steen Talk: The Kevin Steen Shoot Interview*. Highspots, 2012.
8. Llakor. "How El Generico Earned His Cape." *TSM Forums*, 20 Oct. 2005.
9. *Shoot Interview With Kevin Steen*. RF Video, 2014.
10. *Talk Steen Talk: The Kevin Steen Shoot Interview*. Highspots, 2012.
11. *Best on the Indies: Kevin Steen*. Smart Mark Video, 2012.
12. Llakor. "IWS Un F'N Sanctioned Preview." *The Smart Marks*, 7 Sept. 2003. https://forums.thesmartmarks.com/topic/40539-iws-un-fn-sanctioned-preview/
13. *Shoot Interview With Kevin Steen*. RF Video, 2014.
14. Gagnon, Joshua. "PCO Talks Working with Sami Zayn, Giving Kevin Owens Advice Early in His Career." *Wrestling Inc.*, 2 Sept. 2018. https://www.wrestlinginc.com/news/2018/09/pco-talks-working-with-sami-zayn-645437/
15. *Shoot Interview With Kevin Steen*. RF Video, 2014.

PLEASE DON'T GO

1. Gagnon, Joshua. "PCO Talks Working with Sami Zayn, Giving Kevin Owens Advice Early in His Career." *Wrestling Inc.*, 2 Sept. 2018. https://www.wrestlinginc.com/news/2018/09/pco-talks-working-with-sami-zayn-645437/
2. *Shoot Interview With Kevin Steen*. RF Video, 2014.
3. *Shoot Interview with Mr. Wrestling Kevin Steen*. Fortune Video Editing/OJ Productions, 2007.
4. *Shoot Interview with Mr. Wrestling Kevin Steen*. Fortune Video Editing/OJ Productions, 2007.
5. *Best on the Indies: Kevin Steen*. Smart Mark Video, 2012.
6. *Shoot Interview with Mr. Wrestling Kevin Steen*. Fortune Video Editing/OJ Productions, 2007.
7. *Shoot Interview with Mr. Wrestling Kevin Steen*. Fortune Video Editing/OJ Productions, 2007.
8. *Best on the Indies: Kevin Steen*. Smart Mark Video, 2012.
9. *Talk Steen Talk: The Kevin Steen Shoot Interview*. Highspots, 2012.
10. *Fight Owens Fight: The Kevin Owens Story*. WWE. 2017.
11. *Shoot Interview with Mr. Wrestling Kevin Steen*. Fortune Video Editing/OJ Productions, 2007.

NOTES

12. Cagematch.net lists thirteen matches, but there are a lot of matches that slip by unlisted at this time, so it may well be more.
13. Melok, Bobby. "'Familiarity Breeds Contempt.': The Bitter History of Sami Zayn and Kevin Owens." WWE.com, 10 Mar 2016. https://www.wwe.com/article/sami-zayn-kevin-owens-history
14. Melok, Bobby. "'Familiarity Breeds Contempt.': The Bitter History of Sami Zayn and Kevin Owens." WWE.com, 10 Mar 2016. https://www.wwe.com/article/sami-zayn-kevin-owens-history
15. Laprade, Patric. "Kevin Owens Veut Boucler la Boucle à Quebec." TVA Sports, 21 Aug. 2023. https://www.tvasports.ca/2023/08/21/kevin-owens-veut-boucler-la-boucle-a-quebec
16. Gorilla Position. "Kevin Owens Interview: On WWE/NXT career, Steve Austin, Match with Brock Lesnar & John Cena." Youtube, 2 Sept. 2015. https://www.youtube.com/watch?v=m758s-zVP34
17. Gulf News. "WWE NXT Champion Sami Zayn Names his Top 5 Wrestling Influences." Youtube, 2 Feb. 2015. https://www.youtube.com/watch?v=TAfaXG4ahl4
18. Fight Owens Fight: The Kevin Owens Story. WWE, 2017.
19. Ringside Collectibles. "Mattel WWE Entire Panel! - SDCC 2015 - San Diego Comic Con!" July 10, 2015. YouTube, 10 Jul. 2015. https://www.youtube.com/watch?v=t9OREl4mrBM
20. Leroux, Yves. "Steen Believes in Goals, Not Dreams." Slam Wrestling, 7 Mar. 2005. https://slamwrestling.net/index.php/2005/03/07/steen-believes-in-goals-not-dreams/

GRAB THE BRASS RING

1. Best on the Indies: Kevin Steen. Smart Mark Video, 2012.
2. Ryan, Michael. "When We Were Marks: The Kevin Steen Conspiracy." The-W.com, 16 Feb. 2005. http://the-w.com/thread.php/id=24624
3. POST Wrestling. "The Story of Sami Zayn with Pat Laprade | POST Interview." 17 Feb 2023. https://www.youtube.com/watch?v=VH6isAwLmvk
4. Best on the Indies: Kevin Steen. Smart Mark Video, 2012.
5. Best on the Indies: Kevin Steen. Smart Mark Video, 2012.
6. "Jimmy Jacobs." The Kevin Steen Show. Highspots, 2014.

ACTION FIGURES

1. WWE. "WWE Network: Go Behind the Scenes of Kevin Owens & Sami Zayn's Mattel Commercial Shoot." Youtube, 22 Apr. 2018. https://youtu.be/WnN59CQEi9w
2. ThyBostonHeeL. "Generico Sure Does Likes the Women [FUNNY]." Youtube, 26 Apr. 2014. (Original broadcast unknown). https://youtu.be/yMTmxOCx4aQ
3. "Jimmy Jacobs." The Kevin Steen Show. Highspots, 2014.
4. "Matt Hardy." The Kevin Steen Show. Highspots, 2014.
5. Talk Steen Talk: The Kevin Steen Shoot Interview. Highspots, 2012.
6. Shoot Interview with Mr. Wrestling Kevin Steen. Fortune Video Editing/OJ Productions, 2007.
7. Best on the Indies: Kevin Steen. Smart Mark Video, 2012.

NOTES

8. Ryan, Michael. "When We Were Marks: That Rudolph Moment." *TSM Forums*, 25 Jan. 2007. https://forums.thesmartmarks.com/topic/84629-when-we-were-marks-that-rudolph-moment/
9. *Shoot Interview With Kevin Steen*. RF Video, 2014.

JUST WRESTLE

1. "Gabe Sapolsky." *The Kevin Steen Show*. Highspots, 2014.
2. Steen, Kevin. *Hell Rising*. Ring of Honor, 2013.
3. "Jimmy Jacobs." *The Kevin Steen Show*. Highspots, 2014.
4. "Jimmy Jacobs." *The Kevin Steen Show*. Highspots, 2014.
5. "Jimmy Jacobs." *The Kevin Steen Show*. Highspots, 2014.
6. Steen, Kevin. *Hell Rising*. Ring of Honor, 2013.
7. *Shoot Interview With Kevin Steen*. RF Video, 2014.
8. "Jimmy Jacobs." *The Kevin Steen Show*. Highspots, 2014.
9. "Jimmy Jacobs." *The Kevin Steen Show*. Highspots, 2014.
10. "Gabe Sapolsky." *The Kevin Steen Show*. Highspots, 2014.
11. *Best on the Indies: Kevin Steen*. Smart Mark Video, 2012.
12. "Gabe Sapolsky." *The Kevin Steen Show*. Highspots, 2014.
13. "Gabe Sapolsky." *The Kevin Steen Show*. Highspots, 2014.
14. "Gabe Sapolsky." *The Kevin Steen Show*. Highspots, 2014.
15. "Gabe Sapolsky." *The Kevin Steen Show*. Highspots, 2014.
16. "Gabe Sapolsky." *The Kevin Steen Show*. Highspots, 2014.
17. *Shoot Interview With Kevin Steen*. RF Video, 2014.
18. "Gabe Sapolsky." *The Kevin Steen Show*. Highspots, 2014.
19. *Shoot Interview With Kevin Steen*. RF Video, 2014.
20. "Gabe Sapolsky." *The Kevin Steen Show*. Highspots, 2014.

ACROSS THE SEAS

1. Austin, Steve. "Kevin Steen." *The Steve Austin Show* [podcast], 13 Dec. 2013.
2. Owens, Kevin [@FightOwensFight]. "Oh man! Generico hated that match. Not only did I beat the hell out of him, I also kept throwing zingers out and making the crowd laugh. He later said it felt like he was being attacked by an evil stand-up comedian. Oddly enough, I remember loving every second of the match!" Twitter, Feb. 19, 2021. https://twitter.com/FightOwensFight/status/1362763596363673601?s=20
3. "Gabe Sapolsky." *The Kevin Steen Show*. Highspots, 2014.
4. "Gabe Sapolsky." *The Kevin Steen Show*. Highspots, 2014.
5. *Best on the Indies: Kevin Steen*. Smart Mark Video, 2012.
6. *Shoot Interview With Kevin Steen*. RF Video, 2014.
7. *Shoot Interview With Kevin Steen*. RF Video, 2014.
8. Jericho, Chris. "NXT's Sami Zayn & Adrian Neville & Fozzy's Jeff Rouse." *Talk is Jericho* [podcast], 6 Dec. 2014.
9. "Johnny Gargano." *The Kevin Steen Show*. Highspots, 2014.
10. *Shoot Interview with Mr. Wrestling Kevin Steen*. Fortune Video Editing/OJ Productions, 2007.
11. *Talk Steen Talk: The Kevin Steen Shoot Interview*. Highspots, 2012.
12. *Shoot Interview With Kevin Steen*. RF Video, 2014.

NOTES

13. *Shoot Interview with Mr. Wrestling Kevin Steen.* Fortune Video Editing/OJ Productions, 2007.
14. "Gabe Sapolsky." *The Kevin Steen Show.* Highspots, 2014.

MAN UP

1. Counihan, Alan. "Kevin Steen." *DKP* [Podcast], Dec. 2010.
2. "Jay Lethal." *The Kevin Steen Show,* 2013.
3. "Jay Lethal." *The Kevin Steen Show,* 2013.
4. Jericho, Chris. "The Emancipation of Jon Moxley." *Talk is Jericho* [podcast], 29 May. 2019.
5. "Jay Lethal." *The Kevin Steen Show,* 2013.
6. Kevin Owens [@FightOwensFight]. *Jamin* 🩶. Twitter. 19 Jan. 2023. https://x.com/FightOwensFight/status/1615777172467105801
7. "The Super Smash Brothers." *The Kevin Steen Show.* Highspots, 2013.
8. "Gabe Sapolsky." *The Kevin Steen Show.* Highspots, 2014.
9. *Shoot Interview With Kevin Steen.* RF Video, 2014.
10. *Best on the Indies: Kevin Steen.* Smart Mark Video, 2012.
11. *Shoot Interview With Kevin Steen.* RF Video, 2014.

HANDS IN THE AIR

1. "Gabe Sapolsky." *The Kevin Steen Show.* Highspots, 2014.
2. *Talk Steen Talk: The Kevin Steen Shoot Interview.* Highspots, 2012.
3. *Fight Owens Fight: The Kevin Owens Story.* WWE, 2017.
4. *Talk Steen Talk: The Kevin Steen Shoot Interview.* Highspots, 2012.
5. Jacobs, Jimmy. "Final Battle 2021." Ring of Honor.

YEAR OF THE WOLF

1. "Eddie Edwards." *The Kevin Steen Show.* Highspots, 2013.
2. Stories With Brisco And Bradshaw. "ROAD DOGG–FULL EPISODE." Youtube, 26 May 2022. .https://www.youtube.com/watch?v=-uBL2VBrh_o
3. Moxley, Jon. *MOX.* Permuted Press. Pp. 136-137. 2 Nov. 2021.
4. Edwards mostly exits Kevin and Sami's story at this point, but his reputation is made by this match. He'll suffer an even more spectacular injury in 2018, when another wrestler swings at him with a baseball bat and deliberately misses, but then the bat hits a chair and rebounds directly into Eddie's face, gruesomely breaking his eye socket and orbital bone. Edwards has a quote from Rocky 6 tattooed on his arm, embodying the professional wrestler's creed that "It ain't about how hard you hit. It's about how hard you can get hit and keep moving forward." The tattoo is on the forearm of the arm that was broken that night against Kevin and Generico, the ink starting at the elbow.

MOMENT OF CLARITY

1. "Eddie Edwards." *The Kevin Steen Show.* Highspots, 2013.
2. "Jay Lethal." *The Kevin Steen Show.* Highspots, 2013.

NOTES

3. "Jimmy Jacobs." *The Kevin Steen Show*. Highspots, 2014.
4. Zayn, Sami. [@samizayn]. "The Lennon/McCartney of pro wrestling." Twitter, 1 Jun. 2022. https://twitter.com/SamiZayn/status/1531789723525697539?s=20
5. *Shoot Interview With Kevin Steen*. RF Video, 2014.
6. *Shoot Interview With Kevin Steen*. RF Video, 2014.
7. *Shoot Interview with Mr. Wrestling Kevin Steen*. Fortune Video Editing/OJ Productions, 2007.
8. *Shoot Interview With Kevin Steen*. RF Video, 2014.
9. *Shoot Interview With Kevin Steen*. RF Video, 2014.
10. Steen, Kevin. *Hell Rising*. Ring of Honor, 2013.
11. The Indy Corner Wrestling Podcast. "The Indy Corner Interviews Jim Cornette." 8 Dec. 2013. https://www.podomatic.com/podcasts/theindycorner/episodes/2013-12-07T12_28_18-08_00
12. The Indy Corner Wrestling Podcast. "The Indy Corner Interviews Jim Cornette." 8 Dec. 2013. https://www.podomatic.com/podcasts/theindycorner/episodes/2013-12-07T12_28_18-08_00
13. TMPT Empire of Podcasts. "Jim Cornette On Kevin Owens & Sami Zayn's Success and Hating Kenny Omega & Joey Ryan." 18 Apr. 2017. https://www.youtube.com/watch?v=X9J4NmsuD40
14. The Indy Corner Wrestling Podcast. "The Indy Corner Interviews Jim Cornette." 8 Dec. 2013. https://www.podomatic.com/podcasts/theindycorner/episodes/2013-12-07T12_28_18-08_00
15. Steen, Kevin. *Hell Rising*. Ring of Honor, 2013.
16. The Indy Corner Wrestling Podcast. "The Indy Corner Interviews Jim Cornette." 8 Dec. 2013. https://www.podomatic.com/podcasts/theindycorner/episodes/2013-12-07T12_28_18-08_00
17. Steen, Kevin. *Hell Rising*. Ring of Honor, 2013.
18. Zayn, Sami. [@samizayn]. "My… dawg?" Twitter. 7 Nov. 2022. https://twitter.com/SamiZayn/status/1589481109133328385?s=20

BITTER FRIENDS, STIFFER ENEMIES

1. Steen, Kevin. *Hell Rising*. Ring of Honor, 2013.

FIGHT WITHOUT HONOR

1. Sinclair. "History: 2010s." SBGI.net, 2024. https://sbgi.net/who-we-are/history/2010s/
2. Episode 93: Final Battle 2009." *An Honorable Mention with Shane Hagadorn and Jeff Schwartz*. 17 Dec. 2019.
3. Steen, Kevin. *Hell Rising*. Ring of Honor, 2013.
4. "SCUM: Steve Corino & Jimmy Jacobs." *A Full Case of Tales*. Highspots, 2013.
5. Steen, Kevin. *Hell Rising*. Ring of Honor, 2013.
6. Manning, Jake. "Man Scout Puts Over Kevin Steen." *10 Bell Podcast*, 29 Jan. 2020.
7. Jameskelsey. "Last night I was on WWE Raw with Chris Jericho and Kevin Owens. I am, Friendship the Magician! AMaA." *Reddit*, 15 Feb. 2017. https://www.reddit.com/r/IAmA/comments/5u1vn9/last_night_i_was_on_wwe_raw_with_chris_jericho
8. Steen, Kevin. *Hell Rising*. Ring of Honor, 2013.

NOTES

9. "SCUM: Steve Corino & Jimmy Jacobs." *A Full Case of Tales*. Highspots, 2013.
10. *Fight Owens Fight: The Kevin Owens Story*. WWE, 2017.
11. *Talk Steen Talk: The Kevin Steen Shoot Interview*. Highspots, 2012.

FUCK RING OF HONOR

1. Steen, Kevin. *Hell Rising*. Ring of Honor, 2013.
2. *Shoot Interview With Kevin Steen*. RF Video, 2014.
3. WWE. "Kevin Owens Says Goodbye to PWG's Fabled Home Venue: WWE Ride Along (WWE Network Exclusive)" *Youtube*, 19 Nov. 2019. https://www.youtube.com/watch?v=XTT1FOsZ6FI&t=12s
4. Steen, Kevin. *Hell Rising*. Ring of Honor, 2013.
5. Steen, Kevin. *Hell Rising*. Ring of Honor, 2013.
6. Steen, Kevin. *Hell Rising*. Ring of Honor, 2013.
7. Steen, Kevin. *Hell Rising*. Ring of Honor, 2013.
8. Steen, Kevin. *Hell Rising*. Ring of Honor, 2013.
9. Steen, Kevin. *Hell Rising*. Ring of Honor, 2013.

VIEW FROM THE TOP

1. Steen, Kevin. *Hell Rising*. Ring of Honor, 2013.
2. Steen, Kevin. *Hell Rising*. Ring of Honor, 2013.
3. Steen, Kevin. *Hell Rising*. Ring of Honor, 2013.
4. Steen, Kevin. *Hell Rising*. Ring of Honor, 2013.
5. *Fight Owens Fight: The Kevin Owens Story*. WWE, 2017.
6. Steen, Kevin. *Hell Rising*. Ring of Honor, 2013.
7. St-Pierre, Jake. "Zen Arcade Reviews: ROH Showdown In The Sun Day 1." *411Mania*, 11 May 2012. https://411mania.com/wrestling/zen-arcade-reviews-ROH-showdown-in-the-sun-day-1/
8. Good Karma Wrestling. "Sami Zayn on Bloodline, Kevin Owens, World Title and More." *YouTube*, 19 Jul. 2024. https://www.youtube.com/watch?v=pYN3piBD7Ug
9. Middleton, Marc. "How TNA's Lawsuit Against WWE Held Up El Generico's Signing, Possible WWE HOF Inductors." *Wrestling Inc.*, 7 Feb. 2013. https://www.wrestlinginc.com/wi/news/2013/0207/560191/how-tna-lawsuit-against-wwe-held-up-el-generico-signing/
10. El Generico [@elgenerico]. "He is evil & forever my enemy, but @KILLSTEENKILL is tough & most deserve person to hold #ROH champion. I will not be far. EG WEB TRANSLATE." *Twitter*, 2012.
11. Steen, Kevin. *Hell Rising*. Ring of Honor, 2013.
12. Steen, Kevin. *Hell Rising*. Ring of Honor, 2013.

NOTHING WITHOUT YOU

1. *Fight Owens Fight: The Kevin Owens Story*. WWE, 2017.
2. *Fight Owens Fight: The Kevin Owens Story*. WWE, 2017.

NOTES

SEPARATION

1. "Jimmy Jacobs." *The Kevin Steen Show*, 2013.
2. Edge and Christian. "Sami Zayn Talks Turning Heel, Being Motivated by Kevin Owens, and the Evolution of his Character." *E & C's Pod of Awesomeness*, 12 Sept. 2019.
3. Jericho, Chris. "TIJ - EP97 - NXT's Sami Zayn & Adrian Neville & Fozzy's Jeff Rouse." *Talk is Jericho*, 28 Dec. 2018. https://podcasts.apple.com/us/podcast/tij-ep97-nxts-sami-zayn-adrian-neville-fozzys-jeff-rouse/id767016946?i=1000475236807
4. Zayn, Sami. "My Time with Dusty Rhodes." *Twitlonger*, 11 Jun. 2015. https://www.twitlonger.com/show/n_1smklsp
5. Hagadorn, Shane, and Jeff Schwartz. "Kevin Steen: Hell Rising." *An Honorable Mention w/ Shane Hagadorn and Jeff Schwartz* [podcast], 25 Sept. 2018.
6. Comments on JeremyTheMVP. "El Generico in NXT. Unmasked." *Reddit*. 8 Mar. 2013. https://www.reddit.com/r/SquaredCircle/comments/19vur2/el_generico_in_nxt_unmasked/
7. Notsam. "Kevin Owens- NXT, ROH, PWG, Crying, Family, etc - Sam Roberts & Katie Linendoll" *Youtube*, 21 May 2015. https://www.youtube.com/watch?v=vcx24gPdPbs
8. Notsam. "Kevin Owens- NXT, ROH, PWG, Crying, Family, etc - Sam Roberts & Katie Linendoll" *Youtube*, 21 May 2015. https://www.youtube.com/watch?v=vcx24gPdPbs
9. Rickyrockwell. "William Regal was at PWG's BOLA ... Looked to be Scouting Talent." *Reddit*, 1 Sept. 2013. https://www.reddit.com/r/SquaredCircle/comments/1libya/william_regal_was_at_pwgs_bola_looked_to_be/
10. WWE. "Kevin Owens' Parents on the WWE Tape that Changed Their Son's Life: My Son is a WWE Superstar" *Youtube*, 27 Sept. 2018. https://www.youtube.com/watch?v=_a5ewqD0N6I

OUR EVOLUTION

1. Clapp, John. "WWE Signs Kevin Steen to NXT." *WWE.com*, 8 Aug. 2014.
2. Melok, Bobby. "'Familiarity Breeds Contempt.': The Bitter History of Sami Zayn and Kevin Owens." WWE.com, 10 Mar 2016. https://www.wwe.com/article/sami-zayn-kevin-owens-history
3. Austin, Steve. "Kevin Steen." *The Steve Austin Show* [podcast], 13 Dec. 2013.
4. Notsam. "Kevin Owens Live w Sam Roberts - Vince McMahon, Dusty Rhodes, etc." *Youtube*, 6 Sept. 2016
5. *Shoot Interview With Kevin Steen*. RF Video, 2014.
6. *Fight Owens Fight: The Kevin Owens Story.* WWE, 2017.
7. *Fight Owens Fight: The Kevin Owens Story.* WWE, 2017.
8. *Fight Owens Fight: The Kevin Owens Story.* WWE, 2017.
9. *The Kevin Steen Show* with the Young Bucks (2014)
10. Notsam. "Kevin Owens- NXT, ROH, PWG, Crying, Family, etc - Sam Roberts & Katie Linendoll." *Youtube*, 21 May 2015. https://www.youtube.com/watch?v=vcx24gPdPbs
11. Developmentally Speaking. "Matthew Rehwoldt/Aiden English S6 E5 (FCW/NXT)." *YouTube*, 23 May 2023. https://www.youtube.com/watch?v=nlFyCnHAQ4o

NOTES

12. *Fight Owens Fight: The Kevin Owens Story.* WWE, 2017.
13. Notsam. "Kevin Owens- NXT, ROH, PWG, Crying, Family, etc - Sam Roberts & Katie Linendoll." *Youtube,* 21 May 2015. https://www.youtube.com/watch?v=vcx24gPdPbs
14. It's not a *legit* injury to the real person, but considering Neville sells the injured leg for a few weeks, it seems we're meant to believe Neville wasn't feigning an injury to trick Sami, which would have certainly have tipped him from tweener into heel territory.
15. Jericho, Chris. "My Best Friend Kevin Owens Returns to Talk is Jericho - EP281." *Talk is Jericho* [podcast], 10 Sept. 2016.

RIVAL

1. *Fight Owens Fight: The Kevin Owens Story.* Bonus disc. WWE, 2017.

UNSTOPPABLE

1. WWE. "Sami Zayn on Getting Injured Before Facing John Cena: The New Day: Feel the Power, Sept. 28, 2020." *Youtube,* 29 Sept. 2020. https://www.youtube.com/watch?v=FiKvqbEi5QY
2. *Fight Owens Fight: The Kevin Owens Story.* Bonus Disc. WWE, 2017.
3. *Fight Owens Fight: The Kevin Owens Story.* WWE, 2017.
4. *Fight Owens Fight: The Kevin Owens Story.* WWE, 2017.
5. *Fight Owens Fight: The Kevin Owens Story.* WWE, 2017.
6. WWE. "Zayn on Owens' RAW Debut." *Youtube,* 20 May 2015. https://www.youtube.com/watch?v=Ecvi6YwDiHE
7. UpUpDownDown. "ROYAL 1'S (Charlotte/AJ) vs. UP-UPBEATNIKS (Becky/Sami) — Rocket League Tournament SmackDown Semis." *Youtube,* 17 Aug. 2017. https://www.youtube.com/watch?v=RInLo36EJ_g

TIME HEALS ALL WOUNDS

1. Ringside Collectables. "Mattel WWE Entire Panel! - SDCC 2015 - San Diego Comic Con!" *Youtube,* 9 Jul. 2015. https://youtu.be/t9OREl4mrBM?si=51Hs4Z7WoAAqlS0m
2. "Tommaso Ciampa." *The Kevin Steen Show.* Highspots, 2013.

PAYBACK

1. Jericho, Chris. "Sami Zayn Returns to Talk is Jericho." *Talk is Jericho.* 28 Apr. 2016.
2. Jericho, Chris. "Sami Zayn Returns to Talk is Jericho." *Talk is Jericho.* 28 Apr. 2016.
3. The LAW: Live Audio Wrestling. "Chris Jericho Talks About THE LIST, Kevin Owens, Matt Hardy | LAW INTERVIEWS 2016." *YouTube,* 16 Nov. 2016. https://www.youtube.com/watch?v=rQx6UEEUjko&t=1s

NOTES

BATTLEGROUND

1. You can see a couple in the comments responding to this Reddit post: "That Time Sami Zayn Nearly Killed Himself at Battleground" (https://www.reddit.com/r/SquaredCircle/comments/61sil7/that_time_sami_zayn_nearly_killed_himself_at/)
2. Jericho, Chris. "My Best Friend Kevin Owens Returns to Talk Is Jericho - EP281." *Talk is Jericho*, 10 Sept. 2016.
3. Jericho, Chris. "My Best Friend Kevin Owens Returns to Talk Is Jericho - EP281." *Talk is Jericho*, 10 Sept. 2016.

THIS IS OURS

1. WWE. "Kevin Owens." *365*. 2017.
2. Edge and Christian. "WWE's Inaugural Universal Champion—Finn Bálor." *E&C's Pod of Awesomeness*. Spotify podcast. Jan. 2019. https://open.spotify.com/episode/02x80bGMPmAaUK1pvhkIHc
3. Edge and Christian. "WWE's Inaugural Universal Champion—Finn Bálor." *E&C's Pod of Awesomeness*. Spotify podcast. Jan. 2019. https://open.spotify.com/episode/02x80bGMPmAaUK1pvhkIHc
4. *Fight Owens Fight: The Kevin Owens Story*. WWE, 2017.
5. Gulf News. "WWE NXT Champion Sami Zayn Names His Top 5 Wrestling Influences." *Youtube*, 2 Feb 2015. https://www.youtube.com/watch?v=TAfaXG4ahl4
6. Ruse, David. "WWE's Kevin Owens: 'Facing The Undertaker at WrestleMania Would be Huge'." *Sky Sports*, 24 Jan. 2017. https://www.skysports.com/more-sports/wwe/news/14203/10735686/wwes-kevin-owens-facing-the-undertaker-at-wrestlemania-would-be-huge
7. Mrosko, Greg. "So I Guess We're Definitely Getting Sami Zayn vs. Chris Jericho for the US Title at Fastlane." *Cageside Seats*, 11 Feb. 2017. https://www.cagesideseats.com/wwe/2017/2/11/14588604/sami-zayn-vs-chris-jericho-us-title-wwe-fastlane-2017
8. Busted Open Podcast. "Chris Jericho - What Led To AEW Signing, Vince McMahon, WWE, Double Or Nothing." *Youtube*, 17 May 2019. https://www.youtube.com/watch?v=xKqCmuGnvMI
9. WWE Clips. "Sami Zayn Makes CRY Kevin Owens with a Beautiful Words | WWE Clip |" *YouTube*, 26 Mar. 2017. https://www.youtube.com/watch?v=CQS6HzPvw-w

HELL IN A CELL

1. Ryder, James. "Chris Jericho Confirms Vince McMahon's WrestleMania 33 Insult Lead Him to Eventually Signing with AEW." *Web Is Jericho*, 31 Oct. 2019. https://www.webisjericho.com/chris-jericho-confirms-vince-mcmahons-wrestlemania-33-insult-lead-him-to-eventually-signing-with-aew/
2. Jericho, Chris."Jericho's WrestleMania Matches—Live in Belfast." *Talk is Jericho*, Jul. 2022. https://open.spotify.com/episode/13pVM7UGjoIpo5JtrIiY6r?si=b14368d5ca754c09&nd=1
3. Garcia, Lillian. "Kevin Owens: Raw Files from Never-Before-Seen Interview, Kevin Got His Wish." *YouTube*, 2 Feb. 2021. https://www.youtube.com/watch?v=gvIBOnymQUc

NOTES

4. Inside the Ropes. "Chris Jericho SHOCKED Vince McMahon Hated Match Vs Kevin Owens At Wrestlemania 33." *YouTube*, 31 Mar. 2019. https://youtu.be/nsArb U_KRbE?si=tK0aUcJplihNwQDy
5. Garcia, Lillian. "Kevin Owens: Raw Files from Never-Before-Seen Interview, Kevin Got His Wish." *YouTube*, 2 Feb. 2021. https://www.youtube.com/watch?v=gvIBOnymQUc
6. Garcia, Lillian. "Kevin Owens: Raw Files from Never-Before-Seen Interview, Kevin Got His Wish." *YouTube*, 2 Feb. 2021. https://www.youtube.com/watch?v=gvIBOnymQUc

KEVIN'S HEAVEN

1. Benigno, Anthony. "Exclusive Interview: Sami Zayn Suffers Torn Rotator Cuffs, Undergoes Surgery." WWE.com, 21 Jun 2018. https://www.wwe.com/article/sami-zayn-injury-interview
2. Garcia, Lillian. "Kevin Owens: Raw Files from Never-Before-Seen Interview, Kevin Got His Wish." *YouTube*, 2 Feb. 2021. https://www.youtube.com/watch?v=gvIBOnymQUc

THUNDERDOME

1. Upton, Felix. (April 25, 2019). "WWE's Original Plan for Kevin Owens and Why They Turned Him Heel." *Ringside News*, 25 Apr. 2019. https://www.ringsidenews.com/2019/04/25/wwes-original-plan-for-kevin-owens-why-they-turned-him-heel/
2. Nason, Josh. "WWE Bringing WrestleMania Back to Tampa's Raymond James Stadium." *Wrestling Observer Figure Four Online*, 2 Oct. 2020. https://www.f4wonline.com/news/wwe/wwe-bringing-wrestlemania-back-tampas-raymond-james-stadium-321586

INTERLUDE

1. Gorilla Position. "Kevin Owens on the Biggest Night of his Career, Stone Cold Steve Austin, Main Eventing & More!" *Youtube*, Apr. 2, 2022. https://www.youtube.com/watch?v=WYBeiyeLtns
2. Coppinger, Mike. "'The MVP of WWE': Sami Zayn's Rise from Masked Indie Wrestler to Main Event Show Stealer." *ESPN*, Mar. 30, 2023. https://www.espn.com/wwe/story/_/id/35994984/wwe-wrestlemania-39-el-generico-mvp-wwe-sami-zayn-incredible-12-months
3. Coppinger, Mike. "'The MVP of WWE': Sami Zayn's Rise from Masked Indie Wrestler to Main Event Show Stealer." *ESPN*, Mar. 30, 2023. https://www.espn.com/wwe/story/_/id/35994984/wwe-wrestlemania-39-el-generico-mvp-wwe-sami-zayn-incredible-12-months

MIND GAMES AND WARGAMES

1. Lambert, Jeremy. "Paul Heyman Explains The Creative Process Of Bloodline Storyline." *Fightful*, Mar. 6, 2023. https://www.fightful.com/wrestling/paul-heyman-explains-creative-process-bloodline-storyline

ACKNOWLEDGMENTS

A book like this doesn't come into existence without a great deal of help and support. Wrestling history is a slippery, elusive, ephemeral and complex thing, and I was inspired and informed by all the work that has gone before. Pat Laprade's histories of Quebec wrestling, the detailed historical information of Cagematch.net, the rich archive of Ring of Honor reviews at 411mania.com, historical podcasts like *ThROH the Years* and *An Honorable Mention* all were my go-to sources for context and tone. I especially have to thank Shane Hagadorn for giving me access to his ROH files, which let me fill in gigantic gaps in my knowledge.

Huge thanks to my publisher, Jonathan Snowden, for approaching me about this project, and for providing structure, freedom, and patience in equal doses. And a gigantic debt of gratitude to my editor, Kristina Snowden, for polishing my prose, checking my facts, and giving invaluable feedback. Any errors that remain are, of course, entirely my own.

Wrestling is also notoriously hard to capture in words without it becoming a laundry list of moves and technical terms. Jaime Shelhamer's dynamic interior illustrations added invaluable visual references and made everything easier to understand, while Eunice Lai's cover art set the tone for the whole project. I'm in their debt forever.

Non-wrestling-fans supporting a wrestling fan in a big project are always a special and long-suffering group. My father always knew when to ask "How's the book coming along?" and when to keep a prudent silence and let me tear my hair. My sister provided absolutely priceless feedback by reading early drafts as a total outsider to wrestling and letting me know if I was using too much jargon or leaving out important context. And my friend Mina listened to so many late-night rants and insecurities. You all had my back even when you had no idea what I was talking about, and that's the truest kind of support.

I could never have gotten through the rough times of this process without the KOmmunity and the Zayniacs out there sharing their love and enthusiasm. To Andrea, Ashley, Battibat, Bonnie, Corey, Corinne, Dan Young, Danielle, Drea, the Dude, Henry, HT, Irene, Islam, Jayde, Jeffrey, Jessie, Joe King, Kell, Marie, Melissa, Miles, Pat, Rajeev, Ratul, Rowan, Seej, Stina, Tim Kail, and so many others I have failed to mention: we're in the band together. Just keep fighting. And thank you for all the inspiration.

Infinite love and gratitude to my tag team partner of thirty years, Dan Molden, who's been there for every fight and every promo, who always has my back, who's always in the corner ready to make the hot tag and come to the rescue of the babyface in peril. Every day is the main event of *WrestleMania* with you at my side.

And of course, thank you to Kevin Owens and Sami Zayn for the inspiration, the support, the matches and the moments. You taught me what wrestling was and what it could be. You gave me goals and dreams. You've changed my life forever.

ALSO FROM HYBRID SHOOT

Shamrock: The World's Most Dangerous Man

By Jonathan Snowden

"Honestly, this should lead to a movie."
—Dave Meltzer (Wrestling Observer)

"One of the most ambitious MMA or wrestling biographies ever written."
-The Athletic

"There is an incredible amount of new information unearthed in this biography."
-Sports Illustrated

Way of the Blade: 100 of the Greatest Bloody Matches in Wrestling History

By Phil Schneider

"This book rules. Maybe I'll make it into Volume 2!"
—Erik Stevens (Former ROH Wrestler)

"If there are ten people on the planet who have watched more pro wrestling from around than globe than Phil Schneider, I'd love to meet them."
-Jonathan Snowden (Bleacher Report)

www.ingramcontent.com/pod-product-compliance
Lightning Source LLC
Chambersburg PA
CBHW052130070526
44585CB00017B/1765